Supercook's

WORLDWIDE COOKBOOK

Marshall Cavendish London & New York

Edited by Isabel Moore
Designed by Chris Lower

Published by Marshall Cavendish Books Limited
58 Old Compton Street
London W1V 5PA

© Marshall Cavendish Limited 1973, 1974, 1975, 1977

Parts of this material first published by Marshall
Cavendish Limited in the partwork *Supercook*

This volume first published 1977

Printed in Great Britain by
Redwood Burn Limited Trowbridge and Esher

ISBN 0 85685 296 1

Contents

Crêpes Suzette (Grand Marnier crêpes), for recipe see page 188

SPAIN AND MEXICO

Callos Viscainos (Tripe in Wine Sauce), for recipe see page 348

America

American cooking has been a triumph of adaptation and practicality right from the beginning: when the first Thanksgiving Day was celebrated in 1621, it was not the traditional British fare of the Pilgrim Fathers that was given pride of place at the feast, but the staple foods—turkey, corn, pumpkin—of their Indian neighbours.

Tradition has, however, played its part. In those areas which were settled first—New England, Pennsylvania, Virginia—and mainly by the British, food was plain, wholesome and very filling, with few frills and fripperies. Like life in general, it was geared to the practical, and ingenuity was what often made the practical acceptable: hence it was proximity to the sea which dictated the prominence of fish in the New Englanders' diet, but it was creativity which transformed the fish into those delicious chowders.

In rural Pennsylvania, the Pennsylvania

Dutch, a pacifist Protestant sect from Germany settled (their name is confusing, it is a corruption of the German 'deutsch' and has nothing whatsoever to do with Holland) and there is still today a strong community farming in the ways of their ancestors, without cars and tractors and transistor radios. The cooking is still that of their ancestors too, good rib-sticking stuff that relies on nourishing home-grown produce, made more exciting by a liberal use of saffron and the most mouth-watering selection of 'sweets and sours' pickles.

The lands to the south of Virginia did not become part of the United States until 1803 and before that the influence was French or Spanish, with a consequent effect on eating and social habits. The climate was different, too, warmer and lazier, altogether more lush and tropical, and with an abundance of exotic food that probably seemed quite sinful to the

puritans of the north. The heart of Southern cooking was, and remains, in the city of New Orleans, and the cuisine which flourishes there, called Creole, combines the best of French skills and attitudes with the high quality of home-grown American produce. It is a combination that is hard to beat. The 'black' cuisine of the area is unique: the slaves who were brought in to plant cotton did not have access to the fine ingredients available to the whites of the region; their repertoire relied heavily on the food rejected by the white man, or left over from his table. The food which evolved from such unpromising beginnings— called 'soul' food because it hardly kept the body alive, is strong on hot spices and stodge, low on lean meat but manages to be absolutely delicious anyhow.

The states of the Southwest are even younger than those of the 'deep' south. The influence here was predominantly Spanish, or rather Mexican, the way of life out-of-doors and rough-and-ready (before those oil wells

started spouting, even Texas was cattle country), so eating tended to be a casual affair, consisting of food that could safely be mixed together in one pot, thrust over a camp fire and left to cook. The result was barbecue cooking, beans and chillis—and lots of well-fed cowboys!

When the pioneers trekked across to the West, they found the land still teeming with game, the rivers well stocked with fish. Many started ranches for sheep or cattle, so even more meat was available. Hence Western cooking tends to the simple but excellent—lots of large, juicy steaks and roasts, or fish, all garnished liberally with fresh salads and fruits such as citrus fruit, which grow with ease, especially in the Far West.

There are more exotic influences too: the Chinese came to northern California in the late nineteenth century and brought with them new tastes and ideas, which were then adapted to local conditions. Sometimes the adaptations were so complete that they resulted in new

dishes: chop suey, for instance, now a popular menu item in Chinese restaurants all over the world, was actually invented in San Francisco.

Grapes were planted in California by Spanish missionaries eager to secure a local supply for their converts, and the wine produced from them has proved excellent enough to challenge even the better Bordeaux and Burgundies—despite such major discouragements as Prohibition, when the only vineyards allowed to stay in production were those producing wine for communion.

In the closing years of the nineteenth century and the beginning of the twentieth, many Europeans flocked to America in search of a better life—from Italy, Greece, Ireland, Germany, Poland, Russia. Many of the traditional recipes they brought with them proved unsuitable for the new country, but those that could be kept were, and were adapted freely to suit their new way of life. Sourdough bread, which was Middle European in origin, like chop suey is now a

native of San Francisco; breaded veal cutlets, a recognizable cousin to Wiener Schnitzel, are now a standard item in diners and cafés from coast to coast and Pretzels, originally from Germany, are now not just a popular snack but an indispensable part of the American way of life.

America has always seemed in a hurry. Today it seems more so, even when it eats. And naturally in the land where no one walks if he can run or, better still, leap into a car and drive, 'instant' cooking has evolved into a fine art: the difference between a European hamburger and the 'real thing' is almost too painful to contemplate, and the sandwiches are quite definitely the best in the world.

The food is superb, the list of specialities endless and unfortunately limitations of space permits only the most delicious fraction to be included here. Only a country with such diverse traditions, and gifted with a never-ending supply of restless, eager energy, could produce such a range of exciting food.

above: *a Pennsylvania Dutch boy farms in the way of his ancestors, without modern machinery.*

Soups

MANHATTAN CLAM CHOWDER

Chowders originated in New England and are probably the most popular type of soup in the United States. Clams are the most common base, as in the two classic recipes which follow, but fish and even vegetables are sometimes substituted.

	Metric/U.K.	U.S.
Salt pork, diced	125g/4oz	½ cup
Medium onion, chopped	1	1
Large tomatoes, blanched, peeled and chopped	4	4
Medium potatoes, diced	3	3
Salt and pepper to taste		
Dried thyme	½ tsp	½ tsp
Tomato juice	150ml/5floz	⅝ cup
Water	600ml/1 pint	2½ cups
Canned clams, with the juice reserved	425g/14oz	14oz

Fry the salt pork in a saucepan for 5 to 8 minutes, or until it resembles small croûtons and has rendered most of its fat. Transfer to kitchen towels to drain.

Add the onion to the pan and fry for 5 minutes. Stir in the tomatoes, potatoes, salt, pepper and thyme, and fry for 2 minutes. Pour over the tomato juice, water and reserved clam liquid and bring to the boil. Reduce the heat to low, cover and simmer for 12 to 15 minutes, or until the potatoes are tender.

Stir in the clams and reserved salt pork, and simmer for a further 4 to 5 minutes. Transfer to a warmed tureen and serve.

6 Servings

NEW ENGLAND CLAM CHOWDER

	Metric/U.K.	U.S.
Salt pork, diced	75g/3oz	⅜ cup

Manhattan Clam Chowder, a hearty mixture of tomatoes, potatoes and clams, is one of the classic soups of the United States. It is practically a meal in itself, served with lots of crusty bread.

	Metric/U.K.	U.S.
Medium onions, chopped	2	2
Water	175ml/6floz	$\frac{3}{4}$ cup
Milk	250ml/8floz	1 cup
Medium potatoes, chopped	4	4
Canned clams, with the juice reserved	425g/14oz	14oz
Salt and pepper to taste		
Paprika	$\frac{1}{2}$ tsp	$\frac{1}{2}$ tsp
Double (heavy) cream	250ml/8floz	1 cup
Butter	15g/$\frac{1}{2}$oz	1 Tbs

Fry the salt pork in a saucepan for 5 to 8 minutes, or until it resembles small croûtons and has rendered most of its fat. Transfer to kitchen towels to drain.

Add the onions to the pan and fry for 5 minutes. Add the water, milk and potatoes and bring to the boil. Reduce the heat to low, cover and simmer for 12 to 15 minutes, or until the potatoes are tender.

Add the clams, reserved juice, reserved salt pork, salt, pepper and paprika, and simmer for a further 4 to 5 minutes, or until the clams are heated through. Stir in the cream and butter, and heat until the cream is hot but not boiling and the butter has melted. Transfer to a warmed tureen and serve.

6 Servings

GUMBO

This is a delicious Creole speciality from the southern part of the United States.

	Metric/U.K.	U.S.
Butter	25g/1oz	2 Tbs
Medium onions, sliced	2	2
Red pepper, pith and seeds removed and chopped	1	1
Garlic clove, crushed	1	1
Okra, thinly sliced	$\frac{1}{2}$kg/1lb	1lb
Beef stock	1$\frac{1}{4}$l/2 pints	5 cups
Medium tomatoes, blanched, peeled and chopped	4	4
Cayenne pepper	$\frac{1}{2}$ tsp	$\frac{1}{2}$ tsp
Salt and pepper to taste		
Long-grain rice, soaked in cold water for 30 minutes and drained	75g/3oz	$\frac{1}{2}$ cup

Melt the butter in a large saucepan. Add the onions, pepper, garlic and okra and fry for 5 minutes. Pour in the stock, then stir in the tomatoes, cayenne and seasoning. Bring to the boil, reduce the heat to low and cover. Simmer for 1$\frac{1}{2}$ hours. Stir in the rice, re-cover and simmer for a further 30 minutes.

Transfer to a warmed tureen and serve.

4 Servings

PHILADELPHIA PEPPER POT

	Metric/U.K.	U.S.
Veal knuckle, sawn into 3 pieces	1	1
Bouquet garni	1	1
Black peppercorns	6	6
Water	5l/10 pints	6 quarts
Blanched tripe, cut into 2$\frac{1}{2}$cm/1in pieces	$\frac{1}{2}$kg/1lb	1lb
Medium onion, chopped	1	1
Large carrots, chopped	2	2
Celery stalks, chopped	2	2
Salt and pepper to taste		
Red pepper flakes	$\frac{1}{2}$ tsp	$\frac{1}{2}$ tsp
Medium potatoes, diced	2	2
Cornflour (cornstarch), blended with 2 Tbs water	2 Tbs	2 Tbs
Butter	15g/$\frac{1}{2}$oz	1 Tbs
Chopped parsley	2 Tbs	2 Tbs

Put the veal, bouquet garni, peppercorns and water in a large saucepan. Bring to the boil, skimming any scum from the surface. Reduce the heat to low, cover the pan and simmer for 2$\frac{1}{2}$ hours.

Remove the pan from the heat and lift out the knuckle. Put the veal pieces on a chopping board and remove the meat from the knuckle. Discard the fat and bones and cut the meat into small cubes. Strain the stock into a large bowl.

Return the stock to the pan and add the tripe, onion, carrots, celery, salt, pepper· and red pepper flakes. Bring to the boil, reduce the heat to low and cover. Simmer the soup for 1 hour. Add the potatoes and reserved veal cubes and continue to simmer for a further 30 minutes, or until the potatoes are tender.

Stir in the cornflour (cornstarch) and butter until the soup thickens slightly. Transfer to a warmed tureen, sprinkle over the parsley and serve.

6-8 Servings

CHICKEN CORN SOUP

This soup is Pennsylvania Dutch in origin but is now a standard menu item throughout the country.

	Metric/U.K.	U.S.
Vegetable oil	3 Tbs	3 Tbs
Medium onions, sliced	2	2
Celery stalks, sliced	4	4
Chicken stock	1¾l/3 pints	4 pints
Black peppercorns	10	10
Chicken, roasted, flesh removed from the bone, skinned and chopped	1½kg/3lb	3lb
Thick egg noodles	125g/4oz	4oz
Canned sweetcorn, drained	425g/14oz	14oz
Chopped fresh sage	1 tsp	1 tsp
Chopped fresh savory	1 tsp	1 tsp
Salt and pepper to taste		
Saffron threads, soaked in 1 Tbs hot water	½ tsp	½ tsp

Heat the oil in a saucepan. Add the onions and fry until they are soft. Stir in the celery and fry for 5 minutes. Pour over the stock and add the peppercorns. Bring to the boil, reduce the heat to low and simmer for 20 minutes.

Stir in all the remaining ingredients and bring the mixture to the boil. Simmer for 15 to 20 minutes, or until the noodles are just tender. Add more salt if necessary.

Transfer to a warmed tureen and serve.

4-6 Servings

Philadelphia Pepper Pot used to be sold in the streets of Philadelphia before the American Revolution—and it's still just as popular today.

CREAM OF CHICKEN SOUP

	Metric/U.K.	U.S.
Chicken backs and wings	1kg/2lb	2lb
Water	1½l/2½ pints	6¼ cups
Celery stalks	2	2
Small onion, studded with 2 cloves	1	1
Salt and pepper to taste		
Single (light) cream	250ml/8floz	1 cup
Milk	250ml/8floz	1 cup
Cornflour (cornstarch), blended with 3 Tbs water	2 Tbs	2 Tbs

Put the chicken pieces in a large saucepan and pour over the water. Add the vegetables and seasoning, and bring to the boil. Reduce the heat to low, cover the pan and simmer for 2 hours.

Remove from the heat and strain the liquid into a bowl. Pick out the chicken pieces and detach the meat from the bones. Set aside.

Discard the bones and vegetables.

Return the strained liquid to the saucepan and add the cream and milk. Bring to just under boiling point. Stir in the cornflour (cornstarch) mixture and cook, stirring constantly, until the liquid thickens and becomes smooth. Add the chicken meat to the soup and simmer to heat through.

Serve at once.

6 Servings

YANKEE BEAN SOUP

	Metric/U.K.	U.S.
Vegetable oil	50ml/2floz	¼ cup
Large onions, chopped	2	2
Garlic cloves, crushed	2	2
Tomatoes, blanched, peeled and chopped	6	6
Celery stalks, sliced	4	4
Dried red kidney beans, soaked overnight in cold water and drained	225g/8oz	1⅓ cups
Dried black beans, soaked overnight in cold water and drained	225g/8oz	1⅓ cups
Salt and pepper to taste		
Sugar	1 tsp	1 tsp
Lemon juice	1 Tbs	1 Tbs
Dried thyme	2 tsp	2 tsp
Beef stock	2½l/4 pints	5 pints

Heat the oil in a saucepan. Add the onions and garlic and fry until the onions are soft. Stir in all the remaining ingredients and bring to the boil. Reduce the heat to low, cover and simmer for 3 hours.

Transfer to a warmed tureen and serve.

6 Servings

Chicken Corn Soup is one of the finest examples of Pennsylvania Dutch cooking.

Pumpkin Soup is a warming, filling dish based on the traditional American pumpkin.

PUMPKIN SOUP

Pumpkins are part of the American scene; they are hollowed out and used as lanterns at Halloween, their flesh is puréed and made into the classic Thanksgiving dessert, Pumpkin Pie, they form the basis of a delicious stuffing for turkey or other poultry and they are also used as the basis for a delicious soup, as here. If fresh pumpkin is unavailable, canned unsweetened pumpkin purée may be substituted if available.

	Metric/U.K.	U.S.
Butter	25g/1oz	2 Tbs
Small onions, thinly sliced into rings	2	2
Pumpkin flesh, finely chopped	½kg/1lb	2 cups
Chicken stock	1¼l/2 pints	5 cups
Salt	½ tsp	½ tsp
Celery stalk, chopped	1	1
Large potato, chopped	1	1
Lemon juice	1 Tbs	1 Tbs
Tabasco sauce	¼ tsp	¼ tsp
Paprika	1 tsp	1 tsp
Double (heavy) cream	250ml/8floz	1 cup

Melt the butter in a saucepan. Add the onions and pumpkin and cook, stirring occasionally, for 5 minutes. Gradually stir in the stock, salt, celery, potato, lemon juice, Tabasco and paprika, and bring to the boil. Reduce the heat to low, cover and simmer for 30 to 35 minutes, or until the pumpkin and vegetables are cooked and tender.

Remove the pan from the heat and pour the soup through a strainer into a bowl, pressing down on the pulp with the back of a wooden spoon to extract all the juices. Discard the pulp. Stir the cream into the soup and return to a saucepan. Heat, stirring constantly, for 5 to 6 minutes, or until the soup is very hot but not boiling.

Serve at once.

4-6 Servings

Fish and Seafood

CLAM HASH

Clams are among the most popular of American seafood and are used in a variety of ways—from the traditional clam 'bakes' of the northeast to the hearty stews of California.

	Metric/U.K.	U.S.
Butter	75g/3oz	6 Tbs
Small onion, grated	I	I
Cooked potatoes, finely chopped	3	3
Salt and pepper to taste		
Paprika	I tsp	I tsp
Canned minced clams	425g/14oz	14oz
Parmesan or Cheddar cheese, grated	75g/3oz	¾ cup
Double (heavy) cream	75ml/3floz	⅜ cup
Bacon, grilled (broiled) and crumbled	4 slices	4 slices

Melt the butter in a frying-pan. Add the onion and potatoes and fry until the onion is soft. Stir in the seasonings and clams and cook for 10 minutes, pressing down on the mixture occasionally. Stir gently to release some of the crust from the bottom and then press down.

Combine 50g/2oz (½ cup) of the cheese and the cream, and stir into the mixture. Cover and cook for a further 2 to 3 minutes, or until the cheese has melted.

Top with the remaining grated cheese and crumbled bacon before serving.

4-6 Servings

CRAB PATTIES

The eastern coast states of Maryland and Virginia are noted for their seafood, particularly crab and lobster and this is a typical dish of the region. They may be served hot or cold.

	Metric/U.K.	U.S.
Crabmeat, shell and cartilage removed and flaked	½kg/1lb	1lb
Fresh white breadcrumbs	75g/3oz	1½ cups
Egg yolk	I	I
Mayonnaise	2 Tbs	2 Tbs
Spring onions (scallions), finely chopped	12	12
Hard-boiled egg, finely chopped	I	I
Chopped fresh marjoram	I tsp	I tsp
Lemon juice	2 tsp	2 tsp
Salt and pepper to taste		
Cayenne pepper	¼ tsp	¼ tsp
Vegetable oil	125ml/4floz	½ cup
Watercress	½ bunch	½ bunch

Combine the crabmeat, breadcrumbs, egg yolk, mayonnaise, spring onions (scallions), egg, marjoram, lemon juice and seasonings. Mix and knead the mixture until it is well blended. Shape into 5cm/2in balls, then flatten them into patties with the palm of your hands.

Heat the oil in a large frying-pan. Add the patties, a few at a time, and fry for 3 to 5 minutes on each side, or until they are evenly browned. Transfer to kitchen towels to drain while you fry the remaining patties in the same way.

Arrange the patties on a warmed serving dish and garnish with the watercress. Serve at once, if you are serving them hot.

4-6 Servings

CRAB LOUIS

	Metric/U.K.	U.S.
Cos (romaine) lettuce, separated into leaves	I	I
Crabmeat, shell and cartilage removed and flaked	½kg/1lb	1lb
Tomatoes, thinly sliced	2	2
Cucumber, thinly sliced	½	½
Hard-boiled eggs, sliced	4	4

Capers	1 Tbs	1 Tbs
DRESSING		
Mayonnaise	250ml/8floz	1 cup
Olive oil	3 Tbs	3 Tbs
Lemon juice	1 Tbs	1 Tbs
Tomato ketchup	2 Tbs	2 Tbs
Worcestershire sauce	1 tsp	1 tsp
Chopped chives	1 Tbs	1 Tbs
Chopped parsley	1 Tbs	1 Tbs
Salt and pepper to taste		
Double (heavy) cream, stiffly beaten	75ml/3floz	⅜ cup

Crab Louis, a succulent concoction of crabmeat, salad and a spicy dressing, makes a superb main dish for a summer meal.

To make the dressing, combine all the ingredients and beat until they are thoroughly blended.

Arrange the lettuce on a large serving dish and put the crabmeat in the centre of the dish. Spoon over the dressing and garnish with the tomatoes, cucumber, eggs and capers. Serve at once.

4 Servings

SHRIMP CREOLE

Creole is the word given to both the people and cuisine of Louisiana, particularly New Orleans. It has come to mean a classic mixture of fish or meat cooked with onions, peppers and tomatoes, and is traditionally served on a bed of rice. This particular recipe is one of the most popular variations on the theme.

	Metric/U.K.	U.S.
Olive oil	2 Tbs	2 Tbs
Celery stalks, finely chopped	2	2

Large onions, finely chopped	2	2
Dry white wine	250ml/8floz	1 cup
Canned peeled tomatoes, drained and chopped	425g/14oz	14oz
Salt	1 tsp	1 tsp
Red wine vinegar	1 Tbs	1 Tbs
Sugar	1 Tbs	1 Tbs
Large green pepper, pith and seeds removed and chopped	1	1
Cornflour (cornstarch), blended with 50ml/2floz (¼ cup) water	1 Tbs	1 Tbs
Shelled shrimps	700g/1½lb	1½lb

Heat the oil in a large, deep frying-pan. Add the celery and onions and fry until the onions are soft. Pour in the wine and simmer the mixture for 10 minutes, stirring occasionally.

Stir in the tomatoes, salt, vinegar and sugar and simmer for a further 10 minutes. Add the green pepper and simmer for 10 minutes.

Stir the cornflour (cornstarch) mixture into the sauce and cook, stirring constantly, for 2 to 3 minutes, or until it has thickened.

Add the shrimps to the pan and cook for 5 minutes, or until they are heated through. Transfer to a warmed serving dish and serve.

4 Servings

Shrimp Creole is one of the glories of Creole cooking, which has its centre in Louisiana, around the city of New Orleans. It is traditionally served on a bed of rice.

Jambalaya is one of those classic dishes whose fame has spread far beyond its origins—it was Creole to begin with, but is now international in its appeal.

JAMBALAYA

This is a Southern classic, whose popularity has far transcended its Creole origins. It can be—and often is!—made with almost any kind of seafood or meat available, although the ones suggested below are those most usually included. It is a meal in itself, served with crusty bread.

	Metric/U.K.	U.S.
Vegetable oil	1 Tbs	1 Tbs
Lean bacon, chopped	3 slices	3 slices
Medium onion, chopped	1	1
Celery stalks, chopped	2	2
Long-grain rice, soaked in cold water for 30 minutes and drained	350g/12oz	2 cups
Chicken stock	600ml/1 pint	2½ cups
Salt and pepper to taste		
Cayenne pepper	¼ tsp	¼ tsp
Bay leaf	1	1
Large green pepper, pith and seeds removed and chopped	1	1
Canned peeled tomatoes	425g/14oz	14oz
Cooked ham, chopped	125g/4oz	4oz
Cooked shrimps, shelled	225g/8oz	8oz
Cooked chicken, chopped	225g/8oz	8oz
Chopped parsley	1 Tbs	1 Tbs

Heat the oil in a large saucepan. Add the bacon and fry until it is crisp. Transfer it to kitchen towels to drain.

Add the onion to the pan and fry until it is soft. Stir in the celery, then the rice and cook for 3 minutes, or until the rice is coated with the fat. Pour in the stock, then add the seasonings and bay leaf. Reduce the heat to low, cover and simmer for 10 minutes. Add the green pepper and tomatoes and can juice, and continue to simmer, covered, for a further 5 minutes.

Stir in the ham, shrimps, chicken and reserved bacon, and re-cover the pan. Simmer for a further 5 minutes, or until the shrimps and meat are heated through and the rice is cooked.

Transfer the mixture to a warmed serving dish, sprinkle over the parsley and serve immediately.

4-6 Servings

CHIOPINO

Despite its Italian-sounding name, this hearty stew comes from northern California. It is traditionally served in bowls, with lots of garlic bread.

	Metric/U.K.	U.S.
Olive oil	125ml/4floz	½ cup
Garlic cloves, crushed	4	4
Parsley sprigs	3	3
Celery stalk, chopped	1	1
Green pepper, pith and seeds removed and chopped	1	1
Tomatoes, blanched, peeled, seeded and chopped	½kg/1lb	1lb
Tomato purée (paste)	225g/8oz	8oz
Salt and pepper to taste		
Paprika	1 tsp	1 tsp
Red wine	250ml/8floz	1 cup
Dried oregano	½ tsp	½ tsp
White fish fillets (haddock, cod, etc), skinned and chopped	½kg/1lb	1lb
Shrimps, shelled and de-veined	½kg/1lb	1lb
Crabmeat, shell and cartilage removed	125g/4oz	4oz
Mussels or clams, soaked, washed and scrubbed	24	24

Heat the oil in a large saucepan. Add the garlic, parsley, celery and pepper, and fry for 5 minutes. Stir in the tomatoes, tomato purée (paste), salt, pepper, paprika, wine and oregano and reduce the heat to low. Cover and simmer for 1 hour.

Stir in the white fish, shrimps and crabmeat, and cook over moderate heat for 10 minutes, or until the fish are cooked through.

Meanwhile, put enough water into a medium saucepan to make a 2½cm/1in layer and bring to the boil. Put the mussels or clams in the pan and cook for 6 to 8 minutes, or until the shells open (discard any that do not open).

Turn the fish mixture into a warmed tureen or serving bowl and arrange the mussels or clams, in their shells, on top. Serve at once.

6 Servings

LOBSTER NEWBURG

This classic dish can also be made with King (Pacific) prawns or shrimps.

	Metric/U.K.	U.S.
Cooked lobsters, shells split, claws cracked and sac removed	2 × 1kg/ 2lb	2 × 2lb
Butter	40g/1½oz	3 Tbs
Sherry	125ml/4floz	½ cup
Grated nutmeg	¼ tsp	¼ tsp
Salt and pepper to taste		
Egg yolks	3	3
Double (heavy) cream	250ml/8floz	1 cup
Hot buttered toast	6 slices	6 slices

Remove the lobster meat from the shells and claws and cut it into dice.

Melt the butter in a large frying-pan. Add the lobster and fry for 4 minutes. Pour over the sherry and simmer, stirring constantly, for 3 minutes. Stir in the seasonings.

Combine the egg yolks and the cream, then gradually stir into the lobster. Simmer for 3 to 4 minutes, or until the sauce is thick and smooth, and hot but not boiling.

Arrange the toast on a warmed serving dish or individual plates and spoon over the lobster mixture.

4-6 Servings

LOBSTER THERMIDOR

This elegant, rich dish could be described as having dual nationality, since it is the invention of a French chef in the United States. Serve with crusty bread.

	Metric/U.K.	U.S.
Cooked lobsters, shells split, claws cracked and sac removed	4 × 700g/ 1½lb	4 × 1½lb
Dry white wine	150ml/5floz	⅝ cup
Dried chervil	¼ tsp	¼ tsp
Finely chopped fresh tarragon	1 Tbs	1 Tbs
Small shallots, finely chopped	2	2

Chopped parsley	1 Tbs	1 Tbs
Butter	25g/1oz	2 Tbs
Olive oil	2 tsp	2 tsp
Double (heavy) cream	175ml/6floz	$\frac{3}{4}$ cup
Single (light) cream	150ml/5floz	$\frac{5}{8}$ cup
Salt and pepper to taste		
French mustard	1 tsp	1 tsp
Parmesan cheese, grated	50g/2oz	$\frac{1}{2}$ cup

Lobster Thermidor is one of those dishes that could fairly claim dual nationality since it was invented by a French chef in the United States.

Remove the lobster meat from the shells and claws and cut it into dice. Wipe the shells clean and reserve them.

Put the wine, herbs, shallots and parsley into a saucepan and bring to the boil. Reduce the heat to low and simmer for 5 to 8 minutes, or until the liquid has reduced a little. Remove from the heat and set aside.

Melt the butter with the oil in a frying-pan. Add the lobster and fry for 4 minutes. Remove the lobster meat from the pan, set aside and keep hot.

Strain the wine mixture into the pan and stir in the creams, salt, pepper and mustard. Return the pan to low heat and simmer, stirring constantly, for 3 to 4 minutes, or until the sauce is thick and smooth. Remove the pan from the heat and add the reserved lobster. Stir and baste gently to coat the meat thoroughly.

Preheat the grill (broiler) to moderate.

Arrange the reserved lobster shells on a heatproof dish and spoon the lobster mixture into the shells. Sprinkle over the grated cheese and put the dish under the heat. Grill (broil) for 5 minutes, or until the cheese has melted and the top is browned and bubbling. Serve at once.

4 Servings

OYSTERS ROCKEFELLER

This delicious dish, despite the name, originated in New Orleans ; it is traditionally served as an hors d'oeuvre or first course.

	Metric/U.K.	U.S.
Sufficient rock salt to cover the bottom of 2 large baking dishes in a layer about 1cm/½in thick		
Spring onions (scallions), finely chopped	4	4
Celery stalks, finely chopped	2	2
Cooked spinach	225g/8oz	8oz
Parsley sprigs	3	3
Salt and pepper to taste		
Cayenne pepper	¼ tsp	¼ tsp
Single (light) cream	50ml/2floz	¼ cup
Pernod	1 Tbs	1 Tbs
Oysters, one shell removed	36	36

Preheat the oven to very hot 230°C (Gas Mark 8, 450°F).

Spread the rock salt over the bottom of two large baking dishes.

Put the spring onions (scallions), celery, spinach, parsley, salt, pepper, cayenne and cream in an electric blender and blend to a purée. Transfer the purée to a bowl. Stir in the Pernod.

Divide the oysters equally between the baking dishes, then cover each one with a little vegetable purée. Put the dishes into the oven and bake for 4 minutes.

Transfer the oysters to a warmed serving dish and serve.

6 Servings

PAN-FRIED SCROD WITH BUTTER SAUCE

Scrod is a young cod and is usually served filleted in the United States. This simple dish brings out the fresh flavour of the fish ; if you prefer the fish can be grilled (broiled) and the butter sauce served separately. This is a favourite dish in the north eastern states.

	Metric/U.K.	U.S.
Butter	125g/4oz	8 Tbs
Scrod (cod) fillets, skinned and cut into large pieces	700g/1½lb	1½lb
Salt and pepper to taste		
Grated nutmeg	½ tsp	½ tsp
Lemon juice	1½ Tbs	1½ Tbs
Chopped parsley	1 Tbs	1 Tbs

Oysters Rockefeller is a fascinating blend of French and American cooking. It is usually served as a first course, but since it is very rich it should be followed by a light main dish.

Melt half the butter in a large frying-pan. Add the fish fillets, a few at a time, and fry gently for 4 to 6 minutes, turning them carefully from time to time, or until the fish flesh flakes easily.

Transfer the fish to a warmed serving dish, set aside and keep hot while you make the sauce.

Add the remaining butter, seasonings and lemon juice to the pan and simmer gently until the butter has melted. Remove from the heat and pour over the fish.

Sprinkle over the chopped parsley and serve at once.

4 Servings

Meat and Poultry

BRUNSWICK STEW

This simply made stew has been a universal favourite almost since the country began.

	Metric/U.K.	U.S.
Butter	50g/2oz	4 Tbs
Chicken pieces	8	8
Large onion, sliced	1	1
Green pepper, pith and seeds removed and chopped	1	1
Chicken stock	300ml/10floz	1¼ cups
Canned peeled tomatoes, drained	425g/14oz	14oz
Salt	½ tsp	½ tsp
Cayenne pepper	½ tsp	½ tsp
Worcestershire sauce	1 Tbs	1 Tbs
Sweetcorn kernels	225g/8oz	1 cup
Canned or frozen lima beans, drained	½kg/1lb	1lb
Beurre manié (one part butter and two parts flour blended)	2 Tbs	2 Tbs

Melt the butter in a flameproof casserole. Add the chicken and fry until it is evenly browned. Transfer the pieces to a plate.

Add the onion and pepper to the casserole and fry until the onion is soft. Return the chicken to the casserole and stir in the stock, tomatoes, salt, cayenne and Worcestershire sauce. Bring to the boil and reduce the heat to low. Cover and simmer the mixture for 40 minutes.

Add the corn and lima beans, re-cover and simmer for a further 15 minutes. Add the beurre manié, a little at a time, and cook for 3 to 5 minutes, stirring constantly, or until the liquid has thickened and is smooth. Serve at once.

4-6 Servings

CHICKEN POT PIE

Pot pie, in the Pennsylvania Dutch country, doesn't mean meat encased in pastry, but rather cooked chicken with large squares of noodle. This is a traditional version of the dish.

	Metric/U.K.	U.S.
Chicken, cut into serving pieces	1 × 2kg/4lb	1 × 4lb
Leek, chopped	1	1
Celery stalks, halved	2	2
Saffron threads, soaked in 2 Tbs hot water	½ tsp	½ tsp
Salt	1½ Tbs	1½ Tbs
Black pepper	1 tsp	1 tsp
Celery stalks, finely chopped	225g/8oz	8oz
Potatoes, chopped	3	3
POT PIE DOUGH		
Flour	175g/6oz	1½ cups
Salt	¼ tsp	¼ tsp
Eggs, lightly beaten	2	2

Put the chicken, leek, halved celery stalks, saffron, 1 tablespoon of salt, and the pepper into a large saucepan. Add enough water almost to cover the chicken and bring to the boil. Reduce the heat to low, cover and simmer for 1½ to 2 hours, or until the chicken is cooked through and tender. Remove the chicken from the pan and set aside to cool. Strain the cooking liquid and reserve it.

To make the dough, sift the flour and salt into a bowl. Make a well in the centre and add the eggs. Then gradually, using a wooden spoon or your fingers, mix the dry ingredients into the eggs until they are well blended and form a smooth dough. Turn the dough out onto a floured surface and knead, adding more flour as necessary, to make a fairly soft dough. Return to the bowl, cover and 'rest' it for 15 minutes. Roll out the dough until it is very thin and cut it into 5cm/2 in squares.

Return the strained cooking liquid to the saucepan and stir in the remaining salt. Add the chopped celery and potatoes, and bring to the boil. Simmer for 15 minutes. Carefully add the pot pie squares to the broth and continue to simmer for 15 minutes, or until the vegetables and noodle squares are cooked through.

Meanwhile, skin the chicken pieces and remove the meat from the bones. Chop into

bite-sized pieces. Stir the chicken into the mixture in the pan and simmer for a further 5 minutes, or until the chicken is heated through. Serve at once, in bowls.

6-8 Servings

MARYLAND CHICKEN

	Metric/U.K.	U.S.
Milk	350ml/12floz	1½ cups
Seasoned flour	25g/1oz	¼ cup
Chicken breasts	4	4

Egg, lightly beaten with 1 tsp water	1	1
Fresh breadcrumbs	75g/3oz	1½ cups
Butter	125g/4oz	8 Tbs
Vegetable oil	3 Tbs	3 Tbs
Sugar	½ tsp	½ tsp
Flour	1 Tbs	1 Tbs

Pour 4 tablespoons of the milk into a saucer and put the seasoned flour into a shallow dish. Dip the chicken into the milk, then the flour, shaking off any excess. Set the chicken pieces aside for 10 minutes to allow the coating to dry slightly.

Brunswick Stew, a warming dish based on chicken, is popular throughout the United States. Serve with mashed potatoes or noodles for a complete meal.

17

Part of the fun of cooking Maryland Chicken is to decide which of the many traditional garnishes to serve with it—in the recipe above, lightly fried bananas and grilled (broiled) bacon rolls are used, but you could also serve it with sweetcorn fritters, or fried pineapple rings.

Put the egg mixture into one dish and the breadcrumbs on another. Dip the breasts, one at a time, into the egg then the breadcrumbs, shaking off any excess.

Melt 75g/3oz (6 tablespoons) of butter with the oil in a frying-pan. Add the chicken breasts and cook over low heat, turning occasionally, for 20 minutes, or until they are cooked through and tender. Transfer to kitchen towels to drain, cover them and keep them hot while you prepare the sauce.

Melt the remaining butter in a saucepan. Add the sugar, stirring until the mixture caramelizes a little. Stir in the flour and cook for 1 minute, stirring constantly. Remove the pan from the heat and gradually stir in the remaining milk. Return the pan to the heat and cook, stirring constantly with a wooden spoon, for 2 to 3 minutes, or until the sauce is thick and smooth.

Pour the sauce into a sauceboat, arrange the chicken pieces on a warmed serving dish with the garnishes you have chosen, and serve at once.

4 Servings

BURGOO

This dish comes from Kentucky and is probably adapted from the one-pot meal cooked by local trappers over an open fire! Originally the dish contained squirrel, although rabbit as used here, and even chicken, are more common today. It is usually accompanied by corn bread.

	Metric/U.K.	U.S.
Beef chuck	1 × 1kg/2lb	1 × 2lb
Rabbit, skinned, cleaned and cut into serving pieces	1	1
Salt	2 Tbs	2 Tbs
Black peppercorns, crushed	1 Tbs	1 Tbs
Medium potatoes, quartered	3	3
Onions, chopped	2	2
Garlic cloves, crushed	2	2
Carrots, quartered	4	4
Sweetcorn kernels	225g/8oz	1 cup

	Metric/U.K.	U.S.
Canned peeled tomatoes, juice reserved	700g/1½lb	1½lb
Canned butter beans	425g/14oz	14oz
Red peppers, pith and seeds removed and chopped	2	2
Okra, chopped	350g/12oz	1½ cups
Chopped parsley	125g/4oz	1 cup

Put the beef, rabbit, salt and pepper into a very large saucepan and just cover with water. Bring to the boil, skimming off any scum that rises to the surface. Reduce the heat to low, cover and simmer for 2 to 2½ hours, or until the meats are cooked through and tender. Transfer the meats to a chopping board and set aside until they are cool enough to handle.

Add all the remaining ingredients except the parsley to the stock in the pan and bring to the boil. Simmer for 30 minutes.

Meanwhile, chop the beef into cubes and chop the rabbit meat into bite-sized pieces. Discard the rabbit skin and bones. Stir the meats into the vegetables and simmer for a further 15 minutes, or until they are heated through. Stir in the parsley and adjust the seasoning to your taste. Serve at once, in large bowls.

8 Servings

THANKSGIVING TURKEY

The annual festival of Thanksgiving has been celebrated in the U.S. since the Pilgrim Fathers first landed in Massachusetts. This is one of many versions of the Thanksgiving turkey.

	Metric/U.K.	U.S.
Oven-ready turkey, with the liver reserved and finely chopped	1 × 5kg/10lb	1 × 10lb
Salt and pepper to taste		
Butter, melted	125g/4oz	8 Tbs
Apricot jam	4 Tbs	4 Tbs
White wine	150ml/5floz	⅝ cup
Beurre manié (two parts flour and one part butter blended)	2 Tbs	2 Tbs
STUFFING I		
Butter	50g/2oz	4 Tbs
Medium onions, finely chopped	2	2
Pumpkin, peeled, seeded and grated	275g/10oz	1¼ cups
Large carrots, grated	2	2
Sugar	2 tsp	2 tsp
Grated nutmeg	½ tsp	½ tsp
Double (heavy) cream	50ml/2floz	¼ cup
STUFFING II		
Butter	25g/1oz	2 Tbs
Medium onion, finely chopped	1	1
Pork sausagemeat	275g/10oz	10oz
Cranberry jelly	125g/4oz	½ cup
Chopped fresh basil	1 Tbs	1 Tbs
Salt and pepper to taste		
Chopped almonds	50g/2oz	⅓ cup

Rub the turkey, inside and out, with the salt and pepper.

To make stuffing I, melt the butter in a saucepan. Add the onions, pumpkin and carrots and fry until they are soft. Stir in the salt and pepper, sugar, nutmeg and cream, and simmer for 10 minutes, or until the pumpkin is tender and most of the liquid has evaporated. Set aside while you prepare stuffing II.

Melt the butter in a frying-pan. Add the onion and fry until it is soft. Stir in the sausagemeat and fry until it loses its pinkness. Stir in the remaining stuffing ingredients and cook for a further 3 minutes. Set aside.

Preheat the oven to hot 220°C (Gas Mark 7, 425°F).

Stand the turkey upright on a wooden board. Spoon stuffing I into the stomach cavity and press down with the back of a spoon. Spoon stuffing II on top and press down. Secure the openings with a trussing needle and thread or skewers. Brush the turkey liberally with the melted butter.

Put the turkey, breast down, in a large roasting pan and baste liberally with the melted butter. Put the pan into the oven and roast for 15 minutes. Reduce the temperature to moderate 180°C (Gas Mark 4, 350°F) and continue to roast for 2¼ hours, basting occasionally. Remove the pan from the oven and turn the turkey over. Spread over the apricot jam and pour over the wine. Return the pan to the oven and continue to roast for a further 30 minutes, basting occasionally, or until the turkey is cooked through and tender.

Transfer the turkey to a carving board and remove and discard the trussing thread or skewers. Keep hot.

Pour 350ml/12floz (1½ cups) of cooking juices into a saucepan and bring to the boil over high heat. Boil rapidly for 5 minutes or until it has reduced slightly. Add the beurre manié, a little at a time, and reduce the heat to low. Cook, stirring constantly, for 2 to 3 minutes or until the sauce has thickened. Pour into a sauceboat and serve with the turkey.

8-10 Servings

NEW ENGLAND BOILED DINNER

	Metric/U.K.	U.S.
Salt silverside or brisket of beef	1 × 2kg/4lb	4lb
Black peppercorns	6	6
Onion	1	1
Bouquet garni	1	1
Brown sugar	1 Tbs	1 Tbs

Carrots	8	8
Medium potatoes, quartered	8	8
Small onions	6	6
Small beetroots (beets)	8	8
Small head of cabbage, cut into wedges	1	1

Put the beef into a large saucepan and cover with cold water. Bring to the boil, skimming off any scum that rises to the surface. When the scum stops rising, add the peppercorns, onion, bouquet garni and sugar. Reduce the heat to low, half-cover the pan and simmer for 2 hours. Remove and discard the onion and bouquet garni.

Add the carrots, potatoes, onions and beetroots (beets) and simmer gently for a further 30 minutes. Add the cabbage wedges and simmer for a further 15 minutes, or until the vegetables and meat are cooked through and tender.

Transfer the meat to a carving board and cut into thick slices. Arrange on a warmed serving

An indispensable part of the American festive scene, the Thanksgiving Turkey. Here it has two stuffings, one based on pumpkin, the other on pork sausage and cranberries. If you want to be really traditional, serve with Candied Sweet Potatoes (page 37) and Corn Bread (page 58), then follow it with Pumpkin Pie (page 54).

American steaks are famous throughout the world. *Porterhouse Steak with Red Wine Sauce is served here with a simple salad, but for a more formal meal, accompany it with the traditional Baked Potato with Sour Cream and Chives (page 37) and Caesar Salad (page 41).*

dish and surround with the vegetables. Serve at once.

6-8 Servings

RED FLANNEL HASH

Thrifty New Englanders serve this dish as a way to 'stretch' the leftovers from their classic New England Boiled Dinner.

	Metric/U.K.	U.S.
Corned beef, cubed	½kg/1lb	1lb
Medium potatoes, cut into cubes	4	4
Cooked beetroots (beets), cubed	225g/8oz	8oz
Medium onion, chopped	1	1
Double (heavy) cream	175ml/6floz	¾ cup
Chopped parsley	1 Tbs	1 Tbs
Worcestershire sauce	1 tsp	1 tsp
Salt and pepper to taste		
Cayenne pepper	¼ tsp	¼ tsp
Butter	50g/2oz	4 Tbs

Combine the corned beef, potatoes, beetroots (beets) and onion.

Combine the cream, parsley, Worcestershire sauce, salt, pepper and cayenne together. Pour over the corned beef mixture and toss well.

Melt the butter in a large frying-pan. Add the mixture and cook over low heat for 10 minutes, pressing down on the mixture occasionally or until a crust has formed on the base. Remove the pan from the heat and carefully invert the hash so that the crust is now on the top. Cook for a further 10 minutes or until a crust has formed on the other side. Serve at once.

4 Servings

YANKEE POT ROAST

This satisfying dish shows a distinctly Italian influence, but served with mashed potatoes and salad, it is an all-American dish fit for a

President. Bottom round may be substituted for the rump, if you prefer.

	Metric/U.K.	U.S.
Rump steak, rolled and tied	1x3kg/6lb	1x6lb
Red wine	600ml/1 pint	2½ cups
Medium onions, thinly sliced into rings	1	1
Garlic cloves	4	4
Dried basil	1½ tsp	1½ tsp
Butter	25g/1oz	2 Tbs
Olive oil	50ml/2floz	¼ cup
Salt and pepper to taste		
Canned peeled tomatoes, drained	425g/14oz	14oz
Black olives, stoned (pitted)	50g/2oz	⅔ cup
Cornflour (cornstarch), blended with 2 Tbs water	1 Tbs	1 Tbs
Chopped parsley	1 Tbs	1 Tbs

Put the meat in a large bowl and add the wine, onions, garlic and basil. Set aside to marinate at room temperature for 6 hours, basting occasionally. Remove the meat from the marinade and pat dry with kitchen towels. Reserve the marinade.

Preheat the oven to moderate 180°C (Gas Mark 4, 350°F).

Melt the butter with the oil in a large flameproof casserole. Add the meat and fry until it is evenly browned. Add the marinade and bring to the boil. Add salt and pepper to taste and transfer the casserole to the oven. Roast for 2 hours. Add the tomatoes and roast for a further 1 hour, or until the meat is cooked through and tender. Remove from the oven and transfer the meat to a carving board. Cut into thick slices and arrange decoratively on a warmed serving platter. Keep hot while you make the sauce.

Strain the liquid into a saucepan, pressing down on the vegetables with the back of a wooden spoon to extract the juices. Bring to the boil, then add the olives. Reduce the heat to low and stir in the cornflour (cornstarch) mixture. Cook, stirring constantly, until the sauce thickens and is smooth.

Pour over the meat slices, sprinkle over the parsley and serve at once.

10 Servings

PORTERHOUSE STEAK WITH RED WINE SAUCE

Steaks occupy a special place in the American heart, and no wonder. They are simple and quick to make and absolutely fantastic to eat, whether they be T-bone, sirloin or porterhouse, as here. The red wine sauce in the recipe below may be omitted if you prefer your steak unadorned.

	Metric/U.K.	U.S.
Black peppercorns	3 Tbs	3 Tbs
Porterhouse steaks, cut about 1cm/½in thick	4	4
Garlic cloves, crushed	2	2
Salt	1 tsp	1 tsp
Butter	50g/2oz	4 Tbs
Medium onions, thinly sliced	2	2
Mushrooms, thinly sliced	125g/4oz	1 cup
Red wine	125ml/4floz	½ cup
Dried thyme	¼ tsp	¼ tsp
Beurrie manié (two parts flour and one part butter blended)	1 Tbs	1 Tbs

Crush the peppercorns coarsely and put them in a shallow dish. Rub the steaks all over with the garlic and salt, and press each side into the peppercorns.

Melt half the butter in a large frying-pan. Add the onions and fry until they are soft. Stir in the mushrooms and fry for 3 minutes. Transfer the vegetables to a plate while you cook the steaks.

Add the remaining butter to the pan. Add the steaks and fry for 3 minutes on each side over moderate heat. Reduce the heat to moderately low and fry for a further 3 minutes on each side. This will give you rare steaks; double the cooking time for well-done steaks. Transfer the steaks to a warmed serving platter and keep hot.

Return the vegetable mixture to the pan and pour over the wine. Stir in the thyme and boil for 2 minutes. Add the beurre manié, a little at a time, and cook for a further 2 minutes, stirring constantly, or until the sauce has thickened.

Pour over the steaks and serve at once.

4 Servings

LONDON BROIL

Despite its name, this dish is a standard lunch menu item all over the United States. It is often served, cut into diagonal slices, on toast or, as here, with Béarnaise sauce for a more formal meal.

	Metric/U.K.	U.S.
Rump or flank steaks	4 × 225g/8oz	4 × 8oz
MARINADE		
White wine vinegar	50ml/2floz	¼ cup
Olive or vegetable oil	50ml/2floz	¼ cup
Garlic clove, crushed	1	1
Lemon juice	1 Tbs	1 Tbs
Black peppercorns, crushed	4	4
Salt	1 tsp	1 tsp

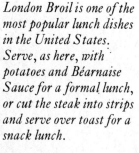

London Broil is one of the most popular lunch dishes in the United States. Serve, as here, with potatoes and Béarnaise Sauce for a formal lunch, or cut the steak into strips and serve over toast for a snack lunch.

Combine all the marinade ingredients in a large shallow dish. Arrange the steaks in the dish and set aside at room temperature for 2 hours, basting occasionally.

Preheat the grill (broiler) to high.

Remove the steaks from the marinade and discard it. Put the steaks on a lined grill (broiler) rack and grill (broil) for 3 minutes on each side. Reduce the heat to low and grill (broil) for a further 3 to 4 minutes on each side, depending on the doneness of the steaks.

Serve at once.

4 Servings

MEAT LOAF I

Meat loaves are standard American fare and are served hot or cold for lunch or dinner, on sandwiches, or as picnic fare.

	Metric/U.K.	U.S.
Butter	25g/1oz	2 Tbs
Large onions, chopped	2	2
Garlic clove, crushed	1	1
Minced (ground) beef	700g/1½lb	1½lb
Pork sausagemeat	225g/8oz	8oz
Tomato purée (paste)	125g/4oz	4oz
Worcestershire sauce	1 tsp	1 tsp
Dried thyme	1 tsp	1 tsp
Salt and pepper to taste		

Preheat the oven to fairly hot 200°C (Gas Mark 6, 400°F).

Melt the butter in a frying-pan. Add the onions and garlic and fry until the onions are

soft. Remove from the heat and transfer the mixture to a bowl. Set aside to cool.

When the mixture has cooled, stir in all the remaining ingredients and mix and beat until they are thoroughly blended. Spoon into a well-greased 1kg/2lb loaf tin, smoothing the top with a knife.

Put the tin into the oven and bake the loaf for 1 hour, or until a skewer inserted into the centre comes out clean.

Remove from the oven and pour off any fat. Turn out on to a warmed serving dish and serve at once, if you are serving the loaf hot.

6-8 Servings

MEAT LOAF II

	Metric/U.K.	U.S.
Minced (ground) beef	½kg/1lb	1lb
Fresh breadcrumbs	75g/3oz	1½ cups
Medium onion, chopped	1	1
Mushrooms, sliced	125g/4oz	1 cup
Eggs, lightly beaten	2	2
Mustard	2 tsp	2 tsp
Worcestershire sauce	1 tsp	1 tsp
Salt and pepper to taste		
Dried marjoram	½ tsp	½ tsp
Dried thyme	½ tsp	½ tsp
Streaky (fatty) bacon	3 slices	3 slices

Preheat the oven to warm 170°C (Gas Mark 3, 325°F).

Combine all the ingredients, except the bacon slices, in a large bowl until they are well blended. Press the mixture into a well-greased 1kg/2lb loaf tin and smooth down the top with a knife. Lay the bacon slices over the top.

Put the tin into a large roasting pan and pour boiling water around it until it comes halfway up the sides. Put the pan into the oven and bake the loaf for 1½ hours. Remove from the oven and remove the tin from the pan. Set aside to cool for 1 hour.

Unmould the meat loaf and turn out on to a plate. Wrap in aluminium foil and chill in the refrigerator for at least 4 hours before serving.

4-6 Servings

Meat loaf used to be what you did with leftover roast, or when you needed to make small amounts of minced (ground) meat go 'further', but the Americans have elevated it into an art form. There are almost as many different meat loaves as there are cooks, but Meat Loaf I above is particularly versatile in that it can be served hot or cold.

25

HAMBURGERS

	Metric/U.K.	U.S.
Minced (ground) beef	1½kg/3lb	3lb
Fresh breadcrumbs	50g/2oz	1 cup
Salt and pepper to taste		
Dried thyme	1 tsp	1 tsp
Egg, lightly beaten	1	1
ACCOMPANIMENTS		
Medium tomatoes, thinly sliced	3	3
Large onion, thinly sliced into rings	1	1
Large lettuce leaves	6	6
Hamburger or large soft buns	6	6
Butter	50g/2oz	4 Tbs

Mix the minced (ground) beef, breadcrumbs, seasonings and egg together. Form the mixture into six balls, then flatten them into patties with the palms of your hands.

Preheat the oven to warm 170°C (Gas Mark 3, 325°F).

Arrange the tomato slices, onion rings and lettuce leaves on a large serving plate.

Split the buns in half and butter each half. Re-assemble them then arrange on a baking sheet. Put the sheet into the oven and leave the buns to heat through while you cook the hamburgers.

Preheat the grill (broiler) to high.

Place the hamburgers on a lined grill (broiler) rack and grill (broil) for 3 minutes on each side, or until they are well browned. Reduce the heat to moderate and continue to grill (broil) the hamburgers for a further 5 to 7 minutes on each side, or until they are cooked through to taste.

To serve, put the hamburgers between the buns and serve at once with the accompaniments.

6 Servings

BOURBON HAM

The bourbon in this recipe refers not to the royal European house but to a whisky lovingly made in the southern and border states of the United States, which provides a classic glaze for ham—among other things, of course!

	Metric/U.K.	U.S.
Smoked ham, scrubbed	1 × 5kg/10lb	1 × 10lb
Bouquet garni	1	1
Peppercorns	8	8
Onion, quartered	1	1
Carrot, quartered	1	1
Celery stalk, quartered	1	1
Dark brown sugar	350g/12oz	2 cups
Dry mustard	2 tsp	2 tsp
Bourbon whisky	175ml/6floz	¾ cup

Hamburgers are an American, even a world-wide, institution. To be really authentic serve on lightly toasted buns with lots of relishes and tomato ketchup, and eat with your hands. If you want to make it into a cheeseburger, as above, just put a slice of Cheddar or other hard cheese on top of the hamburger for the last few minutes of cooking, until it melts slightly.

Cloves	12	12
Oranges, peeled and segmented	2	2

Put the ham in a large bowl and cover with cold water. Soak overnight, then drain. Transfer the ham to a large saucepan and just cover with water. Add the bouquet garni, peppercorns and vegetables. Bring to the boil. Reduce the heat to low and simmer for about 4½ hours (allow about 25 minutes per pound for a fairly large ham, a little more for a smaller one).

Remove the pan from the heat and allow the ham to cool in the liquid.

Preheat the oven to moderate 180°C (Gas Mark 4, 350°F).

Combine the sugar, mustard and 50ml/2floz (¼ cup) of the whisky and set aside.

Remove the ham from the pan and wipe dry with kitchen towels. Cut away the rind then, using the point of a sharp knife, score the fat in a diamond pattern, making cuts through the fat to the meat. Transfer the ham to a rack in a roasting pan. Coat the scored ham with the remaining bourbon. Using a rubber spatula, spread the sugar mixture generously over the

below left: *Spareribs are part of the American scene and all sorts of interesting dishes are made from them—this particular recipe teams them with another American favourite, maple syrup.*

below right: *Barbecued Pork Chops are south-western in origin. Serve with lots of potatoes, salad and crusty bread for a superb and warming meal.*

ham, push the cloves into the fat and arrange the orange segments over the top and sides, securing them with cocktail sticks.

Put the ham into the oven and roast it, basting occasionally, for 1 hour. Serve at once.

10-12 Servings

MAPLE SPARERIBS

Spare ribs are a popular—and inexpensive—meat, and they lend themselves very well to a variety of sauces. Serve these spareribs, as below, with lots of salad for a superb informal meal.

	Metric/U.K.	U.S.
Maple syrup	150ml/5floz	$\frac{5}{8}$ cup
Cayenne pepper	$\frac{1}{4}$ tsp	$\frac{1}{4}$ tsp
Salt and pepper to taste		
Garlic cloves, crushed	2	2
Tomato purée (paste)	2 Tbs	2 Tbs
Prepared French or German mustard	1 Tbs	1 Tbs
Lemon juice	2 Tbs	2 Tbs
Spareribs of pork, trimmed of excess fat and cut into 2-rib serving pieces	2kg/4lb	4lb

Preheat the oven to fairly hot 200°C (Gas Mark 6, 400°F).

Combine all the ingredients, except the spareribs, and beat well to blend.

Arrange the spareribs in a roasting pan and put the pan into the oven. Roast the ribs for 30 minutes. Remove the pan from the oven and remove the spareribs. Discard the fat in the pan, then return the ribs. Pour over the syrup mixture and baste well.

Reduce the oven temperature to moderate 180°C (Gas Mark 4, 350°F) and continue to roast the ribs, basting frequently, for 45 minutes, or until they are browned and glazed. Serve at once.

4 Servings

BARBECUED PORK CHOPS

	Metric/U.K.	U.S.
Butter	1 tsp	1 tsp
Large onion, thinly sliced into rings	1	1
Loin pork chops	6	6
Salt and pepper to taste		
BARBECUE SAUCE		
Red wine vinegar	50ml/2floz	¼ cup
Tomato ketchup	125ml/4floz	½ cup
Sugar	2 tsp	2 tsp
Ground cloves	½ tsp	½ tsp
Celery seeds	1 tsp	1 tsp
Dry mustard	½ tsp	½ tsp
Bay leaf	1	1

Preheat the oven to moderate 180°C (Gas Mark 4, 350°F). With the butter, grease a baking dish large enough to take the chops in one layer. Arrange the onion rings in the dish.

Rub the chops with salt and pepper and put them on top of the onion rings.

Combine all the sauce ingredients and pour over the chops. Put the dish into the oven and bake for 1 hour, or until the chops are cooked through and tender.

Remove and discard the bay leaf and serve at once.

6 Servings

SMOTHERED PORK CHOPS

This is one of the standard items on any 'soulfood' menu. Originally, when it was the festive fare of slaves, the meat was of low quality, cheap pork chops with more fat than meat—the original reason why they were 'smothered' in a rich, spicy gravy. Now that things are at least better than they were, the chops can be of any quality you can afford and like. For a completely authentic soulfood dinner, served Smothered Pork Chops with Collards and Fatback, Hoppin' John and hot Corn Bread.

	Metric/U.K.	U.S.
Pork chops	6	6
Salt and pepper to taste		
Garlic salt	1 tsp	1 tsp
Flour	50g/2oz	½ cup
Cooking oil	50ml/2floz	¼ cup
Water or stock	300ml/10floz	1¼ cups
Worcestershire sauce	1 tsp	1 tsp
Tabasco sauce	¼ tsp	¼ tsp
Medium onion, very finely chopped	1	1

Rub the chops with salt and pepper and sprinkle over half the garlic salt. Set aside for 10 minutes. Gently coat the chops with 40g/1½oz (⅓ cup) of the flour, shaking off any excess.

Heat the oil in a large frying-pan. Add the chops and fry for 10 to 15 minutes, or until they are crisp and evenly browned. Transfer them to a plate.

Stir the remaining flour into the oil in the pan until it forms a smooth paste. Gradually stir in the water or stock and bring to the boil. Stir in the remaining garlic salt, Worcestershire and Tabasco sauces and simmer for 5 minutes. Stir in the onion and simmer for a further 2 minutes.

Return the chops to the pan and cover them with the sauce. Reduce the heat to very low, cover and simmer for 30 to 40 minutes, or until the chops are cooked through and tender.

Remove from the heat, transfer to a warmed serving dish and serve at once.

6 Servings

VEAL PARMESAN

This popular dish is an American adaptation of a traditional Italian favourite. It makes an excellent light meal, served with salad and bread—and lots of red wine.

	Metric/U.K.	U.S.
Veal escalopes, pounded thin and halved	6	6
Lemon juice	2 Tbs	2 Tbs
Large eggs, lightly beaten	2	2
Seasoned flour	125g/4oz	1 cup
Butter	125g/4oz	8 Tbs
Mozzarella cheese, thinly sliced	275g/10oz	10oz
Parmesan cheese, grated	75g/3oz	¾ cup
TOMATO SAUCE Olive oil	50ml/2floz	¼ cup
Medium onions, thinly sliced	2	2
Garlic cloves, crushed	2	2
Canned peeled tomatoes, chopped	450g/1lb	1lb
Tomato purée (paste)	2 Tbs	2 Tbs
Salt and pepper to taste		
Dried basil	½ tsp	½ tsp
Grated Parmesan cheese	2 Tbs	2 Tbs

To make the sauce, heat the oil in a saucepan. Add the onions and garlic and fry until the onions are soft. Add the tomatoes and can juice, the tomato purée (paste), salt, pepper and basil, and stir to mix. Bring the mixture to the boil, reduce the heat to low and simmer for 30 minutes.

Meanwhile, sprinkle the veal with the lemon juice. Preheat the oven to moderate 180°C (Gas Mark 4, 350°F).

Put the eggs in one shallow dish and the flour in another. Dip the veal first in the eggs then in the flour, shaking off any excess.

Melt a third of the butter in a frying-pan. Add a third of the veal pieces and fry, turning occasionally, for 5 to 8 minutes or until they are evenly browned. Transfer to kitchen towels and keep hot while you cook the remaining veal pieces in the same way, using the remaining butter.

Put half the veal pieces on the bottom of an ovenproof casserole. Top with half the cheese slices, then the remaining veal. Cover with the remaining cheese slices.

Remove the sauce from the heat and stir in the grated cheese. Pour the mixture over the mixture in the casserole. Sprinkle over the remaining grated cheese and put the dish into the oven. Bake for 35 to 45 minutes or until the top is brown and bubbling. Serve at once.

6 Servings

BREADED VEAL CUTLETS

This dish is a sort of near cousin to the Austrian

Wiener Schnitzel, except that in Breaded Veal Cutlets, the cutlets or escalopes are not so thin. This dish is often served with a tomato sauce in highway diners all over the United States.

	Metric/U.K.	U.S.
Thin veal cutlets or veal escalopes	4	4
Salt and pepper to taste		
Seasoned flour	50g/2oz	$\frac{1}{2}$ cup
Eggs, lightly beaten	2	2
Fine dry breadcrumbs	50g/2oz	$\frac{2}{3}$ cup
Butter	50g/2oz	4 Tbs
Lemon, cut into slices	I	I

Rub the escalopes with salt and pepper. Put the flour in one shallow dish, the eggs in another and breadcrumbs in a third. Dip the escalopes, one by one, into the flour, then the eggs and finally the breadcrumbs, shaking off any excess.

Melt the butter in a large frying-pan. Add the escalopes and cook for 4 to 5 minutes on each side, turning over very carefully so as not to disturb the coating.

Transfer to a warmed serving dish and garnish with the lemon slices.

4 Servings

CREAMED CHICKEN LIVERS

	Metric/U.K.	U.S.
Butter	50g/2oz	4 Tbs
Onions, thinly sliced into rings	2	2
Chicken livers, cut into strips	12	12
Single (light) cream	250ml/8floz	I cup
Hard-boiled eggs, chopped	2	2
Salt and pepper to taste		
Paprika	2 tsp	2 tsp

Melt half the butter in a deep frying-pan. Add the onion rings and fry until they are golden brown. Using a slotted spoon, transfer them to a large plate and set aside.

Add the chicken liver strips to the pan and fry for 5 minutes, adding more butter if necessary. Using the slotted spoon, transfer the strips to the onion rings, mixing them well.

Add the remaining butter to the pan and melt it. Add the remaining ingredients, including the livers and onions, and cook for 5 minutes, stirring frequently. Transfer to a warmed dish and serve at once.

4 Servings

Creamed Chicken Livers is simple to make, and delicious to eat. Serve, as here, with rice for a filling meal.

Sandwiches are an American speciality and Club Sandwich is one of the very best of them. It can be made 'two-decker' as here or, if you feel really hungry, you can add a 'third deck', with another, contrasting filling in between the extra bread.

CLUB SANDWICH

This is perhaps one of the most popular of all the great American sandwiches, and it comes in a multitude of forms: there are some who make it a 'three-decker', ie with two lots of fillings, there are others who substitute chicken for the turkey, or even ham.

	Metric/U.K.	U.S.
White bread, toasted and kept hot	8 slices	8 slices
Cooked turkey, thinly sliced	275g/10oz	10oz
Salt and pepper to taste		
Large lettuce leaves	4	4
Medium tomatoes, sliced	4	4
Mayonnaise	4 Tbs	4 Tbs

Put half of the bread slices on a board and cover them with turkey slices and salt and pepper to taste. Cover with the lettuce leaves, then the tomato slices. Spread the mayonnaise generously over the four remaining toast slices and put them on top of the filling. Serve at once.

4 Servings

BACON LETTUCE AND TOMATO SANDWICH

This sandwich is so much part of the American scene that it is more usually referred to by its initials (BLT) than by its full name. It makes a perfect lunch dish, or a quick snack meal.

	Metric/U.K.	U.S.
White bread, toasted	8 slices	8 slices
Bacon, chopped and grilled (broiled) until crisp	175g/6oz	6oz
Large lettuce leaves	4	4
Medium tomatoes, sliced	3	3
Mayonnaise	6 Tbs	6 Tbs
Salt and pepper to taste		

Put half the toast slices on a board and arrange the bacon over them. Cover with the lettuce and tomato and salt and pepper to taste. Spread the mayonnaise generously over the four remaining slices and cover the filling. Cut in half and serve at once.

4 Servings

Vegetables and Salads

CORN ON THE COB

	Metric/U.K.	U.S.
Ears of corn	4	4
Sugar	1 tsp	1 tsp

Remove the husks and silk threads from the corn.

Half-fill a large saucepan with water and add the sugar. Bring to the boil. Add the corn ears and return to the boil. Boil for 10 to 20 minutes, depending on the age of the corn, or until the kernels are cooked and have turned bright yellow.

Remove the pan from the heat and drain the corn. Transfer to a warmed serving dish and serve at once, with lots of butter.

4 Servings

CORN PUDDING

This is a dish probably adapted by the early settlers from native American Indian fare. For convenience, creamed sweetcorn has been substituted for fresh corn—but fresh corn and double (heavy) cream can, of course, be used instead of the ingredients suggested below.

	Metric/U.K.	U.S.
Canned creamed sweetcorn	700g/1½lb	1½lb
Eggs, lightly beaten	2	2
Flour	4 Tbs	4 Tbs
Salt and pepper to taste		
Cayenne pepper	¼ tsp	¼ tsp
Butter	25g/1oz	2 Tbs
Single (light) cream	250ml/8floz	1 cup

Preheat the oven to warm 170°C (Gas Mark 3, 325°F). Put the sweetcorn into a large bowl and beat in the eggs, flour and seasonings. Melt the butter in a small saucepan, then stir into the mixture with the cream. Beat gently until the ingredients are thoroughly blended.

Pour the mixture into a well-greased baking dish and put the dish in a deep roasting pan.

Corn cobs are native to the Americas and were a staple food of the Indians long before Christopher Columbus (or Eric the Red . . .) first sighted land. Corn on the Cob, served with knobs of butter, remains a popular vegetable accompaniment throughout the country.

*Boston Baked Beans—
one of the glories of New
England cooking. Once
you've eaten these, you'll
never touch a can of beans
again . . . Serve them with
frankfurters or pastrami.*

Pour enough boiling water into the pan to come about halfway up the sides of the dish. Put the dish in the oven and bake the pudding for 1½ hours, or until a knife inserted into the centre comes out clean.

Serve at once.

4-6 Servings

BOSTON BAKED BEANS

One of the most famous dishes in the United States, Boston Baked Beans predates the Revolution. Traditionally, it used to be baked in the oven with the week's bread.

	Metric/U.K.	U.S.
Dried haricot (dried white), pea or kidney beans, soaked overnight in cold water and drained	1kg/2lb	5⅓ cups
Salt	2 tsp	2 tsp
Large onion	1	1
Salt pork, soaked in cold water for 3 hours, drained and thickly sliced	225g/8oz	8oz
Brown sugar	75g/3oz	½ cup
Molasses or dark treacle	75ml/3floz	6 Tbs
Dry mustard	1 Tbs	1 Tbs
Black pepper	1 tsp	1 tsp

Put the beans in a large saucepan and add enough water just to cover. Stir in half the salt and bring to the boil. Reduce the heat to low, half-cover the pan and simmer for 30 minutes. Drain the beans and discard the liquid.

Preheat the oven to very cool 130°C (Gas Mark ½, 250°F.)

Put the onion on the bottom of a large flameproof casserole. Add a layer of beans, then arrange a layer of salt pork slices over the beans. Add the remaining beans, topped by the remaining salt pork.

Mix the sugar, molasses or treacle, mustard, black pepper and remaining salt together and spoon over the mixture. Add enough boiling water to cover. Cover and put the casserole in the oven. Bake for 5 hours, adding boiling water from time to time so that the beans remain covered.

Remove the cover and bake the beans for a further 45 minutes, or until a slight crust has formed on top. Serve at once.

6-8 Servings

HARVARD BEETS

	Metric/U.K.	U.S.
Sugar	50g/2oz	¼ cup
Cornflour (cornstarch)	1 tsp	1 tsp
Vinegar	50ml/2floz	¼ cup
Water	125ml/4floz	½ cup
Cooked beetroots (beets), sliced	½kg/1lb	1lb

Combine the sugar and cornflour (cornstarch).

Put the vinegar and water in a saucepan and heat over low heat. When the mixture is lukewarm, gradually stir in the sugar mixture until it is completely absorbed. Bring to the boil and cook, stirring constantly, for 2 minutes, or until the sauce is fairly thick and smooth.

Stir in the beetroots (beets) and baste well. Simmer for 4 to 5 minutes, or until they are heated through. Serve at once.

4 Servings

BOSTON STUFFED EGGPLANT

	Metric/U.K.	U.S.
Medium aubergines (eggplants), halved lengthways and dégorged	2	2
Olive oil	75ml/3floz	⅜ cup
Butter	40g/1½oz	3 Tbs
Medium onion, finely chopped	1	1
Mushrooms, sliced	225g/8oz	2 cups
Salt and pepper to taste		
Cayenne pepper	⅛ tsp	⅛ tsp
Grated Parmesan cheese	4 Tbs	4 Tbs
BECHAMEL SAUCE		
Butter	25g/1oz	2 Tbs
Flour	2 Tbs	2 Tbs

34

Milk	125ml/4floz	½ cup
Stock	125ml/4floz	½ cup

Hoppin' John, one of the staples of the soul food repertoire, is a spicy mixture of rice and black-eye beans. For an authentic 'soul' meal, serve it with Smothered Pork Chops (page 29), Collards with Fatback (page 37) and warm Corn Bread (page 58).

Squeeze the aubergines (eggplants) to remove as much liquid as possible, then dry with kitchen towels.

Preheat the oven to fairly hot 200°C (Gas Mark 6, 400°F).

Heat the oil in a large frying-pan. Put the aubergine (eggplant) halves in the pan and cook until they are lightly and evenly browned. Transfer to a plate.

Wipe out the pan and add the butter. When it has melted, add the onion and fry until it is soft. Stir in the mushrooms and cook for a further 2 minutes. Stir in the salt, pepper and cayenne and transfer to a bowl.

Using a spoon, scoop out the aubergine (eggplant) flesh, leaving the skins intact. Add the flesh to the vegetable mixture and blend thoroughly. Carefully spoon about a quarter of the mixture into each aubergine (eggplant) shell.

To make the béchamel sauce, melt the butter in a saucepan. Remove the pan from the heat and stir in the flour to form a smooth paste. Gradually stir in the milk and stock and return to the heat. Bring to the boil, and cook for 2 to 3 minutes, stirring constantly, or until the sauce is thick and smooth.

Put the stuffed aubergines (eggplants) into a shallow baking dish and pour over the béchamel sauce. Sprinkle over the grated cheese. Put the dish into the oven and bake for 10 minutes, or until the topping is golden brown.

Serve at once.

4 Servings

HOPPIN' JOHN

Hoppin' John, a mixture of black-eye beans and rice, is an indispensable part of the Southern 'soul food' repertoire. It is traditionally served with ham hocks or smothered pork chops, collards and corn bread.

	Metric/U.K.	U.S.
Dried black-eye beans, soaked in cold water overnight and drained	225g/8oz	1⅓ cups
Water	1¼ l/2 pints	5 cups
Salt	½ tsp	½ tsp
Long-grain rice, soaked in cold water for 30 minutes and drained	225g/8oz	1⅓ cups
Vegetable oil	1 Tbs	1 Tbs
Medium onion, finely chopped	1	1
Canned peeled tomatoes	425g/14oz	14oz
Cayenne pepper	¼ tsp	¼ tsp
Black pepper	½ tsp	½ tsp

Put the beans in a large saucepan and pour over the water and salt. Bring to the boil, reduce the heat to low and half-cover the pan. Simmer for 1½ hours. Stir in the rice, re-cover and simmer for 15 minutes.

Meanwhile, heat the oil in a frying-pan. Add the onion and fry until it is soft. Remove the pan from the heat and stir in the tomatoes and can juice, and seasonings. Pour the mixture into the beans and rice, and stir to blend. Re-cover and simmer for a further 15 to 20 minutes, or until the rice and beans are cooked and tender. Serve at once.

4-6 Servings

COLLARDS WITH FATBACK

This dish was once a staple part of the diet of most of the black people in the United States. Now that 'soul food' is popular, even trendy, its popularity is increasing among whites as well. Since collards aren't available in many places, we have substituted spring greens.

	Metric/U.K.	U.S.
Spring greens (collard greens), cleaned	1½kg/3lb	3lb
Salt pork (fatback), preferably in one piece	225g/8oz	8oz
Garlic salt	1 tsp	1 tsp
Vinegar	2 Tbs	2 Tbs
Chilli peppers, seeded and chopped	3	3

Wash the greens very carefully, leaf by leaf and shake dry. Chop finely and set aside.

Half-fill a large saucepan with water and bring to the boil. Add the salt pork (fatback), reduce the heat to low and cover. Simmer for 1 hour.

Remove the salt pork from the pan. Add the greens, salt and vinegar and replace the salt pork (fatback) so that it is in the middle of the greens. Bring to the boil, reduce the heat to low and simmer for 2 hours.

Fifteen minutes before the end of the cooking time, sprinkle the chopped chillis over the top of the greens.

6-8 Servings

BAKED POTATOES WITH SOUR CREAM AND CHIVES

This is the classic accompaniment to a steak in the United States. Idaho is the potato usually used there—large King Edwards are probably best in Britain and elsewhere.

	Metric/U.K.	U.S.
Large potatoes, scrubbed	4	4
Butter	50g/2oz	4 Tbs
Salt and pepper to taste		
Sour cream	175ml/6floz	¾ cup
Chopped chives	2 Tbs	2 Tbs

Preheat the oven to hot 225°C (Gas Mark 7, 425°F). Arrange the potatoes on a baking sheet and put them into the oven. Bake for 1 to 1½ hours (depending on the size of the potatoes).

Remove the potatoes from the oven and gently slit the tops. Squeeze the sides slightly to loosen the flesh. Divide the butter equally among them and season with salt and pepper.

Combine the sour cream and chives and spoon the mixture into the slits. Serve at once.

4 Servings

CANDIED SWEET POTATOES

This is the traditional accompaniment to the Thanksgiving turkey in the United States, and has been popular since Cape Cod was first colonized.

Mayonnaise was actually invented by the French but it has definitely been adopted by America, and it is now used as the basis for many interesting salad dressings.

	Metric/U.K.	U.S.
Sweet potatoes, boiled for 20 minutes, drained and thickly sliced	1kg/2lb	2lb
Brown sugar	75g/3oz	6 Tbs
Maple syrup	125ml/4floz	½ cup
Lemon juice	50ml/2floz	¼ cup
Grated lemon rind	1 tsp	1 tsp
Butter	25g/1oz	2 Tbs
Salt and pepper to taste		

Preheat the oven to moderate 180°C (Gas Mark 4, 350°F).

Arrange the sweet potato slices in one layer if possible in a well-greased medium-sized baking dish.

Combine the sugar, syrup, lemon juice and rind and pour over the potato slices. Cut the butter into small pieces and dot over the slices. Season to taste.

Put the dish into the oven and bake, basting frequently, for 30 minutes, or until the potatoes are well glazed.

Serve at once.

4 Servings

MAYONNAISE

Mayonnaise originated in France but has been 'adopted' by the Americans with great enthusiasm and forms the basis of many of the most interesting salad dressings. And it makes an excellent 'extra' filling for sandwiches, eggs and baked potatoes, too.

	Metric/U.K.	U.S.
Egg yolks, at room temperature	2	2
Salt and pepper to taste		
Dry mustard	¾ tsp	¾ tsp
Olive oil, at room temperature	300ml/10floz	1¼ cups

Green Goddess Dressing is one of those delicious dressings which has mayonnaise as its base— and added to it are anchovies, spring onions (scallions), herbs and sour cream. It is often served with a mixed salad, and it makes an excellent filling for baked potatoes, too.

White wine vinegar or lemon juice	1 Tbs	1 Tbs

Put the egg yolks, seasoning and mustard in a mixing bowl and, using a wire whisk, beat until they are thoroughly blended and have thickened. Add the oil, a few drops at a time, whisking constantly. Do not add the oil too quickly or the mayonnaise willl curdle. (After the mayonnaise has thickened, the oil may be added a little more rapidly.)

Beat in a few drops of vinegar or lemon juice from time to time to prevent the mayonnaise from becoming too thick. When all the oil has been added, stir in the remaining vinegar or lemon juice.

Taste for seasoning and add more salt, pepper, mustard or lemon juice or vinegar if desired.

The mayonnaise is now ready to be used. Store in the refrigerator until ready to add to sauces or dressings.

About 300ml/10floz (1¼ cups)

GREEN GODDESS DRESSING

	Metric/U.K.	U.S.
Mayonnaise	250ml/8floz	1 cup
Anchovy fillets, finely chopped	3	3
Spring onions (scallions), finely chopped	3	3
Finely chopped parsley	2 Tbs	2 Tbs
Finely chopped fresh tarragon	2 tsp	2 tsp
Tarragon vinegar	1 Tbs	1 Tbs
Black pepper to taste		
Sour cream	150ml/5floz	⅝ cup

Combine all the ingredients, except the sour cream, and beat well until they are thoroughly blended. Fold in the sour cream.

Store in the refrigerator until ready to use.

About 350ml/12floz(1½ cups)

THOUSAND ISLAND DRESSING

	Metric/U.K.	U.S.
Mayonnaise	450ml/15floz	2 cups
Tabasco sauce	1¼ tsp	1¼ tsp
Chopped pimiento or sweet pickle	2 Tbs	2 Tbs
Stuffed olives, finely chopped	10	10
Hard-boiled eggs, finely chopped	2	2
Spring onion (scallion), finely chopped	1	1
Olive oil	3 Tbs	3 Tbs
Wine vinegar	1 Tbs	1 Tbs
Salt and pepper to taste		

Combine the mayonnaise, Tabasco, pimiento or pickle, olives, eggs and spring onion (scallion), and beat until they are thoroughly blended. Mix the remaining ingredients together, beating well to blend. Beat into the mayonnaise mixture.

Store in the refrigerator until ready to use.

About 600ml/1 pint(2½ cups)

BLUE CHEESE DRESSING

	Metric/U.K.	U.S.
Blue cheese (Stilton, Danish Blue, Dolcelatte, etc.), crumbled	125g/4oz	½ cup
Mayonnaise	125ml/4floz	½ cup
Double (heavy) cream or sour cream	125ml/4floz	½ cup
Salt and pepper to taste		

Combine the ingredients, beating until they are thoroughly blended.

Store in the refrigerator until ready to use.

About 300ml/10floz(1¼ cups)

Coleslaw is almost as popular outside the United States as within it, and it is as nutritious as it is tasty. Serve as a sandwich filling, as well as a salad accompaniment to cold meats, frankfurters or hamburgers.

COLESLAW

	Metric/U.K.	U.K.
Large white cabbage, shredded	1	1
Medium onion, finely chopped or grated	1	1
Green pepper, pith and seeds removed and finely chopped	½	½
Lemon juice	½ tsp	½ tsp
Caraway seeds	1 Tbs	1 Tbs
DRESSING		
Double (heavy) cream	175ml/6floz	¾ cup
Sour cream	75ml/3floz	⅜ cup
French mustard	1 Tbs	1 Tbs
Lemon juice	3 Tbs	3 Tbs
Sugar	1 Tbs	1 Tbs
Salt and pepper to taste		

Arrange the cabbage, onion, pepper and lemon juice in a salad bowl.

Combine all the dressing ingredients, beating until they are thoroughly blended. Pour over the cabbage mixture and add the caraway seeds. Toss until the salad is completely saturated.

Chill for at least 1 hour in the refrigerator before serving, and toss well before serving.

8 Servings

CAESAR SALAD

This very popular salad was created during the Roaring Twenties and remains identified with the era. It is the classic accompaniment to charcoal grilled (broiled) steak.

	Metric/U.K.	U.S.
Olive oil	150ml/5floz	⅝ cup
White bread, crusts removed and cut into small cubes	4 slices	4 slices
Garlic clove, halved	1	1
Wine vinegar	2 Tbs	2 Tbs
Lemon juice	1 tsp	1 tsp
Worcestershire sauce	½ tsp	½ tsp
Mustard	¼ tsp	¼ tsp
Sugar	¼ tsp	¼ tsp
Salt and pepper to taste		
Cos (romaine) lettuces, separated into leaves	2	2
Anchovy fillets, cut into small pieces	6	6
Egg, cooked in boiling water for 1 minute	1	1
Parmesan cheese, grated	50g/2oz	½ cup

Heat 50ml/2floz (¼ cup) of oil in a heavy frying-pan. Add the bread cubes and fry until they resemble small croûtons. Transfer them to kitchen towels to drain.

Rub the garlic halves around the inside of a large salad bowl, then discard them. Combine the remaining oil, vinegar, lemon juice, Worcestershire sauce, mustard, sugar and salt and pepper together.

Arrange the lettuce leaves in the bowl and pour over the dressing. Toss gently to blend. Stir in the reserved croûtons, anchovy fillets, egg and grated cheese, and toss vigorously until the ingredients are thoroughly blended. Serve at once.

8 Servings

CELERY VICTOR

Celery Victor is the creation of the chef at one of San Francisco's most famous hotels.

	Metric/U.K.	U.S.
Large celery hearts, halved	3	3
Chicken stock	350ml/12floz	1½ cups
Salt and pepper to taste		
Bay leaves	2	2
Olive oil	125ml/4floz	½ cup
Wine vinegar	4 Tbs	4 Tbs
Lettuce leaves	6	6
Anchovies, halved	6	6
Pimiento strips	12	12

Put the celery hearts in a saucepan and pour over the stock and seasonings. Bring to the boil, reduce the heat to low and cover the pan. Simmer for 20 minutes, or until the celery is tender. Drain and arrange the hearts in a bowl.

No cuisine would be complete without at least one potato salad—and the United States has many. This is one particularly delicious version. Serve with steaks or cold meats, or as one of a summer buffet selection.

Combine the oil and vinegar and pour over the celery. Set aside in the refrigerator for about 1½ hours, or until the hearts have cooled completely.

Arrange the lettuce leaves on a serving dish. Put the hearts on top and garnish with a lattice pattern of anchovies and pimiento strips. Serve at once.

6 Servings

POTATO SALAD

Almost every culture has at least one potato salad to its credit—and most have many. This recipe is a typical American version.

	Metric/U.K.	U.S.
Cooked potatoes, sliced	½kg/1lb	1lb
Mayonnaise	125ml/4floz	½ cup
Lemon juice	1 Tbs	1 Tbs
Olive oil	1 Tbs	1 Tbs
Salt and pepper to taste		
Chopped chives	2 Tbs	2 Tbs
Chopped leeks	4 Tbs	4 Tbs

Put three-quarters of the potatoes in a salad bowl. Pour over the mayonnaise, lemon juice and oil and season to taste with salt and pepper, and half the chives. Toss until the potatoes are thoroughly coated.

Arrange the remaining potato slices on top of the salad and sprinkle over the remaining chives and the leeks. Cover and chill in the refrigerator for 30 minutes before serving.

4 Servings

CHEF'S SALAD

This is a marvellous way to make left-over cooked meat into a superb meal—and you can use almost any type you like although the meats suggested below are traditional.

	Metric/U.K.	U.S.
Medium lettuce, chilled	1	1
Cold cooked chicken, cut into strips	125g/4oz	4oz
Cold cooked tongue, cut into strips	125g/4oz	4oz
Gruyére cheese, cut into pieces	125g/4oz	4oz
Large hard-boiled egg, thinly sliced	1	1
Finely chopped onion	1 Tbs	1 Tbs
Chopped black olives	3 Tbs	3 Tbs
Olive oil	75ml/3floz	6 Tbs
Red wine vinegar	2 Tbs	2 Tbs
Lemon juice	½ tsp	½ tsp
French mustard	¼ tsp	¼ tsp
Salt and pepper to taste		

Put the lettuce leaves in a large salad bowl. Add the chicken, tongue, cheese, egg, onion and olives.

Combine all the remaining ingredients, beating to blend thoroughly. Pour the dressing over the salad and toss well before serving.

4 Servings

WALDORF SALAD

The Waldorf-Astoria Hotel in New York is probably one of the most famous hostelries in the world—and its immortality is guaranteed in this delicious salad created by one of its Maîtres d'Hotel.

	Metric/U.K.	U.S.
Large red apples, cored and chopped	2	2
Lemon juice	1 Tbs	1 Tbs
Celery stalks, chopped	2	2
Walnuts, chopped	125g/4oz	⅔ cup
Mayonnaise	175ml/6floz	¾ cup
Salt and pepper to taste		

Put the apples in a salad bowl and sprinkle over the lemon juice. Stir in the celery and walnuts.

Combine the remaining ingredients, then pour over the salad. Toss gently until the ingredients are thoroughly coated with the dressing.

Serve at once.

4 Servings

Desserts and Cakes

Desserts in the United States are a very special thing and the repertoire of delicious cakes and pies is never-ending. Banana Cream Pie is one of many absolutely superb desserts.

APPLE BROWN BETTY

This dessert has been found in American cook books since the 18th century and continues to be popular today. Serve with whipped cream or custard.

	Metric/U.K.	U.S.
Fresh breadcrumbs	175g/6oz	3 cups
Butter, cut into small pieces	50g/2oz	4 Tbs
Apples, cored, peeled and thinly sliced	1kg/2lb	2lb
Brown sugar	125g/4oz	⅔ cup
Grated nutmeg	¼ tsp	¼ tsp
Grated rind of ½ lemon		
Raisins	125g/4oz	⅔ cup
Lemon juice	2 Tbs	2 Tbs
Sherry	75ml/3floz	⅜ cup

Preheat the oven to fairly hot 190°C (Gas Mark 5, 375°F).

Put about one-third of the breadcrumbs on the bottom of a well-greased baking dish. Dot with some of the butter pieces. Cover with half the apples, sugar, nutmeg, lemon rind and raisins and sprinkle over 1 tablespoon of lemon juice. Top with another third of breadcrumbs and repeat the layers as before with the

44

remaining ingredients, finishing with the remaining breadcrumbs dotted with butter pieces.

Put into the oven and bake for 40 minutes, or until the apples are tender and the topping is golden brown. Pour the sherry over the pudding and bake for a further 5 minutes. Serve hot.

4-6 Servings

BANANA CREAM PIE

	Metric/U.K.	U.S.
Shortcrust pastry dough	175g/6oz	6oz
FILLING		
Egg yolks	3	3
Castor (superfine) sugar	75g/3oz	⅜ cup
Salt	¼ tsp	¼ tsp
Cornflour (cornstarch)	2 Tbs	2 Tbs
Butter, melted	1 Tbs	1 Tbs
Milk	450ml/15floz	2 cups
Vanilla essence (extract)	1 tsp	1 tsp
Ripe bananas, sliced	2	2
TOPPING		
Egg whites	3	3
Castor (superfine) sugar	175g/6oz	¾ cup
Shredded almonds	2 Tbs	2 Tbs

Preheat the oven to fairly hot 200°C (Gas Mark 6, 400°F).

Roll out the pastry dough to about ½cm/¼in thick and use it to line a 23cm/9in pie dish. Chill in the refrigerator for 10 minutes. Prick the bottom with a fork and line with foil and weigh down with dried beans or peas. Put the dish on a baking sheet and put into the oven. Bake for 10 minutes. Remove the foil and beans or peas and return the pie shell to the oven for a further 10 minutes, or until it is browned and cooked through.

Reduce the oven to cool 150°C (Gas Mark 2, 300°F).

Beat the egg yolks in a heatproof bowl, then gradually whisk in the sugar, salt, cornflour (cornstarch) and butter. Bring the milk to the boil, then gradually stir into the egg mixture. Put the bowl over a pan of simmering water and set over low heat. Cook the mixture, stirring constantly, until it thickens. Remove the pan from the heat and the bowl from the

pan, and set aside to cool. Stir in the vanilla. Arrange the banana slices over the pastry shell and pour over the custard.

Beat the egg whites until they form stiff peaks. Beat in 1 tablespoon of sugar, then fold in the remaining sugar, beating until the mixture is stiff. Pile the meringue on top of the custard and spread to cover the top completely. Sprinkle over the shredded almonds.

Put the dish into the oven and bake for 15 to 20 minutes, or until the meringue is lightly browned. Serve cold.

6 Servings

BLUEBERRY GRUNT

The oddly named 'Grunt' is a warming pudding dating from early colonial New England. Many fruits can be made into grunts but the most popular is blueberry.

	Metric/U.K.	U.S.
Blueberries	½kg/1lb	1lb
Sugar	50g/2oz	¼ cup
Ground allspice	1 tsp	1 tsp
Lemon juice	2 Tbs	2 Tbs
Lemon rind	1 tsp	1 tsp
Maple syrup	50ml/2floz	¼ cup
CRUST		
Flour	125g/4oz	1 cup
Baking powder	1½ tsp	1½ tsp
Salt	¼ tsp	¼ tsp
Butter	50g/2oz	4 Tbs
Single (light) cream	125ml/4floz	½ cup

First make the crust. Sift the flour, baking powder and salt into a bowl. Cut the butter into small pieces and add to the flour, rubbing it in with your fingertips until it resembles coarse breadcrumbs. Stir in the cream until the mixture forms a soft dough. If it is too stiff, add a little milk. Set aside.

Put the blueberries, sugar, allspice, lemon juice, rind and syrup into a saucepan and warm over low heat, stirring constantly, until the sugar has dissolved. Cook gently for 5 minutes, stirring constantly.

Drop tablespoons of the dough mixture over the blueberry mixture, so that it is completely covered. Cover the pan and simmer for 20

45

above: *Cranberries, like corn and pumpkins, are particularly popular in the United States, and are incorporated into the eating ritual. Cranberry Mousse is a rather unusual, but delicious, dessert based on this unusual fruit.*

right: *Cherries Jubilee is usually served over vanilla ice-cream.*

minutes, or until the topping is puffed up and browned. Serve hot.

4 Servings

CHERRIES JUBILEE

	Metric/U.K.	U.S.
Canned, unsweetened, stoned (pitted) cherries	425g/14oz	14oz
Ground cinnamon	¼ tsp	¼ tsp
Castor (superfine) sugar	1 Tbs	1 Tbs
Arrowroot	2 tsp	2 tsp
Brandy	50ml/2floz	¼ cup

Drain the cherries and set aside, reserving about 250ml/8floz (1 cup) of the can juice.

Heat the reserved can juice in a saucepan and stir in the cinnamon, sugar and arrowroot. Cook for 3 to 4 minutes, stirring constantly, or until the juice is warmed through and has

thickened. Add the cherries to the mixture and simmer gently for a further 1 to 2 minutes, or until they are heated through. Remove from the pan and pour into a serving bowl.

Warm the brandy over very low heat until it is hot but not boiling. Pour over the cherries and ignite. Serve as soon as the flames have died away.

6 Servings

CRANBERRY MOUSSE

	Metric/U.K.	U.S.
Egg yolks	4	4
Bottled or canned cranberry juice	125ml/4floz	½ cup
Canned whole cranberries, drained	225g/8oz	8oz
Orange juice	1 Tbs	1 Tbs
Egg whites	2	2

Sugar	50g/2oz	¼ cup
Double (heavy) cream, chilled	150ml/5floz	⅝ cup

Put the egg yolks in a heatproof bowl and beat with a wire whisk until they are pale and thick. Whisk in the cranberry juice. Place the bowl over a pan of simmering water and set the pan over moderate heat. Continue whisking the mixture until it is thick enough to coat the wires of the whisk. (Do not boil, or the eggs will curdle.) Remove the pan from the heat and the bowl from the pan, and stir in the cranberries and orange juice. Chill in the refrigerator for 30 minutes.

Beat the egg whites until they form soft peaks. Fold in the sugar and continue to beat until they form stiff peaks.

Beat the cream until it forms stiff peaks. Fold the cream into the cranberry mixture, then gently fold in the egg whites. When the mixture is thoroughly blended pour into a medium mould.

Put the mould into the refrigerator and chill for at least 6 hours, or until the mousse has set. Serve cold.

4 Servings

PANDOWDY

Pandowdy is another of those oddly named but delicious New England desserts. This one is made with apples but rhubarb can also be used.

	Metric/U.K.	U.S.
Cooking apples, peeled, cored and thinly sliced	1½kg/3lb	3lb
Ground cinnamon	1½ tsp	1½ tsp
Grated nutmeg	¾ tsp	¾ tsp
Salt	¼ tsp	¼ tsp
Black treacle or molasses	3 Tbs	3 Tbs
Brown sugar	50g/2oz	⅓ cup
PASTRY Flour	175g/6oz	1½ cups
Baking powder	1 tsp	1 tsp
Salt	¼ tsp	¼ tsp
Butter	50g/2oz	4 Tbs
Double (heavy) cream	5 Tbs	5 Tbs

Preheat the oven to fairly hot 190°C (Gas Mark 5, 375°F).

To make the pastry, sift the flour, baking powder and salt into a bowl. Add the butter, cut into small pieces and, using your fingertips, rub it into the flour until the mixture resembles fine breadcrumbs. Add the cream and mix it into the flour with a table knife. Mix and knead the dough until it is smooth, adding more cream if the dough is too dry. Shape into a ball and chill in the refrigerator while you prepare the filling.

Arrange about a third of the apples in a well-greased baking dish. Sprinkle over a third of the seasonings, then continue making layers until all the ingredients have been used up. Pour over the treacle or molasses and sprinkle over the sugar.

Remove the dough from the refrigerator and roll out until it is about 5cm/2in larger than the baking dish. Dampen the edge of the dish with water, lift the dough on a rolling pin and lay over the dish. Crimp the edges to seal—do not stretch the dough as it will shrink during baking. Make a small slit in the centre.

Put the dish into the oven and bake for 40 minutes, or until the pastry is golden brown. Serve at once.

6 Servings

ICE-CREAM

The Americans did not invent ice-cream—but they did adopt it, adapt it and make it in a seemingly endless variety of delicious and unusual flavours. Many recipes call for an ice-cream churn, but the recipe below is a simplified basic recipe, which has been adapted to a medium-sized freezing compartment of the refrigerator.

	Metric/U.K.	U.S.
Milk	600ml/1 pint	2½ cups
Vanilla pod, split in half	1	1
Egg yolk	1	1
Custard powder	1 Tbs	1 Tbs
Sugar	3 Tbs	3 Tbs
Gelatine, dissolved in 2 Tbs boiling water	1½ tsp	1½ tsp
Egg white	1	1

Set the thermostat of your refrigerator to its coldest setting.

Scald the milk with the vanilla pod (bring it to just below boiling point) over moderate heat. Remove from the heat, cover and set aside to infuse for 20 minutes.

Beat the egg yolk, custard powder, sugar and 2 tablespoons of the scalded milk together with a wooden spoon. Strain the remaining milk on to the mixture, stirring constantly. Pour back into the saucepan and return it to low heat. Cook, stirring constantly, for 5 minutes, or until the custard starts to simmer and becomes thick enough to coat the back of the spoon. Remove from the heat and stir in the gelatine. Pour the custard into a bowl and set aside. When the custard is cool, cover and put in the refrigerator to chill for 1 hour.

When the custard is cold, spoon it into a cold freezing tray and put it into the frozen food storage compartment of the refrigerator to freeze for 30 minutes. Remove the tray and spoon the mixture into a chilled bowl. Beat well.

Beat the egg white until it forms stiff peaks. Fold the egg white into the custard. Return to the freezing tray and return to the frozen food compartment to freeze for 1 hour, or until the mixture is firm. Remove the ice-cream from the compartment and put into a bowl. Beat it well. Return it to the freezing tray and return it to the compartment for another hour, or until it is firm.

It is now ready to serve.

6 Servings

KNICKERBOCKER GLORY

	Metric/U.K.	U.S.
Fresh peaches, peeled	4	4
Fresh strawberries, hulled	225g/8oz	8oz
Vanilla ice-cream	250ml/8floz	1 cup
Chocolate ice-cream	250ml/8floz	1 cup
Chocolate, cut into small pieces	50g/2oz	2 squares
Brandy	3 Tbs	3 Tbs
Double (heavy) cream	150ml/5floz	⅝ cup
Large cherries	4	4

Halve and stone the peaches, then cut them into thin slices. Set aside.

Halve the strawberries. Place about a quarter

of the strawberries in each of four tall sundae glasses.

Scoop the vanilla ice-cream into each of the glasses, then top with a layer of peaches. Cover with a scoop of chocolate ice-cream.

Melt the chocolate in the brandy over low heat, stirring constantly until it dissolves. Pour a little sauce over each scoop of chocolate ice-cream.

Beat the cream until it forms stiff peaks. Arrange it decoratively on top of the chocolate sauce and garnish with the cherries before serving.

4 Servings

BRANDY ALEXANDER PIE

	Metric/U.K.	U.S.
Digestive biscuits (graham crackers), crushed	225g/8oz	1⅓ cups
Castor (superfine) sugar	50g/2oz	¼ cup
Butter, melted	75g/3oz	6 Tbs
FILLING		
Water	125ml/4floz	½ cup
Gelatine	15g/½oz	½ oz
Castor (superfine) sugar	75g/3oz	⅜ cup
Salt	⅛ tsp	⅛ tsp
Egg yolks	3	3
Brandy	50ml/2floz	¼ cup
Crème de cacao	50ml/2floz	¼ cup
Egg whites	3	3
Double (heavy) cream, chilled	300ml/10floz	1¼ cups

Put all the piecrust ingredients into a bowl and blend well. Press into the bottom and sides of a well-greased 23cm/9in pie dish and chill in the refrigerator for 30 minutes.

Meanwhile, to make the filling, pour the water into a saucepan. Sprinkle over the gelatine and set over low heat. Stir in half the sugar, the salt and egg yolks and cook, stirring constantly, until the gelatine dissolves and the mixture thickens. Do not allow to come to the boil. Remove from the heat and stir in the brandy and crème de cacao.

Pour the mixture into a bowl and set aside to cool. Transfer to the refrigerator to chill. When the mixture begins to set, remove the bowl from the refrigerator and set the mixture aside.

Beat the egg whites until they form soft peaks. Add the remaining sugar and beat until they form stiff peaks. Fold into the thickening egg yolk mixture. Put 250ml/8floz (1 cup) of the chilled cream into a chilled bowl and beat until it forms stiff peaks. Fold into the egg yolk mixture.

Pour the mixture into the piecrust, cover with foil and chill in the refrigerator for several hours, or overnight.

Before serving, stiffly whip the remaining cream. Pipe around the edge of the pie and serve cold.

6-8 Servings

Ice-cream is a particular favourite in American cooking and many traditional desserts have an ice-cream base. Knickerbocker Glory uses a combination of chocolate and vanilla ice-cream, together with fruit and brandy to create a truly superb dessert.

49

DEVIL'S FOOD CAKE

This is one of the most popular American cakes. It is usually served as a dessert.

	Metric/U.K.	U.S.
Dark cooking (semi-sweet) chocolate, chopped	125g/4oz	4 squares
Milk	250ml/8floz	1 cup
Brown sugar	175g/6oz	1 cup
Egg yolks	3	3
Sifted flour	275g/10oz	2½ cups
Salt	¼ tsp	¼ tsp
Bicarbonate of soda (baking soda)	1 tsp	1 tsp
Butter	125g/4oz	8 Tbs
Castor (superfine) sugar	175g/6oz	¾ cup
Water	50ml/2floz	¼ cup
Vanilla essence (extract)	1 tsp	1 tsp
Egg whites	2	2
FUDGE FROSTING		
Single (light) cream	250ml/8floz	1 cup
Sugar	½kg/1lb	2 cups
Salt	⅛ tsp	⅛ tsp
Dark cooking (semi-sweet) chocolate, grated	50g/2oz	2 squares
Butter	40g/1½oz	3 Tbs
Vanilla essence (extract)	½ tsp	½ tsp
Chopped walnuts	50g/2oz	⅓ cup

Devil's Food Cake, one of the glories of American cake-making. It is usually served as a succulent, and unfortunately calorie-packed, dessert.

Preheat the oven to moderate 180°C (Gas Mark 4, 350°F).

Put the chocolate, milk, brown sugar and 1 egg yolk in the top part of a double boiler, or in a heatproof bowl placed over a saucepan of simmering water. Set the boiler or pan over low heat and simmer the mixture, stirring constantly with a wooden spoon, until the chocolate melts and the mixture thickens slightly. Remove the mixture from the heat and set aside while you prepare the rest of the batter.

Put the flour, salt and soda into a bowl.

Put the butter into a second bowl and beat with a wooden spoon until it is creamy. Gradually add the castor (superfine) sugar, beating constantly. Add the remaining egg yolks, one at a time, beating well after each addition. Lightly mix in about a third of the flour, followed by half the water. Add the remaining flour and water, and beat until the batter is smooth. Stir in the vanilla and chocolate mixture until they are thoroughly blended.

Beat the egg whites until they form stiff peaks. Lightly fold them into the batter.

Pour the batter into three shallow greased cake tins lined with greased greaseproof or waxed paper. Place the tins in the oven and bake for 25 minutes, or until a skewer inserted into the centres comes out clean. Remove from the oven, loosen the cakes with a knife and turn them on to a wire rack to cool.

To make the frosting, bring the cream to the boil in a heavy-based saucepan. Remove from the heat and stir in the sugar, salt and grated chocolate. Return the pan to the heat and cook the mixture, covered, for 3 minutes. Do not stir. Uncover, reduce the heat to low and cook until the mixture reaches 120°C (238°F) on a sugar thermometer, or until a teaspoon of the mixture dropped into iced water forms a soft ball. Remove the pan from the heat and plunge it into a larger saucepan filled with cold water.

When the mixture has cooled to 45°C (110°F), or the bottom of the pan is cold enough to touch, beat in the butter and vanilla. Continue beating until the frosting thickens and reaches spreading consistency. Stir in the walnuts.

Sandwich the three rounds of cake together with three-quarters of the frosting and spread the remaining frosting over the top and sides, using a palette knife or spatula to make swirling decorative patterns. Leave the frosting to cool before serving.

8 Servings

LADY BALTIMORE CAKE

This is one of the earliest known cakes in America and originated in Maryland. The filling varies considerably, depending on which source you use—this is one of the most luscious.

	Metric/U.K.	U.S.
Flour	275g/10oz	2½ cups
Salt	½ tsp	½ tsp
Baking powder	2 tsp	2 tsp
Butter	175g/6oz	12 Tbs
Sugar	225g/8oz	1 cup
Milk	175ml/6floz	¾ cup
Vanilla essence (extract)	½ tsp	½ tsp
Rum essence (extract)	½ tsp	½ tsp
Egg whites, stiffly beaten	6	6
FROSTING		
Egg whites	2	2
Sugar	350g/12oz	1½ cups
Water	5 Tbs	5 Tbs
Cream of tartar	¼ tsp	¼ tsp
Vanilla essence (extract)	½ tsp	½ tsp
Seedless raisins, chopped	175g/6oz	1 cup
Walnuts, chopped	75g/3oz	½ cup
Maraschino cherries	175g/6oz	1 cup
Flaked almonds	65g/2½oz	½ cup

Preheat the oven to fairly hot 190°C (Gas Mark 5, 375°F).

Sift the flour, salt and baking powder into a large bowl.

Beat the butter and sugar together until they are creamy. Beat in the milk, a little at a time, beating in about ½ tablespoon of the flour mixture with each addition. Beat in the vanilla and rum essences (extracts) and carefully fold in the remaining flour mixture. Fold in the egg whites.

Divide the mixture equally among three well-greased 20cm/8in sandwich tins. Put the tins into the oven and bake for 20 to 30 minutes, or until a skewer inserted into the centres of the cakes comes out clean. Remove from the oven and place them, cake side down, on wire racks to cool. Cool completely before turning the cakes out of the tins.

Meanwhile, to make the frosting, put the egg whites, sugar, water and cream of tartar into the top of a double boiler or heatproof bowl set over a pan of simmering water. Cook, stirring constantly, for 7 minutes. Remove from the heat and beat in the vanilla. Continue beating the frosting until it is thick enough to spread. Divide among three small mixing bowls. To one bowl, add the raisins and walnuts and beat well; chop half the maraschino cherries and add to the second with the almonds. Halve the remaining cherries and set aside.

Place one of the cakes on a serving dish. Spread the raisin and walnut frosting over the cake. Place the second cake on top and spread over the maraschino and almond frosting. Top with the third cake. Spread the plain frosting on top. Decorate with the reserved cherries before serving.

8 Servings

PINEAPPLE UPSIDE-DOWN CAKE

	Metric/U.K.	U.S.
Butter	150g/5oz	10 Tbs
Brown sugar	2 Tbs	2 Tbs
Medium fresh pineapple, peeled, cored and cut into 9 rings	1	1
Glacé cherries	9	9
Sugar	125g/4oz	½ cup
Eggs	2	2
Self-raising (self-rising) flour, sifted	175g/6oz	1½ cups
Milk	3 Tbs	3 Tbs
Piece of angelica, cut into 18 leaves (optional)	2½cm/1in	1in

Preheat the oven to moderate 180°C (Gas Mark 4, 350°F).

Cut 25g/1oz (2 tablespoons) of butter into small pieces and dot them over the base of a well-greased 20cm/8in square cake tin. Sprinkle the brown sugar over the top. Arrange the pineapple slices on top of the sugar and put a cherry in the centre.

Beat the remaining butter until it is creamy. Add the sugar and beat until it is light and fluffy. Beat in the eggs, one by one, until they

are thoroughly blended, then fold in the flour. Stir in enough of the milk to give the batter a dropping consistency.

Spoon the batter into the cake tin and put the tin into the oven. Bake for 50 minutes to 1 hour, or until a skewer inserted into the centre of the cake comes out clean. Remove the tin from the oven and set aside for 5 minutes in the tin. Run a knife around the sides of the cake and invert on to a serving dish. Decorate each cherry with angelica leaves if wished.

Serve immediately or cool before serving.

9 Servings

CREAM CHEESECAKE

Cheesecake was probably originally a Middle European invention, but it has been embraced and adapted with great enthusiasm—and ingenuity—by Americans so that it is now a standard menu item. Black currants or redcurrants can be substituted for the blackberries, or they can be omitted entirely.

	Metric/U.K.	U.S.
Digestive biscuits (graham crackers), crumbled	175g/6oz	1 cup
Sugar	225g/8oz	1 cup
Butter, melted	75g/3oz	6 Tbs
Cream cheese, softened	700g/1½lb	1½lb
Eggs	4	4
Lemon juice	1 tsp	1 tsp
Grated lemon rind	2 tsp	2 tsp
Cornflour (cornstarch), blended with 1 Tbs water	2 tsp	2 tsp
Blackberries	350g/12oz	12oz
Water	3 Tbs	3 Tbs

Preheat the oven to moderate 180°C (Gas Mark 4, 350°F).

Combine the crushed biscuits (crackers), 75g/3oz (⅜ cup) sugar and melted butter. Press the mixture into the bottom and sides of a well-greased 20cm/8in cake tin with a removable base.

Beat the cream cheese until it is smooth, then gradually beat in the remaining sugar, eggs, lemon juice and half the lemon rind. Pour the mixture into the lined cake tin and put into the oven. Bake for 35 minutes, then set aside to cool. Chill in the refrigerator overnight.

Put the remaining lemon rind and the remaining ingredients into a saucepan and bring to the boil, stirring constantly. Reduce the heat to low and simmer for 3 minutes, stirring occasionally. Remove from the heat and spread over the cheese filling. Serve at once.

6 Servings

COCONUT CREAM PIE

	Metric/U.K.	U.S.
Shortcrust pastry dough	175g/6oz	6oz
FILLING		
Sugar	225g/8oz	1 cup
Flour	65g/2½oz	⅝ cup
Lukewarm milk	725ml/24floz	3 cups
Egg yolks	3	3
Butter	25g/1oz	2 Tbs
Vanilla essence (extract)	1 tsp	1 tsp
Desiccated (shredded) coconut	65g/2½oz	⅝ cup

Preheat the oven to very hot 230°C (Gas Mark 8, 450°F).

Roll out the pastry to about ½cm/¼in thick and use to line a 23cm/9in pie dish. Prick the bottom and line with foil and weigh down with dried beans. Bake for 10 minutes. Remove the beans and foil and return the shell to the oven for a further 10 minutes, or until it is browned and cooked through. Set aside to cool.

Cheesecake is another of those dishes that originated in Europe and has been adopted and perfected into many forms in the United States. This particular version has a biscuit (cracker) crust and a creamy cream cheese filling. If you prefer, you can omit the fruit topping.

Pumpkin Pie, the glorious finale to the Thanksgiving Feast—but there's nothing to stop you enjoying it the whole year round. Serve with lots of cream.

Put the sugar and flour in a saucepan and gradually stir in the milk. Cook, stirring constantly, for 10 minutes or until the mixture thickens. Set aside to cool for 5 minutes.

Beat the egg yolks with 3 tablespoons of the mixture, then stir into the remaining mixture. Return to the heat and cook, stirring constantly, for a further 3 minutes, or until the mixture is thick. Remove from the heat and stir in the remaining ingredients, reserving 2 tablespoons of coconut. Spoon the mixture into the pastry case and sprinkle over the reserved coconut.

Put the dish into the oven and bake for 15 minutes. Remove from the oven and cool completely before serving.

8 Servings

PUMPKIN PIE

This rich, smooth pie is the traditional Thanksgiving Dinner dessert.

	Metric/U.K.	U.S.
Shortcrust pastry dough	175g/6oz	6oz
FILLING		
Brown sugar	125g/4oz	$\frac{2}{3}$ cup
Salt	$\frac{1}{8}$ tsp	$\frac{1}{8}$ tsp
Ground cinnamon	$1\frac{1}{2}$ tsp	$1\frac{1}{2}$ tsp
Ground ginger	$\frac{1}{2}$ tsp	$\frac{1}{2}$ tsp
Ground cloves	$\frac{1}{4}$ tsp	$\frac{1}{4}$ tsp
Canned puréed pumpkin	700g/1$\frac{1}{2}$lb	1$\frac{1}{2}$lb
Eggs, lightly beaten	3	3
Single (light) cream	300ml/10floz	1$\frac{1}{4}$ cups

Preheat the oven to fairly hot 190°C (Gas Mark 5, 375°F).

Roll out the dough to about $\frac{1}{2}$cm/$\frac{1}{4}$in thick and use to line a 23cm/9in pie dish. Chill in the refrigerator for 10 minutes.

Combine the sugar, salt, cinnamon, ginger and cloves in a bowl. Put the puréed pumpkin in another bowl and gradually beat in the eggs. Stir in the sugar mixture until it is smooth and

creamy. Pour into the flan case and put the case on a baking sheet. Put the sheet into the oven and bake the pie for 45 to 50 minutes, or until a knife inserted into the centre of the filling comes out clean. Serve either hot or cold.

4-6 Servings

PECAN PIE

This rich, delicious pie is found all over the United States now, although it originated in the South.

	Metric/U.K.	U.S.
Shortcrust pastry dough	175g/6oz	6oz
FILLING		
Whole pecans	50g/2oz	½ cup
3 eggs	3	3
Golden (light corn) syrup	250ml/8floz	1 cup
Brown sugar	75g/3oz	½ cup
Vanilla essence (extract)	½ tsp	½ tsp
Salt	¼ tsp	¼ tsp

Preheat the oven to hot 220°C (Gas Mark 7, 425°F).

Roll out the dough to about ½cm/¼in thick and use to line a 23cm/9in pie dish. Chill in the refrigerator for 10 minutes. Prick the bottom with a fork and line with foil and weigh down with dried beans or peas. Put the dish on a baking sheet and bake for 10 minutes. Remove the foil and beans or peas and return the pie shell to the oven for a further 10 minutes, or until it is browned and cooked through. Set aside to cool.

When the case is cool, arrange the pecans, in concentric circles, on the bottom.

Beat the eggs until they are light and frothy. Beat in the syrup, then the sugar, and continue beating until it has dissolved. Stir in the vanilla and salt.

Pour the mixture into the flan case, taking care not to disturb the pecan circles—the pecans will rise to the top but will keep their pattern. Put the pie into the oven and bake for 10 minutes. Reduce the temperature to moderate 180°C (Gas Mark 4, 350°F) and continue to bake the pie for a further 30 minutes. Cool completely before serving—the filling will firm up as it cools.

4-6 Servings

Pecan Pie has a rich filling of pecan nuts and syrup. Serve with lots of cream.

SHOOFLY PIE

This is a Pennsylvania Dutch speciality and so named, tradition has it, because when the pie was baked and left to set, the flies buzzed around and the proud cook would say " shoo flies ".

	Metric/U.K.	U.S.
Shortcrust pastry dough	175g/6oz	6oz
FILLING		
Flour	175g/6oz	1½ cups
Butter	125g/4oz	8 Tbs
Soft brown sugar	175g/6oz	1 cup
Bicarbonate of soda (baking soda)	1 tsp	1 tsp
Boiling water	250ml/8floz	1 cup
Molasses or dark treacle	125ml/4floz	½ cup
Clear honey	125ml/4floz	½ cup

Preheat the oven to fairly hot 190°C (Gas Mark 5, 375°F).

Roll out the dough to about ½cm/¼in thick and use to line a 23cm/9in pie dish. Chill in the refrigerator for 10 minutes.

Sift the flour into a bowl. Add the butter and cut into small pieces with a knife. Using your fingers, rub the butter into the flour until the mixture resembles coarse breadcrumbs. Stir in the sugar and set aside.

Dissolve the soda in the boiling water, then stir in the molasses or treacle and honey. Pour this mixture into the pie case. Sprinkle the flour and butter mixture over the top.

Put the pie into the oven and bake for 10 minutes. Reduce the oven temperature to moderate 180°C (Gas Mark 4, 350°F) and bake for a further 25 to 30 minutes, or until the filling has set.

Remove from the oven and set aside to cool completely before serving. Cut into wedges and serve.

4-6 Servings

DEEP DISH PEACH PIE

	Metric/U.K.	U.S.
Butter, softened	50g/2oz	4 Tbs
Cream cheese	125g/4oz	4oz
Flour	150g/5oz	1¼ cups
Sugar	2 Tbs	2 Tbs
Salt	¼ tsp	¼ tsp
Double (heavy) cream	50ml/2floz	¼ cup
Egg, lightly beaten with 1 Tbs milk	1	1
Slivered almonds	1 Tbs	1 Tbs
FILLING		
Fresh peaches, blanched, peeled, stoned and thinly sliced	14	14
Flour	2 Tbs	2 Tbs
Soft brown sugar	3 Tbs	3 Tbs
Melted butter	3 Tbs	3 Tbs
Vanilla essence (extract)	1 tsp	1 tsp

Beat the butter and cream cheese together until the mixture is light and smooth. Sift the flour, sugar and salt into the mixture and blend well. Fold in the cream. Mix the ingredients together until the mixture forms a stiff dough, adding more cream or flour if necessary. Form the dough into a ball and dust with flour. Put into a bowl, cover and chill in the refrigerator for 15 minutes.

Preheat the oven to moderate 180°C (Gas Mark 4, 350°F).

Combine the peaches, flour, sugar, melted butter and vanilla, stirring gently to coat the fruit thoroughly. Carefully turn the mixture into a medium, deep pie dish.

Roll out the dough on a floured surface to about 5cm/2in larger than the dish. Place the dough over the pie dish and secure by gently crimping the edges to seal. Brush the top of the dough with the egg and milk mixture and make a small slit in the centre.

Put the pie dish into the oven and bake for 50 minutes to 1 hour, or until the crust is golden brown. Remove from the oven and serve at once.

6 Servings

STRAWBERRY SHORTCAKE

	Metric/U.K.	U.S.
Flour	225g/8oz	2 cups
Icing (confectioners') sugar	50g/2oz	½ cup
Butter, softened	175g/6oz	12 Tbs
Egg yolk	1	1

Double (heavy) cream	300ml/10floz	1¼ cups
Strawberries, hulled	½kg/1lb	1lb
Castor (superfine) sugar	2 Tbs	2 Tbs

Sift the flour and icing (confectioners') sugar into a medium bowl. With a table knife, cut the butter into small pieces and add to the mixture. Mix and knead together until the mixture forms a smooth dough. Stir in the egg yolk and 2 tablespoons of the cream, and blend well. Cover the dough with waxed paper and chill in the refrigerator for 30 minutes.

Preheat the oven to fairly hot 190°C (Gas Mark 5, 375°F).

Divide the dough into two equal pieces and roll out each piece to a 23cm/9in circle. Put the circles on a well-greased baking sheet and put the sheet into the oven. Bake for 12 to 15 minutes, or until the edges of the shortcakes are golden brown.

Meanwhile, thinly slice the strawberries. Beat the remaining cream until it forms stiff peaks, then lightly fold the strawberries into the cream. Spoon the mixture into a heap in the centre of one of the shortcakes. Cut the other circle into eight equal triangles. Pile the triangles up against the strawberry mixture, sprinkle over the castor (superfine) sugar and serve.

8 Servings

A real, old-fashioned Strawberry Shortcake that looks almost as good as it tastes.

Breads and Cookies

PARKER HOUSE ROLLS

These rolls were invented by the chef at the Boston hotel of the same name and are now a popular breakfast roll all over the northeast.

	Metric/U.K.	U.S.
Fresh yeast	15g/½oz	½oz
Sugar	75g/3oz	⅜ cup
Lukewarm water	2 tsp	2 tsp
Milk	350ml/12floz	1½ cups
Butter	125g/4oz	8 Tbs
Flour	700g/1½lb	6 cups
Salt	1 tsp	1 tsp
Egg, lightly beaten	1	1
Butter, melted	1 Tbs	1 Tbs

Crumble the yeast into a small bowl and mash in ½ teaspoon of the sugar. Add the lukewarm water and cream the mixture to a smooth paste. Set aside in a warm, draught-free place for 15 to 20 minutes, or until the mixture is puffed up and frothy.

Scald the milk (bring to just below boiling point) and add 75g/3oz (6 tablespoons) of the butter. Set over low heat until the butter has melted. Remove from the heat and set aside.

Sift the flour, remaining sugar and salt into a bowl. Make a well in the centre and pour in the yeast, milk and butter mixture and egg. Using your fingers or a spatula, gradually draw the flour into the liquid until it is incorporated and the dough comes away from the sides of the bowl.

Turn out on to a floured surface and knead for 10 minutes. The dough should be elastic and smooth.

Shape the dough into a ball and return it to a clean, greased bowl. Cover and put in a warm draught-free place for 1 to 1½ hours, or until it has almost doubled in bulk.

Turn the dough out on to the floured surface and knead for a further 3 minutes. Roll out to about 1cm/½in thick. Spread the remaining butter over the dough in a thin layer. Cut the dough into 7½cm/3in rounds. Make a shallow cut in the centre of each round and fold in half to make a semi-circle, pressing the edges together to seal. Transfer to well-greased baking sheets, keeping the rolls well spaced apart.

Brush each roll with a little of the melted butter, cover with a damp cloth and return to a warm, draught-free place for 30 to 45 minutes, or until they have risen and expanded.

Preheat the oven to very hot 240°C (Gas Mark 9, 475°F) and put the baking sheets in the oven. Bake the rolls for 15 to 20 minutes, or until they are golden brown. Transfer the rolls to a wire rack to cool to warm before serving.

About 40 rolls

CORN BREAD

Corn bread is the traditional accompaniment to all sorts of Southern delights.

	Metric/U.K.	U.S.
Flour	175g/6oz	1½ cups
Baking powder	4 tsp	4 tsp
Salt	1 tsp	1 tsp
Yellow corn meal	275g/10oz	2 cups
Sugar	2 tsp	2 tsp
Butter, melted	125g/4oz	8 Tbs
Eggs, lightly beaten	4	4
Milk	250ml/8floz	1 cup
Single (light) cream	50ml/2floz	¼ cup

Preheat the oven to fairly hot 200°C (Gas Mark 6, 400°F).

Sift the flour, baking powder and salt into a bowl. Stir in the corn meal and sugar. Pour in the melted butter, cutting with a knife until the mixture resembles coarse breadcrumbs.

Beat the eggs and milk together, then stir into the corn mixture until well blended. Stir in the cream to form a thick paste.

Spoon the batter into a well-greased 20cm/8in square baking tin and put the tin into the oven. Bake for 25 to 35 minutes, or until a skewer inserted into the centre comes out clean. Set aside to cool in the tin for 5 minutes. Cut into large squares before serving.

6 Servings

SAN FRANCISCO SOURDOUGH BREAD

Sourdough bread originated in Mid-Europe and was probably brought to the United States by immigrants from that area. San Francisco adapted its own version of the bread, which is now famous throughout the country.

	Metric/U.K.	U.S.
STARTER		
Strong white flour	225g/8oz	2 cups
Sugar	125g/4oz	½ cup
Milk	450ml/15floz	2 cups
BREAD		
Strong white flour	1½kg/3lb	12 cups
Sugar	2 Tbs	2 Tbs
Salt	1½ Tbs	1½ Tbs
Water	900ml/ 1½ pints	3¾ cups
Vegetable oil	2 Tbs	2 Tbs
Butter	1 tsp	1 tsp

First make the starter. Combine all the ingredients in a screw-top jar, beating until they form a smooth paste. Screw on the lid and set aside in a warm place for between 3 and 4 days.

Sift the flour, sugar and salt into a bowl. Make a well in the centre and pour in the starter, water and oil. Using your fingers, gradually draw the flour into the liquids until it is incorporated and the dough comes away from the sides of the bowl.

Turn out on to a floured board and knead for 5 minutes. The dough should be elastic and smooth. Shape the dough into a ball and return it to a clean greased bowl. Cover and put in a warm, draught-free place for 2 hours, or until it has risen slightly.

Preheat the oven to fairly hot 190°C (Gas Mark 5, 375°F). Grease a large baking sheet with the butter.

Turn the dough on to a floured board and knead for a further 10 minutes. Cut into two pieces and shape each one into a round, about 15cm/6in in diameter. Make a deep cross on the top of each round. Put the rounds, well spaced apart, on the baking sheet and put the sheet into the oven. Bake for 1 to 1¼ hours.

Remove the bread from the oven and rap the undersides with your knuckles. If the bread sounds hollow, like a drum, it is cooked. If it does not, reduce the oven to warm 170°C (Gas Mark 3, 325°F), return the loaves and bake for a further 5 to 10 minutes. Cool on a wire rack before serving.

2 Loaves

BLUEBERRY MUFFINS

Muffins were originally brought to the United States by British settlers but have been adapted and changed so much over the years, they would now no longer be recognizable as 'muffins' to the average Briton. They are still delicious though and, in a variety of flavours, make a popular breakfast food.

	Metric/U.K.	U.S.
Butter, melted	125g/4oz	8 Tbs
Flour	425g/14oz	3½ cups
Salt	1½ tsp	1½ tsp
Sugar	175g/6oz	¾ cup
Baking powder	4 tsp	4 tsp
Eggs	4	4
Milk	300ml/10floz	1¼ cups
Blueberries	275g/10oz	1¼ cups

Preheat the oven to very hot 230°C (Gas Mark 8, 450°F). Lightly grease about 36 muffin tins with a little butter and sprinkle lightly with a little flour, shaking out any excess. Set aside.

Sift the flour, salt, sugar and baking powder into a bowl. In a second bowl, beat the eggs until they are pale and fall in a steady ribbon from the whisk. Add the remaining melted butter and the milk. Stir the egg mixture into the flour as quickly as possible. Do not overmix—the ingredients should be just combined.

Toss the blueberries in a little flour to prevent them from sinking to the bottom of the muffins, and fold into the batter. Spoon the batter into the prepared muffin tins and bake for 15 minutes, or until a skewer inserted into the centres comes out clean. Cool in the tins for about 5 minutes, then turn out and serve hot.

About 36 muffins

WAFFLES

These favourite American breakfast snacks are made on special irons. They are traditionally

Pretzels came from Germany originally but are now an integral part of the American scene. They are so popular that they are sold from carts in the streets, at baseball games—in fact, anywhere where there is a congregation of hungry people.

served with generous helpings of melted butter and maple syrup.

	Metric/U.K.	U.S.
Flour	225g/8oz	2 cups
Salt	¼ tsp	¼ tsp
Castor (superfine) sugar	2 Tbs	2 Tbs
Butter, melted	50g/2oz	4 Tbs
Milk	300ml/10floz	1¼ cups
Egg, separated	1	1

Sift the flour, salt and sugar into a bowl. Make a well in the centre and beat in the melted butter, milk and egg yolk until the mixture forms a smooth batter. Beat the egg white until it forms stiff peaks, then fold into the flour mixture.

Heat a waffle iron over moderate heat and brush liberally with melted butter. Pour 2 tablespoons of the waffle batter into the iron, close and cook for 2 to 3 minutes on each side or until it has stopped steaming.

Tip the waffle on to a warmed serving plate and keep hot while you cook the remaining batter in the same way, brushing the iron with melted butter between each waffle.

Serve hot.

6 Servings

PRETZELS

Pretzels are crisp crunchy biscuits brought to the United States by German colonists and adopted by the new country with great enthusiasm. They are now a favourite snack, and are sold from street carts in much the same way as hot chestnuts are in Europe.

	Metric/U.K.	U.S.
Fresh yeast	15g/½oz	½oz
Sugar	½ tsp	½ tsp
Lukewarm milk	250ml/8floz	1 cup
Butter	25g/1oz	2 Tbs
Flour	350g/12oz	3 cups
Salt	½ tsp	½ tsp
Caraway seeds	1 Tbs	1 Tbs
Egg, lightly beaten	1	1
Coarse sea salt	2 tsp	2 tsp

Crumble the yeast into a bowl and mash in the sugar. Add 2 tablespoons of the milk and cream the mixture to a smooth paste. Set aside in a warm, draught-free place for 15 to 20 minutes, or until the mixture is puffed up and frothy.

Melt the butter in the remaining milk over low heat. Set aside to cool to lukewarm.

Sift the flour and salt into a bowl. Add 2 teaspoons of caraway seeds. Make a well in the centre and pour in the yeast and milk and butter mixture. Using a spatula, gradually draw the flour into the liquid until it is incorporated and the dough comes away from the sides of the bowl.

Turn out on to a floured surface and knead for about 8 minutes. The dough should be smooth and elastic.

Shape the dough into a ball and return it to a clean, greased bowl. Cover and put in a warm, draught-free place for 45 minutes, or until the dough has risen slightly.

Turn the dough out on to the floured surface and knead for a further 4 minutes. Form the dough into a roll about 30cm/12in long. Cut into 48 equal pieces and roll out each piece into a thin sausage shape about 15cm/6in long. Put each dough piece on a flat surface and curve the ends towards you. Cross the loop halfway along each side and twist once. Carefully bend the ends back and press firmly on to the curve of the loop.

Preheat the oven to fairly hot 190°C (Gas Mark 5, 375°F).

Half-fill a large saucepan with boiling water and bring the water to the boil again over moderately high heat. Drop the dough pieces into the water, a few at a time. Cook for 1 minute or until they rise to the surface. Remove from the water as they rise and drain in a colander. Transfer the drained pretzels to well-greased baking sheets. Coat each one with beaten egg and sprinkle over the remaining caraway seeds. Put the sheets into the oven and bake for 15 minutes, or until the pretzels are golden brown and firm to the touch. Cool completely and sprinkle over the salt before serving.

About 48 pretzels

BROWNIES

The chocolate nut brownie is now part of American culture—children are reared on them, adults survive on them, and everyone enjoys them.

Brownies are not so much a snack food as an indispensable part of American culture—but they're fantastic to eat, too! They're guaranteed to keep children quiet when served with milk, and they make a fabulous 'instant' dessert served with ice-cream or fruit yogurt.

Although they are basically a snack, they make a superb 'instant' dessert with vanilla ice-cream.

	Metric/U.K.	U.S.
Dark cooking (semi-sweet) chocolate	175g/6oz	6 squares
Water	2 Tbs	2 Tbs
Butter	125g/4oz	8 Tbs
Castor (superfine) sugar	125g/4oz	$\frac{1}{2}$ cup
Vanilla essence (extract)	1 tsp	1 tsp
Self-raising (self-rising) flour	125g/4oz	1 cup
Salt	$\frac{1}{8}$ tsp	$\frac{1}{8}$ tsp
Eggs	2	2
Walnuts, chopped	50g/2oz	$\frac{1}{3}$ cup

Preheat the oven to warm 170°C (Gas Mark 3, 325°F).

Put the chocolate, water and butter in a saucepan and heat over low heat, stirring constantly until the chocolate has melted. Remove from the heat and stir in the sugar and vanilla. Cool to room temperature.

Sift the flour and salt into a bowl, then gradually beat in the chocolate mixture, eggs and finally the walnuts. Pour the mixture into a shallow well-greased 20cm/8in square baking tin. Put into the oven and bake for 30 to 35 minutes, or until a knife inserted into the centre comes out clean. Serve cool.

16 Brownies

CHOCOLATE CHIP COOKIES

Serve with chilled milk for the perfect after-school or after work snack.

	Metric/U.K.	U.S.
Butter	125g/4oz	8 Tbs
Sugar	125g/4oz	$\frac{1}{2}$ cup
Brown sugar	75g/3oz	$\frac{1}{2}$ cup
Egg	1	1
Vanilla essence (extract)	$\frac{1}{2}$ tsp	$\frac{1}{2}$ tsp
Flour	175g/6oz	1$\frac{1}{2}$ cups
Salt	$\frac{1}{2}$ tsp	$\frac{1}{2}$ tsp
Bicarbonate of soda (baking soda)	$\frac{1}{2}$ tsp	$\frac{1}{2}$ tsp
Walnuts, chopped	50g/2oz	$\frac{1}{3}$ cup
Dark plain (semi-sweet) chocolate chips	125g/4oz	$\frac{1}{2}$ cup

Preheat the oven to fairly hot 190°C (Gas Mark 5, 375°F).

Beat the butter with a wooden spoon until it is creamy. Mix the sugars together, then gradually add to the butter, beating until the mixture is light and fluffy. Beat in the egg and vanilla.

Sift the flour, salt and soda into a bowl. Stir into the butter mixture until it forms a smooth batter. Stir in the nuts and chocolate chips.

Drop teaspoonfuls of the mixture on to well-greased baking sheets, leaving about 2$\frac{1}{2}$cm/1in between each cookie. Put the sheets

into the oven and bake for 10 to 15 minutes, or until they are lightly browned. Cool on a wire rack before serving.

About 30 cookies

CHOCOLATE COOKIES

You can sandwich these attractive cookies together with cream or buttercream, as in the picture, or serve them as they are.

	Metric/U.K.	U.S.
Butter	225g/8oz	16 Tbs
Castor (superfine) sugar	125g/4oz	½ cup
Self-raising flour	225g/8oz	2 cups
Cinnamon	½ tsp	½ tsp
Cocoa	50g/2oz	½ cup
Vanilla essence (extract)	1 tsp	1 tsp

Preheat the oven to moderate 180°C (Gas Mark 4, 350°F).

Beat the butter with a wooden spoon until it is pale and soft. Gradually add the sugar and beat until the mixture is smooth and creamy. Sift in the flour, cinnamon and cocoa, a little at a time, until the mixture is a smooth paste. Beat in the vanilla.

Using your hands, roll teaspoonfuls of the paste into balls and place them on a well-greased baking sheet, leaving about 5cm/2in between each one. Dip a fork in cold water and use the back of the prongs to flatten out the balls. Put the sheet into the oven and bake the cookies for 12 minutes. Remove from the oven and allow to cool for 5 minutes. Transfer to a wire rack to cool completely before serving.

About 25 biscuits (cookies)

Two fabulous American biscuits (cookies)— Chocolate Chip and Chocolate.

Pickles

CAULIFLOWER AND TOMATO PICKLE

	Metric/U.K.	U.S.
Medium cauliflowers, broken into flowerets	2	2
Tomatoes, quartered	700g/1½lb	1½lb
Medium onions, chopped	4	4
Medium cucumber, chopped	1	1
Salt	175g/6oz	1½ cups
Dry mustard	1 tsp	1 tsp
Ground ginger	1 tsp	1 tsp
Black pepper	1 tsp	1 tsp
Soft brown sugar	225g/8oz	1⅓ cups
Pickling spices	1 tsp	1 tsp
White wine vinegar	600ml/1 pint	2½ cups

Arrange the vegetables in layers in a large deep dish, sprinkling equal amounts of salt on each layer. Pour over enough cold water to cover, cover with foil and set aside in a cool place for 24 hours. Drain the vegetables, discarding the liquid. Put the vegetables into a colander and rinse thoroughly under cold running water to remove the excess salt. Drain off the water and transfer the vegetables to a large saucepan.

Sprinkle over the mustard, ginger, pepper, sugar and pickling spices and pour over the vinegar. Set over moderate heat and bring to boil, stirring frequently. Reduce the heat to low and simmer, stirring occasionally, for 15 to 20 minutes, or until the vegetables are cooked and tender. Remove from the heat.

Using a slotted spoon, transfer the vegetables to pickling jars. Pour in enough of the cooking liquid to fill each jar. Wipe clean with a damp cloth and seal the jars with their vacuum lids. Label the jars and store them in a cool, dry place.

About 6 pounds

CHOW-CHOW

	Metric/U.K.	U.S.
Dried red or white kidney beans, soaked overnight in cold water and drained	350g/12oz	2 cups
Red or green peppers, pith and seeds removed and chopped	4	4
Salt	1½ tsp	1½ tsp
Medium cauliflower, broken into flowerets	1	1
French (green) beans, cut into 5cm/2in lengths	½kg/1lb	1lb
Canned sweetcorn, drained	450g/1lb	1lb
Wine vinegar	1¼l/2 pints	5 cups
Soft brown sugar	175g/6oz	1 cup
Dry mustard	5 Tbs	5 Tbs
Mustard seeds	3 Tbs	3 Tbs
Turmeric	1 tsp	1 tsp

Cook all the vegetables individually until they are just tender. Drain them in colanders and set aside. Transfer all the vegetables to a large bowl and gently toss to mix well.

Put the vinegar, sugar, mustard, mustard seeds and turmeric in a large saucepan and place the pan over low heat. Cook, stirring constantly, until the sugar has dissolved. Increase the heat to high and bring the mixture to the boil. Reduce the heat to moderately low and add the vegetables to the pan. Cook the mixture, stirring occasionally so that all the vegetables are thoroughly basted, for 5 minutes.

Remove from the heat and ladle the pickle into clean, warmed preserving jars. Seal the jars and label them. Store in a cool, dry place until ready to use.

About 3½ pounds

China

The delights of Chinese cooking have only
recently become available to the west, but
nearly everyone now knows just how good,
and how economical, a Chinese meal can be.
What is just beginning to be appreciated by
the public at large is just how very easy it is
to create these same meals, or even better ones,
in your own kitchen, so that the joys of eating
Chinese-style can be experienced regularly
rather than as an occasional treat.

About one-third of the world's population
eat Chinese food every day of their lives, yet it
is much, much more than the daily sustenance
of a great many people. Even if it were only
eaten regularly by a handful of obscure
gourmets, Chinese cooking would still be
important for it is one of the truly great and
original cuisines of the world.

The Chinese were a civilized nation long
before the ancestors of the western world had
advanced to the condition of warring tribes,
whose lives consisted mainly of robbery and
rape, of killing and hunting. And as the Chinese
civilization developed and reached new
heights of achievement, so the cuisine became
more sophisticated and refined. Since it has

always been a large, and rather poor country
from an agricultural point of view (only about
12 per cent of it is arable), and since it has
always had a very large population to support,
there have been many periods of shortage,
even starvation. Chinese cooking therefore
concentrates on the practical art of making a
very little go a very long way, and of making
acceptable anything that is edible. And as the
cuisine flourished, it became inextricably
linked with the philosophy, the religion and
the very social fabric of society. Confucius, the
man who shaped Chinese life 25 centuries ago,
regarded food as a most serious art form. The
practice of the art of cooking and of eating was
encouraged, and even urged, to round-out the
human experience.

China is a vast country, almost equatorial
in the south, almost arctic in the north.
And in such diverse conditions many
different schools of cooking have
evolved, although these are usually
broken down into five 'classical' regional
varieties: Peking and the north, the
Yangtze river and the east, Szechuan
in the west, Fukien and the southern

The Boat People were the original inhabitants of Hong Kong and many of them still spend the greater part of their lives aboard their sampans. In this particular picture the sampans are moored to a floating restaurant.

coast, and Canton and the south.

Peking has been the capital of China throughout most of its history and it remains one of its great cultural and gastronomic centres. The food of Peking is rich to taste, flavoured with dark, strong soy sauce or paste, and the taste known to the west as sweet and sour is very popular. Garlic is often added to food, and although rice is served, wheat-based dishes such as noodles and dumplings are more common. The area to the north of Peking is the only part of China where lamb or mutton is eaten with any enthusiasm, and the border area with Mongolia is the home of the 'firepot', now an accepted part of the Chinese cooking ritual. The fire pot somewhat resembles the western fondue, and is one of only a few Chinese dishes which are

considered to be a meal in themselves.

The eastern part of the Yangtze river includes the cities of Ningpo and Shanghai, the latter being traditionally considered as the most cosmopolitan of Chinese cities. The food tends to saltiness, and is often, in fact, preserved in salt. A lot of fish is eaten since much of the region lies on or near the coast, and rice is the staple accompaniment rather than noodles. The food, even the quickly made stir-fry dishes, is cooked for slightly longer than is usual in other parts of the country since the people prefer their meat and vegetables well done.

Szechuan cooking, from the province of the same name in western China, was virtually unknown in the West until ten or fifteen years ago. Since then, there has been an upsurge

cooked in lavish quantities of soy sauce and called 'red-cooked'—pork and cabbage are two foods considered to be particularly suitable for this treatment.

Cantonese and southern cooking is what most people in the west think of as Chinese cooking, for most of the restaurants and Chinese take-away shops outside China are owned by Cantonese. Many stir-fry dishes originate in Canton for the Cantonese do not like their food to be over-cooked, and light soy sauce predominates rather than the heavier, darker type preferred in the north. Dim sum originated here too, especially the steamed varieties, as did the delicate omelets known as foo yungs. And of course glorious Cantonese Lobster—you will find a slightly simplified version of this magnificent feast dish on page *113*.

In China food is expected not just to taste delicious and be sustaining, but also to look attractive, so the preparation and combination of ingredients is important not just from the point of view of taste but also from an aesthetic one. Menus which start with soups and work their way through to desserts are unknown. Instead, depending on the grandness of the occasion, a selection of four, six, eight or up to almost any number of dishes is placed on the table and the diners are expected to help themselves, and in any order they wish. The only 'rule' is that different dishes are not piled on the plate at the same time or otherwise sampled together as is the practice in the west. Each dish is expected to be savoured separately in order to extract the full goodness. Soups are usually eaten as refreshers during the meal, as are sweetmeats.

There are no laws governing what is served with what, but there are philosophical and practical requirements which are taken into account. At a formal feast, for instance, the menu would probably contain an offering from the air (steamed wood pigeons or a birds' nest soup, perhaps), an offering from the sea (some carp, perhaps, or shrimps, a favourite Chinese seafood), and an offering from the land (meat or vegetables). In addition, or as part of the above, there would be an example of sweet and sour, perhaps something cooked in oyster sauce or black bean sauce, an example of stir-fry, one of steaming and one of long, slow cooking, such as a casserole or a roast. The final choice depends, as it has always done, on the capacities of the cook, both in cooking terms and in terms of the availability of money and ingredients.

of interest in it and although there are as yet few restaurants which specialize in the cooking of this region, many predominantly Cantonese or Pekingese restaurants offer one or two specialities from Szechuan—especially the cousin to Peking Duck, Szechuan Duck, or Szechuan Shrimps. It produces by far the hottest, spiciest food in China, almost as hot sometimes as a curry although the taste is very different, and one of the essential ingredients in many of the traditional dishes is chillis. Garlic and ginger are also used to help sharpen the food.

Fukien and the southern coastal lands are also noted for their fish dishes, and Fukien is famous throughout China as producer of the finest soy sauce in the land. As a result of this, many of the most famous local dishes are

Right: *Sowing rice by the traditional methods in Kwangsi Province. Old ways are changing now, however; much of the land is now operated by communes and modern methods are being introduced.*

Far right: *A traditional ceremony of ancestor worship—in this particular feast incense is burnt and a roast pig offered.*

Rice and noodles, the staple foods of China, are not usually served at banquets or formal feasts, simply because they are considered to belong to the everyday, to the necessary, and are not therefore deemed worthy of a 'special' occasion.

Chinese food can be eaten perfectly adequately with western cutlery such as forks and spoons, but it achieves a greater delicacy when eaten with chopsticks, partly because the diner is then forced to eat smaller portions at a time and also more slowly, therefore savouring the food more completely. The legends which surround the origin and the use of chopsticks vary but there is one which suggests that they are wholly practical implements: by eating small morsels at a time you can make a very little go a very long way— often a necessity in China throughout its long history.

Table-setting is simpler than in the west and consists of chopsticks, a selection of bowls of different sizes (for rice, soup, meat dishes, etc), plus a soup spoon, if soup is to be served. If wine or tea is to accompany the meal, an appropriate small cup is added to the table. Napkins, as they are used in the west, are unknown, but, as in Japan, a hot, damp hand towel is handed to guests both before and during the meal. Since the centre of the table is needed for the selection of dishes being presented, there are no floral or other decorations on the Chinese table.

Etiquette, especially for more formal occasions, used to be quite rigid. In contrast to western custom, the pride of place traditionally reserved for the guest of honour was often as far away from the host as it was possible to be, but always directly across from the doorway or opening through which the food would come. Shao Hsing or rice wine is the drink traditionally served at formal feasts, although tea could be served instead.

Tea, in fact, has almost as long and honoured a history in China as it has in Japan and it is surrounded by almost as much ritual. There is even a 'patron saint' of tea! The types most usually served are a version of oolong, or a 'green' (unfermented) tea. Many flowers and leaves, such as jasmine, are also added to give it a special taste. Chinese tea should be served in small handleless cups, without the addition of milk, lemon or sugar.

Preparation of food

In order to produce the beautiful banquets described above, a good deal of preparation is necessary, but basically Chinese cooking is quite simple. The only prerequisite is to be as orderly as possible and to prepare everything you can before the actual cooking process begins. So before you start experimenting with any of the recipes which follow, prepare all of the ingredients, measure them, slice them, chop them, then line them up beside the stove in the order in which they are to be added to the cooking pot. Many dishes, especially the stir-fry ones, just do not allow time to turn around and scramble amid a chaos of half-prepared ingredients.

The secret of Chinese cooking lies, in fact, in the preparation. Food is sliced, shredded or cut according to certain predetermined rules. For really successful short-cooking dishes, all of the ingredients should be cut or chopped to as near the same size as possible to ensure that they are all cooked to the same degree. For very tender, almost velvety meat, the meat should be sliced along the grain; for a slightly crunchier texture it should be sliced against. (Slightly frozen meat is often easier to slice into very thin strips in this way than meat at room temperature.) Vegetables,

particularly, are often sliced on the diagonal both for aesthetic appeal and for regularity of cooking. The cleaver, an implement indispensable in the Chinese kitchen, is the basic instrument used both to slice and shred food, but you do not have to have one in order to create an authentic Chinese touch— a really sharp knife will do just as well.

The basic traditional Chinese cooking vessel is called a wok, and is a cross between a rather deep frying-pan and a rather shallow saucepan, except that it has sloping sides and a somewhat rounded base. It is available in the west, from larger department stores as well as fancy kitchen shops, and of course can be bought quite cheaply from Chinese provision stores. It is an extremely versatile cooking implement and can be converted very successfully to cooking western food as well as Chinese. The wok is particularly suitable for stir-fry dishes, since its rounded base and sloping sides help to keep the food in motion during the stirring and turning process which is intrinsic to the technique.

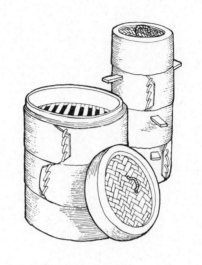

The wok is also used as the base for steamed dishes. Traditional flat, round bamboo steamers are fitted over a wok filled with water (they can be stacked on top of each other, up to four or five at a time). However, an ordinary steamer or even a *couscoussier* is equally effective. Food steamed in the bamboo steamers can be served still in the steamers. Shallow perforated spoons, somewhat similar in appearance to bulb basters, are widely used in deep-frying, another popular method of cooking in China; slotted spoons make an acceptable substitute for the western kitchen.

The rewards of cooking Chinese are obvious to anyone who has ever eaten a well-cooked Sweet and Sour Pork, or been sustained by a succulent Chow Mein. Now that you know how easy and economical it can be, Chinese food need never be a once-a-week restaurant treat again!

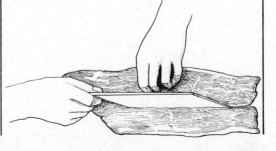

Some popular cooking aids and techniques from the Chinese kitchen: Top: *The most versatile cooking pot in China, the wok;* Second from top: *A typical bamboo steamer— food is often served in it as well as cooked;* Third from top: *A baster, particularly useful for deep-frying;* Second from bottom: *Cutting vegetables diagonally with a traditional cleaver—it has aesthetic appeal and the even cutting ensures even cooking;* Bottom: *Cutting meat with the grain, to ensure velvety softness when cooked.*

Soups

FOONG YIN MUN SUNG
(Birds' Nest Soup with Chicken Cubes and Mushrooms)

This is one of the classics of Cantonese cuisine and is very filling indeed. Birds' nests and quail eggs can be obtained from oriental or Chinese delicatessens.

	Metric/U.K.	U.S.
Birds' nests	225g/8oz	8oz
Vegetable oil	1 Tbs	1 Tbs
Chopped fresh root ginger	1 Tbs	1 Tbs
Cooked chicken, cubed	125g/4oz	4oz
Button mushrooms, quartered	125g/4oz	4oz
Canned quail eggs, drained	225g/8oz	8oz
Chicken stock	1¾l/3 pints	7½ cups

Soak the birds' nests in water for 5 minutes, then drain.

Heat the oil in a saucepan. Add the ginger and fry for 1 minute, stirring constantly. Stir in the chicken, mushrooms, eggs and stock and bring to the boil. Reduce the heat to low and add the birds' nests. Simmer for 5 minutes, stirring occasionally.

Transfer the soup to a warmed tureen or large bowl and serve at once.

6-8 Servings

EGG-DROP SOUP

	Metric/U.K.	U.S.
Vegetable oil	1 Tbs	1 Tbs
Medium onion, thinly sliced	1	1
Small cucumber, finely diced	1	1
Chicken stock	1¾l/3 pints	7½ cups
Tomatoes, blanched, peeled and quartered	4	4
Egg, lightly beaten	1	1

Heat the oil in a large saucepan. Add the onion and fry for 1 minute, stirring constantly. Add the cucumber to the pan and fry for 1 minute, stirring constantly. Pour over the stock and bring to the boil. Reduce the heat to low and simmer for 10 minutes, stirring occasionally. Stir in the tomatoes and simmer for a further 5 minutes.

Remove from the heat and beat in the egg. Serve at once.

6 Servings

CUCUMBER AND PORK SOUP

	Metric/U.K.	U.S.
Chicken stock	1⅓l/2¼ pints	5¾ cups
Salt	1 tsp	1 tsp
Soy sauce	1 Tbs	1 Tbs
Pork fillet (tenderloin), cut into very thin strips	225g/8oz	8oz
Medium cucumbers, peeled, halved lengthways, seeded and cut into ½cm/¼in slices	2	2

Pour the stock, salt and soy sauce into a large saucepan and stir in the pork strips. Bring to the boil over moderate heat and cook for 10 minutes. Add the cucumbers to the pan and return to the boil. Cook for 3 minutes, or until the cucumbers are translucent.

Transfer the soup to a warmed tureen and serve at once.

4 Servings

CRABMEAT SOUP

	Metric/U.K.	U.S.
Water	250ml/8floz	1 cup
Medium onion, chopped	1	1
Fresh root ginger, peeled and halved lengthways	2½cm/1in piece	1in piece
Chicken stock	300ml/10floz	1¼ cups
Crabmeat with the shell and cartilage removed	½kg/1lb	1lb

Salt	1 tsp	1 tsp
Rice wine or dry sherry	3 Tbs	3 Tbs
Chicken stock cube, crumbled	$\frac{1}{2}$	$\frac{1}{2}$
Cornflour (cornstarch)	$1\frac{1}{2}$ Tbs	$1\frac{1}{2}$ Tbs
Milk	300ml/10floz	$1\frac{1}{4}$ cups
Vegetable fat, cut into small cubes	2 tsp	2 tsp

Pour the water into a saucepan and set over moderate heat. Add the onion and ginger and boil until the liquid has been reduced by half. Add the stock, crabmeat, salt and wine or sherry. Reduce the heat to moderately low and slowly bring to the boil, skimming off any scum which rises to the surface.

Blend the stock cube and cornflour (cornstarch) with the milk until smooth and pour into the soup, stirring constantly until the soup has thickened and is smooth. Cook for 2 minutes, stirring constantly, or until the soup is hot but not boiling. Sprinkle over the vegetable fat.

Transfer the soup to a warmed tureen and serve at once.

6 Servings

HOT AND SOUR SOUP

This soup is a speciality of the province of Szechuan in western China and has a most unusual but very attractive taste. Sesame oil can be obtained from health food or Chinese provision stores.

	Metric/U.K.	U.S.
Sesame oil	2 Tbs	2 Tbs
Medium onions, finely chopped	2	2
Flour	2 Tbs	2 Tbs
Chicken stock	$1\frac{1}{4}$l/2 pints	5 cups
Juice of 1 lemon		
Soy sauce	2 Tbs	2 Tbs
Monosodium glutamate (MSG), (optional)	$\frac{1}{4}$ tsp	$\frac{1}{4}$ tsp
Salt and pepper to taste		
Bean sprouts	275g/10oz	10oz
Chinese dried mushrooms, soaked in cold water for 20 minutes, drained and chopped	2	2
Canned bamboo shoot, drained and finely chopped	125g/4oz	4oz
Cooked chicken, finely diced	125g/4oz	4oz

Cucumber and Pork Soup —light, delicious and so easy and quick to make.

Heat the oil in a large saucepan. Add the onions and fry until they are soft. Remove from the heat and stir in the flour to form a smooth paste. Gradually stir in the remaining ingredients until they are well blended and the mixture is smooth. Return the pan to moderate heat and bring to the boil, stirring constantly. Cover the pan, reduce the heat to low and simmer for 1 hour.

Transfer the soup to a warmed tureen and serve at once.

6 Servings

Huang Yu Tang is a traditional and unusual soup in which the fish is first deep-fried then served with a delicious broth.

HUANG YU TANG (Fish Soup)

	Metric/U.K.	U.S.
Herrings or trout, cleaned and boned	½kg/1lb	1lb
Salt	1½ tsp	1½ tsp
Ground ginger	1½ tsp	1½ tsp
Vinegar	2 Tbs	2 Tbs
Sufficient vegetable oil for deep-frying		
Boiling water	900ml/ 1½ pints	3¾ cups
Chicken stock cube	1	1
Soy sauce	1½ Tbs	1½ Tbs
Watercress, stalks removed	1 bunch	1 bunch
Rice wine or dry sherry	2 Tbs	2 Tbs
Black pepper	½ tsp	½ tsp

Rub the insides and outsides of the fish with salt, ginger and half the vinegar. Set aside to marinate for 1 hour. Drain the fish and pat dry with kitchen towels.

Fill a large saucepan one-third full with vegetable oil and heat until it reaches 185°C (360°F) on a deep-fat thermometer, or until a small cube of stale bread dropped into the oil turns golden in 50 seconds. Arrange the fish in a deep-frying basket and carefully lower them into the oil. Fry for 5 to 6 minutes, or until they are crisp. Remove from the oil and drain on kitchen towels.

Put the fish in a large saucepan and pour over the boiling water. Crumble in the stock cube and add the remaining vinegar and the soy sauce. Bring to the boil, reduce the heat to moderately low and simmer for 5 minutes. Carefully stir in the remaining ingredients.

Transfer the soup to a warmed tureen and serve at once.

4 Servings

WONTON DOUGH

Roll out the dough very thinly, to not more than about ⅛cm/1/16 in thick, then cut into shapes as you require (the most usual ones are rectangles or squares).

	Metric/U.K.	U.S.
Flour	450g/1lb	4 cups
Salt	2 tsp	2 tsp

	Metric/U.K.	U.S.
Eggs, lightly beaten	2	2
Water	75ml/3floz	$\frac{3}{8}$ cup

Sift the flour and salt into a bowl. Make a well in the centre and pour in the eggs and water. Using your fingers or a spatula, draw the flour into the liquid until it has been incorporated and the dough comes away from the sides of the bowl.

Turn the dough out on to a lightly floured surface and knead for 10 minutes, or until it is smooth and elastic.

The dough is now ready to use.

Enough dough for 72 wrappers

WONTON SOUP

Wonton wrappers can be bought at most Chinese delicatessens, or they can be made according to the recipe for Wonton dough above.

	Metric/U.K.	U.S.
Lean beef, minced (ground)	$\frac{1}{2}$kg/1lb	1lb
Soy sauce	2 Tbs	2 Tbs
Fresh root ginger, peeled and finely chopped	2$\frac{1}{2}$cm/1in piece	1in piece
Salt	1 tsp	1 tsp
Grated nutmeg	1 tsp	1 tsp
Chopped spinach	275g/10oz	1$\frac{2}{3}$ cups
Wonton dough, thinly rolled and cut into 36 squares, or 36 bought wonton wrappers	225g/8oz	8oz
Chicken stock	1$\frac{3}{4}$l/3 pints	7$\frac{1}{2}$ cups
Watercress, chopped	1 bunch	1 bunch

Put the beef, soy sauce, ginger, salt, nutmeg and spinach in a bowl and mix thoroughly until they are well blended.

Lay the wrappers on a flat surface and put a little filling just below the centre. Wet the edges of the dough, then fold over one corner to make a triangle, pinching the edges together to seal. Pull the corners at the base of the triangle together and pinch to seal.

Half-fill a large saucepan with water and bring to the boil. Drop in the wontons and return to the boil. Cook for 5 minutes, or until the wontons are tender but still firm. Remove from the heat and pour off the water. Return the wontons to the pan and pour in the stock.

Bring to the boil, then stir in the watercress. Return to the boil.

Transfer the soup to a warmed tureen and serve at once.

6 Servings

YU-CHI-TANG (Shark's Fin Soup)

This is one of the great festive dishes of China and is served on special occasions.

	Metric/U.K.	U.S.
Sesame oil	2 Tbs	2 Tbs
Spring onion (scallion), finely chopped	1	1
Fresh root ginger, peeled and finely chopped	2$\frac{1}{2}$cm/1in piece	1in piece
Chinese dried mushrooms, soaked in cold water for 20 minutes, drained and sliced	4	4
Rice wine or dry sherry	2 Tbs	2 Tbs
Chicken stock	2l/3$\frac{1}{2}$ pints	2$\frac{1}{4}$ quarts
Ready-prepared shark's fin, soaked for 1 hour in cold water and drained	125g/4oz	4oz
Boned chicken breast, shredded	225g/8oz	8oz
Peeled small prawns or shrimps	225g/8oz	8oz
Soy sauce	1$\frac{1}{2}$ Tbs	1$\frac{1}{2}$ Tbs
Cornflour (cornstarch), blended with 1 Tbs chicken stock	1$\frac{1}{2}$ Tbs	1$\frac{1}{2}$ Tbs

Heat the oil in a large saucepan. Add the spring onion (scallion), ginger, mushrooms and wine or sherry and fry for 5 minutes, stirring occasionally. Pour over half the chicken stock, add the shark's fin and bring to the boil. Reduce the heat to low and simmer for 10 minutes. Add the chicken, prawns or shrimps and soy sauce. Pour in the remaining chicken stock and the cornflour (cornstarch) mixture, and bring to the boil, stirring constantly. Reduce the heat to low and simmer for a further 10 minutes, stirring occasionally. Serve at once.

8-10 Servings

Firepots are Mongolian in origin but they have been adopted (and improved) by the Chinese and are now a great favourite. This particular version is a rich meal in itself, but you can if you wish make a more modest version by omitting some of the garnishes and serving less expensive fish.

CHICKEN VEGETABLE FIREPOT

'Firepots' are the Chinese equivalent of fondues—the main offering is cooked in a central 'pot' at the table and eaten with garnishes and side dishes grouped around the central dish. This is a simplified version of a Mongolian dish.

	Metric/U.K.	U.S.
Roasting chicken	1x2kg/4lb	1x4lb
Onion, chopped	1	1
Bouquet garni	1	1
Peppercorns	10	10
Bay leaves	2	2
Salt	1 tsp	1 tsp
Water	1¼l/2 pints	5 cups
Lobster meat	175g/6oz	6oz
Large prawns (shrimps), shelled	175g/6oz	6oz
VEGETABLES		
Mushrooms, sliced or whole if small	125g/4oz	4oz
Red pepper, pith and seeds removed and sliced	1	1
Green pepper, pith and seeds removed and sliced	1	1
Celery or Chinese		

	Metric/U.K.	U.S.
cabbage, thinly sliced or shredded	125g/4oz	4oz
Canned water chestnuts, drained and sliced or lotus root, sliced	125g/4oz	4oz
GARNISHES Cooked rice	275g/10oz	4 cups
Chopped spring onions (scallions)	4 Tbs	4 Tbs
Fresh root ginger, peeled and finely chopped	10cm/4in piece	4in piece
Chopped parsley or coriander	4 Tbs	4 Tbs

Remove the skin, bones and flesh from the chicken. Set the flesh aside and put the skin, bones and any giblets into a saucepan with the onion, bouquet garni, peppercorns, bay leaves, salt and water. Bring to the boil, skimming off any scum that rises to the surface. Cover the pan, reduce the heat to low and simmer the stock for 1 to 1½ hours. Remove from the heat and strain. Set the stock aside.

Meanwhile, prepare the meat and fish. Cut the chicken flesh into small bite-sized pieces and arrange decoratively on a large serving dish. Cut the lobster meat and prawns (shrimps) into bite-sized pieces and arrange decoratively with the chicken. Set aside.

To prepare the vegetables, arrange them attractively on a large serving platter and set them aside with the meat and fish.

Put all the garnishes in separate bowls (dividing the rice into individual-bowl servings) and arrange with the other dishes.

Put the fondue or firepot in the centre of the table and arrange the platters around it. Light the spirit burner and pour the boiling stock into the pot. The food is now ready to be cooked, in the same way as fondue.

6 Servings

WONTONS WITH PORK AND SHRIMPS

	Metric/U.K.	U.S.
Vegetable oil	2 Tbs	2 Tbs
Lean pork, minced (ground)	225g/8oz	8oz
Peeled shrimps, finely chopped	225g/8oz	8oz
Soy sauce	2 Tbs	2 Tbs
Rice wine or dry sherry	1 Tbs	1 Tbs
Salt	½ tsp	½ tsp
Bamboo shoots, finely chopped	2 Tbs	2 Tbs
Chinese dried mushrooms, soaked in cold water for 20 minutes, drained and chopped	2	2
Spring onions (scallions), finely chopped	2	2
Cornflour (cornstarch), blended with 1 Tbs water	1 tsp	1 tsp
Wonton dough, thinly rolled and cut into 36 squares, or 36 bought wonton wrappers	225g/8oz	8oz
Sufficient vegetable oil for deep-frying		

Heat the oil in a frying-pan. Add the pork and fry until it loses its pinkness. Stir in the shrimps, soy sauce, wine or sherry, salt, bamboo shoots and vegetables and fry for 1 minute, stirring constantly. Stir in the cornflour (cornstarch) mixture until the pan mixture thickens. Remove from the heat, transfer to a bowl and set aside to cool.

Lay the wrappers on a flat surface and put a little filling just below the centre. Wet the edges of the dough, then fold over one corner to make a triangle, pinching the edges together to seal. Pull the corners at the base of the triangle together and pinch to seal.

Fill a large saucepan one-third full with oil and heat until it reaches 190°C (375°F) on a deep-fat thermometer, or until a small cube of stale bread dropped into the oil turns golden in 40 seconds. Carefully lower the wontons into the oil, a few at a time, and fry for 2 to 3 minutes, or until they are golden brown. Remove from the oil and drain on kitchen towels.

Transfer the wontons to a warmed serving dish and serve piping hot.

8 Servings

SHRIMP DUMPLNGS

	Metric/U.K.	U.S.
Shelled shrimps	225g/8oz	8oz

	Metric/U.K.	U.S.
Spring onions (scallions), finely chopped	2	2
Chopped bean sprouts	2 Tbs	2 Tbs
Soy sauce	2 tsp	2 tsp
Rice wine or dry sherry	1 tsp	1 tsp
Sugar	¼ tsp	¼ tsp
DUMPLINGS		
Flour	225g/8oz	2 cups
Hot water	125ml/4floz	½ cup

To make the dumplings, sift the flour into a large bowl. Make a well in the centre and pour in the water. Using your fingers or a spatula, draw the flour into the liquid until it has been incorporated and the dough comes away from the sides of the bowl. Turn the dough out on to a lightly floured surface and knead for 5 minutes, or until it is smooth and elastic. Return to the bowl, cover and set aside for 30 minutes.

Chop the shrimps finely and transfer them to a bowl. Stir in the spring onions (scallions), bean sprouts, soy sauce, wine or dry sherry and sugar until the mixture is thoroughly blended.

Turn the dough out on to the floured surface and roll out into a sausage about 2½cm/1in in diameter. Cut the dough into slices about 2½cm/1in wide. Flatten the slices evenly with your fingers until they measure about 7½cm/3in in diameter.

Place a teaspoon of filling in the centre of each dough circle. Gather up the dough around the filling and bring it up and over, pleating it slightly as you bring it towards the centre. Turn the ends clockwise slightly to seal the filling in completely.

Half-fill a large saucepan or the bottom half of a steamer with water. Bring to the boil over high heat. Arrange the dumplings in a colander or the top half of the steamer, sealed side up, and place over the boiling water. Reduce the heat to moderate and steam the dumplings for about 10 minutes.

Transfer to a warmed serving dish and serve at once.

4-6 Servings

FENG KUO (Crabmeat Dumplings)

	Metric/U.K.	U.S.
Vegetable oil	2 Tbs	2 Tbs
Chopped spring onions (scallions)	1 Tbs	1 Tbs
Finely chopped fresh root ginger	1 Tbs	1 Tbs
Chinese dried mushrooms, soaked in cold water for 20 minutes, drained and chopped	6	6
Crabmeat, shell and cartilage removed and flaked	225g/8oz	8oz
Salt and pepper to taste		
Sugar	¼ tsp	¼ tsp
Soy sauce	1 tsp	1 tsp
Rice wine or dry sherry	1 Tbs	1 Tbs
DUMPLINGS		
Flour	225g/8oz	2 cups
Hot water	125ml/4floz	½ cup

To make the dumplings, sift the flour into a large bowl. Make a well in the centre and pour in the water. Using your fingers or a spatula, draw the flour into the liquid until it has been incorporated and the dough comes away from the sides of the bowl. Turn the dough out on to a lightly floured surface and knead for 5 minutes, or until it is smooth and elastic. Return to the bowl, cover and set aside for 30 minutes.

Heat the oil in a large frying-pan. Add the spring onions (scallions), ginger, mushrooms and crabmeat and stir-fry for 3 minutes. Stir in the remaining ingredients and fry for a further 1 minute, stirring constantly. Remove from the heat and set aside.

Turn the dough out on to the floured surface and roll out into a sausage about 2½cm/1in in diameter. Cut the dough into slices about 2½cm/1in wide. Flatten the slices evenly with your fingers until they measure about 7½cm/3in in diameter.

Place a teaspoon of filling on one side of each dough circle. Fold over the circles to make a semi-circle and pinch to seal.

Half-fill a large saucepan or the bottom half of a steamer with water. Bring to the boil over high heat. Arrange the dumplings in a colander or the top half of the steamer and place over the boiling water. Reduce the heat to moderate and steam the dumplings for about 10 minutes.

Transfer to a warmed serving dish and serve at once.

4-6 Servings

Meins and Foo Yungs

Noodles are one of the staples of northern China and there are endless delicious recipes based on them. Prawn or Shrimp Chow Mein is one particularly tasty variation.

CHOW MEIN (Fried Noodles)

This is the basic and probably one of the most popular of the Chinese noodle dishes.

	Metric/U.K.	U.S.
Egg noodles or spaghetti	½kg/1lb	1lb
French (green) beans	225g/8oz	8oz
Vegetable oil	50ml/2floz	¼ cup
Medium onion, thinly sliced	1	1
Garlic clove, crushed	1	1
Chicken meat, finely shredded	125g/4oz	4oz
Soy sauce	2 Tbs	2 Tbs
Sugar	1 tsp	1 tsp
Rice wine or dry sherry	1 Tbs	1 Tbs
Butter	1½ Tbs	1½ Tbs
Chicken stock	3 Tbs	3 Tbs
Chicken stock cube, crumbled	½	¼

Cook the noodles or spaghetti in boiling, salted water until they are just tender. Drain, set aside and keep hot. Cook the beans in boiling, salted water for 5 minutes. Drain, set aside and keep hot.

Heat the oil in a large frying-pan. Add the onion and garlic and fry for 2 minutes, stirring constantly. Add the chicken and stir-fry for 1 minute. Add the beans, soy sauce, sugar and wine or sherry and stir-fry for a further 1 minute. Using a slotted spoon, transfer the bean and chicken mixture to a bowl. Keep hot.

Add the butter, stock and stock cube to the oil in the pan. Add the noodles or pasta and fry for 2 minutes, stirring and turning constantly. Add half the bean and chicken mixture. Transfer the mixture to a warmed serving dish, set aside and keep hot.

Return the remaining bean and chicken mixture to the frying-pan and increase the heat to high. Fry for 1 minute, stirring constantly, adding more oil or soy sauce to the pan if necessary. Spoon the bean and chicken mixture over the pasta and serve at once.

4-6 Servings

PRAWN OR SHRIMP CHOW MEIN

	Metric/U.K.	U.S.
Peanut oil for deep-frying		
Thin egg noodles, cooked and drained	225g/8oz	8oz
Vegetable oil	2 Tbs	2 Tbs
Chinese dried mushrooms, soaked in cold water for 20 minutes, drained and sliced	10	10
Carrots, thinly sliced on the diagonal	2	2
Bean sprouts	225g/8oz	8oz
Canned water chestnuts, drained and sliced	225g/8oz	8oz
Chicken stock	125ml/4floz	½ cup
Rice wine or dry sherry	1 Tbs	1 Tbs
Soy sauce	1 Tbs	1 Tbs
Prawns or shrimps, shelled	350g/12oz	12oz

Fill a large saucepan one-third full with oil and heat until it reaches 185°C (360°F) on a deep-fat thermometer, or until a small cube of stale bread dropped into the oil turns golden in 50 seconds. Drop the noodles into the oil and fry for 3 to 4 minutes or until they are golden brown. Remove from the oil and drain on kitchen towels. Arrange the noodles on a serving dish and keep hot while you make the sauce.

Heat the oil in a large frying-pan. Add the vegetables and fry until they are tender but crisp. Stir in the stock and wine or sherry and bring to the boil. Reduce the heat to low and stir in the remaining ingredients. Cover and cook for 3 to 5 minutes, or until the prawns or shrimps are heated through.

Remove from the heat. Pour the sauce over the noodles and serve at once.

3-4 Servings

TAN MEIN (Soup Noodles)

Tan mein is eaten all over China, and primarily as a main or noodle course rather than as a soup course, despite the name.

	Metric/U.K.	U.S.
Egg noodles or spaghetti	350g/12oz	12oz
Vegetable oil	1½ Tbs	1½ Tbs
Small onion, thinly sliced	1	1
Fresh root ginger, peeled and finely chopped	4cm/1½in piece	1½in piece
Lean pork, finely shredded	225g/8oz	8oz
Butter	1 Tbs	1 Tbs
Mushrooms	125g/4oz	4oz
Chinese or white cabbage, blanched for 4 minutes and shredded	125g/4oz	4oz
Bean sprouts, blanched for 1 minute and drained	125g/4oz	4oz
Shrimps or prawns, shelled	125g/4oz	4oz
Soy sauce	1½ Tbs	1½ Tbs
Sugar	1 tsp	1 tsp
Water	300ml/10floz	1¼ cups
Chicken stock cube, crumbled	1	1
Chicken stock	600ml/1 pint	2½ cups

Cook the noodles or spaghetti in boiling, salted water until they are just tender. Drain, set aside and keep hot.

Heat the oil in a large frying-pan. Add the onion, ginger and pork and fry for 2 minutes, stirring constantly. Stir in the butter until it melts. Add the vegetables and shrimps or prawns and fry for 1½ minutes, stirring constantly. Stir in the soy sauce and sugar and stir-fry for a further 1½ minutes. Remove the frying-pan from the heat, set it aside and keep hot.

Pour the water into a saucepan and bring to the boil. Crumble in the stock cube and stir to dissolve it. Add half the pork mixture and the stock and bring the mixture to the boil. Stir in the noodles or spaghetti and simmer for 3 minutes.

Meanwhile, return the frying-pan to high heat and stir-fry the remaining pork mixture for 1 minute to reheat it.

Divide the noodle or spaghetti mixture between four or six individual bowls. Spoon over the remaining pork mixture and serve at once.

4-6 Servings

CHA CHIANG MEIN
(Noodles in Meat Sauce with Shredded Vegetables)

This is one of the classic peasant dishes of Peking and, unlike most Chinese dishes, is a meal in itself. Traditionally, each diner is given a bowl of noodles to which he adds as much meat sauce and shredded vegetables as he likes.

	Metric/U.K.	U.S.
Noodles or spaghetti	½kg/1lb	1lb
Vegetable oil	3 Tbs	3 Tbs
Medium onion, thinly sliced	1	1
Garlic cloves, crushed	2	2
Fresh root ginger, peeled and finely chopped	4cm/1½in piece	1½in piece
Lean pork or beef, minced (ground)	350g/12oz	12oz
Sesame oil	1 Tbs	1 Tbs
Soy sauce	5 Tbs	5 Tbs
Rice wine or dry sherry	2 Tbs	2 Tbs
Sugar	1 Tbs	1 Tbs
Cornflour (cornstarch), blended with 4 Tbs chicken stock	1 Tbs	1 Tbs
SHREDDED VEGETABLES		
Shredded cabbage, blanched for 4 minutes and drained (a heaped side-dishful)	75-125g/3-4oz	3-4oz
Shredded carrots, blanched for 4 minutes and drained (a heaped side-dishful)	75-125g/3-4oz	3-4oz
Bean sprouts, blanched for 1 minute and drained (a heaped side-dishful)	75-125g/3-4oz	3-4oz
Shredded cucumber (a heaped side-dishful)	75-125g/3-4oz	3-4oz
Shredded radishes (a saucerful)	50-75g/2-3oz	4-6 Tbs

	Metric/U.K.	U.S.
Mixed pickles (a saucerful)	25-50g/1-2oz	2-4 Tbs
Chutney (a saucerful)	25-50g/1-2oz	2-4 Tbs

Arrange the shredded vegetables, pickles and chutney on individual serving dishes. Set aside.

Cook the noodles or spaghetti in boiling, salted water until they are just tender. Drain, set aside and keep hot.

Heat the vegetable oil in a large frying-pan. Add the onion, garlic and ginger and fry for $1\frac{1}{2}$ minutes, stirring constantly. Add the pork or beef and stir-fry until it loses its pinkness. Stir in the sesame oil, soy sauce, wine or sherry and sugar, and stir-fry for a further 3 minutes. Stir in the cornflour (cornstarch) mixture and cook, stirring constantly, until the sauce thickens and becomes translucent. Remove from the heat and transfer the sauce to a warmed serving bowl. Keep hot.

Divide the noodles or spaghetti between four individual serving bowls. Serve at once, with the meat sauce and shredded vegetables.

4 Servings

STIR-FRIED BEEF WITH TRANSPARENT NOODLES

	Metric/U.K.	U.S.
Fillet of beef, cut with the grain into thin strips	$\frac{1}{2}$kg/1lb	1lb
Soy sauce	3 Tbs	3 Tbs
Rice wine or dry sherry	1 Tbs	1 Tbs
Peanut oil	75ml/3floz	$\frac{3}{8}$ cup
Cornflour (cornstarch)	2 Tbs	2 Tbs
Transparent noodles	225g/8oz	8oz
Fresh root ginger, peeled and chopped	4cm/$1\frac{1}{2}$in piece	$1\frac{1}{2}$in piece
Chinese cabbage, shredded	125g/4oz	4oz
Bean sprouts	125g/4oz	4oz
Spring onions (scallions), finely chopped	2	2
Sugar	$1\frac{1}{2}$ tsp	$1\frac{1}{2}$ tsp
Salt	1 tsp	1 tsp
Beef stock	50ml/2floz	$\frac{1}{4}$ cup

Put the beef strips into a shallow bowl. Combine 2 tablespoons of soy sauce, the wine or sherry, 1 tablespoon of oil and the cornflour (cornstarch) until they are well blended. Pour the mixture over the beef strips and toss gently to coat them. Set aside to marinate at room temperature for 1 hour.

Meanwhile, turn the noodles into a bowl and pour over enough boiling water to cover completely. Set aside to soak for 5 minutes. Drain.

Heat the remaining oil in a very large frying-pan. Add the ginger and beef strips and stir-fry over high heat for 3 minutes. Push the strips to the side of the pan and add the noodles and remaining ingredients. Fry for 2 minutes, then stir the beef strips into the noodles. Add the remaining soy sauce and fry for a further 2 minutes, stirring frequently.

Transfer the mixture to a warmed serving dish and serve at once.

4 Servings

EGG FOO YUNG

This is the Chinese version of the western omelet. It is usually served either on its own (or with a filling, as the following recipe), or it can be cut into strips and stirred into fried rice as a garnish.

	Metric/U.K.	U.S.
Eggs	4	4
Soy sauce	1 Tbs	1 Tbs
Salt and pepper to taste		
Butter	25g/1oz	2 Tbs
Shallot, very finely chopped	1	1
Bean sprouts	125g/4oz	4oz
Cooked ham, cut into thin strips	50g/2oz	2oz

Beat the eggs, soy sauce and seasoning together until the mixture is light and fluffy.

Melt the butter in a frying-pan. Add the shallot, bean sprouts and ham and fry for 4 to 5 minutes, stirring occasionally. Pour in the egg mixture, stir with a fork and leave to set.

Preheat the grill (broiler) to high.

When the bottom of the omelet is set and golden, transfer the pan to the grill (broiler) and grill (broil) until the top is set and lightly browned.

Serve at once, cut into wedges.

2-3 Servings

SHRIMP EGG FOO YUNG

This particular version of foo yung is crisp, filled with succulent chopped shrimps and is served with a delicate sauce.

	Metric/U.K.	U.S.
Vegetable oil	3 Tbs	3 Tbs
Shelled shrimps, chopped	225g/8oz	8oz
Mushrooms, sliced	125g/4oz	4oz
Bean sprouts	125g/4oz	4oz
Eggs, lightly beaten	4	4
SAUCE		
Chicken stock	250ml/8floz	1 cup
Soy sauce	2 tsp	2 tsp
Salt	$\frac{1}{4}$ tsp	$\frac{1}{4}$ tsp
Cornflour (cornstarch), blended with 1 Tbs water	1 Tbs	1 Tbs

Heat 1 tablespoon of oil in a frying-pan. Add the shrimps and stir-fry for 3 minutes, or until they are heated through. Remove from the heat and set aside.

To make the sauce, combine all the ingredients in a small saucepan and bring to the boil, stirring constantly. Cook for 1 minute, stirring constantly, or until the sauce thickens and becomes translucent. Remove the pan from the heat and set aside.

Combine the vegetables, eggs and shrimps in a large bowl and beat until thoroughly blended.

Return the frying-pan to moderate heat and add the remaining oil. When it is hot, add a quarter of the egg mixture and cook for 1 minute or until the bottom is set and golden brown. Turn the omelet over and cook for a further 1 minute, or until it is just set. Transfer to a serving dish and keep hot while you cook the remaining mixture in the same way, to make three more omelets.

Return the pan with the sauce to the heat and bring to the boil, stirring constantly. Pour a little sauce over the omelets and serve at once, with the remaining sauce.

4 Servings

The Chinese version of the western omelet, but much more delicate and crisp. This particular version is Shrimp Egg Foo Yung.

Meat and Poultry

K'OU TSE NGIU LAN
(Leg of Beef in Fruit Sauce)

	Metric/U.K.	U.S.
Vegetable oil	2 Tbs	2 Tbs
Medium onion, thinly sliced	1	1
Garlic cloves, crushed	2	2
Fresh root ginger, peeled and finely chopped	2½cm/1in piece	1in piece
Boned leg (shin) of beef, cubed	1½kg/3lb	3lb
Juice of 1 lemon		
Juice of 2 oranges		
Soy sauce	4 Tbs	4 Tbs
Dry red wine	300ml/10floz	1¼ cups
Water	600ml/1 pint	2½ cups
Salt and pepper to taste		

Preheat the oven to cool 150°C (Gas Mark 2, 300°F).

Heat the oil in a large flameproof casserole. Add the onion, garlic and ginger and stir-fry for 1 minute. Add the beef and fry until it is evenly browned. Stir in all the remaining ingredients and bring to the boil. Transfer the casserole to the oven and bake for 4 hours, stirring three or four times during the cooking period.

Remove from the oven and serve at once.

6-8 Servings

HAO YIU NGIU JOU PIEN
(Quick-Fried Sliced Beef in Oyster Sauce)

	Metric/U.K.	U.S.
Fillet steak, cut into thin strips about 5cm/ 2in x 2½cm/1in	700g/1½lb	1½lb
Salt and white pepper		
to taste		
Ground ginger	¼ tsp	¼ tsp
Cornflour (cornstarch)	1 Tbs	1 Tbs
Soy sauce	1 Tbs	1 Tbs
Oyster sauce	2½ Tbs	2½ Tbs
Sugar	1 tsp	1 tsp
Rice wine or dry sherry	2 Tbs	2 Tbs
Vegetable oil	75ml/3floz	6 Tbs
Medium onion, thinly sliced	1	1
Garlic clove, crushed	1	1

Rub the beef strips with the salt, pepper, ginger and cornflour (cornstarch).

Combine the soy sauce, oyster sauce, sugar and wine or sherry. Set aside.

Heat the oil in a large frying-pan. Add the onion and garlic and fry for 30 seconds, stirring constantly. Add the beef strips and fry for 2 minutes, stirring constantly. Pour off all but a thin film of oil from the pan. Pour in the reserved sauce and cook for a further 1½ minutes, stirring constantly.

Transfer the mixture to a warmed serving dish and serve at once.

4 Servings

GINGER BEEF

	Metric/U.K.	U.S.
Fillet or rump steak, sliced with the grain into thin strips	½kg/1lb	1lb
Salt and pepper to taste		
Ground ginger	1 tsp	1 tsp
Cornflour (cornstarch)	2 Tbs	2 Tbs
Sesame oil	50ml/2floz	¼ cup
Fresh root ginger, peeled and finely chopped	25g/1oz	3 Tbs
Chopped spring onions (scallions)	2 Tbs	2 Tbs

Put the beef strips in a shallow bowl. Rub them with salt, pepper, ginger and cornflour (cornstarch) and set aside for 10 minutes.

Heat the oil in a frying-pan. Add the root ginger and stir-fry for 2 minutes. Add the beef strips and stir-fry for 3 to 5 minutes, or until they are cooked through.

Unusual but delicious, K'ou Tse Ngiu Lan is leg of beef slowly casseroled in a sauce of fruit and red wine.

Beef with Broccoli takes only a few minutes to cook and the result not only looks fantastic but tastes superb too.

Transfer the strips to a warmed serving dish and sprinkle over the spring onions (scallions). Serve at once.

4 Servings

BEEF WITH BROCCOLI ✓

	Metric/U.K.	U.S.
Fillet of beef, thinly sliced with the grain into 7½cm/3in x 5cm/2in pieces	½kg/1lb	1lb
Soy sauce	3 Tbs	3 Tbs
Rice wine or dry sherry	1 Tbs	1 Tbs
Fresh root ginger, peeled and chopped	2½cm/1in piece	1 in piece
Vegetable oil	50ml/2floz	¼ cup
Broccoli, broken into flowerets	½kg/1lb	1lb

	Metric/U.K.	U.S.
Beef stock	75ml/3floz	$\frac{3}{8}$ cup
Vegetable fat	1 Tbs	1 Tbs
Cornflour (cornstarch), blended with 4 Tbs water	2 tsp	2 tsp

Put the beef strips into a shallow bowl. Combine the soy sauce, wine or sherry, ginger and 1 tablespoon of oil together, then pour over the strips, basting to coat them thoroughly. Set aside to marinate for 15 minutes, stirring and basting occasionally. Meanwhile, cut the broccoli into bite-sized pieces.

Heat the remaining oil in a frying-pan. Add the beef mixture and stir-fry for $1\frac{1}{2}$ minutes. Using a slotted spoon, transfer the beef strips to a plate. Add the stock to the pan and bring to the boil. Add the broccoli and cook for 1 minute, stirring constantly. Reduce the heat to low, cover and simmer the mixture for 4 minutes. Using the slotted spoon, transfer the broccoli to a warmed serving dish. Keep hot.

Add the vegetable fat to the pan and melt it. Return the beef strips to the pan and stir-fry for 30 seconds. Add the cornflour (cornstarch) mixture and stir-fry for 1 minute, or until the sauce becomes translucent. Remove from the heat.

Arrange the beef strips over the broccoli, then pour over the sauce. Serve at once.

4 Servings

CHING-CHIAO-CHAO NIU-JOU
(Steak with Pepper)

	Metric/U.K.	U.S.
Butter	50g/2oz	4 Tbs
Garlic clove, crushed	1	1
Salt and pepper to taste		
Topside (top round) of beef, cut $2\frac{1}{2}$cm/1in thick then into strips	$\frac{1}{2}$kg/1lb	1lb
Soy sauce	4 Tbs	4 Tbs
Sugar	2 tsp	2 tsp
Bean sprouts	175g/6oz	6oz
Tomatoes, blanched, peeled and quartered	2	2
Green peppers, pith and seeds removed and thinly sliced	2	2
Cornflour (cornstarch), blended with 2 Tbs water	$\frac{1}{2}$ Tbs	$\frac{1}{2}$ Tbs
Spring onions (scallions), sliced	4	4

Melt the butter in a large frying-pan. Add the garlic, salt and pepper and stir-fry for 30 seconds. Add the beef strips and stir-fry for 3 minutes. Increase the heat to high. Stir in the soy sauce and sugar, cover and cook for 5 minutes. Uncover, and stir in the bean sprouts, tomatoes and peppers. Re-cover and simmer for 5 minutes. Stir in the cornflour (cornstarch) mixture until the mixture thickens.

Transfer the mixture to a warmed serving dish and sprinkle over the spring onions (scallions). Serve at once.

4 Servings

HUNG SHAO NGIU JOU
(Red-Cooked Beef with Star Anise)

	Metric/U.K.	U.S.
Vegetable oil	75ml/3floz	$\frac{3}{8}$ cup
Boned leg (shin) of beef, cubed	$1\frac{1}{2}$kg/3lb	3lb
Star anise	3 pieces	3 pieces
Water	150ml/5floz	$\frac{5}{8}$ cup
Beef stock cube, crumbled	$\frac{1}{2}$	$\frac{1}{2}$
Soy sauce	7 Tbs	7 Tbs
Fresh root ginger, peeled and finely chopped	4cm/$1\frac{1}{2}$in piece	$1\frac{1}{2}$in piece
Sugar	2 tsp	2 tsp
Red wine	150ml/5floz	$\frac{5}{8}$ cup

Preheat the oven to cool 150°C (Gas Mark 2, 300°F).

Heat the oil in a flameproof casserole. Add the beef cubes and fry until they are evenly browned. Remove from the heat and pour off all the excess oil. Stir in the star anise, water, stock cube and 4 tablespoons of soy sauce. Return the casserole to the heat and bring to the boil, stirring constantly. Transfer to the oven and cook for 1 hour, turning the meat once.

Remove from the oven and stir in the

remaining ingredients. Return to the oven and cook for a further 2 hours, turning the meat every 30 minutes.

Remove from the oven and serve at once.

6-8 Servings

QUICK-FRIED STEAK WITH VEGETABLES

The beef in this dish can either be cut with the grain into thin strips (the traditional Chinese way), or, simpler and probably more to the average western taste, the fillet steaks can simply be cut into two or three pieces, depending on their size.

	Metric/U.K.	U.S.
Sesame oil	50ml/2floz	¼ cup
Leek, separated into layers, then thinly sliced on the diagonal	1	1
Green pepper, pith and seeds removed and thinly sliced	1	1
Red pepper, pith and seeds removed and thinly sliced	1	1
Button mushrooms, sliced	50g/2oz	2oz
Bean sprouts	125g/4oz	4oz
Soy sauce	2 Tbs	2 Tbs
Hoi sin sauce	1 Tbs	1 Tbs
Fillet steaks, cut as above	½kg/1lb	1lb

Heat half the oil in a large frying-pan. Add the leek, peppers and mushrooms and stir-fry for 3 minutes. Add the bean sprouts, soy sauce and hoi sin sauce and stir-fry for a further 1 minute. Transfer the mixture to a warmed serving dish and keep hot while you cook the steak.

Add the remaining oil to the pan. When it is hot, add the steak pieces and either stir-fry (for strips) for 3 to 5 minutes, or until they are cooked through, or cook for 2 to 3 minutes on each side if they are steak pieces.

Arrange the steaks on top of the vegetables and serve at once.

2-3 Servings

SHAO K'O YANG JOU
(Steamed Lamb)

	Metric/U.K.	U.S.
Leg of lamb	1x1½kg/3lb	1x3lb
Crushed black peppercorns	1 tsp	1 tsp
Fresh root ginger, peeled and finely chopped	5cm/2in piece	2in piece
Mixed sweet pickle	125g/4oz	1 cup
Soy sauce	75ml/3floz	⅜ cup
Rice wine or dry sherry	150ml/5floz	⅝ cup
Onions, thinly sliced	2	2
Butter	1 tsp	1 tsp

Half-fill a saucepan with water and bring to the boil. Add the lamb, cover and boil for 4 minutes over moderately high heat. Remove from the heat and drain. Put the lamb on a chopping board and cut it, including the skin, into cubes. Arrange the cubes, skin side down, on the bottom of a heatproof basin. Sprinkle over the peppercorns and ginger and spoon over the pickle.

Combine the soy sauce and wine or sherry and pour over the meat. Arrange the onions on top. Cover with a circle of greaseproof or waxed paper about 10cm/4in wider than the rim of the basin and greased with butter. Cut out a circle of foil the same size, pleat the two and tie securely around the basin with string. Put the basin in a large saucepan and pour in enough boiling water to come about two-thirds of the way up the sides of the basin. Cover the pan and place over low heat. Steam for 2½ hours, adding more boiling water if necessary.

When the lamb has finished steaming, lift the basin out of the water and remove the foil and paper circles. Transfer the mixture to a warmed serving dish and serve at once.

6 Servings

QUICK-FRIED SPINACH WITH SHREDDED PORK

	Metric/U.K.	U.S.
Vegetable oil	3 Tbs	3 Tbs
Pork fillet (tenderloin), cut into thin strips	225g/8oz	8oz
Soy sauce	2 Tbs	2 Tbs

Quick-Fried Steak with Vegetables can either be cooked as in the picture in the western way, or the meat can be cut into strips with the grain and stir-fried in the Chinese way. Both are delicious.

	Metric/U.K.	U.S.
Rice wine or dry sherry	1 Tbs	1 Tbs
Sugar	1 tsp	1 tsp
Black pepper	½ tsp	½ tsp
Vegetable fat	40g/1½oz	3 Tbs
Spinach, trimmed and chopped	½kg/1lb	1lb
Salt	1 tsp	1 tsp

Heat the oil in a large saucepan. Add the pork strips and stir-fry for 2 minutes. Add the soy sauce, wine or sherry, sugar and pepper and stir-fry for a further 2 minutes. Using a slotted spoon, transfer the pork to a plate and keep hot.

Add 25g/1oz (2 tablespoons) of fat to the pan and melt it. Add the spinach and salt and stir-fry for 3 minutes. Add the remaining fat to the pan and stir-fry the mixture for a further 30 seconds. Using the slotted spoon, transfer the spinach to a warmed serving dish.

Increase the heat to moderately high and return the pork strips to the pan. Stir-fry for 30 seconds to reheat them thoroughly. Pour the pork and pan juices over the spinach and serve at once.

2 Servings

SWEET AND SOUR PORK ✓

	Metric/U.K.	U.S.
Soy sauce	4 Tbs	4 Tbs
Fresh root ginger, peeled and grated	2½cm/1in piece	1in piece
Pork fillet (tenderloin), cubed	700g/1½lb	1½lb
Eggs	2	2
Cornflour (cornstarch)	3 Tbs	3 Tbs
Sufficient vegetable oil for deep-frying		
SAUCE		
Vegetable oil	2 Tbs	2 Tbs
Fresh root ginger, peeled and finely chopped	2½cm/1in piece	1in piece
Large carrots, thinly sliced on the diagonal	2	2
Large red pepper, pith and seeds removed and thinly sliced	1	1
Large green pepper, pith and seeds removed and thinly sliced	1	1
Canned pineapple chunks	450g/1lb	1lb
Soy sauce	1 Tbs	1 Tbs
Wine vinegar	3 Tbs	3 Tbs
Soft brown sugar	3 Tbs	3 Tbs
Salt	¼ tsp	¼ tsp
Cornflour (cornstarch), blended with 6 Tbs water	2 Tbs	2 Tbs

Combine the soy sauce and ginger together. Put the pork cubes in a bowl and pour over the soy sauce mixture. Baste the cubes to coat them thoroughly. Cover and set aside for 1 hour.

Mix the eggs and cornflour (cornstarch) together until they are smooth. Pour the batter over the pork cubes and mix well to blend.

Preheat the oven to moderate 180°C (Gas Mark 4, 350°F).

Fill a large saucepan one-third full with oil and heat until it reaches 185°C (360°F) on a deep-fat thermometer, or until a small cube of stale bread dropped into the oil turns golden in 50 seconds. Carefully lower the pork cubes, a few at a time, into the oil and fry for 5 to 6 minutes, or until they are golden brown and crisp. Transfer to an ovenproof dish as they cook and keep hot in the oven while you cook the remaining cubes, and make the sauce.

Heat the oil in a large frying-pan. Add the ginger, carrots and peppers and stir-fry for 3 minutes. Stir in the pineapple chunks with the can juice, the soy sauce, vinegar, sugar and salt and bring to the boil. Cook the sauce for 1 minute, stirring constantly. Stir in the cornflour (cornstarch) mixture until the sauce thickens and becomes translucent.

Remove the pork cubes from the oven. Pour over the sauce and serve at once.

4-6 Servings

LOU JO
(Pork Simmered in Master Sauce)

This dish, a speciality of Peking, is usually made with pork in China, but beef can be substituted if you prefer.

	Metric/U.K.	U.S.
Leg of pork, boned and trimmed of fat	1x1½kg/3lb	1x3lb

SAUCE

Soy sauce	600ml/1 pint	2½ cups
Rice wine or dry sherry	300ml/10floz	1¼ cups
Chicken stock	150ml/5floz	⅝ cup
Soft brown sugar	4 Tbs	4 Tbs
Garlic cloves, crushed	2	2
Fresh root ginger, peeled and sliced	2½cm/1in piece	1in piece
Bouquets garnis	2	2

Put the pork in a large saucepan and just cover with water. Bring to the boil, reduce the heat to moderate and cook for 6 minutes. Remove the pan from the heat, drain the pork and set

aside. Discard the cooking liquid.

To prepare the sauce, combine all the ingredients in a large saucepan. Bring to the boil, stirring frequently. Reduce the heat to low, arrange the pork in the sauce (making sure it is completely submerged), and simmer the mixture for 1½ hours, turning the pork every 30 minutes.

Remove from the heat and transfer the pork to a carving board. Cut into thin slices and arrange them decoratively on a serving dish. Strain the sauce into a sauceboat and pour a little over and around the meat. Serve at once, accompanied by the remaining sauce.

6-8 Servings

No book on Chinese cooking would be complete without Sweet and Sour Pork. In this particular version the pork cubes are deep-fried in batter and the sauce contains a colourful selection of vegetables and pineapple cubes.

SHAO JOU
(Cantonese Roast Pork)

This is one of the great classics of Cantonese cooking, often cooked (and badly) in the west. Hoi sin sauce is a rather spicy, sweet barbecue sauce available in cans or bottles from Chinese delicatessens.

	Metric/U.K.	U.S.
Pork fillet (tenderloin), cut into strips about 15cm/6in x 4cm/1½in	1½kg/3lb	3lb
Vegetable oil	2 Tbs	2 Tbs
MARINADE		
Medium onion, finely chopped	1	1
Soy sauce	5 Tbs	5 Tbs
Sugar	1 Tbs	1 Tbs
Rice wine or dry sherry	1 Tbs	1 Tbs
Ground ginger	1½ tsp	1½ tsp
Hoi sin sauce	1 Tbs	1 Tbs

To make the marinade, combine all the ingredients in a shallow dish. Add the pork strips and coat well. Set aside to marinate at room temperature for 2 hours, basting occasionally.

Preheat the oven to moderate 180°C (Gas Mark 4, 350°F).

Remove the pork from the marinade and reserve the marinade. Arrange the strips in a shallow roasting pan in one layer. Baste with half the reserved marinade and half the oil. Put the pan into the oven and roast the strips for 15 minutes. Remove from the oven and turn the strips over. Baste with the remaining marinade and remaining oil and return the pan to the oven. Roast the strips for a further 15 minutes.

Remove the pan from the oven and transfer the pork to a chopping board. Cut the strips into ½cm/¼in slices and serve at once.

8 Servings

RUN TSA LI CHI
(Plain Deep-Fried Sliced Pork)

	Metric/U.K.	U.S.
Pork fillets (tenderloin)	700g/1½lb	1½lb
Egg whites	2	2

Cornflour (cornstarch)	1½ Tbs	1½ Tbs
Sufficient vegetable oil for deep-frying		
DIP		
Black pepper	1 Tbs	1 Tbs
Salt	1 Tbs	1 Tbs

Slice the pork against the grain into thin slices. Using a mallet, beat the slices until they are very thin, then cut into strips about 7½cm/3in by 5cm/2in. Put the strips into a large bowl and set aside.

Beat the egg whites until they are frothy. Gradually beat in the cornflour (cornstarch) until the mixture forms a smooth batter. Pour the batter over the pork strips and toss to coat thoroughly. Set aside for 10 minutes.

Fill a large saucepan one-third full with oil and heat until it reaches 185°C (360°F) on a deep-fat thermometer, or until a small cube of stale bread dropped into the oil turns golden in 50 seconds. Carefully lower the meat strips, a few at a time, into the oil and cook for 1 minute or until they are golden brown and crisp. Remove from the oil and drain on kitchen towels.

To make the dip, fry the pepper and salt in a small frying-pan over moderately high heat for 4 minutes, stirring constantly. Remove from the heat and transfer the mixture to a small serving bowl.

Serve the pork strips at once, with the dip.

4-6 Servings

CHINESE ROAST PORK

This dish can be eaten either hot or cold and is traditionally accompanied by Chinese mustard.

	Metric/U.K.	U.S.
Loin of pork, boned and trimmed of fat	1x1½kg/3lb	1x3lb
Soy sauce	50ml/2floz	¼ cup
Soft brown sugar	4 Tbs	4 Tbs
Salt and pepper to taste		
Rice wine or dry sherry	2 Tbs	2 Tbs
Fresh root ginger, peeled and sliced	2½cm/1in piece	1in piece

Cut the meat in half. Combine the soy sauce, sugar, salt, pepper, wine or sherry and ginger in a large dish. Add the pork and marinate at

93

Ching-Chiao-Chao Jiu-Jou (steak with pepper—recipe on page 87) and Chinese Roast Pork make a delightful meal served, as here, with fried rice.

room temperature for 4 hours, basting frequently.

Preheat the oven to fairly hot 190°C (Gas Mark 5, 375°F). Put the pork and marinade in a roasting pan and roast for 10 minutes. Turn the meat over and increase the temperature to very hot 230°C (Gas Mark 8, 450°F). Continue to roast for about 40 minutes, turning and basting frequently during cooking, or until the pork is cooked through and tender.

Preheat the grill (broiler) to high.

Put the meat under the grill (broiler) and grill (broil) for 4 to 6 minutes, or until the meat is evenly browned.

Transfer to a serving dish, discarding the marinade, and cut into slices before serving.

6 Servings

KUO PA JOU TIN
(Diced Pork on Crackling Rice)

The English translation of this dish describes the sound the rice is supposed to make when the pork sauce is poured over it.

	Metric/U.K.	U.S.
Pork fillet (tenderloin), cubed	½kg/1lb	1lb
Salt and pepper to taste		
Cornflour (cornstarch)	1½ Tbs	1½ Tbs
Cooked long-grain rice	450g/1lb	6 cups
Sufficient vegetable oil for deep-frying		

SAUCE		
Chicken stock	150ml/5floz	⅝ cup
Soy sauce	3 Tbs	3 Tbs
Sugar	1 Tbs	1 Tbs
Rice wine or dry sherry	2 Tbs	2 Tbs
Corn oil	2 Tbs	2 Tbs
Onion, thinly sliced	1	1
Garlic clove, crushed	1	1
Cornflour (cornstarch), blended with 4 Tbs water	1½ Tbs	1½ Tbs

Preheat the oven to very cool 140°C (Gas Mark 1, 275°F).

Sprinkle the pork cubes with salt, pepper and cornflour (cornstarch), rubbing them into the meat with your fingers.

Put the rice into an ovenproof baking dish and put the dish into the oven. Dry out the rice for 15 to 20 minutes, or until it is slightly crisp.

Meanwhile, fill a large saucepan one-third full with oil and heat until it reaches 185°C (360°F) on a deep-fat thermometer, or until a small cube of stale bread dropped into the oil turns golden brown in 50 seconds. Carefully lower the pork cubes, a few at a time, into the oil and fry for 3 to 4 minutes, or until they are golden brown and crisp. Remove from the oil and drain on kitchen towels.

To prepare the sauce, combine the stock, soy sauce, sugar and wine or sherry.

Heat the corn oil in a large frying-pan. Add the onion and garlic and stir-fry for 1 minute. Pour over the stock mixture and bring to the boil. Add the pork cubes, basting well, and reduce the heat to low. Simmer the mixture for 2 minutes. Stir in the cornflour (cornstarch) mixture and cook until the sauce has thickened and become translucent. Set aside and keep hot.

Remove the rice from the oven.

Return the saucepan with the oil to moderate heat and reheat the oil until it reaches 180°C (350°F) on a deep-fat thermometer, or until a small cube of stale bread dropped into the oil turns golden in 55 seconds. Put the rice in a narrow-meshed deep-frying basket and carefully lower it into the oil. Cook the rice for 1½ minutes, then remove from the oil and drain on kitchen towels.

Arrange the rice on a warmed serving dish and pour over the pork sauce.

Serve at once.

4 Servings

MEE FENG JOU
(Pork in Ground Rice)

This delicious dish is traditionally served with a variety of dips such as tomato-soy sauce (mix together equal quantities of tomato ketchup and soy sauce), garlic-soy (finely chop 3 garlic cloves and mix with 4 tablespoons of soy sauce) and soy-sherry-chilli (3 tablespoons each of soy sauce and sherry with 1 tablespoon of chilli sauce).

	Metric/U.K.	U.K.
Leg or belly of pork	1kg/2lb	2lb
Fresh root ginger, peeled and finely chopped	4cm/1½in piece	1½in piece
Soy sauce	2 Tbs	2 Tbs
Chilli sauce	1½ tsp	1½ tsp
Coarsely ground rice	150g/5oz	1¼ cups

Cut the pork into 7½cm/3in by 4cm/1½in slices, about ½cm/¼in thick.

Mix together the ginger, soy sauce and chilli sauce and rub the mixture over the pork slices so that they are evenly coated on both sides. Set aside to marinate for 1 hour.

Heat a large frying-pan over moderate heat. Add the rice to the pan and cook, stirring constantly, until it begins to brown. Put the pork pieces in the pan and turn them so that they become thickly coated with the rice. Remove from the heat.

Transfer the pork pieces to a heatproof dish, arranging them in 'tile-piece' or 'fish-scale' fashion. Place the dish in a steamer, cover and steam over moderate heat for 35 to 40 minutes, or until the pork is cooked through and tender.

Remove the dish from the steamer and serve the pork, with the dips.

4-6 Servings

JOU SI CHOW CHING TS'AI
Shredded Pork Stir-Fried with Spring Greens)

	Metric/U.K.	U.S.
Lean pork, cut into thin strips	350g/12oz	12oz
Salt and pepper to taste		
Cornflour (cornstarch)	2 tsp	2 tsp
Vegetable oil	3 Tbs	3 Tbs
Spring greens or		

*Jou Yuan Ts'aHui
(meatball chop suey) and
Jou Si Chow Ching Ts'ai
(shredded pork stir-fried
with spring greens) are
two economical and
satisfying traditional
dishes.*

	Metric/U.K.	U.S.
cabbage, shredded	½kg/1lb	1lb
Vegetable fat	15g/½oz	1 Tbs
Beef stock	50ml/2floz	4 Tbs
Soy sauce	2 Tbs	2 Tbs
Sugar	1 tsp	1 tsp
Rice wine or dry sherry	2 Tbs	2 Tbs

Put the pork strips on a plate and sprinkle them with salt, pepper and cornflour (cornstarch), rubbing them into the meat with your fingers.

Heat the oil in a large frying-pan. Add the pork and stir-fry over high heat for 3 minutes. Push the pork to the side of the pan and add the greens or cabbage and vegetable fat. Mix the greens or cabbage with the remainder of the oil and the fat. Reduce the heat to moderate and stir in the stock, soy sauce and sugar. Fry the greens or cabbage, turning constantly, for 3 minutes.

Stir the pork strips into the vegetables, mixing until they are well blended. Pour the wine or sherry over the mixture and stir-fry for a further 1 minute.

Remove from the heat and transfer the mixture to a warm serving dish. Serve at once.

4 Servings

JOU YUAN TS'A HUI
(Meatball Chop Suey)

	Metric/U.K.	U.S.
Lean pork, minced (ground)	350g/12oz	12oz
Canned water chestnuts, drained and chopped	50g/2oz	2oz
Small egg	1	1
Sugar	½ tsp	½ tsp
Salt and white pepper to taste		
Soy sauce	1 Tbs	1 Tbs
Cornflour (cornstarch)	1 Tbs	1 Tbs
Sufficient vegetable oil for deep-frying		
Peanut oil	2 Tbs	2 Tbs
Medium onions, thinly sliced	2	2
Cabbage, shredded	225g/8oz	8oz
Chicken stock	300ml/10floz	1¼ cups
Bean sprouts	225g/8oz	8oz

	Metric/U.K.	U.S.
Small cucumber, shredded lengthways	¼	¼

Combine the pork, water chestnuts, egg, sugar, seasoning, soy sauce and cornflour (cornstarch) until they are smooth. Form the mixture into 10 or 12 small balls and set aside.

Fill a large saucepan one-third full with oil and heat until it reaches 185°C (360°F) on a deep-fat thermometer, or until a small cube of stale bread dropped into the oil turns golden in 50 seconds. Arrange a few of the meatballs in a deep-frying basket and carefully lower them into the oil. Fry for 3 to 4 minutes, or until they are lightly browned and crisp. Remove from the pan and drain on kitchen towels. Keep hot while you fry the remaining meatballs in the same way.

Heat the 2 tablespoons of oil in a flameproof casserole. Add the onions and cabbage and fry until they are soft. Pour in the stock and bring to the boil. Reduce the heat to low and simmer the mixture for 15 minutes, stirring occasionally. Spread the bean sprouts over the cabbage mixture, then top with the shredded cucumber. Arrange the meatballs on top of the vegetables. Simmer the mixture for 8 minutes. Serve at once.

4 Servings

YU HSIANG JOU SI
(Quick-Fried Pork with 'Fish' Ingredients)

	Metric/U.K.	U.S.
Pork fillet (tenderloin), thinly sliced then shredded	½kg/1lb	1lb
Soy sauce	4 Tbs	4 Tbs
Cornflour (cornstarch), blended with 2 Tbs water	2 tsp	2 tsp
Vegetable oil	5 Tbs	5 Tbs
Dried salted black beans, soaked in cold water for 15 minutes, drained and chopped	2 Tbs	2 Tbs
Small dried chillis, finely chopped	2	2
Garlic cloves, crushed	2	2
Chinese dried mushrooms, soaked in cold water for 20 minutes, drained and		

Yu-Lang-Chi (chicken and ham with broccoli—recipe on page 105) and Yu Hsiang Jou Si (quick-fried pork with 'fish' ingredients). The latter is one of the specialities of the province of Szechuan, where meat is often cooked with ingredients more commonly associated with fish or shellfish—hence the translation of the title.

	Metric/U.K.	U.S.
finely chopped	4	4
Leek, white part only, finely chopped	1	1
'Wood ear' fungi	1 Tbs	1 Tbs
Fresh root ginger, peeled and finely chopped	2½cm/1in piece	1in piece
Canned bamboo shoot, drained and chopped	75g/3oz	3oz
Sesame oil	2 tsp	2 tsp
Wine vinegar	1½ Tbs	1½ Tbs
Rice wine or dry sherry	2 Tbs	2 Tbs
Sugar	1½ tsp	1½ tsp

Combine the pork and 2 tablespoons of soy sauce. Work the sauce into the meat with your fingers. Add the cornflour (cornstarch) mixture and stir to blend. Set aside for 10 minutes.

Heat 3 tablespoons of oil in a frying-pan. When it is hot, add the pork mixture, spreading it out over the bottom of the pan. Stir-fry for 1 minute. Using a slotted spoon, transfer the pork strips to a plate.

Add the remaining oil to the pan. Add the black beans and chillis and stir-fry for 10 seconds. Increase the heat to moderately high and add the garlic, vegetables, ginger and bamboo shoot. Stir-fry for 3 minutes. Return the pork to the pan and stir in the sesame oil, remaining soy sauce, vinegar, wine or sherry and sugar. Stir-fry for 1½ minutes, or until the mixture is heated through.

Transfer the mixture to a warmed serving dish and serve at once.

4 Servings

PORK WITH MIXED VEGETABLES

	Metric/U.K.	U.S.
Pork fillet (tenderoin),		

cut into thin strips 5cm/2in x ½cm/¼in	700g/1½lb	1½lb
Vegetable oil	5 Tbs	5 Tbs
Chinese dried mushrooms, soaked in cold water for 20 minutes, drained and sliced	10	10
sliced onion,	1	1
Celery stalks, cut into thin strips	2	2
Green pepper, pith and seeds removed and cut into thin strips	1	1
Canned water chestnuts, drained and sliced	10	10
Bean sprouts	½kg/1lb	1lb
Salt	1 tsp	1 tsp
Sugar	1 tsp	1 tsp
Soy sauce	2 Tbs	2 Tbs
Rice wine or dry sherry	2 Tbs	2 Tbs
MARINADE Soy sauce	2 Tbs	2 Tbs
Fresh root ginger, peeled and finely chopped	2½cm/1in piece	1in piece
Salt	1 tsp	1 tsp
Monosodium glutamate (MSG), (optional)	¼ tsp	¼ tsp
Sugar	2 tsp	2 tsp
Garlic cloves, crushed	2	2
Rice wine or dry sherry	2 Tbs	2 Tbs

To make the marinade, combine all the ingredients in a large bowl. Add the pork strips and stir until the meat is thoroughly coated. Set aside to marinate for 30 minutes.

Heat 2 tablespoons of oil in a large deep frying-pan. Add the mushrooms, onion, celery, pepper and water chestnuts, and stir-fry for 2 minutes. Using a slotted spoon, transfer the vegetables to a plate and keep hot.

Add the remaining oil to the pan. Add the pork slices and marinade and stir-fry for 5 minutes, or until the pork is deeply and evenly browned. Stir in the reserved vegetables and bean sprouts, then the salt, sugar, soy sauce and wine or sherry. Stir-fry for a further 3 minutes.

Transfer the mixture to a warmed serving dish and serve at once.

4-6 Servings

MI TSE HO-TUI
(Ham in Honey Syrup)

Pork with Mixed Vegetables is a filling yet inexpensive dish.

	Metric/U.K.	U.S.
Middle leg of gammon (ham), soaked overnight in cold water and drained	1x1½kg/3lb	1x3lb
SAUCE Sugar	2 Tbs	2 Tbs
Water	4 Tbs	4 Tbs
Clear honey	2 Tbs	2 Tbs
Rice wine or dry sherry	2 Tbs	2 Tbs
Cherry brandy	2 tsp	2 tsp
Cornflour (cornstarch) blended with 3 Tbs water	2 tsp	2 tsp

Half-fill the lower part of a large steamer with boiling water. Put the gammon (ham) in the upper part and place the steamer over moderate heat. Steam the gammon (ham) for 2¼ hours. Remove the steamer from the heat and set the gammon (ham) aside until it is cool enough to handle. When it is cool enough to handle, cut it into ½cm/¼in thick slices. Arrange the slices decoratively on a heatproof serving dish.

To make the sauce, combine all the sauce ingredients in a small saucepan and bring to the boil, stirring constantly. Remove from the heat and pour over the ham slices. Put the serving dish in the top part of the steamer and return the steamer to moderate heat. Steam the meat and sauce for 5 minutes.

Remove the steamer from the heat and carefully remove the dish from the steamer. Serve at once.

6-8 Servings

DEEP-FRIED SWEETBREADS

	Metric/U.K.	U.S.
Sweetbreads, soaked in cold water for 3 hours, drained, skinned and trimmed	1kg/2lb	2lb
Eggs, lightly beaten	2	2
Seasoned cornflour (cornstarch), made with cornflour (cornstarch), salt, pepper and ground ginger to taste	50g/2oz	½ cup
Sufficient vegetable oil for deep-frying		
SAUCE		
Vegetable oil	2 Tbs	2 Tbs
Small onion, finely chopped	1	1
Fresh root ginger, peeled and finely chopped	5cm/2in piece	2in piece
Large green peppers, pith and seeds removed and chopped	2	2
Garlic cloves, chopped	2	2
French (green) beans, cut into 5cm/2in lengths	125g/4oz	4oz
Bean sprouts	125g/4oz	4oz
Canned pineapple chunks	450g/1lb	1lb
Soy sauce	2 Tbs	2 Tbs
White wine vinegar	4 Tbs	4 Tbs
Soft brown sugar	4 Tbs	4 Tbs
Salt	¼ tsp	¼ tsp
Cornflour (cornstarch), blended with 6 Tbs water	2 Tbs	2 Tbs

Put the sweetbreads in a large saucepan and just cover with water. Bring to the boil, remove the pan from the heat and set aside for 10 minutes. Remove the sweetbreads from the pan and drain on kitchen towels. Discard the water. Cut the sweetbreads into 1cm/½in slices and transfer them to a bowl.

Beat the eggs and seasoned cornflour (cornstarch) together until they form a smooth batter. Pour the batter over the sweetbreads and toss gently to coat them thoroughly. Set aside for 10 minutes.

Preheat the oven to cool 150°C (Gas Mark 2, 300°F).

Fill a large saucepan one-third full with oil and heat until it reaches 185°C (360°F) on a deep-fat thermometer, or until a small cube of stale bread dropped into the oil turns golden in

Sweet and Sour Liver—a new way to serve a traditional and nutritious meat. The sauce contains orange juice which blends beautifully with the richness of the liver.

50 seconds. Carefully lower the sweetbread slices into the oil, a few at a time, and fry for 5 to 6 minutes, or until they are golden brown and crisp. Remove the slices from the oil and drain on kitchen towels. Transfer the slices to an ovenproof dish, cover and put the dish into the oven to keep warm while you make the sauce.

Heat the oil in a large frying-pan. Add the onion, ginger, peppers, garlic and beans and fry until they are soft. Stir in the bean sprouts, pineapple chunks and can juice, the soy sauce, vinegar, sugar and salt, and bring to the boil. Cook for 1 minute, stirring constantly. Stir in the cornflour (cornstarch) mixture and cook, stirring constantly, until the sauce thickens and becomes translucent. Remove the pan from the heat.

Remove the sweetbreads from the oven and pour over the sauce.

Serve at once.

6-8 Servings

SWEET AND SOUR LIVER

	Metric/U.K.	U.S.
Lambs' liver, cut into 7½cm/3in x 5cm/2in pieces	700g/1½lb	1½lb
Sufficient vegetable oil for deep-frying		
MARINADE		
Soy sauce	5 Tbs	5 Tbs
Rice wine or dry sherry	2 Tbs	2 Tbs
Sugar	2 tsp	2 tsp
SAUCE		
Wine vinegar	4 Tbs	4 Tbs
Sugar	3 Tbs	3 Tbs
Orange juice	3 Tbs	3 Tbs
Tomato purée (paste)	1 Tbs	1 Tbs
Soy sauce	1½ Tbs	1½ Tbs
Rice wine or dry sherry	1½ Tbs	1½ Tbs

	Metric/U.K.	U.S.
Cornflour (cornstarch), blended with 5 Tbs water	1 Tbs	1 Tbs

Combine all the marinade ingredients in a large shallow bowl. Add the liver pieces and baste well. Set aside at room temperature for 3 hours, basting occasionally. Remove from the marinade and pat dry with kitchen towels. Discard the marinade.

Fill a large saucepan one-third full with oil and heat until it reaches 185°C (360°F) on a deep-fat thermometer, or until a small cube of stale bread dropped into the oil turns golden in 50 seconds. Carefully lower the liver pieces into the oil, a few at a time, and fry for 1 minute or until they are brown and crisp. Remove from the oil and drain on kitchen towels.

Combine all the sauce ingredients in a large saucepan and bring to the boil, stirring constantly. Add the liver pieces to the sauce and cook, stirring constantly, until the sauce thickens and becomes translucent.

Transfer the mixture to a warmed serving dish and serve at once.

6 Servings

RUN TSA CHIN KAN
(Deep-Fried Liver and Kidneys)

	Metric/U.K.	U.S.
Lambs' liver	350g/12oz	12oz
Lambs' kidneys, prepared	350g/12oz	12oz
Soy sauce	5 Tbs	5 Tbs
Rice wine or dry sherry	2 Tbs	2 Tbs
Sugar	2 tsp	2 tsp
Sufficient vegetable oil for deep-frying		
DIP		
Black pepper	1 Tbs	1 Tbs
Salt	1 Tbs	1 Tbs

Slice the liver and kidneys thinly, then cut into thin strips about 4cm/1½in by 2½cm/1in. Put the liver strips in one bowl and the kidney strips in another.

Combine the soy sauce, wine or sherry and sugar, then pour equal quantities of the mixture over the liver and kidneys, gently tossing the strips to coat them thoroughly. Set aside to marinate at room temperature for 3 hours, basting occasionally.

Fill a large saucepan one-third full with oil and heat until it reaches 185°C (360°F) on a deep-fat thermometer, or until a small cube of stale bread dropped into the oil turns golden brown in 50 seconds. Carefully lower the liver strips into the oil and cook for 1 minute or until they are brown and crisp. Remove from the oil and drain on kitchen towels. Keep hot while you fry the kidney strips in the same way.

To make the dip, fry the pepper and salt in a small frying-pan over moderately high heat for 4 minutes, stirring constantly. Remove from the heat and transfer the mixture to a small serving bowl.

Serve the liver and kidney strips at once, accompanied by the dip.

4-6 Servings

LIN-MOUN CHI
(Lemon Chicken)

	Metric/U.K.	U.S.
Chicken, skinned	1x1½kg/3lb	1x3lb
Salt	1½ tsp	1½ tsp
Ground ginger	1 tsp	1 tsp
Egg, lightly beaten	1	1
Ground rice	125g/4oz	1 cup
Sufficient vegetable oil for deep-frying		
Juice of 1 lemon		
Chopped spring onions (scallions)	1 Tbs	1 Tbs
Lemon, cut into thin slices	1	1
SAUCE		
Chicken stock	50ml/2floz	¼ cup
Rice wine or dry sherry	2 Tbs	2 Tbs
Salt	¼ tsp	¼ tsp
Sugar	1 tsp	1 tsp

Cut the chicken through the bone, into 16 or 20 pieces. Sprinkle the pieces with salt and ginger, rubbing them into the flesh. Put the egg in a saucer and dip the chicken pieces in it, one by one, then roll in the ground rice until they are thoroughly coated.

Fill a large saucepan one-third full with oil and heat until it reaches 185°C (360°F) on a deep-fat thermometer, or until a small cube of

stale bread dropped into the oil turns golden in 50 seconds. Put a few of the chicken pieces in a deep-frying basket and carefully lower the basket into the oil. Fry for 3 to 5 minutes, or until the pieces are golden brown and crisp. Remove from the oil and drain on kitchen towels.

To make the sauce, put all the ingredients in a small saucepan and bring to the boil. Remove from the heat and pour over the chicken pieces.

Sprinkle the lemon juice and spring onions (scallions) over the chicken. Arrange the lemon slices around the chicken and serve at once.

4-6 Servings

KUO TIEH CHI
(Egg-Braised Chicken)

	Metric/U.K.	U.S.
Boned chicken breasts, cut into thin strips about 5cm/2in x 2½cm/1in	350g/12oz	12oz
Salt and pepper to taste		
Sugar	2 tsp	2 tsp
Chilli sauce	1 tsp	1 tsp
Dry white wine	2 Tbs	2 Tbs
Cornflour (cornstarch)	1 Tbs	1 Tbs
Sufficient vegetable oil for deep-frying		
Eggs, lightly beaten	3	3
Sesame oil	75ml/3floz	⅜ cup
Chopped parsley	1 Tbs	1 Tbs
Rice wine or dry sherry	1½ Tbs	1½ Tbs
Soy sauce	1½ Tbs	1½ Tbs
Lemon juice	1½ Tbs	1½ Tbs

Sprinkle the chicken strips with the salt, pepper, sugar, chilli sauce, wine and cornflour (cornstarch), rubbing them into the meat with your fingers. Set aside to marinate at room temperature for 1½ hours.

Fill a large saucepan one-third full with oil and heat until it reaches 185°C (360°F) on a deep-fat thermometer, or until a small cube of stale bread dropped into the oil turns golden in 50 seconds. Carefully lower the chicken strips, a few at a time, into the oil and fry for 1 to 2 minutes, or until they are golden brown. Remove from the oil and drain on kitchen towels.

Put the eggs into a shallow bowl. When the chicken strips have been cooked, dip the strips, one by one, into the eggs and coat thickly.

Heat the sesame oil in a frying-pan. Add the chicken strips to the pan, in one layer if possible, and shake and tilt gently to distribute the oil evenly. Fry the strips, turning occasionally, for 2 minutes.

Remove the strips from the pan and arrange them, in one layer, on a very large, warmed serving dish. Sprinkle with the parsley, wine or sherry, soy sauce and lemon juice, and serve at once.

4 Servings

YU-LANG-CHI
(Chicken and Ham)

	Metric/U.K.	U.S.
Chicken stock	1¾l/3 pints	7½ cups
Fresh root ginger, peeled and sliced	2½cm/1in piece	1in piece
Spring onions (scallions), cut into 5cm/2in lengths	2	2
Chicken	1x2kg/4lb	1x4lb
Parma ham, cut into strips	4 slices	4 slices
Broccoli, broken into flowerets	1kg/2lb	2lb
Soy sauce	2 tsp	2 tsp
Cornflour (cornstarch), blended with 1 Tbs water	1 tsp	1 tsp

Put the stock, ginger and spring onions (scallions) into a saucepan and bring to the boil. Add the chicken, and add more boiling water to cover the chicken if necessary. Bring to the boil again. Reduce the heat to low, cover and simmer for 30 minutes. Remove from the heat and set aside for 2 hours. (During this time it will cook through.)

Transfer the chicken to a chopping board. Remove the flesh from the bones, discarding the skin, and cut into serving pieces. Arrange the chicken pieces and ham on a warmed dish. Keep hot.

Pour off and discard all but 450ml/15floz (2 cups) of stock. Strain and return it to the pan and bring to the boil. Add the broccoli and return to the boil. Remove the pan from the

Kuo Pa Jou Tin (diced pork on crackling rice— recipe page 94) is a favourite method of cooking in China. Kuo Tieh Chi (egg-braised chicken) is an unusual and satisfying dish where chicken strips are twice cooked, once by deep frying, once by shallow frying in an egg batter.

heat and soak the broccoli in the stock for 5 minutes.

Drain the broccoli, reserving 125ml/4floz (½ cup) of stock. Arrange the broccoli around the chicken and ham, and keep hot.

Combine the soy sauce and reserved stock in a saucepan and bring to the boil. Add the cornflour (cornstarch) mixture and, when the liquid thickens slightly, remove the pan from the heat. Pour over the chicken and ham and serve.

4-6 Servings

QUICK-FRIED CHICKEN CUBES IN WHITE SAUCE

	Metric/U.K.	U.S.
Chicken breasts, boned	4	4
Ground ginger	¼ tsp	¼ tsp
Salt and pepper to taste		
Cornflour (cornstarch)	1 Tbs	1 Tbs
Butter	1 Tbs	1 Tbs
Vegetable oil	2 Tbs	2 Tbs
Small shelled shrimps	125g/4oz	4oz
Small red pepper, pith and seeds removed and cut into 1cm/½in lengths	1	1
Cucumber, halved and cut into 1cm/½in lengths	¼	¼
SAUCE Chicken stock	75ml/3floz	⅜ cup
Butter	1 Tbs	1 Tbs
Dry white wine	50ml/2floz	¼ cup
Cornflour (cornstarch), blended with 4 Tbs water	1 Tbs	1 Tbs
Single (light) cream	125ml/4floz	½ cup

Cut the chicken breasts into small cubes and rub them with ginger, seasoning and cornflour (cornstarch).

Melt the butter with the oil in a large frying-pan. Add the chicken cubes and stir-fry for 30 seconds. Add the shrimps, pepper and cucumber to the pan and stir-fry the mixture for 2 minutes. Remove from the heat.

To make the sauce, pour the stock into a small saucepan and bring to the boil. Stir in the butter and wine and cook until the butter has melted. Reduce the heat to low and add the

cornflour (cornstarch) mixture, stirring constantly. Simmer for 2 minutes, or until the sauce has thickened. Stir in the cream. Remove from the heat and pour the sauce into the frying-pan. Return the pan to moderate heat and cook, turning the meat and vegetables over in the sauce, for 2 minutes.

Transfer the mixture to a warmed serving dish and serve at once.

4 Servings

HUNG SHAO CHI
(Red-Cooked Chicken)

The chicken suggested for this recipe is a roasting one, but if you wish to economize and use a boiling chicken, increase the cooking time by 40 minutes.

	Metric/U.K.	U.S.
Spring onions (scallions), cut into 5cm/2in lengths	2	2
Fresh root ginger, peeled and chopped	4cm/1½in piece	1½in piece
Oven-ready chicken	1x1½kg/3lb	1x3lb
Vegetable oil	75ml/3floz	⅜ cup
Soy sauce	75ml/3floz	⅜ cup
Water	300ml/10floz	1¼ cups
Chicken stock cube, crumbled	½	½
Sugar	2 tsp	2 tsp
Rice wine or dry sherry	3 Tbs	3 Tbs

Stuff the spring onions (scallions) and ginger into the cavity of the chicken and secure with a skewer or trussing needle and thread.

Heat the oil in a large saucepan. Add the chicken and fry until it is lightly browned all over. Remove the pan from the heat and pour off all the excess oil. Add the soy sauce, water, stock cube, sugar and wine or sherry. Return to the heat and bring to the boil, stirring occasionally. Reduce the heat to low, cover the pan and simmer for 30 minutes. Turn the chicken over and re-cover. Simmer for a further 45 minutes, or until the chicken is cooked through and tender.

Transfer the chicken to a carving board. Untruss and carve into serving pieces. Transfer the pieces to a warmed serving dish. Pour over the cooking liquid and serve at once.

4-6 Servings

Two very different but very tasty quick-fry dishes—on the left Quick-Fried Spinach with Shredded Pork (recipe page 89) and on the right Quick-Fried Chicken Cubes in White Sauce.

HO TAO CHI TIN
(Quick-Fried Chicken Cubes with Walnuts)

	Metric/U.K.	U.S.
Chicken breasts, boned	½kg/1lb	1lb
Salt	1 tsp	1 tsp
Cornflour (cornstarch)	1 Tbs	1 Tbs
Egg white, lightly beaten	1	1
Vegetable oil	75ml/3floz	⅜ cup
Shelled walnuts, halved	225g/8oz	2 cups
Sugar	1 tsp	1 tsp
Soy sauce	1 Tbs	1 Tbs
Rice wine or dry sherry	2 Tbs	2 Tbs

Cut the chicken flesh into bite-sized pieces. Mix the salt and cornflour (cornstarch) together, then rub into the chicken pieces. Put the cubes in a bowl and pour over the egg white. Toss gently to coat the cubes thoroughly.

Heat the oil in a large frying-pan. Add the chicken cubes and stir-fry over high heat for

107

2 minutes. Using a slotted spoon, transfer the cubes to a plate and set aside. Pour off all but 1 tablespoon of oil from the pan and add the walnuts. Reduce the heat to moderate and stir-fry the walnuts for 1 minute. Return the chicken cubes to the pan and stir-fry for a further 1 minute.

Sprinkle over the remaining ingredients and stir-fry for 1½ minutes. Transfer the mixture to a warmed serving dish and serve at once.

4 Servings

PAI CHIU TUNG CHI
(Long-Simmered Chicken in White Wine)

The cooking liquid from this delicious dish is often served as a separate soup course.

	Metric/U.K.	U.S.
Chicken, cleaned	1 x 1¾kg/3½lb	1 x 3½lb
Water	600ml/1 pint	2½ cups
Dry white wine	300ml/10floz	1¼ cups
Soy sauce	3 Tbs	3 Tbs
Sesame oil	1½ Tbs	1½ Tbs
Chinese cabbage, shredded	½kg/1lb	½kg/1lb
STUFFING		
Long-grain rice, soaked in cold water for 30 minutes and drained	75g/3oz	½ cup
Spring onions (scallions), chopped	4	4
Lean bacon, chopped	4 slices	4 slices
Fresh root ginger, peeled and chopped	5cm/2in piece	2in piece
Chicken stock cube, crumbled	1	1
Salt and pepper to taste		

Preheat the oven to cool 150°C (Gas Mark 2, 300°F).

To make the stuffing, combine all the ingredients together then stuff into the cavity of the chicken. Close with a skewer or a trussing needle and thread. Put the chicken into a flameproof casserole and pour over the water. Bring to the boil, then transfer the casserole to the oven and bake for 1 hour.

Add the wine to the casserole and cook the chicken for a further 45 minutes, or until it is

cooked through and tender. Transfer the chicken to a warmed serving dish and keep hot.

Combine the soy sauce and sesame oil in a small bowl, then pour over the chicken and serve at once. If you wish to serve the cooking liquid as a soup course, stir in the cabbage and put the casserole over moderate heat. Cook for 5 minutes, remove from the heat and serve at once.

4-6 Servings

PAI CHOU CHI
(White Cooked Chicken)

	Metric/U.K.	U.S.
Water	2½l/4 pints	5 pints
Chicken, cleaned	1x1½kg/3lb	1x3lb
Spring onions (scallions), finely chopped	5	5
SAUCE A		
Fresh root ginger, peeled and finely chopped	5cm/2in piece	2in piece
Boiling water	5 Tbs	5 Tbs
Hot oil	1 Tbs	1 Tbs
Salt	½ tsp	½ tsp
SAUCE B		
Garlic cloves, crushed	2	2
Soy sauce	3 Tbs	3 Tbs
Vinegar	2 Tbs	2 Tbs

Bring the water to the boil in a large saucepan. Add the chicken and return to the boil. Reduce the heat to low and simmer for 1 hour. Remove from the heat, cover and leave the chicken for 3 hours.

Drain the chicken and discard the cooking liquid. Transfer the chicken to a chopping board and cut, through the bone, into about 20 large-bite pieces. Transfer to a serving plate and set aside.

To make sauce A, put the ginger in a small serving bowl. Add the remaining ingredients and stir to blend.

To make sauce B, put the garlic in a small serving bowl. Add the soy sauce and vinegar and stir to blend.

Sprinkle the chopped spring onions (scallions) over the chicken pieces and serve, with the sauces.

4-6 Servings

SWEET AND SOUR CHICKEN

	Metric/U.K.	U.S.
Chicken breasts, skinned	4	4
Salt and pepper to taste		
Ground ginger	1 tsp	1 tsp
Egg whites, lightly beaten	2	2
Cornflour (cornstarch)	2 Tbs	2 Tbs
Sufficient vegetable oil for deep-frying		
SAUCE		
Vegetable oil	50ml/2floz	¼ cup
Fresh root ginger, peeled and chopped	5cm/2in piece	2in piece
Large green pepper, pith and seeds removed and chopped	1	1
Cucumber, halved lengthways and sliced	½	½
Spring onions (scallions), finely chopped	5	5
Bean sprouts	175g/6oz	6oz
Canned pineapple chunks	225g/8oz	8oz
Wine vinegar	4 Tbs	4 Tbs
Soy sauce	1½ Tbs	1½ Tbs
Tomato purée (paste)	2 Tbs	2 Tbs
Soft brown sugar	2 Tbs	2 Tbs
Cornflour (cornstarch), blended with 3 Tbs water	1 Tbs	1 Tbs

Cut the chicken breasts into bite-sized pieces and rub the flesh with salt, pepper and ground ginger. Put the pieces into a shallow dish. Beat the egg whites and cornflour (cornstarch) together, then pour the mixture over the chicken pieces, tossing gently until they are thoroughly coated. Set aside for 15 minutes, basting occasionally.

Preheat the oven to warm 150°C (Gas Mark 2, 300°F).

Fill a large saucepan one-third full with oil and heat until it reaches 180°C (350°F) on a deep-fat thermometer, or until a small cube of stale bread dropped into the oil turns golden in 55 seconds. Carefully lower the chicken cubes, a few at a time, into the oil and fry for 3 to 4 minutes, or until they are lightly browned and crisp. Remove from the oil and drain on kitchen towels. Transfer the cubes to a serving dish and keep hot in the oven while you cook the sauce.

Heat the oil in a very large frying-pan. Add the ginger and stir-fry for 30 seconds. Add the vegetables and pineapple chunks and stir-fry for 3 minutes. Combine the pineapple can juice and the remaining ingredients, except the cornflour (cornstarch) mixture, and beat well to blend. Pour into the pan and stir-fry for a further 1 minute or until it is heated through. Stir in the cornflour (cornstarch) mixture and cook, stirring constantly, until the sauce thickens and becomes translucent.

Remove the chicken pieces from the oven and pour over the sauce. Serve at once.

4 Servings

Sweet and Sour Chicken— another variation on the sweet and sour theme, this time with chicken as the meat.

Fish and Seafood

PAI CHIU TUNG LI YU
(Carp Steamed in White Wine)

The cooking liquid from this dish is traditionally served as a soup course in China.

	Metric/U.K.	U.S.
Carp, cleaned and gutted	1x1½kg/3lb	1x3lb
Water	150ml/5floz	⅝ cup
Beef stock	150ml/5floz	⅝ cup
Dry white wine	300ml/10floz	1¼ cups
Soy sauce	3 Tbs	3 Tbs
Sesame oil	1½ Tbs	1½ Tbs
Watercress, shredded	1 bunch	1 bunch
STUFFING		
Long-grain rice, soaked in cold water for 30 minutes and drained	4 Tbs	4 Tbs
Lean bacon, chopped	4 slices	4 slices
Spring onions (scallions), finely chopped	4	4
Chicken stock cube, crumbled	1	1
Fresh root ginger, peeled and chopped	7½cm/3in piece	3in piece
Salt and pepper to taste		

To make the stuffing, combine all the ingredients, then stuff the mixture into the carp. Close the cavity with a skewer or a trussing needle and thread.

Arrange the carp in a shallow oval-shaped heatproof casserole and pour over the water. Fill the bottom part of the double boiler or steamer to a depth of 5cm/2in with boiling water. Place the casserole in the top part of the boiler or steamer and cover. Place the boiler or steamer over moderate heat and steam for 45 minutes. Pour the stock and wine into the casserole and continue to steam for a further 45 minutes, or until the fish flakes easily.

Remove the boiler from the heat and lift out the casserole. Transfer the carp to a warmed, oval serving dish. Set aside and keep hot. Reserve the cooking liquid in the casserole. Combine the soy sauce and sesame oil and pour over the fish. Serve the fish at once.

If you wish to serve the cooking liquid as a soup course, stir the watercress into the cooking liquid. Place the casserole over moderate heat and bring to the boil, stirring frequently. Boil for 2 minutes. Remove from the heat and serve.

4-6 Servings

KUO TIEH YU PIEN
(Egg-Braised Sliced Fish)

If you wish to economize, use plaice (flounder) fillets instead of the sole suggested below.

	Metric/U.K.	U.S.
Sole fillets, cut into small strips about 5cm/2in x 2½cm/1in	½kg/1lb	1lb

Salt	2½ tsp	2½ tsp
Ground ginger	½ tsp	½ tsp
Cornflour (cornstarch)	1 Tbs	1 Tbs
Corn oil	1 Tbs	1 Tbs
Eggs, lightly beaten	3	3
Sufficient vegetable oil for deep-frying		
Sesame oil	75ml/3floz	⅜ cup
Chicken stock	50ml/2floz	¼ cup
Rice wine or dry sherry	2 Tbs	2 Tbs
Chopped parsley	1 Tbs	1 Tbs
Soy sauce	1½ Tbs	1½ Tbs
Lemon juice	1½ Tbs	1½ Tbs

Sprinkle the fish strips with 1½ teaspoons of salt, the ginger, cornflour (cornstarch) and corn oil, rubbing them into the flesh with your fingers. Set aside at room temperature for 1 hour.

Beat the eggs and remaining salt together, then set aside.

Fill a large saucepan one-third full with oil and heat until it reaches 185°C (360°F) on a deep-fat thermometer, or until a small cube of stale bread dropped into the oil turns golden in 50 seconds. Carefully lower the fish strips, a few at a time, into the oil and fry for 1½ minutes, or until they are lightly browned and crisp. Remove from the oil and drain on kitchen towels.

Heat the sesame oil in a large frying-pan. Add the fish strips to the pan, in one layer if possible, and fry for 1 minute. Pour in the beaten egg, tilting the pan so that the oil flows freely and the fish strips move and slide in the pan. When the egg is half-set, remove the pan from the heat and turn the fish strips over. Return the pan to the heat. When the egg has completely set, sprinkle over the chicken stock and wine or sherry. Turn the fish strips over once more and cook them in the liquid for 30 seconds.

Transfer the strips to a warmed serving dish, arranging them in one layer. Sprinkle over the remaining ingredients.

Serve at once.

4-6 Servings

Pai Chiu Tung Li Yu (carp steamed in white wine) makes an unusual centrepiece for dinner.

over and cook for a further 1 minute. Remove from the heat and pour off the excess oil.

To make the sauce, melt the fat in a small saucepan. Add the mushrooms and stir-fry for 1 minute. Add the wine, stock, sugar and salt, and bring to the boil. Stir in the cornflour (cornstarch) mixture and cook, stirring constantly, until the sauce thickens and becomes translucent. Remove from the heat and pour the sauce into the frying-pan. Stir carefully around the fish and return the pan to moderate heat. Cook, turning the fish pieces occasionally, for 2 minutes.

Transfer the fish pieces to a warmed serving dish. Pour over the sauce and serve at once.

6 Servings

Abalone is a favourite fish in China and it is used in a number of ways. Above the fish is pictured with its shells and right Pao Yu Tsa'ai Hsin stir-fried abalone and Chinese cabbage a popular dish based on abalone.

LIU YU-PIEN
(Sliced Fish in Wine Sauce)

	Metric/U.K.	U.S.
Sole fillets, cut into 5cm/2in x 2½cm/1in pieces	575g/1¼lb	1¼lb
Salt and pepper to taste		
Ground ginger	½ tsp	½ tsp
Cornflour (cornstarch)	2 tsp	2 tsp
Egg white, lightly beaten	1	1
Vegetable oil	75ml/3floz	⅜ cup
SAUCE Vegetable fat	2 tsp	2 tsp
Chinese dried mushrooms, soaked in cold water for 20 minutes, drained and chopped	8	8
Dry white wine	75ml/3floz	⅜ cup
Chicken stock	50ml/2floz	¼ cup
Sugar	1 tsp	1 tsp
Salt	½ tsp	½ tsp
Cornflour (cornstarch), blended with 3 Tbs water	2 tsp	2 tsp

Put the fish pieces on a board and rub them with salt, pepper, ground ginger and cornflour (cornstarch), rubbing them into the flesh with your fingers. Pour over the egg white and toss carefully to coat the pieces thoroughly.

Heat the oil in a large frying-pan. Add the fish pieces, in one layer if possible, and cook for 30 seconds, tilting the pan so that the oil flows freely around the fish. Turn the pieces

QUICK-FRIED ABALONE WITH MUSHROOMS

Abalone is a shellfish, very popular in Chinese cooking.

	Metric/U.K.	U.S.
Chicken stock	450ml/15floz	2 cups
Canned water chestnuts, drained and sliced	125g/4oz	4oz
Chinese dried mushrooms, soaked in cold water for 20 minutes, drained and sliced	8	8
Canned or fresh abalone, drained and thinly sliced	½kg/1lb	1lb
Spring onions (scallions), chopped	4	4
Soy sauce	2 Tbs	2 Tbs
Cornflour (cornstarch), blended with 2 Tbs water	1½ Tbs	1½ Tbs

Pour the stock into a deep frying-pan or saucepan and bring to the boil. Add the water chestnuts and mushrooms and reduce the heat to low. Simmer for 5 minutes. Add the abalone, spring onions (scallions) and soy sauce, and bring to the boil. Reduce the heat to low and simmer for a further 1 minute.

Stir in the cornflour (cornstarch) mixture and cook, stirring constantly, until the sauce thickens and becomes translucent. Transfer to a warmed serving bowl and serve at once.

4-6 Servings

PAO YU TS'AI HSIN
(Stir-fried Abalone and Chinese Cabbage)

	Metric/U.K.	U.S.
Peanut oil	3 Tbs	3 Tbs
Fresh root ginger, peeled and finely chopped	2½cm/1in piece	1in piece
Small leek, white part only, thinly sliced into rings	1	1
Small Chinese cabbage, shredded	1	1
Monosodium glutamate (MSG), (optional)	¼ tsp	¼ tsp
Salt and pepper to taste		
Soy sauce	2 tsp	2 tsp
Lemon juice	1½ Tbs	1½ Tbs
Canned or fresh abalone, drained and sliced	½kg/1lb	1lb

Heat the oil in a large, deep frying-pan. Add the ginger and leek and stir-fry for 2 minutes. Add the cabbage and stir-fry for 4 minutes, or until it is cooked through but still crisp. Sprinkle over the monosodium glutamate (MSG) if you are using it, salt, pepper, soy sauce and lemon juice and stir in the abalone. Cook the mixture, stirring constantly, for 5 minutes.

Transfer the mixture to a warmed serving dish and serve at once.

4-6 Servings

CANTONESE LOBSTER

This is one of the most popular Chinese dishes outside China and exemplifies Cantonese cooking. To be truly authentic, live lobsters should be used, but for convenience (and the squeamish!), the recipe has been adapted to the cooked lobsters obtainable at fish merchants or larger supermarkets. The traditional Chinese recipe is complicated in the extreme and is also very expensive—this recipe has therefore been slightly simplified.

	Metric/U.K.	U.S.
Cooked lobster, shell split, claws cracked and sac removed	1 x 1kg/2lb	1 x 2lb
Peanut oil	75ml/3floz	⅜ cup
Garlic cloves, crushed	2	2
Fresh root ginger, peeled and chopped	7½cm/3in piece	3in piece
Lean pork, minced (ground)	125g/4oz	4oz
Chicken stock	250ml/8floz	1 cup
Rice wine or dry sherry	1 Tbs	1 Tbs
Soy sauce	1 Tbs	1 Tbs
Monosodium glutamate (MSG), (optional)	¼ tsp	¼ tsp
Sugar	1 tsp	1 tsp
Cornflour (cornstarch), blended with 2 Tbs water	1 Tbs	1 Tbs
Spring onions (scallions), chopped	4	4
Eggs	2	2

Shrimps and prawns are abundant and popular in China and Deep-Fried Prawns or Shrimps is one particularly superb yet simple way of serving them.

Chop the lobster into pieces and set aside. (You can, if you wish, remove the shell but it is traditional to cook this dish with the shell on.)

Heat half the oil in a large, deep frying-pan. Add the garlic and stir-fry for 1 minute. Add the lobster pieces to the pan and stir-fry for 3 to 5 minutes, or until they are heated through. Transfer to a warmed serving dish and keep hot while you make the sauce.

Heat the remaining oil in the same frying-pan. Add the ginger and pork and fry until the pork loses all its pinkness. Pour over the stock and bring to the boil. Combine the wine or sherry, soy sauce, monosodium glutamate (MSG) and sugar, then stir the mixture into the pan. Stir-fry for 1 minute. Stir in the cornflour (cornstarch) mixture and cook, stirring constantly, until the sauce thickens and becomes translucent. Stir in the spring onions (scallions) and cook for 1 minute, stirring

Turn off the heat and beat the eggs a few times just to combine them. Gently pour over the mixture, stirring and lifting the sides of the mixture to allow the egg to run over and under. When the egg mixture becomes creamy and slightly 'set', spoon the sauce over the lobster. Serve at once.

2-4 Servings

BEAN CURD WITH CRABMEAT

	Metric/U.K.	U.S.
Fresh bean curd	3 cakes	3 cakes
Groundnut oil	3 Tbs	3 Tbs
Spring onions (scallions), chopped	2	2
Fresh root ginger, peeled and chopped	5cm/2in piece	2in piece
Salt	1½ tsp	1½ tsp
Chicken stock	3 Tbs	3 Tbs
Crabmeat, with the shell and cartilage removed and flaked	225g/8oz	8oz
Cornflour (cornstarch), blended with 5 tsp water	½ tsp	½ tsp
Watercress sprigs	5	5

Slice each bean curd cake into ½cm/¼in slices, then cut each slice in half.

Heat a heavy frying-pan over high heat for 30 seconds. Add the oil, tilting the pan so that it covers the bottom completely, and heat for 30 seconds. Reduce the heat to moderately high. Add the spring onions (scallions) and ginger and stir-fry for 1 minute. Add the bean curd, salt and stock, and bring to the boil. Cover and cook for 3 minutes. Stir in the crabmeat and cook for 1 minute. Stir in the cornflour (cornstarch) and cook, stirring constantly, until the liquid has thickened and become translucent.

Transfer the mixture to a warmed serving dish, garnish with the watercress and serve at once.

4 Servings

DEEP-FRIED PRAWNS OR SHRIMPS

	Metric/U.K.	U.S.
Tomato purée (paste)	3 Tbs	3 Tbs
Soy sauce	2 Tbs	2 Tbs
Chilli sauce	1 tsp	1 tsp
Sugar	1 tsp	1 tsp
Large prawns or shrimps	700g/1½lb	1½lb
Egg, lightly beaten	1	1
Flour	3 Tbs	3 Tbs
Cornflour (cornstarch)	2 tsp	2 tsp
Fresh root ginger, peeled and finely chopped	2½cm/1in piece	1in piece
Salt	½ tsp	½ tsp
Water	75ml/3floz	⅜ cup
Sufficient vegetable oil for deep-frying		

Combine the tomato purée (paste), soy sauce, chilli sauce and sugar together, then pour into a sauceboat. Set aside.

Remove the shells from the prawns or shrimps, leaving the tails intact. Under cold running water, gently remove the black veins from the flesh, then drain on kitchen towels.

Put the beaten egg into a bowl and beat in the flour, cornflour (cornstarch), ginger, salt and water until the mixture forms a smooth batter.

Fill a large saucepan one-third full with oil and heat until it reaches 180°C (350°F) on a deep-fat thermometer, or until a small cube of stale bread dropped into the oil turns golden in 55 seconds. Holding the prawns or shrimps by the tails, dip each one in the batter, then arrange them, a few at a time, in a deep-frying basket. Carefully lower the basket into the oil and fry for 2 to 3 minutes, or until they are golden brown. Remove from the oil and drain the prawns or shrimps on kitchen towels.

Transfer to a serving dish and serve at once, with the sauce.

4-6 Servings

QUICK-FRIED SHRIMPS, CHICKEN AND PETITS POIS

	Metric/U.K.	U.S.
Vegetable oil	2 Tbs	2 Tbs
Cooked chicken meat, cut into small cubes	225g/8oz	8oz
Ground ginger	½ tsp	½ tsp
Frozen petits pois, thawed	½kg/1lb	1lb
Small frozen shrimps, thawed	175g/6oz	6oz
Butter	25g/1oz	2 Tbs
Chicken stock cube, crumbled	½	½

	Metric/U.K.	U.S.
Water	75ml/3floz	$\frac{3}{8}$ cup
Rice wine or dry sherry	2 Tbs	2 Tbs
Soy sauce	1 Tbs	1 Tbs
Soft brown sugar	1 Tbs	1 Tbs
Cornflour (cornstarch), blended with 3 Tbs water	1 Tbs	1 Tbs

Quick-Fried Shrimps on Crackling Rice is rich, delicious and very filling. 'Crackling' rice is so called because, after being deep-fried, it 'crackles' as the sauce is poured over.

Heat the oil in a saucepan. Add the chicken cubes and ginger and stir-fry for 1 minute. Add the petits pois, shrimps and butter and stir-fry for a further 30 seconds. Add the stock cube, water, wine or sherry, soy sauce and sugar, and bring to the boil, stirring constantly. Stir-fry for a further 30 seconds.

Stir in the cornflour (cornstarch) mixture and cook, stirring constantly, until the sauce thickens and becomes translucent. Remove from the heat and transfer the mixture to a warmed serving dish. Serve at once.

4 Servings

STIR-FRIED SHRIMPS WITH CASHEWS

	Metric/U.K.	U.S.
Small shelled shrimps	$\frac{1}{2}$kg/1lb	1lb
Rice wine or dry sherry	1 Tbs	1 Tbs
Egg white, lightly beaten	1	1
Cornflour (cornstarch)	$1\frac{1}{2}$ Tbs	$1\frac{1}{2}$ Tbs

Salt and pepper to taste		
Ground ginger	½ tsp	½ tsp
Vegetable oil	50ml/2floz	¼ cup
Unsalted cashew nuts	125g/4oz	1 cup
Fresh root ginger, peeled and finely chopped	5cm/2in piece	2in piece
Spring onions (scallions), finely chopped	4	4
Canned bamboo shoot, drained and finely chopped	75g/3oz	3oz

Put the shrimps into a shallow bowl. Combine half the wine or sherry, the egg white, 1 tablespoon of cornflour (cornstarch), seasoning and ground ginger until the mixture forms a smooth batter. Pour the batter over the shrimps and toss gently to coat them thoroughly. Set aside to marinate for 30 minutes.

Heat the oil in a large, deep frying-pan. Add the cashews and fry, turning occasionally, for 5 minutes or until they are deep golden. Push them to the side of the pan and add the shrimps. Stir-fry for 3 minutes or until they are crisp. Stir in the remaining ingredients except the remaining wine or sherry and cornflour (cornstarch). Stir-fry for 2 minutes. Stir in the remaining wine or sherry and cornflour (cornstarch) and stir the cashews back into the shrimp mixture. Cook until the sauce thickens and becomes translucent.

Transfer the mixture to a warmed serving dish and serve at once.

6 Servings

QUICK-FRIED SHRIMPS ON CRACKLING RICE

	Metric/U.K.	U.S.
Shelled shrimps	225g/8oz	8oz
Boned chicken breast, cut into cubes	225g/8oz	8oz
Salt	2 tsp	2 tsp
White pepper	1 tsp	1 tsp
Cornflour (cornstarch)	1 Tbs	1 Tbs
Cooked rice	450g/1lb	6 cups
Sufficient vegetable oil for deep-frying		

SAUCE		
Vegetable oil	2 Tbs	2 Tbs
Onion, very finely chopped	1	1
Beef stock	150ml/5floz	⅝ cup
Tomato purée (paste)	2 Tbs	2 Tbs
Soy sauce	1½ Tbs	1½ Tbs
Sugar	1½ Tbs	1½ Tbs
Wine vinegar	1½ Tbs	1½ Tbs
Rice wine or dry sherry	2 Tbs	2 Tbs
Chilli sauce	1 tsp	1 tsp
Cornflour (cornstarch)	4 tsp	4 tsp

Pre-heat the oven to very cool 140°C (Gas Mark 1, 275°F).

Sprinkle the shrimps and chicken cubes with the salt, pepper and cornflour (cornstarch), rubbing them into the flesh with your fingers.

Place the rice in an ovenproof dish and put the dish into the oven. Dry out the rice for 15 to 20 minutes, or until it is slightly crisp.

Meanwhile, to make the sauce, heat the oil in a large frying-pan. Add the onion and fry until it is soft. Stir in all the remaining ingredients and bring to the boil. Cook the sauce, stirring constantly, until it thickens and becomes translucent. Remove the pan from the heat and set aside.

Fill a large saucepan one-third full with oil and heat until it reaches 185°C (360°F) on a deep-fat thermometer, or until a small cube of stale bread dropped into the oil turns golden in 50 seconds. Put the shrimps and chicken cubes in a deep-frying basket and carefully lower them into the oil. Fry for 1 minute. Remove from the oil and drain on kitchen towels. Transfer the shrimps and chicken cubes to the sauce in the saucepan and return the pan to moderate heat. Cook, stirring constantly, for 2 minutes.

Meanwhile, return the saucepan containing the oil to moderate heat and heat until the oil reaches 180°C (350°F) on a deep-fat thermometer, or until a small cube of stale bread dropped into the oil turns golden in 55 seconds. Remove the rice from the oven and arrange it in a narrow-meshed deep-frying basket. Carefully lower the basket into the oil and fry the rice for 1½ minutes. Remove from the oil and drain on kitchen towels.

Arrange the rice on a warmed serving dish and pour over the shrimp mixture and sauce. Serve at once.

4-6 Servings

SHRIMP FRITTERS

	Metric/U.K.	U.S.
Shrimps, shelled, with the tails left on and de-veined	700g/1½lb	1½lb
Cornflour (cornstarch)	6 Tbs	6 Tbs
Salt	1 tsp	1 tsp
Cayenne pepper	¼ tsp	¼ tsp
Eggs, separated	2	2
Water	3 Tbs	3 Tbs
Sufficient vegetable oil for deep-frying		
SAUCE		
Wine vinegar	1 Tbs	1 Tbs
Soft brown sugar	1 Tbs	1 Tbs
Tomato purée (paste)	1 Tbs	1 Tbs
Soy sauce	1 Tbs	1 Tbs
Vegetable oil	1 Tbs	1 Tbs
Salt	¼ tsp	¼ tsp
Rice wine or dry sherry	50ml/2floz	¼ cup
Cornflour (cornstarch), blended with 125ml/ 4floz water	1 Tbs	1 Tbs
Lemons, cut into wedges	2	2

Wash the shrimps in cold water then drain on kitchen towels.

Combine the cornflour (cornstarch), salt and cayenne together. Make a well in the centre and add the egg yolks and water. Beat gently until the mixture forms a smooth batter. Set aside for 20 minutes.

Meanwhile make the sauce. Put all the ingredients, except the cornflour (cornstarch) mixture and lemons, into a saucepan and bring to the boil, stirring constantly. Reduce the heat to low and stir in the cornflour (cornstarch) mixture. Cook, stirring constantly, until the sauce thickens and is smooth. Remove from the heat and set aside.

Beat the egg whites until they form stiff peaks. Quickly fold them into the egg yolk batter.

Fill a large saucepan one-third full with oil and heat until it reaches 190°C (375°F) on a deep-fat thermomemter, or until a small cube of stale bread dropped into the oil turns golden in 40 seconds. Holding the shrimps by the tails, dip each one in the batter then drop carefully into the oil. Fry, a few at a time, for 3 to 4 minutes, or until they are golden brown. Remove from the oil and drain on kitchen towels.

Arrange the fritters on a warmed serving dish and garnish with the lemon wedges. Reheat the sauce, then pour into small individual bowls. Serve at once, with the fritters.

6-8 Servings

HWANG CHI HSIA REN
(Shrimps in Tomato Sauce)

	Metric/U.K.	U.S.
Shelled shrimps	½kg/1lb	1lb
Salt	1 tsp	1 tsp
Ground ginger	¼ tsp	¼ tsp
Cornflour (cornstarch)	1½ tsp	1½ tsp
Vegetable oil	75ml/3floz	⅜ cup
SAUCE		
Butter	1½ Tbs	1½ Tbs
Medium tomatoes, blanched, peeled and quartered	3	3
Soy sauce	2½ Tbs	2½ Tbs
Tomato purée (paste)	2 Tbs	2 Tbs
Cornflour (cornstarch)	2 tsp	2 tsp
Chicken stock	75ml/3floz	⅜ cup
Rice wine or dry sherry	2 Tbs	2 Tbs
Sugar	1 tsp	1 tsp

Put the shrimps in a shallow dish. Sprinkle over the salt, ginger and cornflour (cornstarch), rubbing them into the flesh with your fingers. Heat the oil in a large frying-pan. Add the shrimps and fry for 2 minutes, stirring constantly. Transfer the shrimps to a plate, cover and keep hot. Pour off the excess oil from the pan and return it to moderate heat. Add the butter. When it melts, add the tomatoes and stir-fry for 2 minutes. Add the soy sauce and tomato purée (paste) and stir-fry for a further 30 seconds.

Combine the cornflour (cornstarch), stock, wine or sherry and sugar. Pour the mixture into the frying-pan and cook, stirring constantly, until the sauce thickens and becomes translucent. Return the shrimps to the sauce and coat them thoroughly. Stir-fry for a further 1½ minutes.

Transfer the mixture to a warmed serving dish and serve at once.

4-6 Servings

WINTER PRAWNS OR SHRIMPS

	Metric/U.K.	U.S.
Egg whites	10	10
Cornflour (cornstarch)	2 tsp	2 tsp
Salt	½ tsp	½ tsp
Shelled prawns or shrimps	175g/6oz	6oz
Sufficient vegetable oil for deep-frying		
Monosodium glutamate (MSG), (optional)	¼ tsp	¼ tsp
Cooked chicken, minced (ground)	50g/2oz	2oz
Chopped chives	2 Tbs	2 Tbs

Beat 1 egg white, the cornflour (cornstarch) and salt together until they form a smooth paste. Arrange the prawns or shrimps in the paste and stir gently until they are coated.

Fill a large saucepan one-third full with oil and heat until it reaches 185°C (360°F) on a deep-fat thermometer, or until a small cube of stale bread dropped into the oil turns golden brown in 50 seconds. Put the prawns or shrimps in a deep-frying basket and carefully lower them into the oil. Fry for 1 minute. Remove from the oil and drain on kitchen towels. Set aside.

Beat the remaining egg whites with the monosodium glutamate (MSG), if you are using it, until they form stiff peaks. Pile half the mixture on a dish and arrange the prawns or shrimps over it. Using a spatula, gently and carefully spread the remaining egg white mixture over the prawns or shrimps.

Tilt the dish over the saucepan containing the hot oil and very carefully slide the egg and prawn or shrimp mixture into the oil. Fry the mixture for 3 minutes, basting the top with oil if it is not fully covered. Remove the pan from the heat and carefully lift out the mixture. Drain on kitchen towels, then transfer to a warmed serving dish.

Sprinkle over the chicken and chives and serve at once.

4-6 Servings

Unusual, delicate, fabulous to eat, Winter Prawns or Shrimps.

Vegetables and rice

CHOW BARG CHOY (Fried Cabbage)

	Metric/U.K.	U.S.
Vegetable oil	2 Tbs	2 Tbs
Garlic clove, crushed	1	1
Chinese cabbage, shredded	700g/1½lb	1½lb
Water	75ml/3floz	⅜ cup
Soy sauce	2 tsp	2 tsp
Flour	1 tsp	1 tsp
Sugar	½ tsp	½ tsp

Heat the oil in a large frying-pan. Add the garlic and stir-fry for 1 minute. Add the cabbage and cook for 6 minutes, stirring.

Mix the water, soy sauce and flour together to form a smooth paste. Stir in the sugar then stir into the pan. Stir-fry for 2 minutes.

Serve at once.

4-6 Servings

HUNG SHAO PAI TS'AI
(Red-Cooked Cabbage)

	Metric/U.K.	U.S.
Butter	40g/1½oz	3 Tbs
Vegetable oil	3 Tbs	3 Tbs
Chinese cabbage, shredded	1	1
Sugar	3½ tsp	3½ tsp
Soy sauce	5 Tbs	5 Tbs
Water	3 Tbs	3 Tbs
Chicken stock cube, crumbled	½	½
Rice wine or dry sherry	3 Tbs	3 Tbs

Melt the butter with the oil in a large frying-pan. Add the cabbage and, using wooden spoons, turn the cabbage in the oil mixture until it is thoroughly coated. Reduce the heat to low, cover and simmer for 5 minutes.

Stir in the sugar, soy sauce, water, stock cube, wine or sherry and simmer, covered, for a further 5 minutes.

Transfer the mixture to a warmed serving dish and serve at once.

6 Servings

NAI-YU-TS'AI HSIN
(Chinese Cabbage in Cream Sauce)

	Metric/U.K.	U.S.
Butter	1 Tbs	1 Tbs
Sesame oil	1 Tbs	1 Tbs
Spring onions (scallions), thinly sliced	3	3

Small Chinese cabbages, coarsely shredded	2	2
Salt and pepper to taste		
White wine vinegar	1 Tbs	1 Tbs
Single (light) cream	125ml/4floz	½ cup
Soy sauce	2 tsp	2 tsp

Melt the butter with the oil in a large frying-pan. Add the spring onions (scallions) and cabbages and stir-fry for 3 minutes. Sprinkle over the salt, pepper and vinegar and stir-fry for a further 3 minutes, or until the cabbage is cooked but still crisp.

Stir in the remaining ingredients and cook, stirring constantly, for 4 minutes, or until the sauce comes to the boil. Remove from the heat and transfer the mixture to a warmed serving dish. Serve at once.

6 Servings

BEAN SPROUTS WITH GINGER

	Metric/U.K.	U.S.
Vegetable oil	3 Tbs	3 Tbs
Large onion, thinly sliced	1	1
Fresh root ginger, peeled and finely chopped	2½cm/1in piece	1in piece
Salt	1 tsp	1 tsp
Bean sprouts	½kg/1lb	1lb

Heat the oil in a large frying-pan. Add the onion and fry until it is soft. Add the ginger and stir-fry for 3 minutes. Stir in the remaining ingredients, increase the heat to moderately high and stir-fry for 3 minutes, or until the bean sprouts are cooked through but still crisp.

Two fine examples of Fukien food, where the 'red cooking' technique using lots of soy sauce is traditional. On the left Hung Shao-Ngiu Jou (red-cooked beef with star anise—recipe page 87) and Hung Shao Pai Ts'ai (red-cooked cabbage). Top right: Bok Choy or Chinese cabbage. Bottom right: Bean curd, in dried lengths and in its usual form used extensively in Chinese cooking, soft white cakes about 7½cm/ 3in square.

Transfer to a warmed serving dish and serve at once.

4-6 Servings

FRIED CUCUMBER AND PINEAPPLE

	Metric/U.K.	U.S.
Vegetable oil	2 Tbs	2 Tbs
Small cucumbers, thinly sliced crosswise	2	2
Salt	½ tsp	½ tsp
Vinegar	1 Tbs	1 Tbs
Canned pineapple chunks, drained	225g/8oz	8oz
Water	175ml/6floz	¾ cup
Flour	2 tsp	2 tsp
Sugar	1 tsp	1 tsp
Soy sauce	1 tsp	1 tsp

Heat the oil in a frying-pan. Add the cucumber slices, salt and vinegar and cook for 4 minutes, stirring frequently. Add the pineapple to the pan and cook for a further 2 minutes, stirring occasionally.

Beat the water, flour, sugar and soy sauce together until the mixture is smooth. Pour into the frying-pan and bring to the boil, stirring constantly. Cook for a further 4 minutes, stirring occasionally.

Transfer the mixture to a warmed serving dish and serve at once.

4-6 Servings

BAMBOO SHOOT WITH MUSHROOMS

	Metric/U.K.	U.S.
Groundnut oil	50ml/2floz	¼ cup
Canned bamboo shoot, drained and sliced	350g/12oz	12oz
Chinese dried mushrooms, soaked in cold water for 20 minutes, drained and chopped	12	12
Rice wine or dry sherry	2 Tbs	2 Tbs
Soy sauce	4 Tbs	4 Tbs
Sugar	1 Tbs	1 Tbs
Monosodium glutamate (MSG), (optional)	¼ tsp	¼ tsp
Water	75ml/3floz	⅜ cup

Heat a heavy-based frying-pan over moderately high heat for 30 seconds. Add the oil and swirl it around the pan. Add the bamboo shoot and mushrooms and stir-fry for 5 minutes. Stir in the remaining ingredients and reduce the heat to low. Cover the pan and simmer for 5 minutes.

Transfer the mixture to a warmed serving dish and serve at once.

4-6 Servings

FRIED MIXED VEGETABLES

	Metric/U.K.	U.S.
Vegetable oil	3 Tbs	3 Tbs
Garlic clove, crushed	1	1
Fresh root ginger, peeled and finely chopped	2½cm/1in piece	1in piece
Salt and pepper to taste		
Carrots, thinly sliced on the diagonal	2	2
Small green pepper, pith and seeds removed and chopped	1	1
Very small cauliflower, broken into small flowerets	1	1
Bean sprouts	50g/2oz	2oz
Chicken stock	150ml/5floz	⅝ cup
Soy sauce	2 tsp	2 tsp
Soft brown sugar	1 tsp	1 tsp

Heat the oil in a large frying-pan. Add the garlic, ginger, salt and pepper, and stir-fry for 1 minute. Add the carrots and stir-fry for 1 minute. Add the green pepper and cauliflower and stir-fry for 3 minutes. Add the bean sprouts and stir-fry for 1 minute. Stir in the remaining ingredients and bring to the boil. Reduce the heat to low, cover and simmer for a further 4 minutes.

Transfer the mixture to a warmed serving dish and serve at once.

4-6 Servings

STIR-FRIED MIXED VEGETABLES WITH WATER CHESTNUTS

This dish has a delightfully crunchy flavour. If mange-tout (snow peas) are not available, green or French beans may be substituted. Bamboo shoot and water chestnuts may be obtained from Chinese provision stores.

	Metric/U.K.	U.S.
Vegetable oil	50ml/2floz	¼ cup
Fresh root ginger, peeled and finely chopped	5cm/2in piece	2in piece
Mange-tout (snow peas), cut into 5cm/2in lengths	½kg/1lb	1lb
Canned bamboo shoot, drained and sliced	50g/2oz	2oz
Water chestnuts, sliced	4	4
Rice wine or dry sherry	1 Tbs	1 Tbs
Sugar	¼ tsp	¼ tsp

Heat the oil in a large frying-pan. Add the ginger and stir-fry for 30 seconds. Add the mange-tout (snow peas) and bamboo shoot and stir-fry for 4 minutes. Stir in all of the remaining ingredients until they are thoroughly mixed.

Transfer the mixture to a warmed serving dish and serve at once.

4-6 Servings

BEAN CURD WITH SPICY MEAT AND VEGETABLES

This dish is an adaptation of one of the more fiery dishes from the Szechuan province of China.

	Metric/U.K.	U.S.
Peanut oil	50ml/2floz	¼ cup
Garlic clove, crushed	1	1
Fresh root ginger, peeled and finely chopped	7½cm/3in piece	3in piece
Spring onions (scallions), finely chopped	4	4
Chinese dried mushrooms, soaked in cold water for 20 minutes, drained and chopped	4	4
Red pepper flakes	1 tsp	1 tsp
Dried red chillis, chopped	2	2
Minced (ground) beef	175g/6oz	6oz
Soy sauce	2 Tbs	2 Tbs
Chicken stock	250ml/8floz	1 cup
Fresh bean curd, mashed	3 cakes	3 cakes
Cornflour (cornstarch), blended with 2 Tbs chicken stock	1 Tbs	1 Tbs

Heat the oil in a large saucepan. Add the garlic, ginger, spring onions (scallions) and mushrooms, and stir-fry for 3 minutes. Stir in the red pepper flakes and chillis and stir-fry for a further 1 minute. Add the minced (ground) meat and fry until it loses its pinkness. Pour over the soy sauce and stock and bring to the boil, stirring constantly. Stir in the mashed bean curd and stir-fry for 5 minutes. Add the cornflour (cornstarch) mixture and cook, stirring constantly, until the sauce thickens.

Transfer the mixture to a warmed serving dish and serve at once.

6-8 Servings

SWEET AND SOUR VEGETABLES

The basic sweet and sour sauce is usually served with pork, chicken or fish in the west, but it can be served with vegetables, too, and the result is delicious.

	Metric/U.K.	U.S.
Peanut oil	50ml/2floz	¼ cup
Carrots, thinly sliced on the diagonal	3	3
Bamboo shoot, drained and sliced	50g/2oz	2oz
Leek, white part only, thinly sliced on the diagonal	1	1
Green pepper, pith and seeds removed and thinly sliced	1	1
Bean sprouts	125g/4oz	4oz
Pineapple juice and water mixed	250ml/8floz	1 cup

	Metric/U.K.	U.S.
Wine vinegar	2 Tbs	2 Tbs
Soy sauce	1½ Tbs	1½ Tbs
Soft brown sugar	2 Tbs	2 Tbs
Cornflour (cornstarch), blended with 2 Tbs water	2 Tbs	2 Tbs

Heat the oil in a large frying-pan. Add the vegetables and stir-fry for 5 minutes. Combine the pineapple juice, vinegar, soy sauce and sugar together and blend well. Pour over the vegetables and bring to the boil. Cook for 2 minutes, stirring occasionally. Stir in the cornflour (cornstarch) mixture and cook, stirring constantly, until the sauce thickens and becomes translucent.

Transfer the mixture to a warmed serving dish and serve at once.

4-6 Servings

BASIC BOILED RICE

	Metric/U.K.	U.S.
Long-grain rice, soaked in cold water for 30 minutes and drained	225g/8oz	1⅛ cups
Water	450ml/15floz	2 cups
Salt	1 tsp	1 tsp

Put the rice into a saucepan and pour over the water and salt. Bring to the boil, reduce the heat to low and cover the pan. Simmer for 15 to 20 minutes, or until the rice is cooked and tender. Serve.

4 Servings

BASIC FRIED RICE

	Metric/U.K.	U.S.
Long-grain rice, soaked in cold water for 30 minutes and drained	225g/8oz	1⅛ cups
Water	450ml/15floz	2 cups
Salt	1 tsp	1 tsp
Peanut oil	2 Tbs	2 Tbs
Soy sauce	2 tsp	2 tsp

Put the rice into a saucepan and pour over the water and salt. Bring to the boil, reduce the heat to low and cover the pan. Simmer for 15 to 20 minutes, or until the water has been absorbed and the rice is cooked and tender. Remove from the heat.

Heat the oil in a large frying-pan. Add the rice and cook for 1 minute, stirring constantly to coat the rice with the oil. Stir in half the soy sauce and fry, stirring constantly, until the rice is lightly browned. Remove from the heat and stir in the remaining soy sauce.

Transfer to a warmed serving dish and serve at once.

4 Servings

CHOW FARN
(Fried Rice)

This is one of the basic dishes of Chinese cuisine and can be either served on its own, or used as an elaborate rice accompaniment dish.

	Metric/U.K.	U.S.
Long-grain rice, soaked in cold water for 30 minutes and drained	225g/8oz	1⅛ cups
Water	450ml/15floz	2 cups
Salt	1½ tsp	1½ tsp
Vegetable oil	2 Tbs	2 Tbs
Medium onions, finely chopped	2	2
Cooked ham, finely chopped	225g/8oz	8oz
Petits pois	2 Tbs	2 Tbs
Medium tomatoes, blanched, peeled and quartered	2	2
Frozen shrimps, thawed and shelled	225g/8oz	8oz
Soy sauce	1 Tbs	1 Tbs
Egg, lightly beaten	1	1

Put the rice into a saucepan and pour over the water and 1 teaspoon of salt. Bring to the boil, reduce the heat to low and cover the pan. Simmer for 15 to 20 minutes, or until the water has been absorbed and the rice is cooked and tender. Remove from the heat.

Heat the oil in a large saucepan. Add the onions and fry until they are soft. Stir in the ham, petits pois, tomatoes, shrimps and remaining salt and cook for 1 minute, stirring

constantly. Stir in the cooked rice and cook for 2 minutes, stirring constantly. Add the soy sauce and egg and cook for 2 minutes, stirring constantly.

Transfer the mixture to a warmed serving dish and serve at once.

4-6 Servings

HAM FRIED RICE

	Metric/U.K.	U.S.
Long-grain rice, soaked in cold water for 30 minutes and drained	225g/8oz	1⅓ cups
Water	450ml/15floz	2 cups
Salt	1 tsp	1 tsp
Butter	15g/½oz	1 Tbs
Eggs, lightly beaten	2	2
Vegetable oil	50ml/2floz	¼ cup
Green beans, cut into 2½cm/1in lengths	125g/4oz	4oz
Cooked ham, diced	275g/10oz	10oz
Black pepper	½ tsp	½ tsp
Spring onions (scallions)	4	4

Put the rice into a saucepan and pour over the water and 1 teaspoon of salt. Bring to the boil, reduce the heat to low and cover the pan. Simmer for 15 to 20 minutes or until the water has been absorbed and the rice is cooked and tender. Remove from the heat.

Melt the butter in a large frying-pan. Add the eggs and cook for 2 to 3 minutes, or until they are set on the underside. Stir the eggs and cook for 2 to 3 minutes more or until they are just set. Remove from the heat and transfer the eggs to a bowl, breaking them up with a fork. Set aside.

Add the oil to the frying-pan and heat over moderately high heat. Add the cooked rice, beans, ham and pepper, and cook for 2 minutes, stirring constantly. Reduce the heat to moderately low and add the spring onions (scallions) and eggs. Cook for 2 minutes, stirring constantly, or until the mixture is very hot.

Transfer the mixture to a warmed serving dish and serve at once.

4 Servings

Fried rice can be very basic or plain, or it can be very complex and rich. Ham Fried Rice could be served as a light meal on its own rather than as an accompaniment to meat or fish dishes.

Sweets

WONTONS WITH ALMONDS AND DATES

The Chinese rarely eat desserts as they are known in the west, but they are fond of sweetmeats, and this wonton sweetmeat stuffed with fruit, nuts and finely grated orange rind is a particular favourite. A recipe for basic wonton dough is given on page 72.

	Metric/U.K.	U.S.
Stoned dates, finely chopped	175g/6oz	1 cup
Slivered almonds	50g/2oz	⅓ cup
Sesame seeds	2 tsp	2 tsp
Finely grated rind of 1 orange		
Orange-flower water	2 Tbs	2 Tbs
Wonton dough, thinly rolled and cut into 36 squares or 36 bought wonton wrappers	225g/8oz	8oz
Sufficient vegetable oil for deep-frying		
Icing (confectioners') sugar	2 Tbs	2 Tbs
Orange, thinly sliced	1	1

Put the dates, almonds, sesame seeds, orange rind and orange-flower water in a bowl and knead the mixture until the ingredients are thoroughly combined.

Lay the wonton wrappers on a flat surface and put a little filling just below the centre. Wet the edges of the dough, then fold over one corner to make a triangle, pinching the edges together to seal. Pull the corners at the base of the triangle together and pinch to seal.

Fill a large saucepan one-third full with oil and heat until it reaches 190°C (375°F) on a deep-fat thermometer, or until a small cube of stale bread dropped into the oil turns golden in 40 seconds. Carefully lower the wontons into the oil, a few at a time, and fry for 2 minutes, or until they are golden brown and crisp. Remove from the oil and drain on kitchen towels.

Arrange the cooked wontons on a warmed serving dish. Sprinkle over the icing (confectioners') sugar and garnish with the orange slices.

Serve at once.

4-6 Servings

HONEY APPLES

One of the favourite Chinese desserts both inside China and outside, Honey Apples is apple rings dipped in syrup then in batter and finally deep-fried.

	Metric/U.K.	U.S.
Cooking apples, peeled, cored and cut into 4 rings	5	5
SYRUP		
Soft brown sugar	125g/4oz	⅔ cup
Clear honey	4 Tbs	4 Tbs
Water	250ml/8floz	1 cup
Juice of 2 lemons		
BATTER		
Flour	125g/4oz	1 cup

Wontons can be sweet as well as savoury and can be served as sweetmeats as well as dim sum. Wontons with Almonds and Dates are crisp, deep-fried packets of wonton dough stuffed with nuts and fruit.

	Metric/U.K.	U.S.
Salt	¼ tsp	¼ tsp
Sugar	2 tsp	2 tsp
Egg yolks	3	3
Water	175ml/6floz	¾ cup
Egg whites, stiffly beaten	3	3
Sufficient vegetable oil for deep-frying		
DECORATION Icing (confectioners') sugar	75g/3oz	¾ cup
Lemon, sliced	1	1

To make the syrup, put the sugar, honey and water into a large saucepan. Bring to the boil, then boil for 5 minutes. Remove from the heat and stir in the lemon juice. Drop the apple rings into the syrup and, using a wooden spoon, carefully stir the apples to coat the rings thoroughly with the syrup. Set aside for 1 hour.

Meanwhile, make the batter. Sift the flour and salt into a bowl and stir in the sugar. Beat in the egg yolks and water until the mixture forms a smooth batter. Quickly fold in the egg whites. Using a slotted spoon, transfer the apple rings to the batter, and stir to coat them completely. Discard the syrup. Set the apples aside.

Fill a large saucepan one-third full with oil and heat until it reaches 180°C (350°F) on a deep-fat thermometer, or until a small cube of stale bread dropped into the oil turns golden in 55 seconds. Carefully lower the apple rings into the oil, a few at a time, and fry for 2 to 3 minutes, or until they are golden brown and crisp. Remove from the oil and drain on kitchen towels.

Put the icing (confectioners') sugar on a large plate. Dip the apples in the sugar and arrange them on a warmed serving dish. Decorate with the lemon slices and serve at once.

6-8 Servings

MELON SHELLS FILLED WITH FRUIT

	Metric/U.K.	U.S.
Melon, cut in half lengthways	1	1
Canned lychees, drained	20	20
Peaches, blanched, peeled and sliced	4	4
White grapes, peeled and seeded	½kg/1lb	1lb

Melon Shells Filled with Fruit makes a refreshing end to a Chinese meal.

Carefully scoop out the flesh of the melon and cut it into cubes, removing as many seeds as possible. Transfer the diced flesh to a bowl. Add the remaining ingredients and carefully and gently toss the mixture to mix the fruit.

Divide the mixture equally between the two melon shells. Put the shells into the refrigerator to chill for 30 minutes.

Serve at once.

6 Servings

127

Glossary

Bamboo shoots: Cone-shaped, light-coloured shoots of tropical bamboo, usually sold canned in Chinese or oriental provision stores. Leftover shoots can be stored for up to two weeks if they are transferred to a screw-top container, immersed in water, and kept in the refrigerator. Change the water daily. There is no real substitute, although celery hearts have a similar texture.

Bean curd: Fermented soya beans pressed into a slab. Sold fresh in cakes that look and feel rather like a soft, pale cheese, from oriental provision stores. It can be kept for up to 10 days if drained and then stored, immersed in water, in a sealed container. Change the water daily. It is also available canned.

Bean sprouts: The young sprouts of the mung bean, the plant which also produces the product from which soy sauce and soya protein are derived. Bean sprouts are used extensively as a vegetable in Chinese cooking and can be obtained fresh from Chinese or oriental provision stores. Fresh sprouts will keep for about two days in the refrigerator. To keep longer, transfer to a screw-top container, immerse in cold water, and keep in the refrigerator. They will keep for up to two weeks, providing the water is changed every two or three days. If fresh sprouts are not available, canned can be substituted but rinse canned bean sprouts thoroughly under cold running water before using.

Black beans, fermented: Soya beans, strongly flavoured and preserved, are an important ingredient in both Cantonese and Szechuan cooking. Sold in plastic bags or in cans. Transfer leftover beans to a screw-top container and store in the refrigerator. They will keep for up to six months. Extra soya sauce may be substituted.

Chinese cabbage: A light green brassica, similar in shape to cos (romaine) lettuce and more delicate to taste than western cabbage. Prepare as for white or savoy—that is, discard the outer leaves, wash thoroughly and shred or chop finely with a sharp knife. If Chinese cabbage is not available, cos (romaine) lettuce, or celery can be substituted.

Chinese dried mushrooms: Black fungi, which are sold by weight in plastic bags (not to be confused with European dried mushrooms) in Chinese or oriental provision stores. They will keep for up to a year. 'Wood ear fungi', a popular ingredient in Szechuan cooking, is a type of mushroom.

Five-spice powder: A popular condiment in Chinese cooking. Only really available from oriental provision stores, but check larger spice manufacturers too. It can be made at home by combining freshly ground black pepper with ground star anise, fennel, cinnamon and cloves. If five-spice powder is not obtainable, substitute cloves or allspice.

Ginger root: Knobbly and light brown, root ginger is an essential ingredient in both Indian and Chinese cooking. It can be obtained from any oriental or Indian provision store, or larger food stores or supermarkets. Ground ginger does not taste the same but *in extremis* can be used as a substitute: about ½ teaspoonful ground ginger equals 4cm/1½in of chopped ginger root. Wrap tightly, unpeeled, in plastic film and store in the refrigerator for up to six weeks.

Hoi sin sauce: A sweet, brownish-red Chinese barbecue sauce (not to be confused with western or American barbecue sauce), and usually containing soya beans, garlic, chillis and other seasonings. It can be obtained from Chinese or oriental provision stores. It is sold in both cans and bottles—if you use it only rarely, it is better to buy a bottle, which will keep better. If you are using canned, remove any leftover sauce and store it in a screw-top container in the refrigerator. It will keep for up to six months. There is no substitute for hoi sin sauce—omit from the recipe if you cannot obtain it.

Oyster sauce: A brown, delicate sauce made from oysters and soy sauce. Available in cans or bottles from Chinese or oriental provision stores. No substitute—omit from the recipe if unavailable.

Rice wine: Called Shao Hsing in China. A dry, strong wine made from rice. If rice wine is not available, Japanese sake or dry sherry can be substituted.

Soy sauce: A highly flavoured brown liquid made from fermented soya beans. Always try to buy Chinese soy sauce when cooking Chinese food, Japanese for Japanese. They are quite different. It can be obtained from Chinese or oriental provision stores, or from larger supermarkets. Soy sauce will keep for up to a year at room temperature.

Star anise: A popular seasoning in Chinese cooking, this spice resembles an eight-pointed star and is usually broken into 'sections' or 'pieces' before being used in cooking. Only available as a rule from Chinese or oriental provision stores, but try larger spice manufacturers too.

Water chestnuts: These are white bulbs about the same size as large chestnuts. Usually available canned from Chinese or oriental provision stores, or larger supermarkets. Store leftover chestnuts in a screw-top container, immersed in water, in the refrigerator. They will keep for up to one month, providing the water is changed daily.

France

French cuisine is generally acknowledged, especially by the French, to be the best and most imaginative in the world. Any claims from Italy or China, who between them have contributed some of the history and many of the spices, are brushed aside. And the rest of the world, dazzled, agrees—even to the point of feeling faintly guilty if they DO prefer a plate of pasta to a pork noisette!

Perhaps what the French do have, in the end, is not so much a cuisine par excellence as an attitude par excellence. Time spent agonizing over menus, prodding vegetables to make sure they are of the correct ripeness, choosing just the 'right' cut of meat, then cooking all to perfection, is not considered to be time wasted as it so often is in the English-speaking world, but one of the most creative and useful ways of spending one's days. And it is an art as much practised by the suburban housewife as by the chef of a great restaurant. A difference in attitude which could be summed up by the treatment of leading chefs: in France they are showered with money, fame, honours, all the reverence that being the excellent exponent of a respected profession can bring, while in most of the rest of the world they are lucky if they earn a decent salary and are merely ignored.

There are two main and very distinct strands of French cooking. The first is *haute* or *grande cuisine*, practised since the beginning by a few very distinguished chefs, employed originally by royalty or the nobility but now more often

right: *A peasant family in the Dordogne have breakfast.*

far right: *Transporting the catch from the Marennes oyster beds off the coast of Bordeaux.*

by leading restaurants or hotels. The second is of course provincial or bourgeois cooking, the cooking of the regions and the people. The latter is what the people actually eat most of the time, the former what the heart (and that famous French liver . . .) aspires to.

The history of *haute cuisine* actually began in Italy, something the French somewhat gloss over, for until the sixteenth century the cooking of France was simple and rustic, with the accent on domestic meat and dairy produce. In the sixteenth century, however, the young Catherine de Medici came to France to marry the French king Henry II and with her she brought her cooks, steeped in the traditions of Renaissance Florence, and their creations, especially their pastries and ice-creams, revolutionized French cuisine.

Haute cuisine owes its prominence to a few giants, whose effect on even the cooking of everyday dishes has been profound. But even among the giants, two stand out. Carême who was the first, and Escoffier who was perhaps the greatest. Antonin Carême was born in 1784, one of twenty-five children, in a slum just outside Paris. Legend has it that at the age of eleven he was told to fend for himself and this he did by apprenticing himself in a local cook shop. Luckily his talents soon became evident

and he quickly became employed by the most famous *patissier* of the time, Bailly. One of Bailly's most distinguished clients was Talleyrand, and it was in his house that Carême really began his life's work—a career that was to see him as chef to Napoleon and to the Prince Regent of Britain (later George IV) among others (he cooked for him in his so-called cottage retreat at Brighton, an astonishing piece of architecture that closely resembled some of Carême's more ostentatious pastry *pièces monté*). He was, in fact, fascinated by design and at one point wished to be an architect, a preoccupation apparent in some of his *pièces montés* (set pieces), which he was in the habit of planning by sketching a series of blueprints. In between, he invented, amended, taught, wrote—and designed.

George Auguste Escoffier who was born almost a century after Carême, came from the south of France near Nice. When he was quite young he was among other things, an army cook (he cooked for the troops during the Franco-Prussian War when he apparently did rather wonderful things with horse meat). He then formed a partnership with César Ritz, the founder of the luxury hotel chain, and together they carried the message and reputation of the excellence of French food

as for the master chef cooking for a wide range of discriminating clients.

There were, of course, others who contributed greatly to the development of *haute cuisine*—Prosper Montagné, who wrote many books on the subject and who was the first to question the need for unnecessary embellishment, and Brillat-Savarin who was more gourmet than chef and considered himself to be a 'philosopher' of the kitchen. He wrote one of the most entertaining books on food ever published, *La Physiologie de Goût*, which is still widely read and translated today some 200 years after it was written.

The tradition goes on: in France the natural heirs of Carême and Escoffier are still at work, experimenting and shaping the cuisine to the needs of today. The leading exponents number about a dozen now and are called *La Bande* in France, and most of them own and cook in their own restaurants, which are located throughout the country. One of them, Michel Guérard, has even invented a new form, called *cuisine minceur*, which adapts the skills of *haute cuisine* to the reality of a low cholesterol life.

The 'other' cuisine of France is more modest—few fancy sauces or extravagant concoctions requiring architectural plans (although there is an area of overlap as the two different forms of cooking meet and learn from each other). Originally, many of the dishes were specialities of specific regions of the country. Most extol the virtues of patience and thrift, taking care to use even the most modest scraps, and using cheaper cuts of meat which are tenderized and cooked slowly to increase their succulence. And since France is a large country, stretching from dull, rainy northern coasts to sunny, southern Mediterranean ones, from the German border to the Swiss and from the Spanish to the Italian, the foods of these varying areas are in themselves very different from one another.

In the north there is Brittany and Normandy, lots of coast-line, rather rocky, which makes the seafood good and plentiful, and vast expanses of farmland which makes the meat, particularly the lamb, well regarded. In Brittany, one of the great delights is crêpes, purchasable for a few francs from road-side stalls and filled with anything from Grand Marnier to seafood. Normandy is farming country, lots of apple orchards, dairy produce, cream, butter and eggs, all successfully incorporated into the food, sharp dry cider and a brandy made from apples, called Calvados, which many connoisseurs consider

throughout the world. This was the era of the *belle epoque*, when eating out was not only fashionable but a social necessity and when the great restaurants and hotels, particularly of France and London came into their own. (Restaurants had been 'invented' just before the Revolution in France and must have struck a sympathetic chord in even that part of the population which could not afford them—despite the fact that the greater part of their natural clientele was wiped out during the Terror, they not only survived but prospered.) Paris and Monte Carlo, in particular, seemed to be populated solely by the beautiful, the gifted, the demi-mondaine and the gourmet, and Escoffier duly responded to the excitement of the time, naming several of his most popular creations in honour of actresses, singers or crowned heads of Europe. He did much more than immortalize Melba by calling that toast after her, however, for in addition to refining and simplifying some of the more grandiose ideas of Carême, he also remained true to his origins and incorporated into his repertoire, and therefore into the classical repertoire of France, many traditional dishes from the regions. His book *Ma Cuisine* includes several Provençal dishes, and remains as appropriate a guide for the housewife cooking for her family

right: *French wine is famous throughout the world—this particular vineyard is in one of the less well known wine areas of the country, in the Midi near Le Lavandou.*

far right: *An old man and a boy—a universal scene, yet typically rural French. The bread with pride of place on the back of the bicycle is the French staple,* the *baguette.*

finer than cognac. Normandy also produces what is probably France's most popular cheese, Camembert.

The Loire, Burgundy, the Rhône and Champagne are famous outside France mainly for their delightful wines, which number among the finest in the world. The cooking is excellent too—the *charcuterie* tradition flourishes in the Loire valley, especially around Tours, famous for its *rillettes*, a sort of potted pork, while Burgundian cooking relies on voluminous quantities of the native wine and is immortalized by *boeuf bourguignonne* and *coq au vin*. At Bresse, near Lyons, they consider their chickens to be the finest in France if not the world, and make many imaginative dishes with them.

Savoie is near to Switzerland, just across the lake from Geneva and so the Swiss influence is strong. The wines are white and somewhat flowery, the most commonly used cheese in cooking is Gruyère, and the food is unpretentious but filling. Chartreuse, the only liqueur still made by monks, is made in this region, and by the same order which first had that brilliant idea . . .

Alsace and Lorraine are usually held together by a hyphen and lumped together in the public imagination, although they are not that similar—in fact the main thing they have in common probably is that both, in their time, have formed part of Germany and have been batted back and forth by the two great

powers almost as the mood took them. Alsace produces some of the most delicate white wine in France, akin to the wines of the almost-neighbouring Rhine, and also some of the better French beer. The German influence is evident in the food too—in the popularity of sausages and smoked hams, and in the classic dish of *choucroute garnie*, the basis of which is sauerkraut. In Lorraine, there is that famous quiche—made in a thousand different ways, imitated to the point of unrecognizability, yet still absolutely delicious!

The southwestern border is significant too, for the Pyrenees, which separate France from Spain, house a people who refuse to belong to either, the Basques, who have their own language, customs—and cooking. Here there's lots of saffron, and dried red peppers, Spanish-style omelets and nourishing filling soups, many containing the traditional *confit d'oie* or pressed goose, and *daubes*, warming stews made from beef or lamb.

In the centre of France, there is Bordeaux, famous for its clarets and the best sweet white wine in the world, Sauternes, and the Marennes beds, noted for the excellence of their oysters and mussels. In the Périgord nearby, the local pigs help hunt out the precious truffle, which is so expensive now that delivery of a supply to a largish delicatessen requires a security guard.

Languedoc is different yet again. *Cassoulet* is probably the dish that is best known to the outside world and although there are many variations, a good one should include lamb or mutton, sausages and haricot (dried white) beans. In the south, the influence is Italian (Nice only became officially part of France during the Second Empire): lots of olive oil for cooking, and garlic and olives are almost part of the staple diet. Dishes are highly spiced and colourful and the southern herbs such as basil and rosemary are used with great abundance. In caves high above Marseilles, the blue Roquefort, made from ewe's milk, matures. A great deal of the *vin ordinaire* of France is now grown in this area, including some exceptionally pleasant dry white and rose wines.

The range is enormous and the taste superb—and the surprise is, when you cook even the more complex dishes, just how easy they are to create. And of course in a time of relative austerity the provincial dishes, with their ability to use almost every scrap in the kitchen, become an almost necessary addition to the repertoire of every budget-conscious cook.

Soups and Starters

SOUPE A L'OIGNON
(Onion Soup)

	Metric/U.K.	U.S.
Butter	75g/3oz	6 Tbs
Large onions, thinly sliced into rings	4	4
Flour	2 Tbs	2 Tbs
Salt and pepper to taste		
Beef stock	900ml/ 1½ pints	3¾ cups
French or Italian bread, cut approximately 1½cm/¾in thick and toasted	4 rounds	4 rounds
Garlic cloves, halved	2	2
Parmesan or Gruyère cheese, grated	75g/3oz	¾ cup

Melt the butter in a heavy flameproof casserole. Reduce the heat to low and add the onions.

French Onion Soup, traditionally associated with the old Les Halles market in Paris but eaten and enjoyed throughout the world.

Simmer them, stirring occasionally, for 25 to 30 minutes, or until they are golden brown. Remove from the heat.

Stir in the flour and seasoning, then gradually add the stock. Return to high heat and bring to the boil. Reduce the heat to low, cover the casserole and simmer for 20 minutes.

Preheat the grill (broiler) to high.

Rub each bread round on each side with a garlic clove half, then discard the garlic. Float the rounds on the soup and sprinkle the cheese generously over the top. Put under the grill (broiler) and cook for 5 minutes, or until the top is golden and bubbling. Serve at once.

4 Servings

POTAGE PARMENTIER
(Potato and Leek Soup)

A version of this traditional country soup was adapted by the French chef Louis Diat to summer cooking. By chilling the soup over ice, he created one of the most popular of cold soups, Vichyssoise.

	Metric/U.K.	U.S.
Butter	50g/2oz	4 Tbs
Vegetable oil	2 Tbs	2 Tbs
Large onion, finely chopped	1	1

Medium leeks, white parts only, thinly sliced	3	3
Medium potatoes, finely chopped	6	6
Salt and pepper to taste		
Chicken stock	900ml/ 1½ pints	3¾ cups
Milk	300ml/10floz	1¼ cups

Melt the butter with the oil in a large saucepan. Add the onion and fry until it is soft. Stir in the leeks and potatoes and cook, turning occasionally, until the potatoes are evenly browned. Season with salt and pepper and pour over the stock and milk. Bring to the boil, stirring constantly. Reduce the heat to low, cover the pan and simmer for 20 to 25 minutes, or until the potatoes are very tender.

Pour the soup through a strainer into a bowl, using the back of a wooden spoon to rub the vegetables through. Discard the pulp in the strainer. Alternatively, purée the soup in a blender.

Return the soup to the saucepan and simmer for 5 minutes. Serve at once.

4-6 Servings

CONSOMME JULIENNE
(Vegetable Consommé)

	Metric/U.K.	U.S.
Butter	50g/2oz	4 Tbs
Carrot, cut into small thin strips	1	1
Celery stalks, cut into small thin strips	2	2
Potatoes, cut into small thin strips	2	2
Onion, chopped	1	1
Parsnips, cut into small thin strips	2	2
Canned beef bouillon	1¾l/3 pints	7½ cups
Salt and pepper to taste		
Dried thyme	½ tsp	½ tsp
Chopped fresh chervil or parsley	1 Tbs	1 Tbs

Melt the butter in a saucepan. Add the vegetables and reduce the heat to low. Cook, turning occasionally, for 15 minutes, or until they are just tender. Remove from the heat and

An elegant yet filling representative of haute cuisine, Consommé Julienne.

drain the vegetables in a colander. Set aside and keep hot.

Bring the bouillon to the boil over moderate heat. Add the vegetables, seasoning and herbs, and stir gently.

Serve at once.

6 Servings

SOUPE ALBIGEOISE
(Meat and Vegetable Soup)

This is one of the traditional soups of southwestern France. The confit d'oie or pressed goose, which is a specialty of the area, should be included if the soup is to be completely authentic, but since it is difficult to obtain outside France, it may be omitted.

	Metric/U.K.	U.S.
Beef ribs, separated	700g/1½lb	1½lb
Salt pork, diced	275g/10oz	2 cups
Bouquet garni	1	1
Beef stock	2½l/4 pints	5 pints
Dried broad (fava or lima) beans, soaked overnight in cold water and drained	225g/8oz	1⅓ cups
Medium green cabbage, coarsely shredded	1	1
Medium carrots, diced	4	4
Small turnips, sliced	4	4
Medium leeks, sliced	4	4
Large onions, sliced	2	2
Large potatoes, sliced	4	4
Garlic cloves, crushed	6	6
Garlic sausage, diced	½kg/1lb	1lb
Pressed goose (confit d'oie)	125g/4oz	4oz

Put the ribs, salt pork and bouquet garni in a flameproof casserole and stir in the stock. Bring to the boil, stirring constantly and skimming off any scum with a slotted spoon. Stir in the beans, reduce the heat to low and cover. Simmer the soup for 1 hour.

Increase the heat to moderate, add the vegetables and garlic and bring to the boil. Reduce the heat to low, re-cover and simmer for 1 hour.

Using a slotted spoon, remove the beef bones and bouquet garni from the soup. Cut the meat from the bones and return to the soup. Add the sausage and goose, and simmer the soup for a further 20 minutes.

Serve at once.

8-10 Servings

BOURRIDE
(Mixed Fish Soup)

This is one of the great dishes of Provence, almost rivalling the bouillabaisse in popularity. It can be made from almost any type of firm-fleshed fish but the important not-to-be-omitted essential of the dish is the aioli. If you want to cheat on making it, add three or four crushed garlic cloves to 300ml/10floz (1¼ cups) of commercially prepared mayonnaise. Boiled potatoes are also often added to the soup when serving.

	Metric/U.K.	U.S.
Firm white fish fillets (haddock, cod, John Dory, brill, or bass)	1½kg/3lb	3lb
Fish heads and trimmings from the fillets		
Water	1¼l/2 pints	5 cups
Dry white wine	300ml/10floz	1¼ cups
Onions, thinly sliced	2	2
Wine vinegar	2 Tbs	2 Tbs
Orange peel, blanched	7½cm/3in strip	3in strip
Bay leaf	1	1
Fennel seeds	1 tsp	1 tsp
Salt	1 tsp	1 tsp
French or Italian bread, toasted	6-8 rounds	6-8 rounds
AIOLI		
Dry breadcrumbs	1 Tbs	1 Tbs
Wine vinegar	1 Tbs	1 Tbs
Garlic cloves, crushed	4	4
Egg yolks	6	6
Salt	½ tsp	½ tsp
Dry mustard	¼ tsp	¼ tsp
White pepper	¼ tsp	¼ tsp
Olive oil	300ml/10floz	1¼ cups
Lemon juice	1 Tbs	1 Tbs

Bourride is one of the great fish soups of Southern France, and is a nourishing, warming meal in itself.

Cut the fish fillets into about 7½cm/3in pieces. Put the trimmings and heads into a large saucepan with all the remaining soup ingredients, except the bread and aioli, and bring to the boil. Half-cover the pan and simmer for 30 minutes.

Meanwhile, make the aioli. Soak the breadcrumbs in vinegar for 5 minutes, then squeeze dry. Transfer the crumbs to a bowl and mash in the garlic. Beat in the egg yolks, one at a time, then the salt, mustard and pepper. When the mixture is very thick and smooth, beat in the olive oil, a few drops at a time. Do not add the oil too quickly or the mayonnaise will curdle. When the mayonnaise has thickened, the oil may be added a little more rapidly. When all the oil has been added, beat in the lemon juice. Set aside.

Strain the fish stock, pressing down on the vegetables with the back of a wooden spoon. Rinse out the pan, then return the fish stock to it. Add the fish and bring to the boil. Reduce the heat to low and simmer for 10 minutes, or until the flesh flakes easily. Using a slotted spoon, transfer the fish pieces to a warmed serving bowl. Boil the stock rapidly for 10 minutes or until it has reduced a little.

Very gradually beat about 125ml/4floz (½ cup) of the fish stock into the aioli. Pour the mixture into the saucepan and simmer gently for 1 to 2 minutes, being careful not to let it curdle.

Arrange the toasted bread rounds on the bottom of individual bowls, and cover with fish pieces. Pour over the aioli stock and serve at once.

8 Servings

PATE DE FOIE
(Liver Pâté)

	Metric/U.K.	U.S.
Streaky (fatty) bacon	225g/8oz	8oz
Butter	25g/1oz	2 Tbs
Chicken livers, trimmed	225g/8oz	8oz
Minced (ground) veal	½kg/1lb	1lb
Minced (ground) pork	225g/8oz	8oz
Garlic cloves, crushed	2	2
Juniper berries, coarsely crushed	12	12
Black peppercorns, coarsely crushed	12	12
Salt and pepper to taste		
Mixed spice or allspice	¼ tsp	¼ tsp
Dry white wine	175ml/6floz	¾ cup
Dry sherry	50ml/2floz	¼ cup

Preheat the oven to moderate 180°C (Gas Mark 4, 350°F).

Dice half the bacon and put it into a mixing bowl. Reserve the remaining slices.

Melt the butter in a small frying-pan. Add the chicken livers and fry until they are well browned on the outside but pink on the inside. Transfer the livers to a chopping board. Chop them finely and transfer them to the bowl with the bacon. Add all the remaining ingredients and beat well to mix.

Turn the mixture into a well-greased medium terrine or ovenproof dish. Pack down well and cover the top with the reserved slices of bacon. Cover tightly with foil and a lid. Put the terrine into a roasting pan and pour in enough boiling water to come about two-thirds up the sides of the terrine. Place the pan in the oven and bake for 2 hours.

Remove from the oven and transfer the terrine to a board. Remove the lid and place a weight on top of the pâté. Leave to cool. When the pâté is cool, remove the weight and chill in the refrigerator for 4 hours.

Before serving, unmould on to a serving plate and cut into slices.

8 Servings

ESCARGOTS A LA BOURGUIGNONNE
(Snails with Garlic Butter)

	Metric/U.K.	U.S.
Butter, softened	175g/6oz	12 Tbs
Finely chopped parsley	2 Tbs	2 Tbs
Garlic cloves, crushed	2	2
Salt and pepper to taste		
Brandy	2 Tbs	2 Tbs
Snail shells	24	24
Canned snails, drained or frozen snails	24	24

Preheat the oven to fairly hot 190°C (Gas Mark 5, 375°F).

Cream the butter, parsley, garlic and seasoning together. Add half the brandy and beat until the mixture is soft and smooth.

Using a teaspoon, push a little of the butter mixture into each snail shell. Then push a snail into each shell and seal the entrance with a little more of the butter mixture.

Put the snails into a shallow ovenproof dish and dribble over the remaining brandy. Put the dish into the oven and bake for 15 to 20 minutes, or until the butter is bubbling and beginning to brown. Serve at once.

4 Servings

RILLETTES DE PORC
(Potted Pork)

This is the speciality of the city of Tours in the Loire valley, although versions of it are found all over France.

	Metric/U.K.	U.S.
Pork fat, cut into pieces	700g/1½lb	1½lb
Lean pork belly, cut into 5cm/2in pieces	1kg/2lb	2lb
Water	50ml/2floz	¼ cup
Salt and pepper to taste		
Dried sage	1 tsp	1 tsp
Bouquets garnis	2	2
Dried marjoram	½ tsp	½ tsp
Garlic clove, crushed	1	1

Put the pork fat, belly and water into a large saucepan and bring to the boil. Season generously with salt and pepper and add the sage and bouquets garnis. Cover and simmer the mixture for 4½ hours, checking occasionally to make sure the mixture does not become too dry (add more boiling water if this happens). Remove from the heat and remove the bouquets garnis.

Pour the mixture into a fine strainer and allow the fat to drip through into a bowl. Beat the marjoram, garlic and seasoning to taste into the mixture in the strainer, then shred with a fork. Turn the pork into small stoneware pots (or a terrine if you prefer). Pour a little of the pork fat over the top and set aside to cool completely. Cover with lids or foil and chill in the refrigerator. Use as required.

About 700g/1½lb

SALADE DE TOMATES
(Tomato Salad)

Despite the name, this is one of the most popular hors d'oeuvre dishes in the French cooking repertoire. Obviously the dressing varies from cook to cook, and if you prefer yours to be non-garlic, then the one suggested below can be amended and changed accordingly.

	Metric/U.K.	U.S.
Tomatoes, thinly sliced	450g/1lb	1lb
Chives, chopped	2 Tbs	2 Tbs
Chopped fresh basil	1 Tbs	1 Tbs
DRESSING		
Olive oil	50ml/2floz	4 Tbs
Wine vinegar	2 Tbs	2 Tbs
Garlic clove, crushed	1	1
Salt and pepper to taste		
French mustard	1 tsp	1 tsp

First make the dressing. Put all the ingredients into a screw-top jar and shake vigorously to blend.

Arrange the tomato slices, slightly overlapping, in a serving dish. Pour over the dressing, then sprinkle with chives and basil.

Chill in the refrigerator for 15 minutes before serving.

4 Servings

Snails are a particular French weakness, and a taste sometimes not quite understood outside the country. Escargots à la Bourguignonne (snails with a delicious garlic butter) will help change that opinion!

Fish and Seafood

MAQUERAUX A LA SAUCE MOUTARDE
(Mackerel Fillets in Mustard Sauce)

	Metric/U.K.	U.S.
Olive oil	1 Tbs	1 Tbs
Large mackerel, cleaned	2	2
Lemon juice	1 Tbs	1 Tbs
Butter	75g/3oz	6 Tbs
French mustard	1½ Tbs	1½ Tbs
Egg yolks	2	2
Cider vinegar	1 Tbs	1 Tbs
Salt and pepper to taste		
Chopped fresh herbs (a mixture of chives, thyme, sage and marjoram)	2 Tbs	2 Tbs

Basic French cooking is about doing simply delicious things with simple, plain food and this Maqueraux à la Sauce Moutarde (mackerel fillets with a piquant mustard sauce) is an excellent example.

Preheat the oven to moderate 180°C (Gas Mark 4, 350°F).

Grease two large pieces of aluminium foil with the oil. Lay one mackerel on each piece of foil and sprinkle over the lemon juice. Wrap the fish loosely in the foil, envelope fashion, so that it is completely enclosed, but allowing it some room to 'breathe'. Place the fish parcels in the oven and bake for 20 minutes, or until the fish flesh flakes easily.

Meanwhile, prepare the sauce. Cream the butter with a wooden spoon until it is soft and set aside.

Beat the mustard, egg yolks, vinegar and seasoning together until they are well blended. Gradually add the egg yolk mixture to the butter, beating until they are combined and the sauce is smooth and thick. Stir in the herbs. Spoon the sauce into a sauceboat and chill in the refrigerator.

Remove the mackerel parcels from the oven and open carefully. Pour the cooking juices into a bowl and reserve.

Remove the skin from the mackerel by scraping it off with the point of a knife, being careful not to break the flesh. Cut each fish into four fillets and remove the bones. Arrange the fillets on a shallow serving dish. Strain the reserved cooking juices over the fillets and allow to cool to room temperature. Chill in the refrigerator for 2 hours.

Serve cold, accompanied by the mustard sauce.

4 Servings

ROUGETS A LA NICOISE
(Red Mullets in Tomato Sauce)

Red mullets are one of the most popular of the southern French fish and are cooked in a variety of ways. This recipe assumes that the fish are medium in size, but if you can only obtain small ones, allow two per person.

	Metric/U.K.	U.S.
Olive oil	50ml/2floz	¼ cup
Tomatoes, blanched, peeled, seeded and coarsely chopped	700g/1½lb	1½lb
Garlic cloves, crushed	4	4

	Metric/U.K.	U.S.
Dried thyme	1 tsp	1 tsp
Bay leaf	1	1
Salt and pepper to taste		
Black olives, stoned (pitted)	225g/8oz	2 cups
Lemons, cut into 12 slices	2	2
Red mullets, cleaned and scaled but with the heads and tails left on	6	6

Heat the oil in a large frying-pan. Add the tomatoes, garlic, herbs and seasoning, reduce the heat to low and simmer, stirring occasionally, for 15 to 20 minutes, or until the mixture is very thick.

Stir in the olives and lemon slices, then transfer half the mixture to a second frying-pan. Divide the fish between the pans and baste them with the sauce until they are well coated.

Cover and cook, turning the fish occasionally, for 15 to 20 minutes, or until the flesh flakes easily.

Remove the bay leaf and serve at once.

6 Servings

DARNE DE SAUMON FLORENTINE
(Salmon Steaks with Spinach)

	Metric/U.K.	U.S.
Salmon steaks, cut 2½cm/1in thick	4	4
Unsalted butter, melted	50g/2oz	4 Tbs
Spinach, cooked, drained and kept hot	1½kg/3lb	3lb
Double (heavy) cream	50ml/2floz	¼ cup
Salt and pepper to taste		
SAUCE		
Unsalted butter, melted	175g/6oz	12 Tbs
Lemon juice	1 Tbs	1 Tbs

Colourful, economical and filling—Rougets à la Niçoise.

	Metric/U.K.	U.S.
Salt and white pepper to taste		
Cayenne pepper	⅛ tsp	⅛ tsp

Preheat the grill (broiler) to moderate. Arrange the steaks on the lined rack of the grill (broiler) pan. Coat them with a little of the melted butter. Grill (broil) the fish for 8 to 10 minutes on each side, basting frequently with the remaining butter, or until the flesh flakes easily.

Meanwhile, combine the spinach, cream and seasoning in a bowl. Arrange the mixture over the bottom of a large, warmed serving dish. Transfer the fish steaks to the dish and arrange them over the spinach.

Combine all the sauce ingredients together in a jug and pour over the steaks. Serve at once.

4 Servings

ROULADE DE SAUMON
(Salmon Roll)

This delicious dish is usually served with sour cream. Use fresh herbs if at all possible; if you are using dried, halve the amounts indicated below. If you aren't lucky enough to have fresh salmon handy, frozen or good-quality canned can be substituted although the taste won't be quite as good.

	Metric/U.K.	U.S.
Cooked fresh salmon, skinned	275g/10oz	10oz
Eggs, separated	4	4
Butter, melted	25g/1oz	2 Tbs
Flour	3 Tbs	3 Tbs
Salt and pepper to taste		
Chopped chives	2 tsp	2 tsp
Chopped fresh fennel	1 tsp	1 tsp
Chopped fresh marjoram	½ tsp	½ tsp
White wine vinegar	2 tsp	2 tsp
Double (heavy) cream	2 Tbs	2 Tbs

Line the base and sides of an 18cm/7in x 25cm/ 10in baking pan with greaseproof or waxed paper, allowing the paper to stand about 2½cm/ 1in above the sides of the pan. Grease the paper and set aside. Preheat the oven to moderate 180°C (Gas Mark 4, 350°F).

Purée the salmon in a blender or food mill and set aside.

Put the egg yolks in a large bowl and beat until they are pale and thick. Gradually beat in the melted butter, then stir in the flour, a tablespoon at a time, until the ingredients are thoroughly combined. Stir in the puréed salmon, seasoning, herbs, vinegar and cream until the mixture is smooth.

Beat the egg whites in a second bowl until they form stiff peaks. Carefully fold the egg whites into the salmon mixture until they are thoroughly combined.

Pour the salmon mixture into the pan and smooth the top. Put the pan into the oven and bake for 15 minutes, or until the mixture is just firm to the touch and pale golden brown. Remove from the oven. Turn the mixture out on to a large piece of greaseproof or waxed paper, then remove and discard the paper from the mixture.

Using the greaseproof or waxed paper, roll up the mixture Swiss (jelly) roll style. Transfer to a warmed serving plate and serve at once.

3-4 Servings

SOLE NORMANDE
(Sole Fillets Garnished with Mussels and Shrimps)

This is one of the great regional classics of French cuisine.

	Metric/U.K.	U.S.
Sole fillets, skinned	8	8
Mussels, scrubbed, steamed for 6-8 minutes or until they open, cooking liquid reserved	600ml/1 pint	1¼ pints
Onion, thinly sliced into rings	1	1
Bouquet garni	1	1
Dry white wine	300ml/10floz	1¼ cups
Butter	25g/1oz	2 Tbs
Shallots, halved	4	4
Button mushrooms, stalks removed	225g/8oz	2 cups
Lemon juice	1 Tbs	1 Tbs
Salt and pepper to taste		
Frozen shrimps, thawed	125g/4oz	4oz

The exquisite simplicity and richness of salmon is demonstrated in two very different but delicious dishes: on top Roulade de Saumon, below Darnes de Saumon Florentine.

The most elegant yet easy to make of fish dishes, Sole Meunière.

SAUCE		
Butter	1 Tbs	1 Tbs
Flour	2 Tbs	2 Tbs
Salt and pepper to taste		
Double (heavy) cream	250ml/8floz	1 cup

Roll up the fillets Swiss (jelly) roll style and secure with thread. Arrange the rolls in a large ovenproof dish and set aside.

Strain the reserved mussel liquid into a large saucepan. Add the onion and bouquet garni then pour over the wine. Bring the liquid to the boil. Reduce the heat to moderately low and simmer the stock for 10 minutes. Strain the stock into a large bowl and set aside.

Preheat the oven to moderate 180°C (Gas Mark 4, 350°F).

Melt the butter in a large frying-pan. Add the shallots, mushrooms, lemon juice and seasoning and fry for 5 minutes. Transfer the mixture to the dish containing the fish. Set the pan aside.

Add the mussels and shrimps to the dish and pour over the reserved stock. Put the dish into the oven and cook for 15 to 20 minutes, or until the fish flesh flakes easily. Transfer the fish rolls to a warmed serving dish. Remove and discard the thread. Transfer the shallots, mushrooms, mussels and shrimps to the serving dish and arrange decoratively around the fish. Set aside and keep hot while you make the sauce.

Strain the cooking liquid and set aside. Add the butter to the butter remaining in the frying-pan and melt it over moderate heat. Remove from the heat and, using a wooden spoon, stir in the flour to form a smooth paste. Gradually stir in the reserved cooking liquid and seasoning and return to the heat. Cook the sauce, stirring constantly, for 2 to 3 minutes, or until it is smooth and thick. Remove from the heat and stir in the cream.

Pour the sauce over the fish and serve at once.

4 Servings

SOLE MEUNIERE
(Sole Fillets with Butter Sauce)

	Metric/U.K.	U.S.
Sole fillets, skinned	700g/1½lb	1½lb
Lemon juice	3 Tbs	3 Tbs
Seasoned flour (flour with salt and pepper to taste)	50g/2oz	½ cup
Butter	125g/4oz	8 Tbs
Large lemon, thinly sliced	1	1
Parsley sprigs	6	6

Sprinkle the fillets with 2 tablespoons of the lemon juice and set aside for 5 minutes. Pat dry with kitchen towels. Dip the fillets in the seasoned flour, shaking off any excess.

Melt 75g/3oz (6 tablespoons) of the butter in a large frying-pan. Add the fillets, a few at a time, and cook them for 4 to 6 minutes on each side, or until the flesh flakes easily. Arrange the fillets in a warmed, shallow serving dish.

Wipe the pan clean and add the remaining juice and butter. Place over low heat and simmer until the butter melts, stirring constantly.

Remove from the heat and pour the butter over the fillets. Garnish with lemon slices and parsley.

Serve at once.

6 Servings

TRUITES AUX AMANDES
(Trout with Almonds)

	Metric/U.K.	U.S.
Medium trout, cleaned and with the eyes removed	6	6
Salt and white pepper to taste		
Lemon juice	2 Tbs	2 Tbs
Milk	175ml/6floz	¾ cup
Seasoned flour (flour with salt and pepper to taste)	75g/3oz	¾ cup
Butter	150g/5oz	10 Tbs
Slivered almonds	125g/4oz	1 cup
Lemon quarters	6	6

Gently rub the fish with the seasoning and half the lemon juice.

Dip the fish first in the milk, then in the seasoned flour, shaking off any excess.

Melt 75g/3oz (6 tablespoons) of the butter in a large frying-pan. Add the trout and fry for 4 to 6 minutes on each side, or until the flesh flakes easily. Transfer the fish to a warmed serving dish. Keep warm.

Add the remaining butter in the pan. Stir in the almonds and remaining lemon juice and fry until the almonds are golden brown.

Pour the mixture over the trout and garnish with the lemon quarters. Serve at once.

6 Servings

HARENGS A LA BOULANGERE
(Herrings Baked with Potatoes and Onions)

French cooking isn't just elegant sauces and expensive ingredients, it's also combining the everyday and inexpensive, and making of them something very special. This herring dish is baked with the classic boulangère garnish of potatoes and onions and the result is superb—and cheap and easy to make.

	Metric/U.K.	U.S.
Medium potatoes, parboiled for 5 minutes, then thinly sliced	4	4
Herrings, filleted and cleaned	6	6
Dried marjoram	½ tsp	½ tsp
Dried thyme	½ tsp	½ tsp
Salt and pepper to taste		
Lemon juice	1 Tbs	1 Tbs
Medium onions, thinly sliced into rings	2	2
Water	125ml/4floz	½ cup
Butter	25g/1oz	2 Tbs

Preheat the oven to fairly hot 190°C (Gas Mark 5, 375°F).

Line the bottom of a large, well-greased baking dish with half the potato slices. Lay the fillets on top and sprinkle over the herbs and seasoning. Pour over the lemon juice and cover with onion slices. Lay the remaining potato slices on top. Pour over the water. Cut the butter into small pieces and dot them on top of the potatoes, and season to taste.

Cover the dish and put into the oven. Bake for 40 minutes, or until the potatoes are cooked through and the fish flesh flakes easily.

Serve immediately, from the dish.

4-6 Servings

MOULES MARINIERE
(Mussels in White Wine)

This is one of the most popular of French fish dishes and is a specialty of Brittany. It should be eaten in large bowls, rather like soup—with an extra bowl for the shells.

	Metric/U.K.	U.S.
Shallots, finely chopped	2	2
Garlic clove, crushed	1	1
Bouquet garni	1	1
Parsley sprigs	2	2
Mussels, scrubbed, soaked for 1 hour in cold water and drained	3l/6 pints	3½ qts
Dry white wine	600ml/1 pint	2½ cups
Butter, cut into small pieces	50g/2oz	4 Tbs
Salt and pepper to taste		
Chopped parsley	2 Tbs	2 Tbs

Put the shallots, garlic and herbs in a large buttered saucepan.

Discard any mussels which are not tightly shut or do not close if sharply tapped, and any that have broken shells or have floated in the water. Arrange the remaining mussels in the pan and pour over the wine. Scatter over half the butter, cover and bring to the boil. Cook for 6 to 8 minutes, or until the mussel shells open. Remove the mussels from the pan and remove one shell from each one. Arrange the mussels in a warmed serving dish and keep hot.

Remove the bouquet garni and parsley sprigs from the pan and boil the liquid rapidly until it has reduced by one-third and has thickened. Stir in the seasoning and remaining butter until it has melted.

Pour over the mussels, sprinkle over the

Huitres Marinées, a delicious new way with oysters.

parsley and serve at once.

4 Servings

HUITRES MARINEES
(Marinated Oysters)

There are two main areas of oyster production in France, at Marennes off the coast of Bordeaux, and around the coasts of Brittany. This dish, with regional embellishments is popular in both areas, and is eaten as an hors d'oeuvre or (in double quantities and by afficionados) as a light lunch. The traditional wine to serve with an oyster dish such as this, by the way, is chilled Chablis.

	Metric/U.K.	U.S.
Oysters	16	16
MARINADE		
Dry white wine	175ml/6floz	¾ cup
Olive oil	50ml/2floz	¼ cup
Lemon juice	50ml/2floz	¼ cup
Salt and pepper to taste		
Dried thyme	¼ tsp	¼ tsp
Dried chervil	¼ tsp	¼ tsp
Chopped parsley	1 tsp	1 tsp
Garlic clove, crushed	1	1

First, prepare the marinade. Combine all the ingredients in a large bowl, stirring to blend thoroughly. Set aside for 15 minutes.

Meanwhile, detach the oysters from the shells and put them into a saucepan. Discard the shells. Add the marinade and bring the liquid to the boil.

Transfer the oysters and liquid to a serving bowl and set aside to cool to room temperature. Chill in the refrigerator until required. Serve cold, in the marinade.

2-4 Servings

COQUILLES SAINT-JACQUES A L'AIL
(Scallops with Garlic and Basil)

	Metric/U.K.	U.S.
Scallops, cut into 1cm/½in pieces	700g/1½lb	1½lb
Lemon juice	1 Tbs	1 Tbs
Salt and white pepper to taste		
Seasoned flour (flour with salt and pepper to taste)	50g/2oz	½ cup
Vegetable oil	75ml/3floz	6 Tbs
Shallots, finely chopped	3	3
Garlic cloves, crushed	3	3
Dried basil	¼ tsp	¼ tsp
Butter	25g/1oz	2 Tbs
Chopped parsley	1 Tbs	1 Tbs

A classic dish of scallops, Coquilles Saint-Jacques à l'Ail.

Dry the scallops on kitchen towels and place them on a piece of greaseproof or waxed paper. Sprinkle over the lemon juice, salt and pepper. Set aside for 5 minutes. Dip the scallops in the flour, shaking off any excess.

Heat the oil in a large frying-pan. Add the scallops and fry for 5 minutes, turning occasionally, or until they are lightly browned. Stir in the shallots, garlic and basil and cook for a further 2 minutes. Remove from the heat and stir in the butter and parsley.

Transfer to a warmed serving dish or individual scallop shells and serve at once.

4 Servings

147

Alouettes Sans Têtes is the rather gory name for this superb dish of stuffed beef rolls.

Meat

ALOUETTES SANS TETES
(Stuffed Beef Rolls)

Despite its bizarre name (it means, literally, larks without heads) this dish is really stuffed beef rolls, or paupiettes as they are sometimes called in France. Because of the long slow cooking time, an inexpensive cut of meat can be used, braising or chuck steak, for instance, as well as the more usual paupiette beef topside (top rump).

	Metric/U.K.	U.S.
Lean beef, cut 12½cm/5in square by ½cm/¼in thick	8 slices	8 slices
Vegetable oil	2 Tbs	2 Tbs
Onions, chopped	2	2
Carrots, chopped	2	2
Beef stock	300ml/10floz	1¼ cups
Tomatoes, blanched, peeled, seeded and chopped	3	3
Garlic clove, crushed	1	1
Bay leaf	1	1
Chopped parsley	2 Tbs	2 Tbs
STUFFING		
Minced (ground) pork or veal	175g/6oz	6oz
Small onion, finely chopped	1	1
Butter, softened	25g/1oz	2 Tbs
Fresh white breadcrumbs	25g/1oz	½ cup
Finely chopped parsley	1 Tbs	1 Tbs
Dried sage	1 tsp	1 tsp
Finely grated lemon rind	1½ tsp	1½ tsp
Egg, lightly beaten	1	1
Salt and pepper to taste		

Preheat the oven to moderate 180°C (Gas Mark 4, 350°F).

To prepare the stuffing, mix all the ingredients together until they are thoroughly blended.

Lay the beef slices out flat on a working surface and divide the stuffing among them, spreading it out carefully. Roll up the slices, Swiss (jelly) roll style and tie with string or thread.

Heat the oil in a large saucepan. Add the rolls and fry, turning frequently, until they are evenly browned. Transfer them to a large casserole.

Add the onions and carrots to the pan and fry until they are soft. Stir in the stock, tomatoes, garlic and bay leaf and bring to the boil. Pour the mixture over the beef rolls and cover the casserole tightly. Put the dish into the oven and cook for 1½ hours, or until the rolls are cooked through and tender.

Transfer the beef rolls to a warmed serving dish and remove the string or thread. Keep hot. Strain the cooking liquid into a jug or pan, pressing down on the vegetables and flavourings with the back of a wooden spoon. Bring to the boil and adjust the seasonings if necessary.

Pour the sauce over the beef rolls, sprinkle over the parsley and serve at once.

4 Servings

FONDUE BOURGUIGNONNE
(Beef Fondue with Sauces)

Fondue is traditionally Swiss, but the French have adapted the original cheese idea and applied it to meat—and the result is as below. The beef is speared on special fondue forks and placed in the boiling oil until cooked to taste. The dips and sauces suggested here are just that, suggestions— any sauce or garnish may be used so long as it complements the meat.

	Metric/U.K.	U.S.
Medium onion, finely chopped	1	1
Large dessert apple, cored, finely chopped and sprinkled with a little tarragon vinegar	1	1
Large pickled gherkins, finely chopped	2	2
Capers, finely chopped	1 Tbs	1 Tbs
Chopped fresh herbs (chives, basil, parsley or chervil)	1 Tbs	1 Tbs
French mustard	4 Tbs	4 Tbs
Prepared horseradish sauce or relish	4 Tbs	4 Tbs
Aioli sauce or mayonnaise	125ml/4floz	½ cup
Fillet or rump steak	1kg/2lb	2lb
Vegetable oil	600ml/1 pint	2½ cups
TOMATO SAUCE Butter	25g/1oz	2 Tbs
Tomatoes, blanched, peeled and halved	3	3
Dried basil	1 tsp	1 tsp
Salt and pepper to taste		
Tomato purée (paste)	2 tsp	2 tsp

First make the tomato sauce. Melt the butter in a small saucepan. Add the tomatoes, basil and seasoning and simmer for 10 minutes, stirring occasionally, or until the tomatoes have pulped. Strain into a bowl, rubbing the tomatoes through with the back of a wooden spoon. Stir in the tomato purée (paste). Allow the mixture to cool completely, then transfer to a shallow serving dish. Set aside.

Put the onion, apple, gherkins, capers, herbs, mustard, horseradish and aioli or mayonnaise in small individual serving dishes.

Cut the beef into 2½cm/1in cubes and arrange them on a large serving dish.

Heat the oil in a saucepan until it reaches 190°C (375°F) on a deep-fat thermometer, or until a small cube of stale bread dropped into the oil turns golden brown in 40 seconds. Carefully pour the oil into a fondue pot.

Light the spirit burner and place the fondue pot over it. The oil is now ready for cooking the steak.

6 Servings

BOEUF BOURGUIGNON
(Beef Stew with Red Wine)

This dish, not surprisingly given its name, originated in the province of Burgundy where they produce a lot of wine and can afford to use large amounts of it in cooking! Its popularity,

however, has long since spread beyond its native province and it is now one of the two or three best-known examples of French cuisine both inside and outside France.

	Metric/U.K.	U.S.
Streaky (fatty) bacon, cut into strips	175g/6oz	6oz
Olive oil	1 Tbs	1 Tbs
Chuck or braising steak, cubed	1½kg/3lb	3lb
Carrot, sliced	1	1
Onion, sliced	1	1
Salt and pepper to taste		
Flour	25g/1oz	4 Tbs
Red wine	750ml/1¼ pts	3 cups
Beef stock	450ml/15floz	2 cups
Garlic cloves, crushed	3	3
Dried thyme	½ tsp	½ tsp
Bay leaf	1	1
Chopped parsley	2 Tbs	2 Tbs
VEGETABLES Butter	50g/2oz	4 Tbs
Vegetable oil	1½ Tbs	1½ Tbs
Small pickling or pearl onions	18	18
Beef stock or red wine	150ml/5floz	⅝ cup
Bouquet garni	1	1
Salt and pepper to taste		
Mushrooms, quartered	½kg/1lb	4 cups

Blanch the bacon strips in boiling water for 5 minutes, then dry on kitchen towels. Set aside.

Heat the oil in a large flameproof casserole. Add the bacon and fry until the strips are evenly browned. Transfer the strips to a plate.

Reheat the fat until it is very hot. Add the beef cubes and fry until they are evenly browned. Transfer the cubes to the plate with the bacon. Add the carrot and onion to the casserole and fry until they are soft. Pour off the fat from the casserole and return the beef and bacon to it. Season to taste, sprinkle over the flour and toss lightly with a wooden spoon.

Preheat the oven to warm 170°C (Gas Mark 3, 325°F).

Stir the wine, stock, garlic and herbs into the casserole and bring to the boil. Cover and put the casserole into the oven. Cook for 3½ to 4 hours, or until the meat is very tender.

Meanwhile, prepare the vegetables. Melt half the butter and half the oil in a frying-pan. Add the onions and fry until they are evenly browned. Pour in the stock or wine, bouquet garni and seasoning. Cover and simmer for 40 minutes, or until they are tender but still firm. Transfer to a plate. Discard the juices in the pan.

Add the remaining butter and oil to the pan. Add the mushrooms and fry for 5 minutes, or until they are cooked. Transfer to the onions.

Arrange the meat, onions and mushrooms on a serving dish and keep hot. Strain the casserole juice into a saucepan and boil rapidly until it has reduced and thickened. Pour over the meat and vegetables, and serve at once.

6-8 Servings

DAUBE DE BOEUF A LA PROVENCALE
(Beef Stew with Tomatoes, Mushrooms and Olives)

Daubes are a type of marinated beef stew found all over the southern part of France. They are quite economical to cook since marination tenderizes meat, which means that the cheapest type of stewing steak may be used. This is a local variation on the theme from Provence.

	Metric/U.K.	U.S.
Lean stewing steak, cubed	1½kg/3lb	3lb
Streaky (fatty) bacon, cut into strips	225g/8oz	8oz
Flour	125g/4oz	1 cup
Mushrooms, sliced	225g/8oz	2 cups
Tomatoes, blanched, peeled, seeded and chopped	700g/1½lb	1½lb
Garlic cloves, crushed	3	3
Grated orange rind	1 tsp	1 tsp
Chopped parsley	1 Tbs	1 Tbs
Bouquet garni	1	1
Beef stock	175ml/6floz	¾ cup
Black olives, stoned (pitted) and halved	12	12
MARINADE Dry white wine	300ml/10floz	1¼ cups

Daubes are a type of marinated stew very popular all over France but traditional to the southern part. Daube de Boeuf la Provençale is a superb variation on the theme.

151

	Metric/U.K.	U.S.
Brandy	50ml/2floz	¼ cup
Salt	2 tsp	2 tsp
Black peppercorns	1 tsp	1 tsp
Dried thyme	½ tsp	½ tsp
Bay leaf	1	1
Garlic cloves, crushed	2	2
Medium onions, thinly sliced	4	4
Medium carrots, sliced	4	4

Combine all the marinade ingredients in a large bowl and add the beef cubes. Set aside at room temperature for at least 8 hours (or overnight in the refrigerator), basting occasionally.

Blanch the bacon strips in boiling water for 5 minutes then dry on kitchen towels. Set aside.

Remove the beef cubes from the marinade and pat dry on kitchen towels. Strain the marinade into a bowl, reserving both liquid and vegetables. Discard the bay leaf.

Preheat the oven to warm 170°C (Gas Mark 3, 325°F).

Dip the beef cubes in the flour, shaking off any excess.

Arrange two or three bacon strips over the bottom of a large flameproof casserole. Spoon over a few of the marinated vegetables, then mushrooms and tomatoes. Arrange a layer of beef over the vegetables, and sprinkle with crushed garlic, orange rind and parsley. Add the bouquet garni. Continue making layers as before, ending with a layer of bacon. Pour over the beef stock and reserved marinade liquid, and scatter over the olives. Bring the liquid to the boil, then transfer to the oven. Braise for 4 hours, or until the meat is very tender.

Remove from the oven and skim any fat from the surface. Adjust the seasoning, discard the bouquet garni and serve at once.

6-8 Servings

ENTRECOTES AU POIVRE
(Steaks with Crushed Peppercorns)

	Metric/U.K.	U.S.
Black peppercorns	3 Tbs	3 Tbs
Butter	50g/2oz	4 Tbs
Entrecôte steaks, about 175g/6oz each	4	4
Brandy	2 Tbs	2 Tbs
Double (heavy) cream	150ml/5floz	⅝ cup

Put the peppercorns into a mortar and crush them coarsely with a pestle. Transfer them to a plate. Press the steaks into the crushed peppercorns, coating both sides and shaking off any excess.

Melt the butter in a large frying-pan. Add the steaks and fry for 2 minutes on each side over moderately high heat. Reduce the heat to moderately low and fry for a further 3 minutes on each side. This will give you rare steaks; double the cooking time for well-done steaks. Transfer the steaks to a large, warmed serving platter. Keep hot.

Add the brandy to the pan and stir well. Stir in the cream and cook for 3 minutes, stirring and scraping the bottom of the pan. Pour over the steaks and serve at once.

4 Servings

BOEUF EN CROUTE
(Fillet of Beef in Pastry, Called Beef Wellington)

This is one of the most spectacular dishes in all of haute cuisine *and although it takes a little care in preparation, the end result is more than worth the effort.*

	Metric/U.K.	U.S.
Puff pastry dough	575g/1¼lb	1¼lb
FILLING		
Fillet or côntrefilet of beef, with excess fat removed	1x1½kg/3lb	1x3lb
Brandy	1 Tbs	1 Tbs
Salt and pepper to taste		
Streaky (fatty) bacon	6 slices	6 slices
Pâté de foie gras	225g/8oz	8oz
Egg, lightly beaten	1	1
SAUCE		
Butter	75g/3oz	6 Tbs
Shallots, finely chopped	6	6
Beef stock	600ml/1 pint	2½ cups
Madeira	225ml/7floz	⅞ cup

Preheat the oven to very hot 230°F (Gas Mark 8, 450°F).

Rub the fillet all over with the brandy and

season with salt and pepper. Cover the top with the bacon slices and put the meat in the rack in a roasting pan. Put the pan into the oven and roast the meat for 20 minutes, if you want the meat to be rare, and 10 minutes longer if you prefer medium meat. Remove the pan from the oven and remove the meat from the pan. Discard the bacon and set the meat aside to cool to room temperature. When the meat has cooled, spread the pâté over the top and sides.

Reduce the oven temperature to hot 220°C (Gas Mark 7, 425°F).

Roll out the pastry dough to a rectangle about 45cm/18in x 30cm/12in by $\frac{1}{2}$cm/$\frac{1}{4}$in thick. Put the meat on the dough, top side down, with the long sides of the meat parallel to the long sides of the dough. Wrap the meat in the dough to make a neat parcel, trimming off any excess. Brush the joins with a little beaten egg and crimp to seal. Be careful not to wrap the meat too tightly because the pastry will shrink slightly during cooking.

Arrange the meat on a baking sheet, seam side down. Mark a criss-cross pattern on the top, then brush the top and sides with a little more beaten egg. Roll out the dough trimmings and use them to decorate the top of the parcel.

Put the sheet into the oven and bake the meat for 30 minutes, or until the pastry is golden brown.

Meanwhile, to make the sauce, melt a third of the butter in a saucepan. Add the shallots and fry until they are golden brown. Pour over the stock and 150ml/5floz ($\frac{5}{8}$ cup) of Madeira. Bring to the boil and boil for 30 minutes or until the liquid has reduced by about half. Strain the sauce into a bowl, then return to the saucepan and bring to the boil. Remove from the heat and stir in the remaining butter until it has melted, then the remaining Madeira. Transfer the sauce to a warmed sauceboat. Keep hot.

When the meat has finished cooking, turn off the oven and leave the meat in the oven for 15 minutes.

Remove and serve carved into thin slices. Accompany the meat with the sauce.

8-12 Servings

One of the most elegant and famous of haute cuisine *dishes, Boeuf en Croûte is equally popular outside France, where it is sometimes called Beef Wellington.*

NAVARIN PRINTANIER
(Mutton Stew with Vegetables)

The secret of this French classic is in the vegetables—to be really authentic, fresh young spring vegetables should be used. If mutton is difficult to obtain, lamb may be substituted but needs to cook for only an hour to an hour and a quarter altogether.

Noisettes are small, succulent lamb chops with the bones removed, and they are a feature of haute cuisine. In Noisettes d'Agneau à la Clamart, they are served over small pastry cases filled with fresh, puréed garden peas.

	Metric/U.K.	U.S.
Salt pork, diced	125g/4oz	4oz
Boned breast of mutton, trimmed of excess fat and cubed	700g/1½lb	1½lb
Boned shoulder of mutton, trimmed of excess fat and cubed	700g/1½lb	1½lb
Soft brown sugar	2 Tbs	2 Tbs
Salt and pepper to taste		
Flour	½ Tbs	½ Tbs
Medium tomatoes, blanched, peeled, seeded and chopped	6	6
Chicken stock	1¼l/2 pints	5 cups
Bouquet garni	1	1
Butter	50g/2oz	¼ cup
Small potatoes, peeled	12	12
Small turnips, whole	6	6
Small carrots, whole or halved	6	6

Small pickling or pearl		
onions	12	12
Sugar	½ Tbs	½ Tbs

Fry the salt pork in a large heavy-bottomed saucepan until it resembles small croûtons and has rendered most of its fat. Transfer the salt pork to a plate.

Add the meat to the pan and fry until it is lightly and evenly browned. Transfer the meat to the salt pork.

Remove the pan from the heat and pour off about half of the fat. Return the meat cubes and salt pork to the pan and sprinkle over the sugar and seasoning. Cook for 3 minutes, stirring constantly, or until the sugar has caramelized. Add the flour and cook for a further 3 minutes, stirring constantly. Stir in the tomatoes, stock and bouquet garni, and bring to the boil. Cover and simmer for 1 hour.

Meanwhile, prepare the vegetables. Melt the butter in a large frying-pan. Add the vegetables and fry until the onions are golden brown. Stir in the sugar and fry for a further 3 minutes or until it has dissolved. Remove the pan from the heat and transfer the vegetables to the saucepan containing the meat. Skim off any fat from the surface. Cook for 25 minutes, or until the meat and vegetables are cooked through and tender.

Remove from the heat and skim any fat from the surface of the stew. Discard the bouquet garni and transfer the stew to a large, warmed serving dish.

Serve at once.

6 Servings

SAUTE D'AGNEAU
(Lamb Stew)

	Metric/U.K.	U.S.
Olive oil	3 Tbs	3 Tbs
Lean stewing lamb, cubed	1kg/2lb	2lb
Celery stalk, chopped	1	1
Onion, finely chopped	1	1
Red wine	125ml/4floz	½ cup
Beef stock	250ml/8floz	1 cup
Cornflour (cornstarch), blended with 2 Tbs water	1 Tbs	1 Tbs
Tomato purée (paste)	2 Tbs	2 Tbs

Salt and pepper to taste		
Grated lemon rind	1 tsp	1 tsp
Button mushrooms, sliced	125g/4oz	1 cup

Heat 2 tablespoons of the oil in a flameproof casserole. Add the lamb cubes and fry quickly over moderately high heat until they are deeply and evenly browned. Transfer the meat to a plate and keep warm.

Reduce the heat to moderate and add the remaining oil to the casserole. Add the vegetables and fry until they are soft. Pour over the wine and stock, then stir in the cornflour (cornstarch) mixture and bring to the boil. Return the meat to the pan and stir in the remaining ingredients. Cover the casserole and cook for 15 minutes. (If you prefer your meat well done, increase the final cooking time by 10 minutes.)

Remove from the heat and serve at once.

4 Servings

NOISETTES D'AGNEAU A LA CLAMART
(Boned Lamb Chops in Pastry Cases with Puréed Peas)

	Metric/U.K.	U.S.
Shortcrust pastry	125g/4oz	4oz
Salt	1 tsp	1 tsp
Fresh peas, weighed after shelling	½kg/1lb	2 cups
Butter	40g/1½oz	3 Tbs
Lamb noisettes	8	8

Preheat the oven to fairly hot 200°C (Gas Mark 6, 400°F).

Roll out the pastry dough to a circle about ½cm/¼in thick. Using a 7½cm/3in pastry cutter, cut the dough into circles and use them to line eight well-greased patty tins. Cover with foil and weigh down with beans or rice. Put the tins into the oven and bake blind for 10 minutes. Remove from the oven and remove the beans or rice and foil. Bake the pastry cases for a further 5 minutes, or until they are cooked through and golden brown. Remove the tins from the oven and allow the tartlets to cool in the tins. Turn off the oven. Cover the tartlets with aluminium foil or waxed paper and return to the oven to keep warm while you

Cotelettes d'Agneau au Concombre—elegant enough for the most sophisticated dinner party, simple enough for a quiet supper at home.

prepare the remaining garnish.

Cook the peas in boiling, salted water for 15 to 20 minutes or until they are tender. Drain in a colander and either push them through a strainer using the back of a wooden spoon, or purée them in a blender. Transfer the purée to a saucepan and add 1 tablespoon of the butter. Place the pan over low heat and cook, stirring constantly, until the purée is smooth and hot. Remove from the heat. Remove the pastry cases from the oven and spoon equal portions of the purée into each one. Return to the oven to keep warm while you fry the noisettes.

Melt the remaining butter in a frying-pan. Add the noisettes and fry them for 4 to 6 minutes on each side, or until they are tender but still slightly pink inside. Remove the pan from the heat and transfer the noisettes to a plate.

Transfer the pastry cases to a warmed serving dish. Arrange the noisettes on top of the cases.

Serve at once.

4 Servings

COTELETTES D'AGNEAU AU CONCOMBRE
(Lamb Cutlets with Cucumber and Onion)

	Metric/U.K.	U.S.
Lamb cutlets	8	8
Seasoned flour (flour with salt and pepper to taste)	50g/2oz	½ cup
Egg, lightly beaten	1	1
Dry breadcrumbs	125g/4oz	1⅓ cups
Cucumbers, peeled and cut into chunks	1½	1½
Spring onions (scallions), with 5cm/2in of green tops	18	18
Butter	50g/2oz	4 Tbs
Salt and pepper to taste		
Chopped mint	1 tsp	1 tsp
Vegetable oil	75ml/3floz	⅜ cup
MOUSSELINE SAUCE		
Egg yolks	3	3

Butter, melted	75g/3oz	6 Tbs
Lemon juice	2 Tbs	2 Tbs
Salt and pepper to taste		
Double (heavy) cream	50ml/2floz	¼ cup

To make the sauce, half-fill a saucepan with water and bring to the boil. Reduce the heat to very low. Put the egg yolks and 1 tablespoon of the butter into a heatproof bowl and set the bowl over the pan. Using a wooden spoon, gradually work the butter into the egg yolks. Continue stirring for about 5 minutes, or until the yolks begin to thicken. Stir in the lemon juice. Add the remaining butter, a tablespoon at a time, stirring well after each addition. The butter should be added very slowly. Be careful not to let the bowl become too hot or the egg yolks will curdle. When all the butter has been incorporated and the sauce is smooth and thick, remove the bowl from the pan. Stir in seasoning and cream and set aside.

Dip the cutlets first in the seasoned flour, then in the egg and finally in the breadcrumbs, shaking off any excess. Set aside.

Put the cucumbers and spring onions (scallions) in a large bowl and pour over enough boiling water to cover completely. Leave for 1 minute, then drain thoroughly.

Melt the butter in a saucepan. Add the spring onions (scallions), cucumber and seasoning. Cover and simmer the vegetables for 6 minutes, or until the cucumbers are tender. Remove from the heat and stir in the mint.

Heat the oil in a large frying-pan. Add the cutlets to the pan and fry for 3 to 5 minutes on each side or until they are cooked through.

Two minutes before the cutlets are cooked, replace the bowl with the sauce over the hot water and reheat gently, taking care not to bring to the boil. Remove from the pan and pour into a warmed sauceboat.

Arrange the cutlets on a warmed serving dish standing upright to form a crown. Pile the cucumber and spring onion (scallion) mixture in the centre and serve with the sauce.

4 Servings

CARRE DE PORC AU GUINIEVRE
(Loin of Pork with Juniper Berries)

Juniper berries are quite widely used in French cooking, especially with pork, ham and sauer-kraut. Their addition to this simple dish adds a

piquancy and spice to what otherwise would be somewhat bland.

Carré de Porc au Guinièvre, lean tender pork loin flavoured with juniper berries.

	Metric/U.K.	U.S.
Boned loin of pork, trimmed of excess fat	1x2kg/4lb	1x4lb
Garlic cloves, thinly sliced	2	2
Juniper berriers, coarsely crushed	12	12
Salt and pepper to taste		
Beef stock	300ml/10floz	1¼ cups
Dry white wine	150ml/5floz	⅝ cup

Preheat the oven to fairly hot 190°C (Gas Mark 5, 375°F).

Make small incisions all over the pork and insert the garlic slices. Sprinkle with the juniper berries and seasoning and roll up Swiss (jelly) roll style, securing it at 2½cm/1in intervals with string.

Put the meat on a rack in a roasting pan and put the pan into the oven. Roast for 2 to 2½ hours, or 30 to 35 minutes per half kilo (pound), depending on the thickness of the cut, or until the meat is cooked through and tender.

Remove the pan from the oven. Remove the pork from the pan. Wrap in foil and return to the turned-off oven to keep hot while you make the sauce.

Pour off the fat from the roasting pan. Scrape up any brown bits that have stuck to the bottom and sides. Add the stock and wine and bring to the boil, stirring constantly. Boil for 8 to 10 minutes, or until the liquid has reduced and thickened slightly. Pour into a warmed sauceboat.

Remove the pork from the oven and discard the foil. Arrange the pork on a warmed serving dish and serve at once, accompanied by the sauce.

8-10 Servings

COTES DE PORC CHARCUTIERE
(Pork Chops Braised in Piquant Sauce)

	Metric/U.K.	U.S.
Olive oil	50ml/2floz	¼ cup
Large pork chops	6	6
Medium onions, thinly sliced	3	3
Flour	1 Tbs	1 Tbs
Dry white wine	250ml/8floz	1 cup
Beef stock	125ml/4floz	½ cup
Tomato purée (paste)	1 Tbs	1 Tbs
Dried sage	½ tsp	½ tsp
Dried rosemary	½ tsp	½ tsp
Garlic cloves, crushed	2	2
Salt and pepper to taste		
French mustard	1½ tsp	1½ tsp
Medium gherkin, sliced	1	1
Cornflour (cornstarch), blended with 1 Tbs water (optional)	1 tsp	1 tsp
Chopped parsley	2 Tbs	2 Tbs

Preheat the oven to warm 170°C (Gas Mark 3, 325°F).

Heat the oil in a flameproof casserole. Add the chops and brown on all sides. (You may have to do this in batches.) As the chops brown, transfer them to a heated platter.

Add the onions to the casserole, reduce the heat to low and simmer until they are soft. Stir in the flour until it has dissolved.

Pour the wine and stock into the casserole and stir in the tomato purée (paste), herbs, garlic and seasoning. Bring to the boil, cover and simmer the sauce for 5 minutes. Stir in the mustard, then return the chops to the casserole, basting them well with the sauce. Cover and put the casserole into the oven. Braise for 45 to 55 minutes, or until the chops are cooked through and tender.

Transfer the chops to a warmed serving dish. Put the casserole over the heat and bring to the boil. Cook for 2 to 3 minutes, then stir in the sliced gherkin. Taste and adjust the seasoning if necessary. (If you prefer a thicker sauce, add the cornflour [cornstarch] mixture, stirring until it has dissolved, then cook the sauce for a further 2 to 3 minutes.)

Pour the sauce over the chops, sprinkle over the parsley and serve at once.

6 Servings

TOURTE DE PORC
(Pork Pie)

	Metric/U.K.	U.S.
Puff pastry dough	350g/12oz	12oz
Egg yolk, lightly beaten	1	1
FILLING		
Lean minced (ground) pork	1kg/2lb	2lb
Brandy	50ml/2floz	¼ cup
Butter	15g/½oz	1 Tbs
Vegetable oil	2 Tbs	2 Tbs
Shallots, finely chopped	2	2
Garlic clove, crushed	1	1
Chopped fresh sage	1 Tbs	1 Tbs
Chopped parsley	1 Tbs	1 Tbs
Chopped fresh chervil	1 Tbs	1 Tbs
Salt and pepper to taste		
Cornflour (cornstarch), blended with 1 Tbs water	1 Tbs	1 Tbs

First prepare the filling. Put the pork into a large bowl and pour over the brandy. Set aside to marinate for 1 hour.

Meanwhile, melt the butter with the oil in

The French version of pork pie, Tourte de Porc. It contains a delicious mixture of minced (ground) pork, brandy and herbs.

One of the simplest yet most popular veal stews in the French cooking repertoire, Blanquette de Veau.

a large frying-pan. Add the shallots and garlic and fry until the shallots are soft. Add the pork and brandy and fry, stirring frequently, until the pork loses its pinkness. Stir in the herbs and seasoning and cook, stirring occasionally, for 15 minutes. Remove from the heat and stir in the cornflour (cornstarch) mixture.

Preheat the oven to hot 220°C (Gas Mark 7, 425°F).

Divide the dough in half and roll out one-half into a circle large enough to line a 23cm/9in pie plate. Press gently into the bottom and sides of the plate and trim off any excess. Spoon the filling into the centre, doming it up slightly.

Roll out the remaining dough in the same way and place it over the filling so that it covers it completely. Trim the edges, then crimp the edges together to seal. Cut a large cross in the centre. Roll out the trimmings and use them to decorate the top of the pie. Brush the top of the dough with the beaten egg yolk.

Put the plate into the oven and bake for 5 minutes. Reduce the heat to moderate 180°C (Gas Mark 4, 350°F) and bake for a further 30 minutes or until the pastry is golden brown. Remove from the oven and serve at once.

4-6 Servings

BLANQUETTE DE VEAU
(Veal in Cream Sauce)

	Metric/U.K.	U.S.
Stewing veal, cubed	700g/1½lb	1½lb
Medium onions, each studded with 2 cloves	2	2
Medium carrots, quartered	2	2
Bouquet garni	1	1
Salt and pepper to taste		
Butter	40g/1½oz	3 Tbs
Flour	40g/1½oz	⅓ cup
Single (light) cream	150ml/5floz	⅝ cup
Egg yolks	2	2
White bread, toasted and cut into triangles	4 slices	4 slices
Lemon slices (to garnish)		
Parsley sprigs (to garnish)		

Put the veal cubes into a saucepan and add just enough water to cover. Bring to the boil, then simmer for 2 minutes. Skim off any scum from the surface. Add the vegetables, bouquet

garni and seasoning and cover the pan. Simmer for 1½ to 2 hours, or until the meat is cooked through and tender.

Transfer the meat and carrots to a warmed serving dish. Remove the cloves from the onions and quarter them. Add to the meat. Cover the mixture and keep hot while you make the sauce. Strain the cooking liquid into a bowl and reserve about 725ml/1¼ pints (3 cups) for the sauce.

Melt the butter in a saucepan. Remove from the heat and stir in the flour to form a smooth paste. Gradually stir in the reserved stock. Return to the heat and bring to the boil. Cook the sauce for 2 to 3 minutes, stirring constantly, or until it is thick and smooth. Remove from the heat.

Combine the cream and egg yolks in a small bowl. Gradually stir about 4 tablespoons of the hot sauce into the mixture. Return the mixture to the saucepan, whisking it in, a little at a time, until the sauce is thoroughly blended. Replace the pan over low heat and simmer until the sauce is hot but not boiling.

Pour the sauce over the veal and garnish with the toast triangles, lemon slices and parsley sprigs. Serve at once.

4 Servings

TENDRONS DE VEAU AUX EPINARDS
(Breast of Veal with Spinach)

This inexpensive country dish utilizes two of France's favourite vegetables, spinach and sorrel. If you find it difficult to obtain fresh sorrel, use all spinach instead.

	Metric/U.K.	U.S.
Breast of veal, trimmed of excess fat and cubed	1kg/2lb	2lb
Seasoned flour (flour with salt and pepper to taste)	50g/2oz	½ cup
Eggs, beaten	2	2
Cheddar or Gruyère cheese, grated	125g/4oz	1 cup
Spinach, chopped	1kg/2lb	2lb
Sorrel, chopped	225g/8oz	8oz
Sufficient vegetable oil for deep-frying		

Coat the meat cubes first in the seasoned flour, then in the eggs and finally in the cheese, shaking off any excess.

Put the spinach and sorrel into a saucepan

A simple, economical veal stew with nutritious spinach, that's Tendrons de Veau aux Epinards.

and gently cook for 5 to 8 minutes, or until they are cooked and tender. (You need not add water—there will be sufficient moisture clinging to the leaves to provide enough for cooking.) Remove the pan from the heat and drain the vegetables, pressing down on them with a plate to extract all the liquid. Chop the vegetables and arrange them around the edge of a warmed serving dish. Keep hot while you cook the meat.

Fill a deep-frying pan about one-third full with oil and heat it until it reaches 180°C (350°F) on a deep-fat thermometer, or until a small cube of stale bread dropped into the oil turns golden in 55 seconds.

Carefully lower the meat cubes into the oil, a few at a time, and fry for 6 to 8 minutes, or until they are golden brown and crisp. Drain on kitchen towels and, when all the cubes have been cooked, transfer to the centre of the serving dish. Serve at once.

4 Servings

VEAU MARENGO
(Veal Cooked with Mushrooms and Wine)

Legend has it that a version of this recipe (using chicken) was created by Napoleon's cook just after the Battle of Marengo—hence the rather unusual name.

	Metric/U.K.	U.S.
Lean stewing veal, cubed	1½kg/3lb	3lb
Salt and pepper to taste		
Butter	75g/3oz	6 Tbs
Vegetable oil	50ml/2floz	¼ cup
Medium onions, thinly sliced	2	2
Garlic cloves, crushed	2	2
Dry white wine	125ml/4floz	½ cup
Veal or chicken stock	125ml/4floz	½ cup
Bouquet garni	1	1
Canned peeled tomatoes	225g/8oz	8oz
Tomato purée (paste)	65g/2½oz	2½oz
Paprika	1 tsp	1 tsp
Pickling or pearl onions	12	12
Button mushrooms, sliced	350g/12oz	3 cups
Beurre manié (page 192)	1 Tbs	1 Tbs

Rub the veal cubes with salt and pepper.

Melt 50g/2oz (4 tablespoons) of the butter with the oil in a large flameproof casserole. Add the onions and garlic and fry until they are soft. Stir in the veal and fry until the cubes are evenly browned. Pour over the wine and stock and stir in the bouquet garni, tomatoes and can juice, the tomato purée (paste) and paprika. Bring to the boil, reduce the heat to low and simmer the mixture for 1½ hours. Add the onions and simmer for a further 30 minutes or until the meat is cooked through.

Meanwhile, melt the remaining butter in a frying-pan. Add the mushrooms and cook for 3 minutes, stirring frequently. Transfer the mushrooms to a warmed serving dish. When the veal is cooked, transfer the cubes and onions to the serving dish. Keep warm while you finish the sauce.

Remove the casserole from the heat and strain the contents into a saucepan, pressing down on the vegetables and flavourings with the back of a wooden spoon. Skim any scum from the surface of the cooking liquid and bring to the boil. Boil for about 10 minutes, or until the liquid has reduced by about a third. Stir in the beurre manié, a little at a time, and cook the sauce for 2 to 3 minutes, stirring constantly, or until it has thickened and is smooth.

Pour the sauce over the meat and vegetables and serve at once.

6 Servings

ESCALOPES DE VEAU CORDON BLEU

	Metric/U.K.	U.S.
Cooked ham	4 thin slices	4 thin slices
Gruyère cheese	4 thin slices	4 thin slices
Veal escalopes, pounded thin	8	8
Pepper to taste		
Dried marjoram	½ tsp	½ tsp
Flour	25g/1oz	¼ cup
Eggs, lightly beaten	2	2
Dry white breadcrumbs	50g/2oz	⅔ cup
Butter	125g/4oz	8 Tbs
Lemon slices	4	4

Napoleon's cook is reputed to have created a version of this classic on the battlefield of Marengo, hence Veau Marengo. Its a delicious combination of lean veal, white wine, tomatoes, mushrooms and onions.

163

Put a slice of ham and a slice of cheese on four of the escalopes. Cover with the remaining escalopes to make a 'sandwich'. Pound the edges of the escalopes with a mallet to seal them.

Sprinkle the veal with pepper and the marjoram, then dip them first in the flour, then in the eggs and finally in the breadcrumbs, shaking off any excess. Wrap in greaseproof or waxed paper and chill in the refrigerator for 30 minutes.

Melt the butter in a large frying-pan. Add the escalopes and fry them for 3 minutes on each side. Reduce the heat to low and cook, turning occasionally, for a further 15 minutes, or until the 'sandwiches' are cooked through.

Transfer to a warmed serving dish, garnish with the lemon slices and serve at once.

4 Servings

Cassoulet is one of the great dishes from Languedoc in south western France, Cassoulet de Gascogne is a somewhat simplified but equally tasty version of the classic, from neighbouring Gascony.

ROGNONS DE DIJON
(Kidneys with Mustard Sauce)

	Metric/U.K.	U.S.
Butter	25g/1oz	2 Tbs
Veal kidneys, cleaned and cut into pieces	700g/1½lb	1½lb
Flour	2 Tbs	2 Tbs
Single (light) cream	300ml/10floz	1¼ cups
French mustard	2-3 Tbs	2-3 Tbs
Salt and pepper to taste		
Chopped parsley	6 Tbs	6 Tbs

Melt the butter in a large frying-pan. Add the kidney pieces and fry until they are deeply and evenly browned. Transfer them to a plate.

Remove the pan from the heat and stir in the flour to form a smooth paste. Gradually stir in the cream and mustard and return the pan to the heat. Cook the sauce for 2 to 3 minutes, stirring constantly, or until it is smooth and thick. Stir in the seasoning and parsley. Return the kidneys to the pan and simmer for 5 minutes, or until they are cooked through and tender.

Transfer the mixture to a warmed serving dish and serve at once.

4-6 Servings

FOIE DE VEAU AU VIN BLANC
(Calf's Liver in White Wine)

	Metric/U.K.	U.S.
Calf's liver, thinly sliced	700g/1½lb	1½lb
Seasoned flour (flour with salt and pepper to taste)	50g/2oz	½ cup
Butter	50g/2oz	4 Tbs
Dry white wine	250ml/8floz	1 cup
Single (light) cream	2 Tbs	2 Tbs
Salt and pepper to taste		

Coat the liver slices in the seasoned flour, shaking off any excess.

Melt the butter in a large frying-pan. Add the liver slices and fry for 1 minute on each side. Pour over the wine and bring to the boil. Reduce the heat to low and simmer for 2 minutes, or until the liver is cooked through and tender. Transfer the liver to a warmed serving dish.

Stir the cream and seasoning into the pan and heat gently until hot but not boiling. Pour the sauce over the liver slices and serve at once.

4 Servings

CASSOULET GASCOGNE

(Bean Stew with Sausages and Garlic and Parsley Butter)

	Metric/U.K.	U.S.
Salt pork, cubed	½kg/1lb	1lb
Dried white haricot (dried white) beans, soaked overnight in cold water and drained	½kg/1lb	2⅔ cups
Bouquet garni	1	1
Salt and pepper to taste		
Smoked pork sausages (Italian or Polish), cut into 2½cm/1in pieces	½kg/1lb	1lb
GASCONY BUTTER		
Salt	½ tsp	½ tsp
Garlic cloves	8	8
Butter	75g/3oz	6 Tbs
French mustard	1 tsp	1 tsp
Chopped parsley	2 Tbs	2 Tbs

Preheat the oven to moderate 180°C (Gas Mark 4, 350°F).

Put the salt pork and beans in a casserole and pour over just enough boiling water to cover. Add the bouquet garni and cover. Put the casserole into the oven and cook for 3 hours, or until the beans are tender. Remove from the oven and add seasoning to taste and the sausage pieces. Return to the oven to cook, uncovered, for a further 30 minutes.

Meanwhile, to make the butter, half-fill a saucepan with water. Add the salt and garlic cloves and bring to the boil. Boil for 10 minutes. Transfer the cloves to a mortar and pound or mash them, with the butter, to form a smooth paste. Stir in the mustard and parsley. Remove the casserole from the oven.

Strain off any liquid and remove the bouquet garni. Stir in the garlic butter and serve.

4 Servings

SAUCISSES A LA PUREE DE CELERI RAVE

(Sausages with Puréed Celeriac)

	Metric/U.K.	U.S.
Water	250ml/8floz	1 cup
Salt and pepper to taste		
Dried marjoram	½ tsp	½ tsp
Grated lemon rind	½ tsp	½ tsp
Potatoes, chopped	½kg/1lb	1lb
Celeriac, sliced	½kg/1lb	1lb
Onion, chopped	1	1
Sausages	4-8	4-8
Hot milk	50ml/2floz	¼ cup
Cheddar or Gruyère cheese, grated	75g/3oz	¾ cup

Put the water, seasoning, marjoram and lemon rind into a saucepan and bring to the boil. Add the potatoes, celeriac and onion and reduce the heat to low. Simmer for 20 to 25 minutes, or until the vegetables are cooked through and tender.

Preheat the grill (broiler) to moderate. Arrange the sausages in the lined rack of the grill (broiler) pan and grill (broil) for 6 to 10 minutes, or until they are cooked through.

Drain the vegetables, then purée them in a blender, or rub them through a strainer into a bowl, using the back of a wooden spoon. Stir the hot milk and cheese into the vegetable mixture and beat well until the cheese has melted and the ingredients are thoroughly blended.

Spoon the mixture into a warmed serving dish and top with the sausages. Serve at once.

2-4 Servings

The French touch with sausages is amply demonstrated in this rustic Saucisses à la Purée de Celeri Rave.

165

Poultry and Game

FRICASSEE DE POULET
(Chicken, Tomato and Mushroom Stew)

In French cooking, a fricassée is simply a white meat stew, cooked in white stock or sauce, and although this version is chicken, lamb and veal are also often cooked in this way.

	Metric/U.K.	U.S.
Chicken, skinned and cut into serving pieces	1x2½kg/5lb	1x5lb
Seasoned flour (flour with salt and pepper to taste)	50g/2oz	½ cup
Vegetable oil	50ml/2floz	¼ cup
Chicken stock	450ml/15floz	2 cups
Cornflour (cornstarch), blended with 1 Tbs water	1½ tsp	1½ tsp
Bay leaf	1	1
Garlic clove, crushed	1	1
Medium tomatoes, blanched, peeled and chopped	6	6
Small button mushrooms, sliced	225g/8oz	2 cups
Egg yolks	2	2
Double (heavy) cream	150ml/5floz	⅝ cup
Paprika	½ tsp	½ tsp

Coat the chicken pieces in the seasoned flour, shaking off any excess.

Heat the oil in a large saucepan. Add the chicken pieces and fry until they are deeply and evenly browned. Stir in the stock, cornflour (cornstarch) mixture, bay leaf and garlic, and bring to the boil.

Reduce the heat to low, cover the pan and simmer for 40 minutes. Stir in the tomatoes and mushrooms and simmer for a further 20 minutes. Remove the bay leaf.

Transfer the chicken pieces to a warmed serving dish.

Combine the egg yolks and cream together. Stir about 4 tablespoons of the chicken cooking

Fricassée de Poulet is a classic stew of chicken, tomatoes and mushrooms.

liquid into the mixture, then pour the mixture into the saucepan. Simmer gently, stirring constantly, for 3 to 5 minutes, or until the sauce thickens slightly. Take care not to let the sauce boil, or it will curdle.

Pour the sauce over the chicken pieces, sprinkle over the paprika and serve at once.

6 Servings

POULET VALLEE D'AUGE
(Chicken with Calvados in Cream)

Normandy is the home of the French dairy industry and also of Calvados, a sort of brandy made from apples, so the two types of ingredients are often incorporated into the food of the region as here.

	Metric/U.K.	U.S.
Butter	50g/2oz	4 Tbs
Roasting chicken	1x1½kg/3lb	1x3lb
Calvados (or brandy if you prefer)	50ml/2floz	¼ cup
Shallots, finely chopped	2	2
Celery stalk, chopped	1	1
Large dessert apple, peeled, cored and chopped	1	1
Streaky (fatty) bacon	50g/2oz	2oz
Dried sage	½ tsp	½ tsp
Salt and pepper to taste		
Dry cider or apple juice	300ml/10floz	1¼ cups
Egg yolks	2	2
Double (heavy) cream	75ml/3floz	⅜ cup

Preheat the oven to warm 170°C (Gas Mark 3, 325°F).

Melt the butter in a large flameproof casserole. Add the chicken and fry until it is evenly browned. Remove from the heat. Warm the Calvados or brandy, pour over the chicken and ignite. When the flames have died down, stir in the vegetables, apple, bacon, sage and seasoning.

Return to the heat and fry the vegetables until they are soft. Pour over the cider or apple juice and bring to the boil. Transfer the casserole to the oven and cook for 1 hour, or until the chicken is cooked through.

Remove the chicken from the casserole and transfer to a warmed serving dish.

When Rossini became tired of being a musical prodigy he turned to cooking and one of his 'cooking' friends was the great French chef Auguste Escoffier, who created Suprèmes de Volailles Rossini in his honour. It is a stunning mixture of boned chicken breasts with pâté and a Madeira-based sauce.

Strain the cooking liquid into a small saucepan, pressing down on the vegetables and bacon with the back of a wooden spoon to extract all the juice. Boil rapidly until the sauce has reduced by about one-third.

Beat the egg yolks and cream together, then gradually stir in the sauce. Return the sauce to the saucepan and simmer gently until it is hot but not boiling. When the sauce has thickened, pour a little over the chicken and the remainder into a warmed sauceboat. Serve the chicken at once, accompanied by the sauce.

4 Servings

POULET A L'ESTRAGON
(Chicken with Tarragon)

This is one of the classics of French country cuisine. If at all possible, fresh tarragon should be used—the taste will not be nearly so delicate with the dried variety.

	Metric/U.K.	U.S.
Butter, softened	125g/4oz	8 Tbs
Salt and pepper to taste		
Chopped fresh tarragon	4 Tbs	4 Tbs
Roasting chicken	1x2½kg/5lb	1x5lb
Tarragon sprigs	6	6

Preheat the oven to fairly hot 190°C (Gas Mark 5, 375°F).

Combine the butter, seasoning and chopped tarragon and beat until they form a smooth paste. Stuff half the mixture inside the cavity of the chicken and close with trussing thread or a skewer.

Put the chicken into a roasting pan, then spread the remaining butter mixture over the chicken, particularly over the breast area. Put the pan into the oven and roast for 30 minutes, basting occasionally. Turn the chicken over on to the other side and return to the oven to roast for a further 30 minutes, basting occasionally.

Reduce the oven temperature to moderate

180°C (Gas Mark 4, 350°F). Turn the chicken on to its back and baste well with the melted butter. Roast for a further 30 minutes, basting well, or until the chicken is cooked through and tender.

Remove from the oven and transfer the chicken to a warmed serving dish. Pour the cooking juices over the chicken, garnish with the tarragon sprigs and serve at once.

6 Servings

POULET BONNE FEMME
(Chicken Casserole with Vegetables)

Bonne femme in French means 'good wife' and obviously (in France at least!) the function of a 'good' wife is very much wrapped up with the art of producing good cooking, economically and with little apparent effort. This dish fully merits the description, being economical, unbelievably good to eat—and a nourishingly balanced meal.

	Metric/U.K.	U.S.
Chicken	1x2kg/4lb	1x4lb
Salt and pepper to taste		
Butter	50g/2oz	4 Tbs
Pickling or pearl onions	700g/1½lb	1½lb
Small new potatoes, scrubbed	700g/1½lb	1½lb
Lean bacon, chopped	6 slices	6 slices
Bouquet garni	1	1

Preheat the oven to moderate 180°C (Gas Mark 4, 350°F).

Rub the chicken, inside and out, with salt and pepper.

Melt the butter in a large flameproof casserole. Add the chicken and fry until it is evenly browned. Remove from the casserole. Add the onions, potatoes and bacon and fry for 10 minutes, shaking the casserole frequently so that the bacon does not stick to the bottom.

Return the chicken to the casserole and add seasoning to taste and the bouquet garni. Cover and put into the oven. Cook for 1 hour, or until the chicken is cooked through and tender.

Remove from the oven and remove the bouquet garni. Transfer the chicken to a warmed serving dish and surround with the vegetables and bacon. Serve at once.

4 Servings

SUPREMES DE VOLAILLE ROSSINI
(Boned Chicken Breasts with Pâté)

Auguste Escoffier, by common consent, is one of the two or three most important figures in French cuisine. He lived on into the first years of the 20th century but most of his great masterpieces were created during the Belle Epoque of late 19th century Paris. His abiding interest in music is illustrated in this delicate recipe, dedicated to the Italian composer and chef, Rossini.

	Metric/U.K.	U.S.
Chicken breasts, skinned and boned	6	6
Salt and pepper to taste		
Lemon juice	1 Tbs	1 Tbs
Butter	75g/3oz	6 Tbs
Pâté de foie gras, cut into 6 slices	225g/8oz	8oz
SAUCE		
Medium onion, thinly sliced	1	1
Medium carrot, thinly sliced	1	1
Lean cooked ham, finely chopped	50g/2oz	2oz
Chopped parsley	2 Tbs	2 Tbs
Beef stock	300ml/10floz	1¼ cups
Madeira	50ml/2floz	¼ cup
Beurre manié (page 192)	1 Tbs	1 Tbs

Rub the breasts with salt, pepper and lemon juice.

Melt the butter in a large, deep frying-pan. Add the breasts and fry for 7 to 10 minutes on each side, or until they are cooked through and tender. Transfer the breasts to a warmed serving dish and keep hot while you make the sauce.

Pour off all but 2 tablespoons of the butter. Add the onion, carrot, ham and parsley and fry until the onion is soft. Pour in the stock and Madeira, and bring to the boil, stirring frequently. Strain the liquid into a saucepan, rubbing the vegetables and ham through with the back of a wooden spoon. Return the pan to the heat and bring to the boil. Reduce the heat to low and stir in the beurre manié, a little at a time, until the sauce thickens and is smooth.

Top each chicken breast with a slice of pâté

and pour half the sauce over the top. Pour the remaining sauce into a warmed sauceboat and serve with the meat.

6 Servings

CANETON AUX NAVETS
(Braised Duckling with Turnips)

	Metric/U.K.	U.S.
Duckling, oven-ready and with the giblets reserved	1x2½kg/5lb	1x5lb
Salt and pepper to taste		
Butter	75g/3oz	6 Tbs
Dry white wine	250ml/8floz	1 cup
Duck stock, made with the reserved giblets	350ml/12floz	1½ cups
Bouquets garnis	2	2
Pickling or pearl onions	16	16
Soft brown sugar	2 tsp	2 tsp
Small white turnips, quartered	1kg/2lb	2lb
Lemon juice	½ tsp	½ tsp
Cornflour (cornstarch), blended with 2 Tbs water	2 Tbs	2 Tbs
Chopped parsley	1 Tbs	1 Tbs

Preheat the oven to hot 220°C (Gas Mark 7, 425°F).

Rub the duck all over with salt and pepper.

Melt a third of the butter in a large flame-proof casserole. Add the duck and fry until it is evenly browned. Pour over the wine and stock, and add the bouquets garnis and seasoning. Bring to the boil, then transfer the casserole to the oven. Braise the duck for 30 minutes.

Meanwhile, melt another third of the butter in a frying-pan. Add the onions and half the sugar and fry gently for 5 minutes. Transfer the onions to a plate. Melt the remaining butter in the pan and add the turnips and remaining sugar. Fry gently until the turnips are evenly

A succulent, economical country dish—Caneton aux Navets.

browned. Transfer the turnips to the onions.

Reduce the oven temperature to warm 170°C (Gas Mark 3, 325°F). Arrange the vegetables around the duck, cover and return the casserole to the oven. Braise for a further 1 to 1¼ hours, or until the duck is cooked through and tender. Transfer the duck to a warmed serving dish and untruss. Transfer the onions and turnips to the dish and arrange them decoratively around the duck. Keep hot while you make the sauce.

Strain the cooking liquid into a saucepan and bring to the boil. Boil rapidly for 5 minutes, or until it has reduced by about a third. Stir in the lemon juice and seasoning. Stir in the cornflour (cornstarch) until the sauce has thickened and is smooth.

Pour the sauce into a warmed sauceboat and serve at once, with the duck and vegetables. Garnish with the parsley.

4 Servings

PINTADES FARCIES
(Stuffed Guinea Fowls)

	Metric/U.K.	U.S.
Minced (ground) veal	225g/8oz	8oz
Chicken livers, coarsely chopped	175g/6oz	6oz
Shelled pistachio nuts	25g/1oz	¼ cup
Fresh parsley	1 Tbs	1 Tbs
Chopped fresh tarragon	1 Tbs	1 Tbs
Salt and pepper to taste		
Brandy	1 Tbs	1 Tbs
Guinea fowls, cleaned and boned	2x700g/1½lb	2x1½lb
Streaky (fatty) bacon	6 slices	6 slices
Butter	125g/4oz	8 Tbs
Medium onion, thinly sliced	1	1

Another example of the elegance and superlative taste of haute cuisine *at its best,* Pintades Farcies *(stuffed guinea fowls).*

	Metric/U.K.	U.S.
Dried thyme	½ tsp	½ tsp
Bay leaf	1	1
Chicken stock	250ml/8floz	1 cup
Mushrooms, with stalks removed	½kg/1lb	4 cups
Egg yolk	1	1
Double (heavy) cream	2 Tbs	2 Tbs

Combine the veal, chicken livers, nuts, herbs, seasoning and brandy together.

Lay the guinea fowls out flat on a working surface and spoon half the stuffing mixture into each one. Wrap the guinea fowls around the stuffing and sew them up with a trussing needle and thread. Place three bacon slices over the breast of each fowl and tie them on with string.

Melt half the butter in a large flameproof casserole. Add the guinea fowls and fry until they are evenly browned. Add the onion, herbs and stock and bring to the boil. Reduce the heat to low, cover and simmer for 50 minutes to 1 hour, or until the fowls are cooked through and tender.

Five minutes before the end of the cooking time, melt the remaining butter in a saucepan. Add the mushrooms and cook for 3 minutes. Remove the pan from the heat.

Remove the casserole from the heat and carefully transfer the guinea fowls to a warmed serving dish. Remove the bacon slices. Arrange the mushrooms around the fowls and keep hot while you make the sauce.

Strain the cooking liquid into a saucepan skimming any scum from the surface. Bring to the boil.

Combine the egg yolk and cream in a small bowl. Stir in about 4 tablespoons of the stock, then pour the mixture into the saucepan. Simmer gently for 3 minutes, or until the sauce has thickened and is smooth. Do not let the sauce boil or it will curdle.

Pour the sauce into a warmed sauceboat and serve at once, with the stuffed guinea fowls.

6 Servings

SALMIS DE PIGEONS
(Pigeon Stew)

	Metric/U.K.	U.S.
Pigeons, oven-ready with the giblets reserved	6	6
Salt and pepper to taste		
Butter, melted	175g/6oz	12 Tbs
Streaky (fatty) bacon	6 slices	6 slices
Button mushrooms, cooked and drained	125g/4oz	1 cup
Brandy	50ml/2floz	¼ cup
Truffle, drained and thinly sliced	1	1
SAUCE		
Onion, finely chopped	1	1
Medium carrot, chopped	1	1
Bouquet garni	1	1
Chicken stock	250ml/8floz	1 cup
Dry white wine	250ml/8floz	1 cup
Butter	25g/1oz	2 Tbs
Flour	25g/1oz	¼ cup
Salt and pepper to taste		

Preheat the oven to moderate 180°C (Gas Mark 4, 350°F).

Rub the pigeons, inside and out, with salt and pepper. Place them in a large roasting pan and spoon over the melted butter. Lay a slice of bacon over the breast of each bird. Put the pan into the oven and roast for 40 minutes.

Remove the pan from the oven and remove the bacon from the birds. Transfer the pigeons to a carving board. Skin the pigeons and carve the meat into slices. Arrange the slices in a large flameproof casserole. Cover with mushrooms and sprinkle with half the brandy. Place the truffle slices on top of the mushrooms and sprinkle with the remaining brandy. Set aside while you prepare the sauce.

Chop the pigeon skin and giblets finely.

Pour off all but 125ml/4floz (½ cup) of the cooking liquid from the pan. Strain these juices into a saucepan. Set over moderate heat and add the skin, giblets, the carcasses, onion, carrot and bouquet garni. Pour in the stock and wine, and bring to the boil. Cover and simmer the mixture for 15 minutes, or until it has reduced by about a quarter. Remove from the heat and strain the liquid into a large bowl, pressing down on the ingredients with the back of a wooden spoon to extract all the juices. Skim off any scum from the surface of the strained liquid.

Melt the butter in a small saucepan. Remove from the heat and stir in the flour to form a smooth paste. Gradually stir in the strained liquid and return to the heat. Bring to the boil,

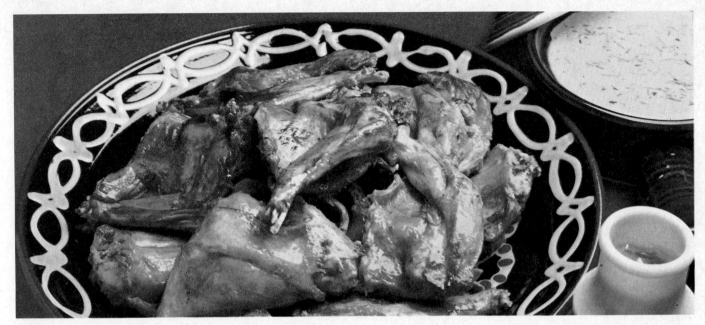

stirring constantly. Cook for 2 to 3 minutes, stirring constantly, or until the sauce is thick and smooth. Season to taste.

Pour the sauce over the pigeon meat, cover and set over moderately low heat. Simmer for 15 minutes. Remove from the heat and transfer the meat to a warmed serving dish. Arrange the mushrooms and truffle around it and pour over half the sauce. Pour the remaining sauce into a warmed sauceboat and serve at once, with the meat and vegetables.

4-6 Servings

LAPIN A LA SAUCE MOUTARDE
(Rabbit with Mustard Sauce)

	Metric/U.K.	U.S.
Rabbit, cleaned and cut into serving pieces	1x2kg/4lb	1x4lb
Butter	50g/2oz	4 Tbs
Salt and pepper to taste		
Dried thyme	½ tsp	½ tsp
Dried rosemary	½ tsp	½ tsp
Single (light) cream	300ml/10floz	1¼ cups
French mustard	1 Tbs	1 Tbs
Cornflour (cornstarch), blended with 2 Tbs single (light) cream	1 Tbs	1 Tbs
MARINADE		
Dry white wine	300ml/10floz	1¼ cups
Olive oil	125ml/4floz	½ cup
Garlic cloves, crushed	2	2
Salt and pepper to taste		
Medium onion, thinly sliced	1	1
Medium carrot, thinly sliced	1	1

To prepare the marinade, mix all the ingredients in a large, shallow bowl. Add the rabbit pieces and marinate them at room temperature for 6 hours, basting occasionally. Remove the rabbit from the marinade and dry on kitchen towels. Reserve the marinade.

Melt the butter in a large, deep frying-pan. Add the rabbit pieces and fry until they are evenly browned. Pour in the marinade and bring to the boil. Stir in seasoning, cover and simmer for 1 to 1¼ hours, or until the pieces are cooked through and tender. Remove the pan from the heat and transfer the rabbit to a warmed serving dish. Keep warm while you make the sauce.

Strain the cooking liquids into a small saucepan, pressing down on the vegetables with the back of a wooden spoon. Bring to the boil, then stir in the herbs. Reduce the heat to low and stir in the cream, a little at a time, then the mustard and cornflour (cornstarch) mixture. Gently warm the sauce, stirring constantly, until it is hot but not boiling, and is thick.

Pour the sauce into a warmed sauceboat and serve at once, with the rabbit.

4 Servings

Rabbit is an under-used meat in most parts of the English-speaking world, but in France its succulence is much appreciated. In Lapin à la Sauce Moutarde it is teamed with a creamy mustard sauce.

173

Vegetables and Salads

PAIN DE CHOU FLEUR
(Cauliflower Loaf)

	Metric/U.K.	U.S.
Medium cauliflowers, separated into flowerets	2	2
Potatoes, cooked and quartered	700g/1½lb	1½ lb
Butter	15g/½oz	1 Tbs
Salt and pepper to taste		
Cayenne pepper	¼ tsp	¼ tsp
Eggs	6	6
Gruyère cheese, finely grated	150g/5oz	1¼ cups

Put the cauliflowers into a large saucepan and add just enough water to cover. Bring to the boil and cook for 12 to 15 minutes, or until the flowerets are very tender. Drain and set aside.

Preheat the oven to moderate 180°C (Gas Mark 4, 350°F).

Put the cauliflowers, potatoes, butter, seasoning and cayenne into a bowl and mash together to form a purée. Add the eggs, one by one, beating well between each addition. Alternatively, purée the cauliflowers with the potatoes, butter, seasonings and eggs in a blender.

Stir in 125g/4oz (1 cup) of the grated cheese and spoon the purée into a well-greased medium ovenproof mould. Cover with foil and put the mould into a roasting pan one-third full of boiling water. Put the pan into the oven and bake for 1 hour.

Remove the pan from the oven and remove the mould from the pan. Remove the foil. Place a heatproof serving dish over the top of the mould and invert quickly. The mould should slide out easily. Sprinkle the remaining cheese over the top and return the mould to the oven for 5 minutes, or until the cheese melts.

Remove from the oven and serve at once.

4-6 Servings

Line a large flameproof casserole with the bacon slices. Add the cabbage, then the onions, garlic and seasoning. Moisten with the wine and stock and bring to the boil. Stir in the chestnuts, cover and put into the oven. Braise for 2 to 2½ hours, or until the cabbage is cooked through and most of the liquid is absorbed.

Remove from the oven and serve at once.

6 Servings

far left: *Pain de Chou Fleur, a delicate vegetable dish with a cauliflower base.*

near left: *Petits Pois à la Française, one of the most famous of French vegetable dishes, a marvellous combination of fresh peas, onion and lettuce.*

PETITS POIS A LA FRANCAISE
(Small Garden Peas, French Style)

	Metric/U.K.	U.S.
Fresh garden peas, weighed after shelling, or frozen petits pois	700g/1½lb	1½lb
Salt and pepper to taste		
Sugar	1 tsp	1 tsp
Medium onion, thinly sliced	1	1
Lettuce leaves, shredded	4	4
Beurre manié (page 192)	25g/1oz	2 Tbs

Put the peas, seasoning, sugar, onion and lettuce into a saucepan. Pour over enough hot water just to cover the peas and bring to the boil. Reduce the heat to very low, cover and simmer the mixture for 20 to 30 minutes, or until the onion is soft and the peas are very tender. Stir in the beurre manié, a little at a time, until the mixture has thickened and is smooth. Simmer for 1 minute.

Remove from the heat and transfer to a warmed serving bowl. Serve at once.

4 Servings

CHOU ROUGE A LA LIMOUSINE
(Red Cabbage with Chestnuts)

The delicious combination of red cabbage and chestnuts is a common one in France—this version is a southwestern one, from the province of Limousin. If you prefer, use canned whole chestnuts instead of as suggested here—and in this case, they should be added to the casserole about 30 minutes before the end.

	Metric/U.K.	U.S.
Streaky (fatty) bacon	6 slices	6 slices
Red cabbage, shredded	1kg/2lb	2lb
Medium onions, finely chopped	2	2
Garlic cloves, crushed	2	2
Salt and pepper to taste		
Red wine	150ml/5floz	⅝ cup
Beef stock	150ml/5floz	⅝ cup
chestnuts, blanched and peeled	20	20

Preheat the oven to warm 170°C (Gas Mark 3, 325°F).

CAROTTES VICHY
(Glazed Carrots)

	Metric/U.K.	U.S.
Carrots, thinly sliced	1kg/2lb	2lb
Water	250ml/8floz	1 cup
Butter	50g/2oz	4 Tbs
Sugar	2 Tbs	2 Tbs
Salt	½ tsp	½ tsp

	Metric/U.K.	U.S.
Chopped parsley	2 Tbs	2 Tbs

Put all the ingredients, except the parsley, into a saucepan and bring to the boil. Simmer, uncovered, for 15 minutes, or until the carrots are tender and the liquid has evaporated, shaking the pan frequently so that the carrots are thoroughly glazed.

Transfer to a warmed serving dish and sprinkle over the parsley. Serve at once.

4-6 Servings

RATATOUILLE
(Mixed Vegetable Casserole)

This colourful mixture of peppers, aubergine (eggplant), courgettes (zucchini) and tomatoes is one of the glories of Provençal cooking. It can be served hot or cold. A 425g/14oz can of tomatoes, with its juice, may be substituted for the fresh tomatoes.

	Metric/U.K.	U.S.
Olive oil	125ml/4floz	½ cup
Medium onions, thinly sliced	3	3
Garlic cloves, crushed	2	2
Medium aubergines (eggplants), sliced and dégorged	2	2
Large green pepper, pith and seeds removed and chopped	1	1
Large red pepper, pith and seeds removed and chopped	1	1
Medium courgettes (zucchini), sliced	4	4
Tomatoes, blanched, peeled, seeded and chopped	6	6
Dried basil	1 tsp	1 tsp
Dried rosemary	1 tsp	1 tsp
Salt and pepper to taste		

Heat the oil in a flameproof casserole. Add the onions and garlic and fry until they are soft. Stir in the aubergines (eggplants), peppers and courgettes (zucchini) and fry for 5 minutes. Stir in the remaining ingredients and bring to

the boil. Cover and simmer for 45 minutes to 1 hour, or until the vegetables are tender but still firm.

Serve at once, if you are serving hot.

4-6 Servings

COURGETTES SAUTEES MAITRE D'HOTEL
(Courgettes [Zucchini] with Lemon, Butter and Parsley Sauce)

Maître d'Hotel is served in many ways in France —as a butter on steaks and chops, as a sauce on fish and vegetables. This combination is a particularly successful one.

	Metric/U.K.	U.S.
Butter	75g/3oz	6 Tbs
Courgettes (zucchini), thinly sliced	8	8
Olive oil	2 Tbs	2 Tbs
Lemon juice	2 Tbs	2 Tbs
Salt and pepper to taste		
Chopped parsley	3 Tbs	3 Tbs

Melt two-thirds of the butter in a large frying-pan. Add the courgette (zucchini) slices to the pan and cook for 8 to 10 minutes, turning occasionally, or until they are evenly browned and cooked through.

Stir in the lemon juice and seasoning, then the remaining butter and parsley. When the butter has melted, transfer the mixture to a warmed serving dish.

Serve at once.

4 Servings

POMMES DE TERRE SOUFFLEES
(Potato Puffs)

	Metric/U.K.	U.S.
Potatoes, cut into ¼cm/⅛in slices	½kg/1lb	1lb
Sufficient vegetable oil for deep-frying		
Salt	1 tsp	1 tsp

Put the slices into a large bowl of water and set aside for 30 minutes. Drain and dry thoroughly on kitchen towels.

Fill two large saucepans one-third full with oil. Heat the oil in one pan until it reaches 170°C (325°F) on a deep-fat thermometer, or until a small cube of stale bread dropped into the oil turns golden in 65 seconds. Heat the oil in the second pan until it reaches 190°C (375°F) on a deep-fat thermometer or until a small cube of stale bread dropped into the oil turns golden in 40 seconds.

Drop the potato slices into the first pan and fry for 4 minutes. Using a slotted spoon, transfer the slices to the second pan and fry for 2 to 3 minutes or until they puff up. Remove from the oil and drain on kitchen towels.

Sprinkle over the salt and serve at once.

2-4 Servings

POMMES DE TERRE AU ROQUEFORT
(Baked Potatoes with Blue Cheese)

Roquefort is rather an expensive cheese outside France, certainly to use in cooking, so for economy's sake, any type of blue cheese may be substituted if you prefer.

	Metric/U.K.	U.S.
Large potatoes, scrubbed	4	4
Sour cream	150ml/5floz	$\frac{5}{8}$ cup
Roquefort cheese, crumbled	125g/4oz	4oz
Chopped chives	2 Tbs	2 Tbs
Pinch of cayenne pepper		
Salt and pepper to taste		

Preheat the oven to fairly hot 190°C (Gas Mark 5, 375°F).

Put the potatoes on a baking sheet and put them into the oven. Bake for 1 to 1½ hours, or until they are cooked through. (Cooking times will depend on the size of the potatoes.)

Remove the potatoes from the oven and set aside to cool a little. When they are cool enough to handle, lay them on their sides. Cut off a thin slice, lengthways, from the top of each potato and, using a spoon, carefully scoop out the inside to within ½cm/¼in of the shell, leaving the shell intact.

Two delicious recipes with potato : Pommes de Terre au Roquefort (baked potato with a blue cheese stuffing) and Pommes de Terre Soufflés (deep-fried potato puffs).

Mash together the scooped out potato flesh, sour cream, cheese, chives, cayenne and seasoning. Stuff equal amounts into the potato shells and return the stuffed potatoes to the baking sheet. Bake for 10 to 15 minutes, or until the top of the filling is lightly browned.

Remove from the oven and serve at once.

4 Servings

SALADE DE RIZ AU SAUCISSON
(Rice Salad with Garlic Sausage)

	Metric/U.K.	U.S.
Long-grain rice, soaked in cold water for 30 minutes and drained	125g/4oz	$\frac{2}{3}$ cup
Salt and black pepper to taste		
Mayonnaise	75ml/3floz	$\frac{3}{8}$ cup
Dried chervil	1 tsp	1 tsp
$\frac{1}{2}$ red pepper, pith and seeds removed and and chopped	$\frac{1}{2}$	$\frac{1}{2}$
Hard-boiled eggs	2	2
Small lettuce, separated into leaves	1	1
Garlic sausage, cut into $\frac{1}{2}$cm/$\frac{1}{4}$in slices	1x20cm/8in	1x8in

Put the rice into a saucepan. Pour over enough water to cover and add about a teaspoon of salt. Bring to the boil, cover and reduce the heat to low. Simmer for 15 to 20 minutes, or until the rice is cooked and all the liquid is absorbed. Transfer the rice to a large bowl and set aside for 5 minutes.

Meanwhile, mix together the seasoning, mayonnaise and chervil. Pour half over the rice and add the red pepper. Using two large spoons, carefullly toss the mixture to blend. Set aside to cool completely.

Meanwhile, cut the eggs in half, lengthways. Remove the yolks and add them to the remaining mayonnaise mixture. Mash well, then return the mixture to the egg whites.

Arrange the lettuce leaves in a salad bowl. Pile the rice mixture on top and arrange the sausage slices around the edges. Garnish with the filled egg whites and serve the salad at once.

4-6 Servings

CAROTTES RAPEES
(Grated Carrot Salad)

	Metric/U.K.	U.S.
Carrots	$\frac{1}{2}$kg/1lb	1lb
DRESSING		
Olive oil	3 Tbs	3 Tbs
White wine vinegar	$1\frac{1}{2}$ Tbs	$1\frac{1}{2}$ Tbs
Lemon juice	1 tsp	1 tsp
Sugar	$\frac{1}{2}$ tsp	$\frac{1}{2}$ tsp
Salt and pepper to taste		

First make the dressing. Put all the ingredients into a screw-topped jar and shake vigorously.

Grate the carrots into a shallow salad bowl. Pour over the dressing and, using two large spoons, carefully toss to blend thoroughly.

Cover and chill before serving.

4 Servings

SALADE NICOISE
(Potato, French Bean and Tomato Salad)

	Metric/U.K.	U.S.
Small lettuce, separated into leaves	1	1
Medium cold cooked potatoes, diced	6	6
Cold cooked French beans, cut into lengths	275g/10oz	$1\frac{2}{3}$ cups
Tomatoes, blanched, peeled and quartered	6	6
Garlic cloves, crushed	2	2
Anchovy fillets, halved	6	6
Black olives, stoned	10	10
Capers	2 Tbs	2 Tbs
DRESSING		
Olive oil	50ml/2floz	$\frac{1}{4}$ cup
Wine vinegar	2 Tbs	2 Tbs
French mustard	1 tsp	1 tsp

Arrange the lettuce leaves in a large salad bowl.

Put the potatoes, beans, tomatoes and garlic into the centre of the bowl. Combine all the ingredients for the dressing together, then pour over the vegetables. Garnish with the anchovies, olives and capers.

6 Servings

An unusual and colourful salad meal in itself, Salade de Riz au Saucisson.

Eggs and Cheese

SOUFFLE DE FROMAGE
(Cheese Soufflé)

	Metric/U.K.	U.S.
Butter	50g/2oz	4 Tbs
Cheese, grated (preferably a mixture of Gruyère and Parmesan)	150g/5oz	1¼ cups
Flour	25g/1oz	4 Tbs
Milk, scalded	300ml/10floz	1¼ cups
Salt and pepper to taste		
Paprika	¼ tsp	¼ tsp
Egg yolks	5	5
Egg whites	6	6
Cream of tartar	¼ tsp	¼ tsp

Preheat the oven to moderate 180°C (Gas Mark 4, 350°F). Using a little of the butter, grease a medium soufflé dish. Sprinkle about 4 tablespoons of the grated cheese around the inside and press on to the bottom and sides.

Melt the remaining butter in a saucepan. Remove the pan from the heat and stir in the flour to form a smooth paste. Gradually stir in the scalded milk and return to the heat. Bring to the boil and cook the sauce, stirring constantly, for 2 to 3 minutes, or until it is thick and smooth.

Remove from the heat again and beat in the seasoning and paprika, then the egg yolks a little at a time. Set aside to cool slightly.

Beat the egg whites until they are foamy. Add salt to taste and the cream of tartar and continue to beat until they form stiff peaks.

Stir the remaining cheese into the egg yolk mixture and when it is thoroughly blended, quickly fold in the egg whites. Transfer the mixture to the prepared soufflé dish. Carefully mark a deep circle in the centre of the soufflé and place the dish in the oven. Bake for 40 to 45 minutes, or until it is lightly browned on top and the soufflé is well risen.

Remove from the oven and serve at once.

4-6 Servings

OMELETTE FINES HERBES
(Omelet with Fresh Herbs)

Fines Herbes is one of the classic fillings for omelets in France and the herbs involved are usually a combination of parsley, chervil and tarragon. Chives and occasionally bay leaves are also sometimes added. If you are going to make this recipe, it is essential that fresh herbs be used to attain the full, delicate taste.

	Metric/U.K.	U.S.
Eggs	6	6
Salt and pepper to taste		
Cold water	2 Tbs	2 Tbs
Chopped fresh herbs	1½ Tbs	1½ Tbs
Butter	15g/½oz	1 Tbs

Beat the eggs, seasoning, water and herbs together until they are thoroughly blended.

Melt the butter in a large omelet pan. Pour in the egg mixture. Stir, then leave for a few seconds until the bottom sets. Reduce the heat to low. Using a palette knife or spatula, lift the edges of the omelet and, at the same time, tilt the pan away from you so that the liquid egg escapes from the top and runs on to the pan. Put the pan down flat over the heat and leave until the omelet begins to set again. Tilt the pan away from you again and, with the help of the knife, flip one half of the omelet over to make a semi-circle.

Remove from the heat and slide the omelet on to a warmed serving dish. Serve at once.

3 Servings

OEUFS ST. GERMAIN
(Eggs with Purée of Peas)

	Metric/U.K.	U.S.
Fresh peas, weighed after shelling	½kg/1lb	1lb
Butter	65g/2½oz	5 Tbs
Chicken stock	65ml/2½floz	⅓ cup
Onion, very finely chopped	1	1
Large lettuce leaves, shredded	4	4
Salt and pepper to taste		
Medium potatoes	2	2

Eggs, soft-boiled	6	6
Triangles of fried bread (to garnish)		

Quiches are part and parcel of French life and they can have many different fillings. This particular filling is courgettes (zucchini) and tomatoes.

Put the peas in a saucepan and just cover with cold water. Bring to the boil, then remove from the heat and drain. Return the peas to the pan and add the butter, stock, onion, lettuce and seasoning. Cover and simmer until the peas are tender and most of the liquid has been absorbed.

Meanwhile, boil the potatoes in salted water for 15 to 20 minutes, or until they are tender. Drain and either purée in a blender or push through a strainer. Transfer to a bowl. Purée the peas in a blender or push them through the strainer. Stir the pea mixture into the potatoes, then season to taste.

. Divide the purée among individual serving plates and arrange a shelled egg on top.

Garnish with the bread triangles and serve at once.

6 Servings

QUICHE LORRAINE
(Bacon and Egg Flan)

This is virtually the national dish of Lorraine, on the border with Germany. Almost as many versions exist as there are villages in the region, but this is a fairly typical version.

	Metric/U.K.	U.S.
Shortcrust pastry dough	275g/10oz	10oz
FILLING		
Smoked or unsmoked bacon, grilled (broiled)		

	Metric/U.K.	U.S.
until crisp and crumbled	175g/6oz	6oz
Single (light) cream	250ml/8floz	1 cup
Egg yolks	3	3
Salt and pepper to taste		

Preheat the oven to fairly hot 200°C (Gas Mark 6, 400°F).

Roll out the pastry dough to about ½cm/¼in thick and use it to line a well-greased 23cm/9in flan tin. Put the tin on a baking sheet. Arrange the crumbled bacon over the bottom of the case.

Beat the remaining ingredients together and pour over the bacon. Put the baking sheet into the oven and bake the quiche for 25 to 30 minutes, or until the filling is set and firm and golden brown on top.

Serve at once, if you are serving the quiche hot, or set aside to cool before serving.

4-6 Servings

QUICHE AUX COURGETTES ET TOMATES
(Courgette [Zucchini] and Tomato Flan)

	Metric/U.K.	U.S.
Shortcrust pastry dough	275g/10oz	10oz
FILLING		
Butter	50g/2oz	4 Tbs
Garlic cloves, crushed	2	2
Courgettes (zucchini), sliced	4	4
Salt and pepper to taste		
Single (light) cream	125ml/4floz	½ cup
Eggs	3	3
Gruyère or Cheddar cheese, grated	50g/2oz	½ cup
Small tomatoes, blanched, peeled and thinly sliced	5	5

Preheat the oven to fairly hot 200°C (Gas Mark 6, 400°F).

Roll out the pastry dough to about ½cm/¼in thick and use it to line a well-greased 23cm/9in flan tin. Put the tin on a baking sheet.

Melt the butter in a large frying-pan. Add the garlic and fry for 1 minute. Add the courgette (zucchini) slices and seasoning to taste. Cook for 8 to 10 minutes, or until they are evenly browned. Remove from the heat.

Beat the cream, eggs and grated cheese together.

Arrange the courgettes (zucchini) and tomatoes in concentric circles in the flan case. Pour over the cream mixture. Put the baking sheet into the oven and bake the quiche for 35 to 40 minutes, or until the filling is set and firm and golden brown on top.

Remove from the oven and serve at once, if you are serving the quiche hot, or set aside to cool before serving.

4-6 Servings

CREPES AU FROMAGE
(Blue Cheese Crêpes)

Crêpes are very popular all over France although they originate in Brittany. This one is a delicious combination of crêpes and the queen of French blue cheeses, Roquefort.

	Metric/U.K.	U.S.
Béchamel sauce (page 192)	250ml/8floz	1 cup
Egg yolk	1	1
Roquefort cheese, crumbled	150g/5oz	5oz
Salt and pepper to taste		
Crêpe batter (savoury) (page 192)	225g/8oz	1 cup
Butter, melted	25g/1oz	2 Tbs
Brandy, warmed	50ml/2floz	¼ cup

To make the filling, pour the béchamel and egg yolk into a bowl and beat together until they are thoroughly blended. Stir in the crumbled cheese and seasoning and beat well to blend. Chill in the refrigerator for 1 hour.

Fry the crêpes according to the instructions in the batter recipe.

Lay the crêpes out flat and put about 2 tablespoons of the filling in the centre of each one. Fold in half, then in quarters to enclose the filling.

Arrange the crêpes on a chafing dish or baking dish and pour over the melted butter. Pour over the warmed brandy and ignite. Shake gently until the flames have died away, then serve at once.

6 Servings

Desserts and Cakes

BAVAROIS AU CHOCOLAT
(Chocolate Bavarian Cream)

This richly flavoured dessert belongs firmly in the tradition of grand cuisine; its origins are very old, but the dessert was revived and refined by the great Careme and is now the glory of many an haute cuisine *restaurant.*

	Metric/U.K.	U.S.
Vegetable oil	1 Tbs	1 Tbs
Milk	725ml/1¼ pints	3 cups
Dark cooking (semi-sweet) chocolate, grated	125g/4oz	4 squares
Castor (superfine) sugar	75g/3oz	⅜ cup
Egg yolks	4	4
Gelatine	15g/½oz	½oz
Strong black coffee	125ml/4floz	½ cup
Vanilla essence (extract)	1 tsp	1 tsp
Double (heavy) cream, beaten until thick	150ml/5floz	⅝ cup
Rum	2 Tbs	2 Tbs

One of the glories of French cuisine, now appreciated the whole world over—Crème Caramel.

Grease the inside of a 1¼l/2 pint (1½ quart) mould with the oil, then place upside down on kitchen towels to drain off any excess. Set aside.

Put the milk and chocolate into a saucepan and cook over low heat, stirring constantly until the chocolate has dissolved. Remove from the heat.

Put the sugar into a heatproof bowl. Make a well in the centre and drop in the egg yolks, one at a time, beating slowly until the sugar has been completely incorporated. Pour over the milk mixture in a thin steady stream, beating constantly. Put the bowl over a saucepan half-filled with hot water and set the pan over low heat. Cook, stirring constantly, until the custard is thick enough to coat the back of a wooden spoon. Do not let the mixture boil or it will curdle. Remove from the heat.

Dissolve the gelatine in the coffee over low heat, then stir into the custard. Strain the custard into a bowl placed over crushed ice. Stir constantly until the custard thickens.

Beat the vanilla into the cream then, using a metal spoon, lightly fold the cream mixture and rum into the thickening custard. Pour the mixture into the prepared mould.

Cover the mould with foil or greaseproof or waxed paper and transfer to the refrigerator to chill for 6 hours, or until the mould has completely set.

Remove from the refrigerator and run a knife around the edge of the cream. Quickly dip the bottom of the mould in hot water and invert quickly on to a serving dish, giving the bottom a sharp tap. The cream should slide out easily.

Serve at once.

4-6 Servings

CREME CARAMEL
(Baked Caramel Custard)

	Metric/U.K.	U.S.
Sugar	125g/4oz	½ cup
Water	65ml/2½floz	⅓ cup
CREME		
Milk	600ml/1 pint	2½ cups
Sugar	90g/3½oz	Scant ½ cup
Eggs	2	2
Egg yolks	2	2
Vanilla essence (extract)	1 tsp	1 tsp

Dissolve the sugar in the water over low heat, stirring constantly until it has dissolved. Increase the heat to moderately high and bring to the boil. Cook for 3 to 4 minutes, without stirring, or until it turns a light nut-brown colour. (Be careful not to overcook or the syrup will darken too much and become bitter.) Pour into individual ramekin dishes or a heat-proof dish. Dissolve the milk and sugar together, stirring constantly. Remove from the heat.

Beat the eggs and egg yolks together in a bowl until they thicken and become pale yellow. Stir in the milk and vanilla.

Preheat the oven to warm 170°C (Gas Mar, 3, 325°F).

Strain the mixture into the ramekins or dish, spooning off any froth which appears on the surface. Put the dishes or dish into a roasting pan and add enough boiling water to come halfway up the sides.

Put the pan into the oven and bake the crème for 40 minutes, or until the centres are firm when pressed with your fingertip. Do not allow the water to boil during baking or the custard will have a grainy texture. (If it does begin to boil, reduce the temperature.)

Bavarois au Chocolat, the perfect end to any meal.

Remove the dishes or dish from the water and set aside to cool completely. Chill in the refrigerator for 1 hour.

Run a knife around the edge of the ramekins or dish and invert on to serving plates. Serve at once.

6 Servings

RIZ A L'IMPERATRICE
(Empress Rice Pudding)

This delicious dessert is said to have been created for, and named after, the Empress Eugenie, wife of Napoleon III of France.

	Metric/U.K.	U.S.
Round-grain rice	75g/3oz	½ cup
Castor (superfine) sugar	50g/2oz	¼ cup
Milk	900ml/1½ pints	3¾ cups
Vanilla essence (extract)	1½ tsp	1½ tsp
Chopped candied peel	2 Tbs	2 Tbs
Chopped glacé cherries	2 Tbs	2 Tbs
Kirsch	2 Tbs	2 Tbs
Egg yolks	3	3
Gelatine, dissolved in 6 Tbs hot water	25g/1oz	1oz
Custard	250ml/8floz	1 cup
Double (heavy) cream, stiffly beaten	300ml/10floz	1¼ cups
Apricot jam	2 Tbs	2 Tbs

Preheat the oven to cool 150°C (Gas Mark 2, 300°F).

Put the rice, sugar, milk and vanilla in a well-greased baking dish and put the dish into the oven. Bake for 3 hours, or until the rice is cooked and all the liquid is absorbed.

Meanwhile, put the candied peel and glacé cherries in a bowl and pour over the kirsch. Set aside to marinate at room temperature.

Remove the dish from the oven and gradually beat in the egg yolks, then the gelatine. Set aside to cool for 15 minutes.

Beat in the fruit and kirsch mixture, then fold in the custard and cream.

Lightly coat the inside of a 1¼l/2 pint (1½ quart) mould with the jam. Pour the rice mixture into the mould, smoothing it down. Put into the refrigerator to chill for 2 hours, or until the rice has set.

To serve, remove the mould from the refrigerator and run a knife around the edge of the rice. Invert quickly on to a serving dish, giving the mould a sharp tap. The rice should slide out easily.

Serve at once.

6 Servings

CHARLOTTE AUX MARRONS
(Chestnut Mould)

The original charlotte was 'invented' by the great Carême, but since his original (charlotte russe), there have been many superlative variations on the theme—this one uses chestnuts, a flavouring very popular with the French.

	Metric/U.K.	U.S.
Milk	225ml/7floz	⅞ cup
Water	75ml/3floz	⅜ cup
Sponge finger biscuits (lady-fingers)	30	30
Sugar	75g/3oz	⅜ cup
Gelatine, dissolved in 4 Tbs hot water	15g/½oz	½oz
Canned unsweetened chestnut purée	165g/5½oz	5½oz
Orange-flavoured liqueur	2 Tbs	2 Tbs
Canned preserved chestnuts	125g/4oz	4oz
Double (heavy) cream	300ml/10floz	1¼ cups

Line the bottom of a 1¼l/2 pint (1½ quart) mould with a circle of greaseproof or waxed paper. Set aside.

Mix together 75ml/3floz (⅜ cup) each of the milk and water. One by one, dip the biscuits (cookies) into the mixture, coating them well, but being careful not to saturate them. Line the sides of the mould with the biscuits (cookies), reserving the extra to use later. Trim the biscuits (cookies) to fit the top of the mould. Set aside.

Dissolve the sugar in the remaining milk, stirring constantly until it has dissolved. Stir in the dissolved gelatine, then the chestnut purée and orange-flavoured liqueur. Remove the pan from the heat and transfer the mixture to a bowl. Chill in the refrigerator for 30 minutes, or until the mixture is beginning to set.

Sumptuous Charlotte aux Marrons—a superb combination of chestnut purée, cream and orange-flavoured liqueur, all moulded together.

The French make apple tart differently from everybody else, but the result is just as delicious, as this Tarte aux Pommes testifies.

Drain the preserved chestnuts, reserving the syrup. Chop coarsely and set aside. Beat the cream until it is thick but not stiff. Beat half the cream into the gelatine mixture, then fold in the remaining cream. Fold in the chopped chestnuts.

Spoon the mixture into the lined mould. Arrange the remaining biscuits (cookies) over the top, to cover the mould completely, and trim off any protruding parts.

Cover with greaseproof or waxed paper and chill in the refrigerator for at least 6 hours or overnight.

To serve, remove the paper and run a knife around the edge of the mould. Invert on to a serving dish, giving a sharp shake. The charlotte should slide out easily.

Pour over the reserved chestnut syrup and serve at once.

10 Servings

CREPES SUZETTE
(Crêpes Flambéed with Grand Marnier)

This is one of the most famous of all French desserts and its range of popularity is such that it can be found on the menu of the most elegant restaurants in the country—and yet it is also, traditionally, served from street stalls all over Paris. If you prefer, use all Grand Marnier rather than mixing it with brandy.

	Metric/U.K.	U.S.
Crêpe batter (sweet) (page 192)	150g/5oz	$\frac{5}{8}$ cup
Medium oranges	2	2
Sugar cubes	4	4
Castor (super fine) sugar	50g/2oz	$\frac{1}{4}$ cup
Unsalted butter, softened	175g/6oz	12 Tbs

	Metric/U.K.	U.S.
Fresh orange juice	75ml/3floz	⅜ cup
Grand Marnier	5 Tbs	5 Tbs
Brandy	3 Tbs	3 Tbs

Fry the crêpes according to the instructions in the basic recipe. Keep hot.

Rub each orange all over with the sugar cubes to extract the zest from the rind. Put the sugar into a bowl and crush with the back of a wooden spoon. Peel the oranges, discarding any pith. Chop the rind very finely and add to the sugar. Stir in half the castor (superfine) sugar and the softened butter. Cream the mixture until it is light and fluffy. Stir in the orange juice, then 3 tablespoons of the Grand Marnier and beat until the mixture is well blended and creamy.

Melt the orange butter in a frying-pan. Holding the outer edges of a crêpe with your fingertips, dip it into the butter mixture until it is well soaked. Carefully fold in half, then in quarters. Transfer to a warmed serving dish. Repeat until all the crepes have been well coated. Sprinkle over the remaining sugar and pour over any remaining melted butter.

Warm the remaining Grand Marnier and brandy together until they are hot. Pour over the crêpes and ignite, shaking the dish gently and carefully. When the flames die away, serve at once.

4-6 Servings

MOUSSE AU CHOCOLAT
(Chocolate Mousse)

For the best results make this dessert the day before you wish to serve it and chill in the refrigerator. As a finishing touch, decorate with grated chocolate and/or whipped cream.

	Metric/U.K.	U.S.
Dark cooking (semi-sweet) chocolate, broken into small pieces	225g/8oz	8 squares
Strong black coffee	3 Tbs	3 Tbs
Unsalted butter, cut into small pieces	40g/1½oz	3 Tbs
Eggs, separated	4	4
Brandy	2 Tbs	2 Tbs

Combine the chocolate and coffee in a heat-proof bowl. Put the bowl over a saucepan half-filled with hot water and set the pan over moderately low heat. Cook the mixture, beating constantly with a wooden spoon, until the chocolate has melted and the mixture is smooth.

Beat in the butter, a few pieces at a time, and continue beating until it is thoroughly blended. Add the egg yolks and cook, beating constantly, for 5 minutes, or until the mixture has thickened and is smooth. Do not let the mixture come to the boil.

Remove the pan from the heat and the bowl from the pan. Stir in the brandy and set the mixture aside for 30 minutes to cool completely.

Meanwhile, beat the egg whites until they form stiff peaks. Quickly fold the egg whites into the chocolate mixture.

Spoon the mousse into individual serving glasses and chill for 4 hours, or overnight.

6 Servings

TARTE AUX POMMES
(Apple Flan)

	Metric/U.K.	U.S.
Shortcrust pastry dough	175g/6oz	6oz
Thick sweet apple purée	300ml/10floz	1¼ cups
Dessert apples, cored, peeled and thinly sliced	½kg/1lb	1lb
Grated rind and juice of ½ lemon		
Redcurrant or apple jelly	4 Tbs	4 Tbs
Brandy	2 Tbs	2 Tbs

Preheat the oven to fairly hot 200°C (Gas Mark 6, 400°F).

Roll out the pastry dough to about ½cm/¼in thick and use it to line a well-greased 23cm/9in flan tin. Put the flan tin on a baking sheet.

Spoon the apple purée over the bottom of the case to cover it completely, then arrange the apple slices on top, in concentric circles. Sprinkle over the lemon rind and juice.

Put the baking sheet into the oven and bake the flan for 40 to 45 minutes, or until the pastry and apples are cooked. Remove from the oven and set aside to cool.

Warm the jelly and brandy together until the jelly has dissolved. Brush the glaze gently over the apples and serve the flan warm or cold.

6 Servings

PROFITEROLES AUX GLACES
(Choux Puffs with Ice-Cream)

	Metric/U.K.	U.S.
PASTRY		
Water	300ml/10floz	1¼ cups
Butter, cut into small pieces	75g/3oz	6 Tbs
Salt	1 tsp	1 tsp
Pinch of grated nutmeg		
Flour	275g/10oz	2½ cups
Large eggs	5	5
Egg, beaten with ½ tsp water		
FILLING		
Vanilla ice-cream	450ml/15floz	2 cups
Dark cooking (semi-sweet) chocolate, melted	125g/4oz	4 squares

Bring the water to the boil in a large saucepan. Add the butter, salt and nutmeg and, when the butter has melted, remove from the heat and gradually beat in the flour. Continue beating until the dough comes away from the sides of the pan.

One by one, beat the eggs into the mixture, making sure each is absorbed before adding the next. When the eggs have been added, the mixture should be thick and glossy.

Preheat the oven to hot 220°C (Gas Mark 7, 425°F). Lightly grease two baking sheets.

Fill a forcing bag, fitted with a plain nozzle, with the pastry dough. Squeeze the dough on to the baking sheets in circular mounds (about 5cm/2in in diameter and 2½cm/1in in height). If you do not have a forcing bag, arrange the dough carefully into mounds on the sheets, using two spoons. The puffs will expand considerably in baking, so allow plenty of space between each one. Coat each puff with the beaten egg mixture and put the sheets into the oven. Bake for 10 minutes. Reduce the oven temperature to fairly hot 190°C (Gas Mark 5, 375°F) and bake the puffs for a further 25 to 30 minutes, or until they have doubled in size and are light brown in colour.

Remove from the oven and make a slit in the side of each puff to allow the steam to escape. Replace the puffs in the turned-off oven for 10 minutes, then transfer to a wire rack to cool to room temperature.

Cut the tops off the puffs and reserve. Fill the puffs with the ice-cream. Replace the tops and arrange the filled puffs on a serving dish.

One of the classic French pastries, with a luscious filling—Profiteroles, puffs of choux pastry baked, then filled with ice-cream and topped with chocolate sauce.

Pour over the melted chocolate and serve at once.

8 Large Puffs

MADELEINES
(Shell-Shaped Sponges)

The invention of the madeleine is generally attributed to one of the great early pastry cooks, Avice, who was in the service of Prince Talleyrand. It has remained a popular part of the French culinary experience ever since, and has even been immortalized in literatiure—it was the action of biting into a madeleine which caused the hero of Proust's Remembrances of Things Past *to remember . . . To be traditionally correct, the cakes should be baked in special moulds; they will, however, taste just as nice if cooked in ordinary muffin tins, even if the shapes aren't strictly 'shell'!*

	Metric/U.K.	U.S.
Butter, melted	125g/4oz plus 2 Tbs	8 Tbs plus 2 Tbs
Flour, sifted	125g/4oz plus 2 Tbs	1 cup plus 2 Tbs
Castor (superfine) sugar	125g/4oz	½ cup
Eggs	4	4
Vanilla essence (extract)	½ tsp	½ tsp

Preheat the oven to fairly hot 200°C (Gas Mark 6, 400°F). Lightly grease 36 madeleine moulds with the 2 tablespoons of butter. Sprinkle the moulds with the 2 tablespoons of flour, tipping and rotating to distribute it evenly, and knocking out any excess.

Beat the sugar, eggs and vanilla together until the mixture is very thick. Very gradually, fold in the remaining flour. Add the remaining butter until it is thoroughly mixed. Spoon the batter into the moulds until they are about three-quarters full. Put the moulds on a baking sheet and put the sheet into the oven. Bake for 7 to 10 minutes, or until a skewer inserted into the centres of the cakes comes out clean.

Remove from the oven and leave the cakes to cool in the moulds for 5 minutes before turning out on to a wire rack to cool completely. Serve cold.

36 Cakes

Basic Recipes

BEURRE MANIE
(Flour and Butter Paste)

	Metric/U.K.	U.S.
Butter	25g/1oz	2 Tbs
Flour	25g/1oz	4 Tbs

Combine the butter and flour together, beating until they are thoroughly blended. Break off small pieces and roll into individual balls. The balls should be added, a little at a time, to whatever mixture is being thickened.

About 50g/2oz (4 Tablespoons)

PATE A CREPES
(Crêpe Batter)

This is a basic crêpe batter—to make a savoury version sift ½ teaspoon of salt with the flour at the beginning of the recipe: to make a sweet batter, beat 1 tablespoon sugar and 2 or 3 drops of vanilla into the batter after adding the milk and water.

	Metric/U.K.	U.S.
Flour	225g/8oz	2 cups
Eggs	4	4
Butter, melted	50g/2oz	4 Tbs
Milk	250ml/8floz	1 cup
Water	225ml/7floz	$\frac{7}{8}$ cup
Vegetable oil	2 Tbs	2 Tbs

Sift the flour into a bowl. Make a well in the centre and add the eggs and melted butter. Gradually beat in the milk and water until the mixture forms a smooth batter. Strain the batter if necessary to get rid of any lumps. Cover and set aside in a cool place for 2 hours.

Brush a heavy frying-pan with a little of the oil. Place over moderate heat and heat the oil until it is very hot. Remove the pan from the heat and pour about 4 tablespoons of batter into the centre of the pan. Quickly tilt the pan in all directions to spread out the batter. Return the pan to the heat and cook the crêpe for just over 1 minute. Shake the pan to loosen the crêpe. To see if it is cooked, lift one edge of it with a spatula; it should be light golden underneath. If it is not, cook for a further 10 seconds.

Turn the crêpe over by lifting it up and over. Brown the other side for 30 seconds. This side will be less evenly browned and is the side on which fillings should be spread.

Slide the crêpe on to a warmed plate and keep hot while you cook the remaining crêpes in the same way.

About 225g/8oz (1 cup) batter

SAUCE BECHAMEL
(White Sauce)

This is the single most important sauce in the whole of French cooking and is reputed to have been introduced into the national cooking repertoire during the reign of Louis XIV. It is used as a base for mushroom, cheese, tomato and many other sauces.

	Metric/U.K.	U.S.
Milk	450ml/15floz	2 cups
Bay leaf	1	1
Peppercorns	6	6
Mace blade	1	1
Pinch of grated nutmeg		
Butter	33g/1¼oz	2½ Tbs
Flour	25g/1oz	4 Tbs
Salt and pepper to taste		

Put the milk and flavourings into a saucepan and heat for 10 minutes, or until warm; do not let the milk come to the boil. Strain into a small bowl and set aside to cool.

Melt the butter in a saucepan. Remove from the heat and stir in the flour to form a smooth paste. Gradually stir in the strained milk and return to the heat. Bring to the boil, stirring constantly, or until it has thickened and is smooth.

The sauce is now ready to use.

About 450ml/15floz (2 cups)

India

Indian cooking is a story of geography and of religion. The main cooking divisions can be separated, roughly but fairly satisfactorily, into north and south (with some deviations along the coast line), and many eating and cooking habits can be traced directly to the dietary restrictions of the main religions of the sub-continent; Moslem and Hindu.

The differences between the north and south are many. In the north, various waves of conquerors have come and gone and left their influence, some of their culture—and much of their food (except for the British, who built roads). The Moghuls, particularly, have left their mark on Indian cuisine and the rich diversity of their cooking still finds echoes in many of the finer dishes of the north to this day, such as Huseini Kebabs. The Persians also contributed their share, particularly their

fondness for rice-based dishes (many of the famous pulaos of the north are Persian in influence if not in origin). The northern cuisine evolved basically in the courts of the many royal princelings so it is not a cuisine of necessity but rather one that is rich with spices, herbs and sauces.

In the south, the outside influences are less obvious although the Portuguese have left traces of their occupation. The food is hotter, less subtle than in the north and rice is very much a staple of the diet—much more so than in the north. The south abounds in fresh vegetables and fruit, and both are not only incorporated into the cuisine but form the basis of many of the most popular dishes.

The south is predominantly Hindu, and in consequence vegetarian, although adherence to the stricter aspects of the faith vary

near right: *A watermelon seller divides up his merchandise on the streets of Gujurat.*
far right: *Women harvest the tea crop.*

according to caste (the higher the caste the more strictly the adherence—the Brahmin are not supposed to eat eggs or fish as well as meat) and practical necessity (there are communities of Hindus along the coast who eat fish, which is plentiful there, claiming that it is not forbidden 'meat' but rather 'fruit of the sea' and therefore not taboo). But most of the people are at least vegetarian in that they do not eat meat and a vast and superb vegetarian cuisine has therefore developed in this area. In the absence of meat, pulses form an important part of the diet and simple lentil dishes such as Sambar and Khichri have become classics.

There are Hindus in the north too, but there the dietary laws are interpreted more leniently, only beef from the sacred cow being forbidden. In Pakistan, of course, where the population is predominantly Moslem, only pork is refused and both beef and lamb are much enjoyed.

The sub-continent has other minorities which have also made their culinary contribution. The Parsees, for instance, who settled many centuries ago in west India to escape religious persecution, are renowned for their cooking, and several of their dishes are now part of the standard Indian repertoire—Dhansak, an unusual combination of chicken and lentils and Ekuri, a sort of spicy scrambled eggs dish, are perhaps the best known.

The Syrian Christians have contributed Vath, a ceremonial duck dish, and the Goans, descended at least in spirit from the Portuguese conquerors of their island, are famous for their seafood and for their almost soup-like curries.

Outside India, Indian cooking is often dismissed in one word—curry. Indeed most dishes are reckoned to taste very much the same, with perhaps the only variation being in the main ingredient. Nothing could be further from the truth. The 'curry' so misinterpreted in the west is, in fact, merely a corruption of the Tamil word for sauce and, correctly used, describes only one type of Indian stew, and one of the simplest in the cooking repertoire at that.

That the variety and range of Indian cooking is huge can be seen by even a quick perusal of the recipes which follow in this book. But what is perhaps not quite so apparent is the quite bewildering, and very sophisticated, number of different techniques or styles of cooking. *Tandoori* is probably the best known outside India and is simple in the extreme, being primarily based on four traditional dishes cooked in a clay oven called a *tandoor*, which is a popular feature in parts of north India.

And although other types of food are now cooked in this way, especially fish, the four (Tandouri Murg or Chicken, Boti Kebabs or lamb on skewers, and two types of bread) remain the standards. Recipes are given later in the book for the two meat recipes, which are adapted to standard ovens. *Biryanis* and *pulaos* are both dishes based on rice—in the former the meat ingredient predominates and the overall dish is more complicated and richer than is the custom in *pulaos*, although both dishes are north Indian in origin. Many versions of both dishes use saffron to give a subtle flavour—and colour—to the finished dish.

Other important techniques include *korma*, the name given to a method of braising, usually in yogurt, although cream can be used (lamb is the meat traditionally used although pork can be substituted); *vindaloo*, where vinegar is traditionally added to the spices to create a hot and slightly sour flavour; and *chasnidarh*, which is the Indian version of sweet and sour.

But the real glory and challenge of Indian cooking lies in obtaining just the 'right' combination of the many spices which go to create the flavour called 'curry'. The combination is called *masala*, and each of the components of a *masala* should be carefully measured so that it will retain its own particular flavour in the dish, yet combine with the other spices so that none predominates. (Occasionally, it will happen that, deliberately, one spice *will* be chosen to 'stand out', but this is the exception rather than the rule.) It is an art which, of necessity, must be practised by individual cooks until they attain the final flavour most pleasing to their palate. In many of the recipes which follow, whole spices are recommended for *masalas* rather than ground ones, simply because they retain their flavour longer. Like the final taste of the *masala*, however, it is left to the particular cook to decide which is used—they are of course interchangeable. If you intend to grind your own whole spices, it is worth reserving a specific pestle and mortar for this purpose.

Menus, as they are constructed in the west, are unknown in India and, as in China, the dishes to be presented at a meal are placed on the table together. On average, a main meal will consist of a meat and/or fish offering, with three or four vegetable dishes, usually including lentils or rice, and one or more of the Indian breads. Sweetmeats are usually served after the meal, and bowls of hot water are passed around afterwards so that guests may wash their hands. Traditionally each diner is served separately from a *thali*, or round tray, upon which are placed individual bowls of the food being served. It is considered extremely rude either to eat from someone else's *thali*, or to offer anything from your own.

Although knives and forks can be used to eat Indian food, in many areas the custom is to eat with your hands, or rather right hand. (The left being considered unclean and therefore used neither to eat nor to serve food). Depending on which part of the country you find yourself (and presumably your state of hunger), you will either delicately lower your fingers into the food and scoop it up, or plunge in with more or less your whole hand. In the south, meals are often served from banana leaves rather than bowls. Alcohol is not served during the meal, although in the west lager is sometimes drunk as an accompaniment. Tea is often served after the meal.

Whether you choose to serve Indian food according to the customs of the sub-continent or whether you serve it within the context of a western menu, is up to you; it is most versatile. For Indian cooking is easily mastered—and the rewards for doing so are great: delicious and 'different' meals, often at little cost, with a variety of tastes guaranteed to tempt even the most jaded of palates.

Vegetarian Dishes

Channa Dhal (curried chick-peas)—one of the glories of a superb Indian vegetarian cuisine. Served with a selection of other vegetable or lentil dishes, and some chutney or salad, it makes a delicious meal.

CHANNA DHAL
(Curried Chick-Peas)

	Metric/U.K.	U.S.
Dried chick-peas, soaked in cold water overnight and drained	350g/12oz	2 cups
Salt	1 tsp	1 tsp
Ghee or clarified butter	40g/1½oz	3 Tbs
Cumin seeds	1 tsp	1 tsp
Medium onion, chopped	1	1
Fresh root ginger, peeled and chopped	2½cm/1in piece	1in piece
Turmeric	1 tsp	1 tsp
Ground cumin	½ tsp	½ tsp
Ground coriander	1 tsp	1 tsp
Garam masala	1 tsp	1 tsp
Hot chilli powder	¼ tsp	¼ tsp
Chopped coriander leaves	1 Tbs	1 Tbs

Put the chick-peas in a saucepan and cover with about 1½l/2½ pints (6 cups) of water and

the salt. Bring to the boil. Reduce the heat to low, half-cover the pan and simmer for 1 hour.

Melt the ghee or clarified butter in a saucepan. Add the cumin seeds and cook for 1 minute. Add the onion and ginger and fry until the onion is golden brown.

Combine the turmeric, ground cumin, coriander, garam masala, and chilli powder with 2 tablespoons of water to make a smooth paste. Add the paste to the onion mixture in the pan and fry for 3 minutes, stirring constantly. Add the chick-peas and cooking liquid and bring the mixture to the boil, stirring constantly. Reduce the heat to low, cover and simmer for 30 minutes, or until the chick-peas are tender but still firm. Adjust the seasoning if necessary.

Transfer the mixture to a warmed serving dish and sprinkle over the coriander leaves before serving.

6 Servings

BAINGAN BHARTA
(Curried Aubergine [Eggplant] Purée)

Bhartas are popular all over northern India where they are served as part of a main meal, or as a sort of side 'salad'.

	Metric/U.K.	U.S.
Aubergines (eggplants)	1kg/2lb	2lb
Canned peeled tomatoes	425g/14oz	14oz
Ground coriander	2 tsp	2 tsp
Ground cumin	1 tsp	1 tsp
Turmeric	1 tsp	1 tsp
Chopped coriander leaves	2 Tbs	2 Tbs
Ghee or vegetable oil	5 Tbs	5 Tbs
Onion, finely chopped	1	1
Garlic cloves, crushed	2	2
Fresh root ginger, peeled and finely chopped	4cm/1½in piece	1½in piece
Green chilli, chopped	1	1
Salt	1 tsp	1 tsp
Juice of ½ lemon		

Preheat the oven to moderate 180°C (Gas Mark 4, 350°F).

Cut the aubergines (eggplants) in half, lengthways, and make two or three slits in the flesh. Place the halves, flesh side up, in a baking dish. Cover with foil and put the dish into the oven. Bake for 1 hour, or until they are soft. Remove from the oven and set aside to cool.

When the aubergines (eggplants) are cool enough to handle, scoop the pulp from the skins and transfer to a bowl. Discard the skins. Mash the pulp to a smooth purée, then beat in the tomatoes, coriander, cumin, turmeric and 1 tablespoon of the coriander leaves. Set aside.

Heat the ghee or oil in a large frying-pan. Add the onion and fry until it is soft. Stir in the garlic, ginger and chilli and fry for 5 minutes, stirring frequently. Stir in the aubergine (eggplant) mixture and salt and cook, stirring frequently, until the liquid has evaporated and the mixture is thick and smooth.

Transfer the bharta to a warmed serving dish, sprinkle over the lemon juice and remaining coriander leaves, and serve at once.

6 Servings

WENGYACHEN BHARIT
(Curried Aubergines [Eggplants])

	Metric/U.K.	U.S.
Aubergines (eggplants)	1kg/2lb	2lb
Butter	40g/1½oz	3 Tbs
Medium onions, finely chopped	3	3
Garlic cloves, crushed	4	4
Fresh root ginger, peeled and finely chopped	5cm/2in piece	2in piece
Green chillis, seeded and finely chopped	2	2
Coriander leaves, chopped	½ bunch	½ bunch
Turmeric	1 tsp	1 tsp
Ground cumin	1 tsp	1 tsp
Salt	1 tsp	1 tsp
Yogurt	175ml/6floz	¾ cup
Sugar	2 tsp	2 tsp

Preheat the oven to moderate 180°C (Gas Mark 4, 350°F).

Make three slits in each aubergine (eggplant) and arrange them in a baking dish. Put the dish into the oven and bake the aubergines (eggplants) for 1 hour, or until they are soft. Remove from the oven and set aside to cool.

Vendai Kai Kari is a southern Indian vegetable dish which has okra as the main ingredient.

When they are cool enough to handle, scoop the pulp from the skins and transfer to a bowl. Mash to a smooth purée. Discard the skins.

Melt the butter in a large saucepan. Add the onions and fry until they are golden brown. Stir in the garlic, ginger and chillis and fry for 3 minutes, stirring constantly. Stir in the coriander, turmeric and cumin. Cook for 1 minute, stirring constantly. Stir in the aubergine (eggplant) purée and salt. Cook for 5 minutes, stirring frequently.

Stir in the yogurt and sugar, then remove from the heat. Transfer to a warmed serving dish.

Serve at once.

4 Servings

PAKORAS
(Vegetable Fritters)

Pakoras are usually served as a snack in India, and although cauliflower has been used here, the dish may be made from any raw vegetable, or shrimps can also be used.

	Metric/U.K.	U.S.
Chick-pea flour	175g/6oz	1½ cups
Salt	1 tsp	1 tsp
Ground coriander	1 tsp	1 tsp
Cayenne pepper	1 tsp	1 tsp
Water	175-250ml/6-8floz	¾-1 cup
Medium cauliflower, broken into flowerets	1	1
Sufficient vegetable oil for deep-frying		

Sift the flour, salt, coriander and cayenne into a bowl. Gradually pour in enough of the water to make a smooth pouring batter, stirring constantly with a wooden spoon. Set aside for 30 minutes.

Add the cauliflower flowerets to the batter and turn and toss to coat well.

Fill a deep-frying pan one-third full with oil and heat until it reaches 185°C (360°F) on a deep-fat thermometer, or until a small cube of stale bread dropped into the oil turns golden in 50 seconds.

Carefully lower the flowerets, a few at a time, into the oil and fry for 3 to 4 minutes, or until they are crisp and golden brown. Remove from the oil and drain on kitchen towels.

Transfer the cooked flowerets to a warmed serving dish and serve at once.

4 Servings

VENDAI KAI KARI
(Curried Okra)

This spicy dish comes from south India. If you prefer a less pungent curry, seed the chillis before adding them to the dish.

	Metric/U.K.	U.S.
Tamarind	50g/2oz	¼ cup
Boiling water	250ml/8floz	1 cup
Vegetable oil	60ml/2½floz	5 Tbs
Okra, cut into pieces	700g/1½lb	1½lb
Medium onions, sliced	2	2
Fresh root ginger, peeled	2½cm/1in	1in
and finely chopped	piece	piece
Garlic cloves, crushed	2	2
Green chillis, chopped	2	2
Turmeric	1 tsp	1 tsp
Ground coriander	1 Tbs	1 Tbs
Coconut milk	300ml/10floz	1¼ cups
Salt	1 tsp	1 tsp
Mustard seeds	1 tsp	1 tsp
Curry or bay leaves	4	4

Put the tamarind into a small bowl and pour over the boiling water. Set aside until the mixture is cool. Pour the mixture through a strainer into a bowl, using the back of a wooden spoon to push through as much of the softened tamarind pulp as possible. Pour over a little more water if necessary to make the tamarind juice up to 250ml/8floz (1 cup). Discard the contents of the strainer.

Heat 50ml/2floz (¼ cup) of the oil in a saucepan. Add the okra and fry until they are golden brown. Transfer to a plate and set aside.

Add the onions, ginger, garlic and chillis to

Pakoras are tasty vegetable fritters which are very popular as a snack dish in India. In this particular recipe, cauliflower has been used but any type of vegetable can be substituted.

the pan and fry until the onions are golden brown. Add the turmeric and coriander and fry for 3 minutes, stirring constantly. Add a spoonful or two of water if the mixture becomes too dry.

Pour in the tamarind juice, return the okra to the pan and bring to the boil. Reduce the heat to low, cover the pan and simmer for 5 minutes. Stir in the coconut milk and salt, and bring to the boil again. Reduce the heat to low and simmer, uncovered, for 10 minutes.

Meanwhile, heat the remaining oil in a small frying-pan. Add the mustard seeds and curry or bay leaves. Cover the pan and fry until the seeds pop. Stir the contents of this pan into the okra mixture and cook for 1 minute.

Transfer the curry to a warmed serving dish and serve at once.

4 Servings

CURRIED POTATOES AND PEAS

This dish is eaten all over India, either on its own with chappati or puris, or as part of a meal.

	Metric/U.K.	U.S.
Ghee or vegetable oil	3 Tbs	3 Tbs
Medium onion, finely chopped	1	1
Fresh root ginger, peeled and finely chopped	2½cm/1in piece	1in piece
Garlic cloves, chopped	2	2
Green chilli, chopped	1	1
Turmeric	1 tsp	1 tsp
Frozen or fresh peas, thawed	½kg/1lb	1lb
Potatoes, cubed	225g/8oz	8oz
Salt	1 tsp	1 tsp
Chopped coriander leaves	2 Tbs	2 Tbs
Juice of ½ lemon		

Heat the ghee or oil in a saucepan. Add the onion and fry until it is soft. Stir in the ginger, garlic and chilli and cook for a further 5 minutes, stirring frequently. Stir in the turmeric, then the peas, potatoes and salt. Reduce the heat to low, cover the pan and simmer for 20 minutes. Add a spoonful or two of water if the mixture becomes too dry.

Stir in the coriander leaves and lemon juice, and simmer for a further 10 to 15 minutes, or until the vegetables are tender. Serve at once.

4 Servings

JUMPING POTATOES

This dish is an essential part of a special festive dish called Alu Makhala, a speciality of a small group of Middle Eastern Jews living in India. They can, of course, be served as an accompaniment to other Indian meat or vegetable dishes.

	Metric/U.K.	U.S.
Medium potatoes, peeled	1kg/2lb	2lb
Salt	1 tsp	1 tsp
Turmeric	½ tsp	½ tsp
Vegetable oil	950ml/32floz	4 cups

Put the potatoes into a large saucepan and barely cover them with cold water. Add the salt and turmeric and bring to the boil. Boil for 30 seconds, remove from the heat and drain the potatoes.

Heat the oil in a large deep-frying pan (one that is large enough to take the potatoes in one layer). When it is hot, but not hot enough to fry the potatoes, add the potatoes. Simmer for

Sabzi Kari is a filling, easy-to-make mixed vegetable curry.

10 to 15 minutes or until they begin to soften. (Test by prodding them with a fork.) Remove from the heat and let the potatoes cool in the oil.

Twenty minutes before serving, return the pan to high heat and heat the oil until it is very hot. When the potatoes float to the top continue cooking, stirring constantly, for 5 to 6 minutes, or until the potatoes are crisp and golden brown.

Run enough cold water into the sink to make a depth of about 5cm/2in. Remove the pan from the heat and place it in the water. Stir the potatoes gently for 2 minutes. Using a slotted spoon, remove the potatoes from the oil and arrange them on a warmed serving dish. Serve very hot.

4-6 Servings

SABZI KARI
(Vegetable Curry)

The vegetables given below are only suggestions—this delightful dish can be made with others, too.

	Metric/U.K.	U.S.
Vegetable oil	3 Tbs	3 Tbs
Medium onions, chopped	2	2
Fresh root ginger, peeled and finely chopped	4cm/1½in piece	1½in piece
Garlic cloves, crushed	2	2
Green chillis, chopped	2	2
Turmeric	1 tsp	1 tsp
Ground coriander	1 Tbs	1 Tbs
Paprika	1 Tbs	1 Tbs
Cayenne pepper	½ tsp	½ tsp
Ground fenugreek	¼ tsp	¼ tsp
Black pepper	¼ tsp	¼ tsp
Lemon juice	2 Tbs	2 Tbs
Potatoes, cubed	½kg/1lb	1lb
Turnip, cubed	1	1
Carrots, sliced	3	3
French beans, sliced	125g/4oz	⅔ cup
Fresh peas, weighed after shelling	125g/4oz	⅔ cup

There are over 60 varieties of lentil in India so it is almost inevitable that there are some superb Indian lentil dishes. Sambar (recipe on the following page) is a southern Indian speciality.

Salt	1 tsp	1 tsp
Canned peeled tomatoes, rubbed through a strainer with the juice	425g/14oz	14oz

Heat the oil in a large saucepan. Add the onions, ginger, garlic and chillis and fry until the onions are golden brown.

Meanwhile, combine the turmeric, coriander, paprika, cayenne, fenugreek and pepper. Add the lemon juice and a little water, if necessary, to make a smooth paste. Add the spice paste to the onion mixture and fry for 5 minutes, stirring constantly. Add a spoonful or two of water if the mixture becomes too dry. Add the vegetables to the pan and fry for 5 minutes, stirring constantly. Stir in the salt and tomatoes and bring to the boil. Reduce the heat to low,cover the pan and simmer the curry for 25 minutes, or until the vegetables are tender.

Transfer the curry to a warmed serving dish and serve at once.

4-6 Servings

SAMBAR
(Lentils Cooked with Spices)

There are over sixty varieties of lentils to be found in India, and their popularity is what you might expect from a population that is, at least in theory, overwhelmingly vegetarian. This particular south Indian dish calls for toovar dhal (lentils) but any available type may be substituted.

	Metric/U.K.	U.S.
Toovar dhal (lentils), washed, soaked for 1 hour and drained	225g/8oz	1 cup
Ground fenugreek	½ tsp	½ tsp
Water	1¼l/2 pints	5 cups
Salt	1½ tsp	1½ tsp
Fresh coconut, chopped	50g/2oz	⅓ cup
Whole cumin seeds	2 tsp	2 tsp
Coriander seeds	1 Tbs	1 Tbs
Ground cinnamon	½ tsp	½ tsp
Tamarind	50g/2oz	¼ cup
Boiling water	250ml/8floz	1 cup
Soft brown sugar	2 tsp	2 tsp
Hot chilli powder	1 tsp	1 tsp
Chopped coriander leaves	2 Tbs	2 Tbs
Vegetable oil	2 Tbs	2 Tbs
Mustard seeds	1 tsp	1 tsp
Turmeric	1 tsp	1 tsp
Asafoetida (optional)	¼ tsp	¼ tsp
Garlic cloves, crushed	2	2
Green chilli, chopped	1	1

Put the dhal, fenugreek, water and 1 teaspoon of salt into a saucepan and bring to the boil. Reduce the heat to low and simmer for 1 hour, or until the dhal is soft. Remove from the heat.

Meanwhile, cook the coconut, cumin, coriander and cinnamon in a frying-pan, stirring constantly with a wooden spoon, for 3 minutes. Remove from the heat and allow the mixture to cool. Purée in a blender with 4 tablespoons of cold water, then transfer the mixture to a bowl and set aside.

Put the tamarind in a small bowl and pour over the boiling water. Set aside until the mixture is cool. Pour the mixture through a strainer into a saucepan, using the back of a wooden spoon to push through as much of the softened tamarind pulp as possible. Discard the contents of the strainer.

Put the saucepan over moderate heat. Stir in the sugar, chilli powder, coriander leaves and remaining salt and simmer the mixture for 5 minutes. Remove from the heat and set aside.

Heat the oil in a small frying-pan. Add the mustard seeds. Cover the pan and fry until they pop. Stir in the turmeric, asafoetida, if you are using it, the garlic and chilli. Reduce the heat to low and fry for 2 minutes, stirring constantly. Spoon the contents of the pan into the dhal with the tamarind mixture and coconut and spice purée. Return the pan to low heat and simmer the dhal mixture for 10 minutes, stirring frequently.

Remove from the heat and transfer to a warmed serving dish. Serve at once.

4 Servings

KHICHRI
(Rice with Lentils)

This is the dish from which evolved the Anglo-Indian breakfast dish of Kedgeree. It is usually served with spiced vegetables in India.

	Metric/U.K.	U.S.
Butter	75g/3oz	6 Tbs
Onion, finely chopped	1	1
Fresh root ginger, peeled and finely chopped	2½cm/1in piece	1in piece
Garlic clove, chopped	1	1
Peppercorns	6	6
Bay leaf	1	1
Long-grain rice, soaked in cold water for 1 hour and drained	225g/8oz	1⅓ cups
Moong dhal (yellow lentils), soaked with the rice in cold water for 1 hour and drained	125g/4oz	½ cup
Salt	1 tsp	1 tsp
Turmeric	½ tsp	½ tsp
Boiling water	600ml/1 pint	2½ cups

Fried onion rings
(to garnish)

Melt 50g/2oz (4 tablespoons) of the butter in a large saucepan. Add the onion and fry until it is soft. Stir in the ginger, garlic, peppercorns and bay leaf and fry for 3 minutes, stirring constantly.

Add the rice, dhal, salt and turmeric. Stir and toss the mixture gently. Reduce the heat to moderately low and continue cooking and stirring for 5 minutes. Pour in the boiling water and stir once. Reduce the heat to low, cover the pan and simmer for 15 to 20 minutes, or until the rice and dhal are cooked and the water has been absorbed. Stir in the remaining butter.

Turn the khichri into a warmed serving dish and scatter over the fried onion rings. Serve at once.

4 Servings

Rice with Aubergine (Eggplant) and Potatoes can be served either as an accompaniment to a meat or fish curry or, with other vegetable dishes, as a light meal.

Pulao with Cashew Nuts makes a delightful accompaniment to meat or poultry dishes. Scatter over some blanched almonds for a particularly effective garnish.

RICE WITH AUBERGINE (EGGPLANT) AND POTATOES

	Metric/U.K.	U.S.
Long-grain rice, soaked in cold water for 30 minutes and drained	275g/10oz	$1\frac{2}{3}$ cups
Water	600ml/1 pint	$2\frac{1}{2}$ cups
Salt	$1\frac{1}{2}$ tsp	$1\frac{1}{2}$ tsp
Turmeric	1 tsp	1 tsp
Ground cumin	1 tsp	1 tsp
Ground coriander	1 Tbs	1 Tbs
Cayenne pepper	$\frac{1}{2}$ tsp	$\frac{1}{2}$ tsp
Sugar	$\frac{1}{2}$ tsp	$\frac{1}{2}$ tsp
Lemon juice	1 Tbs	1 Tbs
Chick-pea flour	2 tsp	2 tsp
Ghee or clarified butter	50g/2oz	4 Tbs
Potatoes, cubed	350g/12oz	12oz
Aubergine (eggplant), cubed and dégorged	1	1
Butter, melted	50g/2oz	4 Tbs

Put the rice into a large saucepan. Pour over the water and 1 teaspoon of salt. Bring to the boil. Cover the pan and simmer for 15 to 20 minutes, or until the rice is tender and the water has been absorbed. Remove from the heat, set aside and keep warm.

Meanwhile, combine the turmeric, cumin, coriander, cayenne, sugar, lemon juice, flour and remaining salt to a paste, adding more lemon juice if necessary. Set aside.

Preheat the oven to moderate 180°C (Gas Mark 4, 350°F).

Melt the ghee or clarified butter in a large frying-pan. Add the potato and aubergine (eggplant) cubes and fry for 10 minutes, stirring constantly. Add a spoonful or two of water if the mixture becomes too dry. Reduce the heat to low, cover the pan and simmer for 15 to 20 minutes, or until the vegetables are tender. Set aside.

Spread half the rice over the bottom of an ovenproof dish. Sprinkle 25g/1oz (2 tablespoons) of the melted butter over the rice. Spread the vegetable mixture over the rice and cover with the remaining rice. Sprinkle the remaining melted butter over the top. Cover and put the dish into the oven. Cook for 25 minutes.

Remove from the oven and serve immediately.

4 Servings

PULAU WITH CASHEW NUTS

This dish is filling enough to constitute a light meal on its own (with, perhaps, some poppadums), or it makes a filling accompaniment to meat or fish.

	Metric/U.K.	U.S.
Butter	75g/3oz	6 Tbs
Small pineapple, peeled, cored and cut into chunks	1	1
Raisins	3 Tbs	3 Tbs
Spring onions (scallions), chopped	12	12
Unsalted cashew nuts	75g/3oz	½ cup
Coriander seeds, crushed	1 Tbs	1 Tbs
Cayenne pepper	¼ tsp	¼ tsp
Long-grain rice, soaked in cold water for 30 minutes and drained	350g/12oz	2 cups
Salt	1 tsp	1 tsp
Chicken stock	600ml/1 pint	2½ cups
Hard-boiled eggs, quartered	2	2
Chopped coriander leaves	1 Tbs	1 Tbs

Melt half the butter in a frying-pan. Add the pineapple chunks and raisins and fry until the pineapple is lightly browned. Remove the pan from the heat and set aside.

Melt the remaining butter in a large saucepan. Add the spring onions (scallions) and fry until they are golden brown. Stir in the cashew nuts, coriander seeds and cayenne and fry for 4 minutes, stirring occasionally. Stir in the rice and salt and fry for 5 minutes, stirring constantly. Stir in the pineapple mixture, then pour over the stock and bring to the boil. Reduce the heat to low, cover the pan and simmer for 20 to 25 minutes, or until the rice is tender and the liquid has been absorbed.

Transfer the pulau to a warmed serving dish, sprinkle over the coriander.

Serve at once.

4 Servings

EKURI
(Scrambled Eggs with Chilli)

This is one of the eating delights of the Parsees, a religious community in western India.

	Metric/U.K.	U.S.
Butter	40g/1½oz	3 Tbs
Medium onion, finely chopped	1	1
Fresh root ginger, peeled and finely chopped	1cm/½in piece	½in piece
Green chilli, finely chopped	1	1
Turmeric	½ tsp	½ tsp
Chopped coriander leaves	2 Tbs	2 Tbs
Salt	½ tsp	½ tsp
Eggs, lightly beaten	8	8
Bread, slightly toasted	4 slices	4 slices
Tomatoes, quartered	2	2

Melt the butter in a medium frying-pan. Add the onion and ginger and fry until the onion is soft. Stir in the chilli, turmeric, 1½ tablespoons of coriander leaves and salt and fry for 1 minute.

Pour in the beaten eggs, reduce the heat to low and cook the eggs until they are softly scrambled, stirring constantly.

Spoon the mixture on to the toast, garnish with the tomato quarters and remaining coriander leaves.

Serve at once.

4 Servings

Meat

KOFTA KARI
(Meatball Curry)

These small spicy meatballs are served in a hot sauce (the original meaning of kari, or curry, was sauce). Although this version is made with minced (ground) beef, lamb may be substituted if you prefer.

	Metric/U.K.	U.S.
MEATBALLS		
Minced (ground) beef	700g/1½lb	1½lb
Chick-pea flour	3 Tbs	3 Tbs
Fresh root ginger, peeled and chopped	1cm/½in piece	½in piece
Garlic cloves, crushed	2	2
Hot chilli powder	½ tsp	½ tsp
Salt	1 tsp	1 tsp
Egg	1	1
Turmeric	½ tsp	½ tsp
Juice and finely grated rind of ½ lemon		
Onion, finely chopped	1	1
Vegetable oil	50ml/2floz	¼ cup
SAUCE		
Vegetable oil	2 Tbs	2 Tbs
Onions, finely chopped	2	2
Fresh root ginger, peeled and chopped	1cm/½in piece	½in piece
Garlic cloves, crushed	2	2
Green chillis, chopped	2	2
Turmeric	1 tsp	1 tsp
Ground coriander	1 Tbs	1 Tbs
Ground cumin	1 tsp	1 tsp
Paprika	2 tsp	2 tsp
Creamed coconut	2½cm/1in slice	1in slice
Boiling water	450ml/15floz	2 cups
Curry leaves (optional)	3	3
Salt	1 tsp	1 tsp

First, make the meatballs. Put all the ingredients, except the oil, in a bowl and, using your hands, knead well to blend. Shape the mixture into about 24 small balls.

Heat the oil in a large frying-pan. Add the meatballs and fry until they are golden brown all over. (Don't crowd the pan; if necessary fry the balls in two or three batches.) Transfer the meatballs to a plate as they brown.

To make the sauce, heat the oil in a large saucepan. Add the onions and fry until they are golden brown. Stir in the ginger, garlic and chillis, and fry for 3 minutes. Stir in the turmeric, coriander, cumin and paprika and fry for 5 minutes. Add a spoonful or two of water if the mixture becomes too dry.

Meanwhile, dissolve the creamed coconut in the water, then stir into the saucepan with the curry leaves, if you are using them, and salt. Bring to the boil and reduce the heat to low. Cover and simmer the sauce for 15 minutes.

Add the meatballs to the pan, turning them over gently in the sauce to coat them well. Bring to the boil again. Reduce the heat to low, re-cover the pan and simmer for a further 20 minutes.

Remove from the heat and transfer the mixture to a warmed serving dish. Serve at once.

4 Servings

KHEEMA
(Curried Minced [Ground] Meat)

This dish is often combined with peas or cabbage in India to provide a light main dish. If you prefer a mild curry, reduce the amount of chilli powder.

	Metric/U.K.	U.S.
Vegetable oil	50ml/2floz	¼ cup
Medium onions, thinly sliced	4	4
Fresh root ginger, peeled and finely chopped	2½cm/1in piece	1in piece
Garlic cloves, crushed	2	2
Turmeric	1 tsp	1 tsp
Hot chilli powder	1 tsp	1 tsp
Ground coriander	1 tsp	1 tsp
Minced (ground) beef	700g/1½lb	1½lb
Salt	½ tsp	½ tsp
Tomatoes, blanched, peeled and chopped	3	3

	Metric/U.K.	U.S.
Chopped coriander leaves	2 Tbs	2 Tbs

Heat the oil in a saucepan. Add the onions, ginger and garlic and fry until the onions are soft. Stir in the turmeric, chilli powder and coriander, and fry for 3 minutes, stirring constantly. Stir in the meat and fry until it is well browned. Add the salt and tomatoes. Stir well, reduce the heat to moderately low and cover the pan. Simmer the kheema for 10 minutes.

Uncover the pan and cook for a further 5 minutes. Adjust seasoning and serve at once.

4 Servings

DRY BEEF CURRY

This is a very basic and easy-to-make dish. If you wish it to be less pungent, seed the chillis before cooking them. Serve with plain rice and a selection of raitas, sambals and chutney.

	Metric/U.K.	U.S.
Vegetable oil	50ml/2floz	$\frac{1}{4}$ cup
Green chillis, chopped	2	2
Medium onions, chopped	2	2
Stewing or chuck steak, cubed	1kg/2lb	2lb
Salt	$\frac{1}{2}$ tsp	$\frac{1}{2}$ tsp
Tomatoes, blanched, peeled and chopped	2	2
Turmeric	1 tsp	1 tsp
Ground cumin	1 tsp	1 tsp
Ground coriander	2 tsp	2 tsp
Garam masala	$1\frac{1}{2}$ tsp	$1\frac{1}{2}$ tsp
Yogurt	300ml/10floz	$1\frac{1}{4}$ cups
Chopped coriander leaves	1 Tbs	1 Tbs

Heat the oil in a saucepan. Add the chillis and fry for 1 minute. Stir in the onions and fry until they are golden brown. Add the beef cubes and salt. Fry for 10 to 15 minutes, or until they are deeply browned all over. Stir in the tomatoes and cook for 10 minutes, or until most of the liquid has evaporated.

Combine the turmeric, cumin, coriander and 1 teaspoon of the garam masala. Beat in the yogurt. Stir this mixture into the mixture in the pan, reduce the heat to low and half-cover. Simmer for $1\frac{1}{2}$ hours.

Remove the lid from the pan and simmer the curry for a further 30 minutes, or until the liquid has evaporated leaving the meat covered in a thick gravy. If the curry becomes too dry too quickly, cover and continue cooking.

Transfer the mixture to a warmed serving dish and sprinkle over the remaining garam masala and the coriander leaves.

Serve at once.

4-6 Servings

Kofta Kari are savoury little meatballs covered with a hot, spicy sauce.

GOSHT AUR ALOO
(Beef and Potato Curry)

Succulent beef and small new potatoes form the basis of this unusual dish, called Gosht aur Aloo.

	Metric/U.K.	U.S.
Ghee or clarified butter	50g/2oz	4 Tbs
Onions, finely chopped	2	2
Garlic clove, crushed	1	1
Fresh root ginger, peeled and chopped	4cm/1½in piece	1½in piece
Green chillis, chopped	2	2
Turmeric	1 tsp	1 tsp
Ground coriander	1 Tbs	1 Tbs
Hot chilli powder	¼ tsp	¼ tsp
Ground cumin	1 tsp	1 tsp
Cardamom seeds, crushed	1 Tbs	1 Tbs
Ground cloves	½ tsp	½ tsp
Lean stewing or chuck steak, cubed	1kg/2lb	2lb
Water	450ml/15floz	2 cups
Salt	1 tsp	1 tsp
Bay leaves	2	2
Small potatoes, scrubbed	½kg/1lb	1lb

Melt the ghee or butter in a large saucepan. Add the onions and garlic and fry until they are golden brown. Stir in the ginger and chillis and fry for 4 minutes. Stir in the turmeric, coriander, chilli powder, cumin, cardamom and cloves and fry for 6 minutes, stirring frequently. Add a spoonful or two of water if the mixture becomes too dry.

Add the meat cubes and fry until they are evenly browned. Stir in the water, salt and bay leaves, and bring to the boil. When the mixture begins to bubble, reduce the heat to low and simmer for 1¼ hours.

Add the potatoes and bring to the boil again. Cover and simmer for a further 45 minutes, or until the meat is cooked through and tender. Taste and add more salt if necessary.

Transfer the mixture to a warmed serving dish and serve at once.

4-6 Servings

TURKARI MOLEE
(Lamb and Coconut Curry)

A molee in Indian cooking is a curry in which coconut is used as one of the main flavourings. This is one of the basic molees.

	Metric/U.K.	U.S.
Ghee or clarified butter	50g/2oz	4 Tbs
Medium onions, sliced	2	2
Garlic cloves, crushed	6	6
Fresh root ginger, peeled and finely chopped	5cm/2in piece	2in piece
Turmeric	1½ tsp	1½ tsp
Hot chilli powder	2 tsp	2 tsp
Black pepper	½ tsp	½ tsp
Ground fenugreek	½ tsp	½ tsp
Ground coriander	2 tsp	2 tsp
Ground cumin	1 tsp	1 tsp
Paprika	2 tsp	2 tsp
Lean lamb, cubed	1kg/2lb	2lb
Coconut milk	600ml/1 pint	2½ cups
Salt	1½ tsp	1½ tsp
Curry leaves (optional)	2	2

Melt the ghee or clarified butter in a large saucepan. Add the onions and fry until they are golden brown. Add the garlic, ginger, turmeric, chilli powder, pepper, fenugreek, coriander, cumin and paprika and fry for 5 minutes, stirring constantly. Add a spoonful or two of water if the mixture becomes too dry.

Add the lamb cubes and fry for 10 minutes, turning them frequently. Pour in the coconut milk and add the salt and curry leaves, if you are using them. Bring to the boil. Reduce the heat to low, cover the pan and simmer for 1 hour or until the lamb is cooked through and tender.

Transfer to a warmed serving dish and serve at once.

4-6 Servings

KABAB MASSALAM
(Minced [Ground] Lamb kebabs)

These spicy cigar-shaped kebabs are popular all over India. The thick wooden skewers traditionally used for kebabs in India should be used in this dish—the mixture adheres to it better than it would to a metal skewer. Serve on a bed of rice, or over bread as in the picture overleaf and a selection of chutneys.

kebabs for 5 minutes. Turn, then brush with the remaining melted butter and grill (broil) for a further 5 minutes, or until the kebabs are cooked through.

Arrange the skewers on a warmed serving dish and garnish with the lemon quarters. Serve at once.

4 Servings

ZEERA GOSHT
(Cumin Lamb)

In Indian cooking, the masala, or combination of spices, is usually such that no one spice 'stands out' in the finished dish—but occasionally, to provide a different taste for a dish, one is allowed to predominate. The 'zeera' in this succulent lamb dish means that the singled-out taste is cumin.

The Indians are very fond of kebabs and they are cooked in many different ways. This particular Kabab Massalam is simply minced (ground) meat wrapped around traditional thick wooden skewers and grilled (broiled). The result is absolutely delicious.

	Metric/U.K.	U.S.
Garlic cloves, crushed	3	3
Fresh root ginger, peeled and finely chopped	4cm/1½in piece	1½in piece
Green chillis, finely chopped	2	2
Medium onion, chopped	1	1
Chopped coriander leaves	2 Tbs	2 Tbs
Yogurt	3 Tbs	3 Tbs
Turmeric	½ tsp	½ tsp
Lemon juice	1 Tbs	1 Tbs
Salt	1 tsp	1 tsp
Fresh breadcrumbs	15g/½oz	¼ cup
Minced (ground) lamb	700g/1½lb	1½lb
Butter, melted	25g/1oz	2 Tbs
Lemons, quartered	2	2

Combine all the ingredients, except the melted butter and lemons, in a large bowl. Using your hands, lightly knead until the ingredients are blended and the mixture is stiff. Cover and set aside to 'rest' for 30 minutes.

Preheat the grill (broiler) to high. Lightly grease 12 skewers with a little of the melted butter. With dampened hands, remove small pieces of the meat mixture and shape them into cigar shapes around the skewers, two to a skewer.

Lay the skewers on the lined grill (broiler) pan and brush them with about half the remaining melted butter. Grill (broil) the

	Metric/U.K.	U.S.
Whole cumin seeds	1 Tbs	1 Tbs
Fresh root ginger, peeled and chopped	2½cm/1in piece	1in piece
Garlic cloves	3	3
Cardamom seeds	2 tsp	2 tsp
Whole cloves	2	2
Blanched almonds	12	12
Sesame seeds	2 tsp	2 tsp
Cayenne pepper	1 tsp	1 tsp
Salt	1 tsp	1 tsp
Soft brown sugar	1 tsp	1 tsp
Yogurt	175ml/6floz	¾ cup
Butter	40g/1½oz	3 Tbs
Medium onion, finely chopped	1	1
Large green or red peppers, pith and seeds removed and sliced	2	2
Boned leg of lamb, cubed	1kg/2lb	2lb
Ground saffron	¼ tsp	¼ tsp

Put the cumin seeds, ginger, garlic, cardamom seeds, cloves, almonds, sesame seeds, cayenne, salt, sugar and 2 tablespoons of the yogurt into a blender and blend to a purée, adding more yogurt if the mixture becomes too dry. Transfer the mixture to a small bowl and set aside.

Melt the butter in a large flameproof casserole. Add the onion and fry until it is golden brown. Stir in the spice paste and fry for 5 minutes, stirring constantly, adding a spoonful or two of water if the mixture becomes too dry. Add the peppers and fry for 2 minutes. Add the lamb and fry for 10 minutes, turning the cubes frequently.

Meanwhile, beat the remaining yogurt and saffron together, then pour the mixture into the casserole and mix well. Bring to the boil, reduce the heat to very low and cover the casserole. Simmer for 50 minutes.

Meanwhile, preheat the oven to cool 150°C (Gas Mark 2, 300°F).

Transfer the casserole to the oven and cook the lamb for 25 minutes. Remove from the oven and serve at once.

4-6 Servings

SAG GOSHT
(Lamb and Spinach Curry)

You can substitute lean veal cubes for the lamb in this dish, if you prefer.

	Metric/U.K.	U.S.
Ghee or clarified butter	50g/2oz	4 Tbs
Mustard seeds	1½ tsp	1½ tsp
Garlic cloves, crushed	2	2
Cardamom seeds, crushed	2 tsp	2 tsp
Ground coriander	1 Tbs	1 Tbs
Fresh root ginger, peeled and chopped	4cm/1½in piece	1½in piece
Lean boned lamb, cubed	1kg/2lb	2lb
Medium onion, chopped	1	1
Green chillis, chopped	3	3
Sugar	1 tsp	1 tsp
Turmeric	1 tsp	1 tsp
Spinach, trimmed, washed and chopped	1kg/2lb	2lb
Salt	1½ tsp	1½ tsp
Black pepper	½ tsp	½ tsp
Yogurt	3 Tbs	3 Tbs

Melt the ghee or butter in a flameproof casserole. Add the mustard seeds and cover.

Sag Gosht is a nutrious—and delicious—mixture of lean lamb cubes and velvety leaf spinach cooked together in a yogurt-based sauce.

Fry until the seeds begin to pop. Stir in the garlic, cardamom, coriander and ginger and fry for 1 minute, stirring constantly. Add the lamb cubes and fry until they are evenly browned.

Stir in the onion, chillis and sugar and fry until the onion is golden brown. Stir in the turmeric and spinach and cook for 3 minutes. Add the remaining ingredients and reduce the heat to low. Cover and simmer for 1 hour, or until the meat is cooked through and tender and the spinach is smooth and soft. Uncover and stir well.

Preheat the oven to cool 150°C (Gas Mark 2, 300°F). Put the casserole into the oven and cook for 20 minutes. Remove from the oven and serve at once.

4-6 Servings

ROGHAN JOSH
(Spiced Lamb)

This dish is one of the classics of Kashmiri cooking, although it is now eaten all over northern India. It is traditionally eaten with chappati or naan, rather than rice.

	Metric/U.K.	U.S.
Yogurt	250ml/8floz	1 cup
Asafoetida (optional)	$\frac{1}{4}$ tsp	$\frac{1}{4}$ tsp
Cayenne pepper	$\frac{1}{2}$ tsp	$\frac{1}{2}$ tsp
Boned leg of lamb, cubed	1kg/2lb	2lb
Fresh root ginger, peeled and chopped	4cm/1$\frac{1}{2}$in piece	1$\frac{1}{2}$in piece
Garlic cloves	4	4
White poppy seeds	1 tsp	1 tsp
Cumin seeds	1 tsp	1 tsp
Coriander seeds	1 Tbs	1 Tbs
Cloves	4	4
Cardamom seeds	1 Tbs	1 Tbs
Peppercorns	8	8
Whole unblanched almonds	2 Tbs	2 Tbs
Ghee or clarified butter	50g/2oz	4 Tbs
Medium onion, chopped	1	1
Turmeric	1 tsp	1 tsp
Water	250ml/8floz	1 cup
Garam masala	1 tsp	1 tsp
Chopped coriander leaves	1 Tbs	1 Tbs

Combine the yogurt, asafoetida, if you are using it, and cayenne in a large bowl. Add the lamb cubes, baste well, cover and set aside.

Put the ginger, garlic, poppy, cumin and coriander seeds, cloves, cardamom, peppercorns and almonds in a blender with 4 tablespoons of water and blend until the mixture forms a smooth paste. Add more water if necessary. Transfer the mixture to a small bowl and set aside.

Melt the ghee or clarified butter in a flameproof casserole. Add the onion and fry until it is golden brown. Stir in the turmeric and spice paste and fry for 8 minutes, stirring constantly. Add a spoonful or two of water if the mixture becomes too dry.

Increase the heat to high. Add the lamb cubes and marinade and fry for 10 minutes, stirring constantly. Reduce the heat to very low, cover and simmer for 45 minutes.

Uncover the casserole, increase the heat to moderate and stir in 50ml/2floz ($\frac{1}{4}$ cup) of water until it has been absorbed. Add another 50ml/2floz ($\frac{1}{4}$ cup) and stir until it has been absorbed. Pour in the remaining water, re-cover and simmer the lamb for a further 15 minutes.

Preheat the oven to very cool 140°C (Gas Mark 1, 275°F).

Stir in the garam masala and coriander leaves. Cover and put the casserole into the oven. Cook for 25 minutes. Remove from the oven, transfer the mixture to a warmed serving dish and serve at once.

4-6 Servings

SHAKOOTI RASSA
(Lamb Cooked with Coconut)

This spicy dish of lamb with vegetables comes from the west coast of India.

	Metric/U.K.	U.S.
Chillis, seeded	6	6
Chopped coriander leaves	6 Tbs	6 Tbs
Garlic cloves	3	3
Fresh root ginger, peeled and chopped	5cm/2in piece	2in piece

Salt	1 tsp	1 tsp		White poppy seeds	1 Tbs	1 Tbs
Thick coconut milk	475ml/16floz	2 cups		Black peppercorns	1 tsp	1 tsp
Boned leg of lamb, cubed	1kg/2lb	2lb		Turmeric	1 tsp	1 tsp
Ghee or clarified butter	65g/2½oz	5 Tbs		Grated nutmeg	½ tsp	½ tsp
Fresh coconut, grated	½	½		Medium onions, chopped	2	2
Whole cumin seeds	1 Tbs	1 Tbs		Potatoes, cubed	½kg/1lb	1lb

Lamb and vegetables cooked with coconut, Shakooti Rassa is a western Indian speciality.

213

Raan is a classic Indian dish in which leg of lamb is marinated in yogurt and spices for 48 hours before being roasted until it is so tender the meat almost falls off the bones.

Put the chillis, coriander leaves, garlic, ginger and salt into a blender and blend, adding 2 to 3 tablespoons of coconut milk, to make a smooth paste. Alternatively, pound the ingredients in a mortar with a pestle. Transfer the spice paste to a large mixing bowl and add the meat cubes. Mix well, then set aside to marinate at room temperature for 6 hours, basting occasionally.

Melt 25g/1oz (2 tablespoons) of the ghee or clarified butter in a frying-pan. Add the grated coconut, cumin and poppy seeds, peppercorns, turmeric and nutmeg and fry, stirring constantly, for 5 minutes or until the ingredients are lightly browned. Remove from the heat and set aside to cool. When cool, put the mixture into the blender with 125ml/4floz ($\frac{1}{2}$ cup) of the remaining coconut milk and blend until it forms a smooth purée. Alternatively, pound in a mortar with a pestle. Set aside.

Melt the remaining ghee or clarified butter in a saucepan. Add the onions and fry until they are golden brown. Stir in the coconut and spice purée and fry for 5 minutes, stirring constantly. Stir in the meat mixture and fry for 10 minutes, or until the cubes are evenly browned. Pour in the remaining coconut milk, stir well and bring to the boil. Reduce the heat to low, cover the pan and simmer for 40 minutes.

Add the potatoes and more salt if necessary. Continue cooking, uncovered, for 20 minutes, or until the potatoes are tender and the sauce has thickened. Remove from the heat and transfer the shakooti to a warmed serving dish. Serve at once.

4-6 Servings

KORMA
(Lamb and Almond Curry)

Korma is a method of cooking in India, akin to braising in western cuisine. In this particular basic korma the braising agents are yogurt and cream, although stock and even water are sometimes used. Kormas can be made with most kinds of meat and vegetables.

	Metric/U.K.	U.S.
Medium onions, chopped	2	2
Fresh root ginger, peeled and chopped	4cm/1½in piece	1½in piece
Garlic cloves, crushed	3	3
Ground saffron	½ tsp	½ tsp
Yogurt	150ml/5floz	⅝ cup
Boned leg of lamb, cut into cubes	1kg/2lb	2lb
Butter	50g/2oz	4 Tbs
Hot chilli powder	½ tsp	½ tsp
Dill seed, crushed	1 tsp	1 tsp
Salt	1 tsp	1 tsp
Ground almonds	50g/2oz	⅓ cup
Double (heavy) cream	150ml/5floz	⅝ cup

Combine half the onions, half the ginger, half the garlic, the saffron and 2 to 3 tablespoons of yogurt in a large bowl. Add the meat and baste well. Set aside to marinate for 1 hour.

Melt the butter in a large saucepan. Add the remaining onions, ginger and garlic and fry until they are deep golden brown. Using a slotted spoon, transfer the mixture to a plate.

Add the meat mixture to the pan and fry until they are evenly browned. Moisten the meat with a spoonful or two of yogurt while frying. As it dries, add more yogurt. Stir in the onion mixture, chilli powder, dill, salt and any remaining yogurt. Reduce the heat to low and simmer the meat, stirring occasionally, for 40 minutes. Add a spoonful or two of water if the mixture becomes too dry.

Mix the almonds and cream together, then stir the mixture into the lamb. Cover the pan and continue to simmer the korma for a further 15 to 20 minutes, or until the lamb is cooked through and tender.

Transfer to a warmed serving dish and serve at once.

4-6 Servings

RAAN
(Leg of Lamb Marinated in Spiced Yogurt and Roasted)

	Metric/U.K.	U.S.
Leg of lamb, trimmed of fat	1x3kg/6lb	1x6lb
Fresh root ginger, peeled and chopped	125g/4oz	4oz
Large garlic cloves, peeled	12	12
Thinly pared rind of 1 lemon		
Lemon juice	5 Tbs	5 Tbs
Cumin seeds	2 tsp	2 tsp
Cardamom seeds	1 Tbs	1 Tbs
Whole cloves	8	8
Turmeric	1 tsp	1 tsp
Hot chilli powder	1½ tsp	1½ tsp
Salt	1 Tbs	1 Tbs
Unblanched almonds	150g/5oz	1 cup
Soft brown sugar	4 Tbs	4 Tbs
Yogurt	300ml/10floz	1¼ cups
Saffron threads, soaked in 2 Tbs boiling water	½ tsp	½ tsp

Prick the leg of lamb all over. Make several deep gashes in the flesh, then transfer to a large, deep roasting pan. Set aside.

Put the ginger, garlic, lemon rind and juice, cumin seeds, cardamom seeds, cloves, turmeric, chilli powder and salt in a blender and blend to a purée. Scrape the purée out of the blender and spread it all over the lamb. Set aside for 1 hour.

Put the almonds, 2 tablespoons of the sugar and half the yogurt into the blender and blend until they form a purée. Transfer to a small bowl and stir in the remaining yogurt. Spread this mixture all over the lamb, on top of the spice purée. Cover the pan and chill in the refrigerator for 48 hours.

Preheat the oven to hot 220°C (Gas Mark 7, 425°F).

Remove the pan from the refrigerator and allow the lamb to warm to room temperature. Sprinkle over the remaining sugar. Put the pan into the oven and roast for 20 minutes. Reduce the oven temperature to moderate 180°C (Gas Mark 4, 350°F) and roast for a further 1 hour. Reduce the temperature to warm 170°C (Gas Mark 3, 325°F), cover the pan and roast, basting occasionally, for 4 hours.

Remove from the oven and, using two large forks or spoons, transfer the lamb to a large piece of foil. Cover the meat completely and return to the oven.

Remove any excess fat from the pan, then stir in the saffron mixture. Place the pan over high heat and boil the sauce rapidly for 15 to 20 minutes, or until it is reduced by half. Remove from the heat.

Remove the lamb from the oven and discard the foil. Arrange on a warmed serving dish, spoon over the sauce and serve at once.

8-10 Servings

TALAWA GOSHT
(Deep-Fried Lamb and Potatoes)

	Metric/U.K.	U.S.
Butter	25g/1oz	2 Tbs
Fresh root ginger, peeled and finely chopped	4cm/1½in piece	1½in piece
Garlic cloves, crushed	3	3
Boned leg of lamb, cubed	700g/1½lb	1½lb
Turmeric	1 tsp	1 tsp
Hot chilli powder	2 tsp	2 tsp
Salt	½ tsp	½ tsp
Yogurt	50ml/2floz	¼ cup
Sufficient vegetable oil for deep-frying		
Potatoes, boiled until nearly tender, drained and cubed	½kg/1lb	1lb
Lemons, cut into wedges	2	2
BATTER		
Chick-pea flour	225g/8oz	2 cups
Salt	1 tsp	1 tsp
Hot chilli powder	½ tsp	½ tsp
Yogurt	75ml/3floz	⅜ cup
Water	250ml/8floz	1 cup

Melt the butter in a deep frying-pan. Add the ginger and garlic and fry for 3 minutes, stirring frequently. Add the meat cubes and fry until they are evenly browned.

Meanwhile, combine the turmeric, chilli powder, salt and yogurt together in a small bowl. Stir the mixture into the pan and cook, uncovered, for 30 minutes or until the lamb is just cooked through. Set aside to cool.

To make the batter, sift the flour, salt and chilli powder into a large bowl. Beat in the yogurt and stir in the water, a little at a time, until the mixture forms a smooth batter. Set aside for 30 minutes.

Fill a deep-frying pan one-third full with oil and heat until it reaches 185°C (360°F) on a deep-fat thermometer, or until a small cube of stale bread dropped into the oil turns golden in 50 seconds. Dip the lamb and potato cubes into the batter, then carefully lower them, a few at a time, into the hot oil. Fry for 3 to 4 minutes, or until they are golden brown and crisp. Remove from the oil and drain on kitchen towels.

Serve at once, garnished with the lemon wedges.

4 Servings

BADAMI GOSHT
(Lamb with Almonds)

	Metric/U.K.	U.S.
Ghee or clarified butter	65g/2½oz	5 Tbs
Cinnamon sticks	2x10cm/4in	2x4in
Whole cloves	6	6
Cardamom seeds	1 Tbs	1 Tbs
Large onion, chopped	1	1
Garlic cloves, crushed	2	2

Fresh root ginger, peeled and finely chopped	4cm/1½in piece	1½in piece
Boned leg of lamb, cubed	700g/1½lb	1½lb
Yogurt	300ml/10floz	1¼ cups
Saffron threads, soaked in 2 Tbs boiling water	1 tsp	1 tsp
Hot chilli powder	½ tsp	½ tsp
Ground almonds	75g/3oz	½ cup
Salt	1 tsp	1 tsp
Coconut milk	350ml/12floz	1½ cups
Dried red chillis	2	2

Melt the ghee or butter in a saucepan. Add the cinnamon, cloves and cardamom seeds and fry for 1 minute, stirring constantly. Add the onion and fry until it is soft. Add the garlic and ginger and fry for 2 minutes, stirring constantly. Add the lamb cubes to the pan and fry until they are evenly browned.

Combine the yogurt, saffron mixture and chilli powder in a small bowl, beating to blend thoroughly. In a second bowl, combine the almonds with enough water to make a smooth paste.

Stir the yogurt mixture and almond paste into the lamb cubes, then stir in the salt. Simmer the mixture for 15 minutes. Stir in the coconut milk and red chillis, and simmer for a further 40 minutes, or until the lamb is cooked through and tender. Cover the lamb for the last 10 minutes of cooking.

Serve at once.

4 Servings

Almonds and coconut form the flavourful base of this lamb curry known as Badami Gosht.

YAKHNI PULAO
(Lamb Cooked with Rice)

Yakhni in Indian cooking is similar to a western stock and is used as a basis for many dishes. The stock can be made with almost any type of meat or poultry, although lamb, as here, and chicken are the most popular.

Yakhni in India is a type of highly flavoured stock, and in this dish it is cooked with lean lamb cubes and rice to make a superb Yakhni Pulao.

	Metric/U.K.	U.S.
Boned leg of lamb, cubed and with the bones reserved	1kg/2lb	2lb
Pared rind of 1 lemon		
Fresh root ginger, peeled and thinly sliced	1cm/½in piece	½in piece
Cinnamon stick, bruised	2x5cm/2in pieces	2x2in pieces
Grated nutmeg	¼ tsp	¼ tsp
Green chilli, chopped	1	1
Black peppercorns	12	12
Yogurt	150ml/5floz	⅝ cup
Cayenne pepper	½ tsp	½ tsp
Juice of ½ lemon		
Salt	1½ tsp	1½ tsp
Butter	125g/4oz	8 Tbs
Medium onion, finely chopped	1	1
Whole cloves, bruised	4	4
Cardamom seeds, bruised	4	4
Whole cumin seeds	1 tsp	1 tsp
Long-grain rice, soaked in cold water for 30 minutes and drained	350g/12oz	2 cups
GARNISH		
Slivered almonds, lightly toasted	2 Tbs	2 Tbs

Medium onion, thinly sliced and fried until golden	1	1
Raisins, lightly fried	2 Tbs	2 Tbs
Hard-boiled eggs, quartered	2	2

Put the lamb, the reserved bones, lemon rind, ginger, cinnamon, nutmeg, chilli and peppercorns in a large saucepan. Add enough water to cover the lamb and bones generously and bring to the boil. Reduce the heat to low, cover and simmer the mixture for 40 minutes, or until the lamb cubes are cooked through and tender.

Using a slotted spoon, transfer the lamb cubes to a bowl. Re-cover the pan and continue simmering the stock for 2 hours. Remove from the heat and strain into a bowl, discarding the contents of the strainer. Set the stock aside to cool. When it is cold, skim off and discard the fat on the surface.

Meanwhile, combine the yogurt, cayenne, lemon juice and half the salt. Pour the mixture over the lamb cubes and coat well. Cover the bowl and set aside for 2 hours.

Melt half the butter in a large saucepan. Add the onion and fry until it is golden brown. Stir in the cloves, cardamom and cumin and fry for 2 minutes. Stir in the rice and fry for 6 to 8 minutes, or until the rice becomes translucent.

Preheat the oven to very cool 140°C (Gas Mark 1, 275°F).

Meanwhile, pour the stock into a saucepan and bring to the boil. Remove from the heat and pour the stock over the rice, to cover it by about 1cm/½in. Add the remaining salt and, when the mixture comes back to the boil, reduce the heat to low and cover the pan. Simmer for 15 to 20 minutes, or until the rice is tender and the stock has been absorbed. Remove from the heat.

Meanwhile, melt the remaining butter in a frying-pan. Add the lamb cubes and marinade and fry for 5 minutes, stirring constantly. Reduce the heat to low and simmer for 10 minutes, stirring frequently. Remove from the heat.

Layer the rice and lamb into a large baking dish, beginning and ending with a layer of rice. Cover tightly with foil. Put the dish into the oven and bake for 20 minutes.

Combine the almonds, onion and raisins together and set aside.

Remove the dish from the oven and sprinkle over the garnish and eggs.

4-6 Servings

BOTI KEBABS
(Lamb on Skewers)

This is one of the basic tandoori dishes—dishes cooked in the clay oven called tandoor.

	Metric/U.K.	U.S.
Boned leg of lamb, cubed	1kg/2lb	2lb
Yogurt	150ml/5floz	⅝ cup
Ground coriander	1 Tbs	1 Tbs
Turmeric	1 tsp	1 tsp
Hot chilli powder	½ tsp	½ tsp
Salt	1 tsp	1 tsp
Garlic cloves, crushed	2	2
Fresh root ginger, peeled and finely chopped	2½cm/1in piece	1in piece
Chopped coriander leaves	1 Tbs	1 Tbs
Lemons, cut into wedges	2	2

Put the lamb cubes into a large bowl. Combine the yogurt, coriander, turmeric, chilli powder, salt, garlic and ginger and beat well. Pour over the lamb cubes, baste well and cover the bowl. Chill in the refrigerator for 6 hours, or overnight, basting occasionally.

Preheat the grill (broiler) to high.

Stir the meat mixture well, then thread the cubes on to skewers. Put the skewers on to the lined rack of the grill (broiler) pan and grill (broil) the cubes for 5 to 8 minutes on each side, or until they are cooked through.

Transfer the skewers to a warmed serving dish and sprinkle over the coriander leaves. Garnish with the lemon wedges before serving.

6 Servings

VINDALOO
(Vinegar Pork Curry)

Vindaloos come from the west coast of India and, although they are traditionally made with pork, chicken and even duck are sometimes substituted. This type of curry relies on vinegar rather than coconut milk to moisten and is rather hot.

	Metric/U.K.	U.S.
Fresh root ginger, peeled and chopped	5cm/2in piece	2in piece

A simple dish of braised, curried lambs' kidneys, Gurda Korma can be served with a selection of chutneys to make the centrepiece for a beautiful meal.

Garlic cloves, chopped	4	4
Hot chilli powder	1½ tsp	1½ tsp
Turmeric	2 tsp	2 tsp
Salt	1 tsp	1 tsp
Cardamom seeds	1 Tbs	1 Tbs
Whole cloves	6	6
Peppercorns	6	6
Cinnamon stick	5cm/2in	2in
Coriander seeds	2 Tbs	2 Tbs
Cumin seeds	1 Tbs	1 Tbs
Wine vinegar	150ml/5floz	⅝ cup
Pork fillet (tenderloin), cubed	1kg/2lb	2lb
Curry leaves (optional)	4	4
Vegetable oil	3 Tbs	3 Tbs
Mustard seeds	1 tsp	1 tsp
Water	150ml/5floz	⅝ cup

Put the ginger, garlic, chilli powder, turmeric, salt, cardamom, cloves, peppercorns, cinnamon, coriander, cumin seeds and vinegar into a blender and blend to a purée. Scrape down the sides of the blender and blend for a further 30 seconds. Add more vinegar if necessary to form a smooth liquid paste.

Put the pork in a large bowl and pour over the spice paste. Cover and set aside to marinate for 1 hour. Lay the curry leaves, if you are using them, on top. Re-cover and put the bowl into the refrigerator for 24 hours, turning the meat two or three times during the period.

Two hours before cooking time, remove the bowl from refrigerator and set aside.

Heat the oil in a large saucepan. Add the mustard seeds and cover the pan. Fry the seeds until they pop, then add the pork, marinade and water and bring to the boil, stirring constantly. Reduce the heat to low, cover the pan and simmer for 30 minutes. Uncover and simmer for a further 30 minutes, or until the pork is cooked through and tender.

Transfer the vindaloo to a warmed serving dish and serve at once.

4-6 Servings

KOFTA CHASNIDARH
(Sweet and Sour Meatballs)

The Indians, too, have a sweet and sour taste although it is perhaps not so well known as the Chinese version. This is a basic version of the technique using meatballs as the meat ingredient, but cubed beef, lamb or pork could equally be used providing the cooking time is adjusted to suit.

	Metric/U.K.	U.S.
Minced (ground) pork	700g/1½lb	1½lb
Small onion, grated	1	1
Paprika	1 tsp	1 tsp
Ground cumin	2 tsp	2 tsp
Salt and pepper to taste		
Chick-pea flour	3 Tbs	3 Tbs
Ghee or clarified butter	50g/2oz	4 Tbs
Sugar	50g/2oz	¼ cup
Lime or lemon juice	125ml/4floz	½ cup
Cornflour (cornstarch)	1 Tbs	1 Tbs
Fresh root ginger, peeled and finely chopped	2½cm/1in piece	1in piece
Carrots, cut into lengths	2	2
Medium onions, quartered	2	2
Green pepper, pith and seeds removed and chopped	1	1
Chicken stock	300ml/10floz	1¼ cups
Saffron threads, soaked in 2 Tbs boiling water	¼ tsp	¼ tsp
Ground fenugreek	2 tsp	2 tsp

Put the pork, onion, paprika, cumin, seasoning and flour into a large bowl and mix well. Using your hands, shape the mixture into walnut-sized balls.

Melt three-quarters of the ghee or butter in a large frying-pan. Add the meatballs, a few at a time, and fry until they are deeply and evenly browned. Remove from the heat and keep hot while you make the sauce.

Mix the sugar, lime or lemon juice and cornflour (cornstarch) in a bowl until they are well blended. Set aside.

Melt the remaining ghee or butter in a saucepan. Add the ginger and fry for 1 minute, stirring constantly. Add the vegetables and fry until they are soft. Pour over the stock and bring to the boil. Stir in the sugar mixture and cook, stirring constantly, until the liquid thickens and becomes smooth. Stir in the remaining ingredients, including the reserved meatballs, and bring the liquid to the boil again. Reduce the heat to low, cover the pan and simmer for 30 to 40 minutes, or until the

Small onions, chopped	2	2
Hot chilli powder	¼ tsp	¼ tsp
Ground turmeric	¼ tsp	¼ tsp
Ground coriander	1 tsp	1 tsp
Ground cumin	¼ tsp	¼ tsp
Salt and pepper to taste		
Lambs' kidneys, prepared and quartered	8	8
Small green pepper, pith and seeds removed and thinly sliced	1	1

Melt the butter with the oil in a frying-pan. Add the garlic and ginger and fry for 30 seconds. Stir in the onions and fry until they are soft. Stir in the chilli powder, turmeric, coriander and cumin and cook for 1 minute. Add the seasoning and kidneys. Stir well to coat the kidneys, then cook, stirring occasionally, for 15 minutes, or until the kidneys are only faintly pink inside.

Transfer the mixture to a warmed serving dish and arrange the green pepper on top. Serve at once.

4 Servings

Samosas are the Indian equivalent of western turnovers and are served as snacks and at picnics all over India. This particular version contains a spicy meat filling.

meatballs are cooked through and tender and the sauce has thickened.

Transfer the mixture to a warmed serving dish.

Serve at once.

4 Servings

GURDA KORMA
(Curried Kidneys)

This dish is simple in the extreme, yet the end result is both appetizing and attractive to look at (see the photograph on the previous page). Serve with plain boiled rice and a selection of chutneys and raitas.

	Metric/U.K.	U.S.
Butter	25g/1oz	2 Tbs
Vegetable oil	1 Tbs	1 Tbs
Garlic clove, crushed	1	1
Fresh root ginger, peeled and finely chopped	1cm/½in piece	½in piece

NARGISI KOFTAS
(Meatballs Stuffed with Hard-Boiled Eggs)

This dish is the Indian equivalent of the western Scotch eggs and, like Scotch eggs, is usually served as a snack or picnic dish. They can, however, be served with a tomato or curry sauce over rice.

	Metric/U.K.	U.S.
Minced (ground) lamb	575g/1¼lb	1¼lb
Fresh root ginger, peeled and finely chopped	2½cm/1in piece	1in piece
Hot chilli powder	½ tsp	½ tsp
Ground cumin	1 tsp	1 tsp
Ground coriander	1 Tbs	1 Tbs
Onion, finely chopped	1	1
Garlic cloves, crushed	2	2
Chick-pea flour	40g/1½oz	⅓ cup
Salt and pepper to taste		
Egg	1	1
Hard-boiled eggs	8	8

Sufficient vegetable oil
for deep-frying

Combine the lamb, ginger, chilli powder, cumin, coriander, onion, garlic, flour, seasoning and egg. Using your hands, mix and knead well until the ingredients are thoroughly blended. Alternatively, purée the ginger, onion and garlic together in a blender before adding them to the other ingredients.

Divide the mixture into eight equal portions. Using wet hands, roll each portion into a ball, then flatten and put a hard-boiled egg in the centre. Bring the meat mixture up and around the egg to enclose it completely. Put the balls into a greased dish and chill in the refrigerator for 30 minutes.

Fill a deep-frying pan one-third full with oil and heat until it reaches 190°C (375°F) on a deep-fat thermometer, or until a small cube of stale bread dropped into the oil turns golden in 40 seconds. Carefully lower the balls into the oil, a few at a time, and fry for 2 to 3 minutes or until they are golden brown and crisp. Remove the koftas from the oil and drain on kitchen towels.

Arrange on a warmed serving dish and serve at once.

4-6 Servings

SAMOSAS
(Stuffed Savoury Pastries)

These spicy little pastries are served both as picnic or other snacks, or as part of a meal in India. This version contains meat, but a selection of finely chopped vegetables can be substituted if you prefer.

	Metric/U.K.	U.S.
PASTRY		
Flour	225g/8oz	2 cups
Salt	$\frac{1}{2}$ tsp	$\frac{1}{2}$ tsp
Butter	25g/1oz	2 Tbs
Water	50-75ml/ 2-3floz	$\frac{1}{4}$ to $\frac{3}{8}$ cup
FILLING		
Butter	25g/1oz	2 Tbs
Small onion, finely chopped	1	1
Garlic cloves, crushed	2	2
Green chillis, chopped	2	2
Fresh root ginger, peeled and finely chopped	2$\frac{1}{2}$cm/1in piece	1in piece
Turmeric	$\frac{1}{2}$ tsp	$\frac{1}{2}$ tsp
Hot chilli powder	$\frac{1}{2}$ tsp	$\frac{1}{2}$ tsp
Lean minced (ground) beef	350g/12oz	12oz
Salt	1 tsp	1 tsp
Garam masala	2 tsp	2 tsp
Juice of $\frac{1}{2}$ lemon		
Sufficient vegetable oil for deep-frying		

First make the pastry. Sift the flour and salt into a bowl. Add the butter, cut into small pieces, and rub it into the flour until the mixture resembles fine breadcrumbs. Pour in 50ml/ 2floz ($\frac{1}{4}$ cup) of water and mix with a knife to a smooth dough. Add a little more water if the dough looks too dry. Pat the dough into a ball and turn it out on to a lightly floured surface. Knead it well for 10 minutes, or until the dough is smooth and elastic. Return the dough to the bowl, cover and set aside while you make the filling.

Melt the butter in a frying-pan. Add the onion, garlic, chillis and ginger and fry until the onion is golden brown. Stir in the turmeric and chilli powder, then the meat and salt. Cook, stirring constantly, until the meat is cooked through and all the moisture has been absorbed. Stir in the garam masala and lemon juice and cook for a further 5 minutes. Remove the pan from the heat and set aside to cool.

Divide the dough into 15 equal portions. Roll each portion into a ball. Flatten each ball and roll out to a circle about 10cm/4in in diameter. Cut each circle in half. Dampen the cut edges of each semi-circle with water and shape them into cones. Fill the cones with a little of the filling, dampen the top and bottom edges of the cones and pinch together to seal. Set aside.

Fill a deep-frying pan one third full with oil and heat until it reaches 185°C (360°F) on a deep-fat thermometer, or until a small cube of stale bread dropped into the oil turns golden in 50 seconds.

Carefully lower the samosas into the oil, a few at a time, and fry them for 2 to 3 minutes, or until they are golden brown. Remove from the oil and drain on kitchen towels.

Pile on to a warmed serving dish and serve at once.

30 Samosas

Poultry and Game

Masalas in Indian cooking are spice mixtures, which form the basis of many dishes. Usually the ingredients for a masala are balanced finely so that although each one can be tasted separately, no one dominates the mixture. However, occasionally one spice is deliberately allowed to predominate. In this superb chicken dish, Zeera Murg, the principal spice is cumin, and the result is absolutely fantastic!

TANDOORI MURG
(Marinated Spiced Chicken)

Tandoori in Indian cooking indicates that the main ingredient (usually lamb or chicken) has been cooked in a special clay oven called a tandoor. You can, however, use a domestic oven instead—in this case, either put the chicken on a rack in a roasting pan or on a spit. Traditionally tandoori chicken is served with sliced onions, tomatoes and green chillis.

	Metric/U.K.	U.S.
Chicken, skinned	1x1½kg/3lb	1x3lb
Hot chilli powder	1 tsp	1 tsp
Salt and pepper to taste		
Lemon juice	2 Tbs	2 Tbs
Butter, melted	50g/2oz	4 Tbs
MARINADE		
Yogurt	3 Tbs	3 Tbs
Garlic cloves	4	4
Raisins	1 Tbs	1 Tbs
Fresh root ginger, peeled and finely chopped	5cm/2in piece	2in piece
Cumin seeds	1 tsp	1 tsp
Coriander seeds	1 Tbs	1 Tbs
Dried red chillis	2	2
Orange or red food colouring	½ tsp	½ tsp

Make gashes in the thighs and on each side of the breast of the chicken. Mix the chilli powder, seasoning to taste and lemon juice together, then rub the mixture all over the bird, especially into the gashes. Set aside for 20 minutes.

Meanwhile, prepare the marinade. Put all the ingredients, except the red food colouring, into a blender and purée until smooth. Transfer the mixture to a small bowl and stir in the food colouring. Put the chicken in a large bowl and spread the yogurt mixture all over the chicken, rubbing it well into the gashes. Cover the bowl and chill in the refrigerator for 24 hours.

Preheat the oven to fairly hot 200°C (Gas Mark 6, 400°F).

Put the chicken, on its back, on a rack in a roasting pan. Pour in enough water just to cover the bottom of the pan—this is to prevent the drippings from burning. Spoon all the marinade left in the bowl over the chicken, then a tablespoon of the melted butter. Roast the chicken for 1 hour, or until it is very tender, basting frequently with the remaining melted butter and the drippings in the pan.

Remove the pan from the oven. Put the chicken on a carving board and cut into serving pieces. Arrange the pieces on a warmed platter. Scrape any drippings from the pan and spoon over the chicken. Serve at once.

2-3 Servings

ZEERA MURG
(Cumin Chicken)

	Metric/U.K.	U.S.
Chicken, cut into 8 serving pieces	1x2½kg/5lb	1x5lb
Juice of 2 lemons		
Salt	1 tsp	1 tsp
Cayenne pepper	1 tsp	1 tsp
Flour	25g/1oz	¼ cup
Butter	50g/2oz	4 Tbs
Onions, sliced	2	2
Garlic cloves, crushed	2	2
Fresh root ginger, peeled and finely chopped	2½cm/1in piece	1in piece
Cumin seeds	2 tsp	2 tsp
Yogurt	300ml/10floz	1¼ cups
Double (heavy) cream	150ml/5floz	⅝ cup
Thinly pared rind of 1 lemon, in one piece		

Put the chicken pieces on a large plate and rub them all over with the lemon juice. Set aside for 20 minutes, then pat dry with kitchen towels.

Mix the salt, cayenne and flour together on a second plate and roll the chicken pieces in it, shaking off any excess.

Melt the butter in a frying-pan. Add the chicken pieces and fry until they are evenly

browned. As they brown, transfer the pieces to a plate.

Add the onions, garlic, ginger and cumin seeds to the pan and fry until they are golden brown. Stir in the yogurt, cream and lemon rind. Return the chicken pieces to the pan and turn in the mixture to coat thoroughly. Bring to the boil, reduce the heat to low and cover. Simmer the chicken for 1 hour, or until it is cooked through and tender. Uncover the pan for the last 20 minutes to allow the sauce to thicken somewhat.

Discard the lemon rind and transfer the chicken and sauce to a warmed serving dish. Serve at once.

6 Servings

Chicken Tikka is a popular Pakistani dish in which small cubes of chicken meat are marinated overnight in yogurt, then grilled (broiled).

CHICKEN TIKKA
(Spicy Chicken Kebabs)

This is one of the most popular Pakistani dishes, and is usually accompanied by naan or chappati.

	Metric/U.K.	U.S.
Yogurt	150ml/5floz	$\frac{5}{8}$ cup
Garlic cloves, crushed	4	4
Fresh root ginger, peeled and finely chopped	4cm/1½in piece	1½in piece
Small onion, grated	1	1
Hot chilli powder	1½ tsp	1½ tsp
Ground coriander	1 Tbs	1 Tbs

	Metric/U.K.	U.S.
Salt	1 tsp	1 tsp
Chicken breasts, skinned and boned	4	4
GARNISH		
Large onion, thinly sliced into rings	1	1
Large tomatoes, thinly sliced	2	2
Chopped coriander leaves	2 Tbs	2 Tbs

Combine the yogurt, garlic, ginger, onion, chilli powder, coriander and salt together. Set aside.

Cut the chicken meat into 2½cm/1in cubes. Add the cubes to the marinade and mix well. Cover the bowl and chill in the refrigerator for at least 6 hours, or overnight.

Preheat the grill (broiler) to high.

Thread the chicken cubes on to skewers. Place the skewers on a lined rack in the grill (broiler) pan and grill (broil) the cubes, turning them occasionally, for 5 to 8 minutes, or until they are cooked through.

Remove the skewers from the heat and slide the kebabs on to a warmed serving dish. Garnish with the onion rings, tomatoes and coriander leaves and serve at once.

4 Servings

GOAN VINEGAR CURRY

The Goan Christians are a minority religious group who live in the former Portuguese colony of Goa on the west coast of India. Their cooking, like that of the Syrian Christians, is distinctively different from that of their Indian neighbours, and includes (unusual in India) a great many pork dishes. This particular curry uses chicken but pork could be substituted if you prefer.

	Metric/U.K.	U.S.
Vegetable oil	75ml/3floz	⅜ cup
Fresh root ginger, peeled and finely chopped	7½cm/3in piece	3in piece
Green chillis, chopped	3	3
Garlic cloves, chopped	4	4
Chicken, cut into 8 serving pieces	1x2kg/4lb	1x4lb
Ground cardamom	½ tsp	½ tsp

	Metric/U.K.	U.S.
Ground cloves	½ tsp	½ tsp
Ground cinnamon	½ tsp	½ tsp
Turmeric	1½ tsp	1½ tsp
Ground coriander	1 Tbs	1 Tbs
Hot chilli powder	½ tsp	½ tsp
Vinegar	250ml/8floz	1 cup
Large onions, sliced	4	4
Water	150ml/5floz	⅝ cup
Salt	1 tsp	1 tsp

Heat the oil in a large saucepan. Add the ginger, chillis and garlic and fry for 2 minutes, stirring constantly. Add the chicken pieces and fry until they are evenly browned. Transfer the chicken pieces to a plate and set aside.

Mix the cardamom, cloves, cinnamon, turmeric, coriander and chilli powder with enough of the vinegar to make a paste.

Add the onions to the pan and fry until they are golden brown. Stir in the spice paste and fry for 8 minutes, stirring constantly. Add a spoonful or two of vinegar if the mixture becomes too dry.

Return the chicken pieces to the pan and pour in the remaining vinegar, the water and salt. Bring to the boil, cover the pan and reduce the heat to low. Simmer for 1 hour, or until the chicken is cooked through and tender.

Transfer to a warmed serving dish and serve at once.

4-6 Servings

MURGHI BIRYANI
(Chicken with Rice)

The only real difference between biryanis and pulaos is that in the former the rice is partially and the meat completely cooked before being baked together.

	Metric/U.K.	U.S.
Ghee or clarified butter	125g/4oz	8 Tbs
Garlic cloves, crushed	3	3
Fresh root ginger, peeled and finely chopped	4cm/1½in piece	1½in piece
Cayenne pepper	½ tsp	½ tsp
Cumin seeds	1½ tsp	1½ tsp
Chicken cut into serving pieces	1x2½kg/5lb	1x5lb

	Metric/U.K.	U.S.
Cinnamon stick	1x10cm/4in	1x4in
Cloves	10	10
Peppercorns	8	8
Cardamom seeds	1 tsp	1 tsp
Yogurt	350ml/12floz	1½ cups
Salt	2 tsp	2 tsp
Long-grain rice, soaked in cold water for 30 minutes and drained	450g/1lb	2⅔ cups
Saffron threads, soaked in 2 Tbs boiling water	1 tsp	1 tsp
Onions, thinly sliced	2	2
Slivered almonds	75g/3oz	½ cup
Sultanas or seedless raisins	50g/2oz	⅓ cup

Melt half the ghee or clarified butter in a large saucepan. Add the garlic, ginger, cayenne and cumin seeds and fry for 3 minutes. Add the chicken pieces and fry until they are evenly browned. Stir in the cinnamon, cloves, peppercorns, cardamom, yogurt, and half the salt. Add 125ml/4floz (½ cup) of water and bring to the boil. Reduce the heat to low, cover the pan and simmer for 1 hour, or until the chicken is cooked through and tender.

Bring 1½l/3 pints (4 pints) water to the boil in a large saucepan. Add the remaining salt and pour in the rice. Boil briskly for 1½ minutes. Remove from the heat, drain the rice and set aside.

Preheat the oven to moderate 180°C (Gas Mark 4, 350°F).

Melt 1 tablespoon of the remaining ghee in a large flameproof casserole. Put one-third of the parboiled rice over the bottom, then cover with one-third of the chicken. Sprinkle one-third of the saffron mixture over it. Cover with another one-third of the chicken pieces, then with rice, sprinkled with saffron water. Remove all the remaining chicken pieces from the pan and arrange them on top. Finish with a final layer of rice, sprinkled with saffron water. Pour over the pan liquid. Cover the casserole tightly and put into the oven. Cook for 20 to 30 minutes, or until the rice is tender and the liquid is absorbed.

Melt the remaining ghee or clarified butter in a small frying-pan. Add the onions and fry until they are golden brown. Using a slotted spoon, transfer to a plate. Add the almonds and sultanas or seedless raisins to the pan and fry for 3 minutes, or until the almonds are toasted. Using the slotted spoon, transfer the nuts and raisins to the onions.

Transfer the rice and chicken to a large warmed serving dish and sprinkle over the onions, almonds and raisins. Serve at once.

6-8 Servings

RUSTOM'S CHICKEN

	Metric/U.K.	U.S.
Garlic cloves, crushed	2	2
Salt	1½ tsp	1½ tsp
Lemon juice	2 Tbs	2 Tbs
Chicken, cut into serving pieces	1x2kg/4lb	1x4lb
Vegetable oil	50ml/2floz	¼ cup
Medium onions, sliced	3	3
Green chillis, chopped	2	2
Fresh root ginger, peeled and finely chopped	2½cm/1in piece	1in piece
Turmeric	1 tsp	1 tsp
Ground almonds	2 Tbs	2 Tbs
Chicken stock	250ml/8floz	1 cup
RICE		
Butter	25g/1oz	2 Tbs
Medium onion, chopped	1	1
Sugar	1½ tsp	1½ tsp
Water	125ml/4floz	½ cup
Long-grain rice, soaked in cold water for 30 minutes and drained	350g/12oz	2 cups
Cardamom seeds	1 Tbs	1 Tbs
Salt	1 tsp	1 tsp
GARNISH		
Butter	25g/1oz	2 Tbs
Large bananas, peeled, sliced in half lengthways, then halved	2	2
Chopped unsalted cashew nuts, roasted	3 Tbs	3 Tbs
Chopped coriander leaves	1 Tbs	1 Tbs

Combine the garlic, salt and lemon juice together and rub all over the chicken pieces. Set aside for 1 hour.

Heat the oil in a large frying-pan. Add the onions and fry until they are golden brown.

Rustom's Chicken is an exotic mixture of chicken with ground almonds, served with a garnish of roasted cashew nuts and bananas.

Dhansak is a classic Parsee dish from the west coast of India, a mixture of chicken, lentils and vegetables.

Stir in the chillis, ginger and turmeric and fry for 1 minute. Add the chicken pieces and fry until they are evenly browned. Stir in the ground almonds and fry for 1 minute. Pour in the stock and stir to mix. Reduce the heat to low, cover the pan and simmer for 50 minutes, or until the chicken is cooked through.

Meanwhile, cook the rice. Melt the butter in a saucepan. Add the onion and fry until it is soft. Stir in the sugar and cook until it is brown and caramelized. Stir in the water and bring to the boil, stirring constantly. Add the rice, cardamom seeds and salt and stir to mix. Add just enough water to cover the rice by about 1cm/½in. Bring to the boil, reduce the heat to low and cover the pan. Simmer the rice for 15 to 20 minutes, or until it is tender.

While the rice is cooking, prepare the garnish. Melt the butter in a small frying-pan. Add the banana slices and fry for 3 minutes, or until they are golden.

Spoon the rice on to a serving dish. Arrange the chicken pieces on top and pour over the cooking juices from the pan. Scatter the cashew nuts over the top and sprinkle over the coriander leaves. Arrange the banana slices around the chicken and serve at once.

4-6 Servings

DHANSAK
(Chicken with Lentils and Vegetables)

The Parsees are an important religious sect whose members fled from Persia hundreds of years ago and settled mainly on the west coast of India. They have remained intact as a community and their cooking is quite distinctive. This is one of their most famous dishes, and although it is normally made with chicken, as here, lamb can be substituted. The dhals mentioned here are merely different forms of lentils; if you cannot obtain them all, the more common red or yellow lentils may be substituted.

	Metric/U.K.	U.S.
Tur dhal (lentils)	125g/4oz	½ cup
Channa dhal (lentils)	25g/1oz	⅛ cup
Masoor dhal (lentils)	50g/2oz	¼ cup
Moong dhal (lentils)	25g/1oz	⅛ cup
Water	900ml/1½ pints	3¾ cups
Salt	2 tsp	2 tsp
Ghee or clarified butter	40g/1½oz	3 Tbs
Fresh root ginger, peeled and finely chopped	2½cm/1in piece	1in piece

Garlic clove, finely chopped	1	1
Chicken pieces	8	8
Chopped fresh mint	1 Tbs	1 Tbs
Aubergine (eggplant), cubed	1	1
Pumpkin, peeled and cubed	225g/8oz	1⅓ cups
Spinach, chopped	125g/4oz	1 cup
Large onion, sliced	1	1
Canned peeled tomatoes, drained	425g/14oz	14oz
MASALA		
Ghee or clarified butter	50g/2oz	4 Tbs
Large onion, sliced	1	1
Fresh root ginger, peeled and sliced	4cm/1½in piece	1½in piece
Green chillis, finely chopped	2	2
Garlic cloves, crushed	3	3
Ground cinnamon	½ tsp	½ tsp
Ground cardamom	½ tsp	½ tsp
Ground cloves	½ tsp	½ tsp
Turmeric	1½ tsp	1½ tsp
Ground coriander	1 tsp	1 tsp
Hot chilli powder	½ tsp	½ tsp
Chopped coriander leaves	3 Tbs	3 Tbs

Wash all the dhals thoroughly and soak them for 30 minutes in cold water. Drain and transfer them to a large saucepan. Add the water and salt and bring to the boil, skimming off any scum. Reduce the heat to low, cover the pan and simmer for 40 minutes.

Meanwhile, heat the ghee or clarified butter in a large frying-pan. Add the ginger and garlic and fry for 2 minutes, stirring constantly. Add the chicken pieces and fry until they are deeply and evenly browned. Transfer the mixture to the dhal.

Add the mint, aubergine (eggplant), pumpkin, spinach, onion and tomatoes. Increase the heat to high, stir to mix and bring to the boil. Reduce the heat to low, cover the pan and simmer for 45 minutes, or until the chicken is cooked through and tender. Transfer the chicken pieces to a plate. Purée the vegetables and dhal in a blender and set aside.

Rinse out and dry the saucepan. To make the masala, heat the ghee or clarified butter in the saucepan. Add the onion and fry until golden brown. Stir in the ginger, chillis and garlic and fry for 3 minutes. Stir in all the remaining ingredients, except the coriander leaves, and fry for 8 minutes, stirring constantly. Add a spoonful or two of water if the mixture becomes too dry. Pour the puréed vegetables and dhal mixture into the pan and stir well. Bring to the boil, reduce the heat to low and cover the pan. Simmer the mixture for 20 minutes. Stir in the chicken pieces and simmer for a further 10 minutes, basting the chicken with the sauce.

Transfer the dhansak to a warmed serving dish, sprinkle over the coriander leaves and serve at once.

6-8 Servings

MURG KASHMIRI
(Chicken with Almonds and Raisins)

	Metric/U.K.	U.S.
Chicken, skinned	1x2kg/4lb	1x4lb
Juice of ½ lemon		
Coriander seeds	1 Tbs	1 Tbs
Black peppercorns	1 tsp	1 tsp
Cardamom seeds	1 tsp	1 tsp
Whole cloves	6	6
Fresh root ginger, peeled and finely chopped	4cm/1½in piece	1½in piece
Salt	1 tsp	1 tsp
Hot chilli powder	½ tsp	½ tsp
Butter	75g/3oz	6 Tbs
Medium onions, very finely chopped	2	2
Double (heavy) cream	300ml/10floz	1¼ cups
Saffron threads, soaked in 2 Tbs boiling water	¼ tsp	¼ tsp
Slivered almonds	50g/2oz	⅓ cup
Raisins	50g/2oz	⅓ cup

Preheat the oven to fairly hot 200°C (Gas Mark 6, 400°F). Prick the chicken all over, then rub over the lemon juice. Set aside.

Using a mortar and pestle, or grinder, crush the coriander seeds, peppercorns, cardamom seeds and cloves. Sift the spices through a fine strainer into a small bowl. Stir in the ginger, salt and chilli powder. Using a small wooden spoon, cream in half the butter to make a smooth paste. Rub the paste all over the chicken, then transfer the chicken to a flameproof casserole. Put the casserole into the oven and roast the chicken for 15 minutes.

Meanwhile, melt the remaining butter in a saucepan. Add the onions and fry until they are golden brown. Remove from the heat and stir in the cream, saffron mixture, almonds and raisins. Pour over the chicken.

Reduce the oven temperature to moderate 180°C (Gas Mark 4, 350°F) and roast the chicken, basting every 10 minutes with the cream and almond mixture, for a further 1 hour, or until it is cooked through and tender.

Remove from the oven and transfer the chicken to a carving board. Carve into serving pieces and arrange them on a warmed serving dish. Keep hot while you finish the sauce.

Skim off most of the fat from the surface of the cooking liquid. Return to low heat and simmer the sauce for 2 minutes, stirring constantly. Pour over the chicken pieces and serve at once.

4 Servings

MURG MASSALAM
(Baked Spiced Chicken)

This is one of the great Moghul dishes of northern India, rich yet rather delicate. Although traditionally the chicken is baked whole, if you prefer, it can be cut into serving pieces.

	Metric/U.K.	U.S.
Chicken	1x2kg/4lb	1x4lb
Juice of 1½ lemons		
Salt	2 tsp	2 tsp
Cayenne pepper	1 tsp	1 tsp
Saffron threads, soaked in 2 Tbs boiling water	¼ tsp	¼ tsp
Butter, melted	50g/2oz	4 Tbs
MARINADE		
Raisins	50g/2oz	⅓ cup
Flaked almonds	75g/3oz	½ cup
Clear honey	1 Tbs	1 Tbs
Garlic cloves	2	2
Fresh root ginger, peeled and finely chopped	5cm/2in piece	2in piece
Cardamom seeds	½ tsp	½ tsp
Cumin seeds	½ tsp	½ tsp
Turmeric	1 tsp	1 tsp
Yogurt	150ml/5floz	⅝ cup
Double (heavy) cream	125ml/4floz	½ cup

Make diagonal cuts in the breast and thighs of the chicken. Combine the lemon juice, salt and cayenne, then rub the mixture all over the chicken, pushing it well into the slits. Put the chicken into a bowl and set aside for 30 minutes.

Meanwhile, make the marinade. Put the raisins, almonds, honey, garlic, ginger, cardamom, cumin and turmeric into a blender. Add 4 tablespoons of yogurt and purée to a smooth paste, adding more yogurt if necessary. Transfer the purée to a bowl and stir in the remaining yogurt and cream.

Pour the marinade over the chicken, cover the bowl and marinate in the refrigerator for 24 hours, turning the chicken over occasionally. Remove from the refrigerator and set aside at room temperature for 1 hour.

Preheat the oven to fairly hot 200°C (Gas Mark 6, 400°F).

Put the chicken into a deep roasting pan. Combine the saffron mixture with the remaining marinade in the bowl and pour over the chicken. Spoon a little of the melted butter over the top. Pour 150ml/5floz (⅝ cup) of water into the pan and put the pan into the oven. Roast the chicken, basting frequently with the liquid in the pan, for 1 hour, or until the chicken is cooked through and tender.

Remove the pan from the oven and transfer the chicken to a warmed serving dish. Spoon the cooking juices over the chicken and serve at once.

4 Servings

PAKISTANI PULAO
(Curried Chicken with Rice)

	Metric/U.K.	U.S.
Ghee or clarified butter	50g/2oz	4 Tbs
Large onion, sliced	1	1
Fresh root ginger, peeled and finely chopped	4cm/1½in piece	1½in piece
Garlic cloves, crushed	2	2
Green chillis, chopped	2	2
Chicken, cut into		

serving pieces	1x2kg/4lb	1x4lb
Turmeric	1 tsp	1 tsp
Hot chilli powder	½ tsp	½ tsp
Ground coriander	1 Tbs	1 Tbs
Salt	1½ tsp	1½ tsp
Black pepper	½ tsp	½ tsp
Yogurt	150ml/5floz	⅝ cup

Juice of 1 small lemon		
Long-grain rice, soaked in cold water for 30 minutes and drained	350g/12oz	2 cups
Boiling water	350ml/12floz	1½ cups

Melt the ghee or butter in a large saucepan. Add the onion and fry until it is soft. Add the ginger, garlic and chillis, reduce the heat to low

Murg Massalam, below left, is one of the great Moghul chicken dishes of northern India ; below right is a delicate, unusual dish of Curried Partridges.

An unusual and pungent curry, Duck Curry is cooked in a vinegar-based masala and coconut milk.

and fry for 4 minutes, stirring occasionally. Add the chicken pieces and fry them until they are evenly browned.

Combine the remaining spices, salt, pepper, yogurt and lemon juice in a bowl. Pour the mixture into the pan and mix well. Reduce the heat to low, cover and simmer for 35 to 40 minutes, or until the chicken is almost cooked.

Uncover the pan and increase the heat to moderately high. Stir in the rice and cook, stirring frequently, until most of the liquid in the pan has been absorbed. Pour in the water and cover the pan. When the water begins to boil again, reduce the heat to low and simmer for 15 to 20 minutes, or until the rice is tender

and all the liquid has been absorbed.

Remove from the heat and serve at once.

4-6 Servings

CURRIED PARTRIDGES

	Metric/U.K.	U.S.
Juice of 1 lemon		
Salt	1½ tsp	1½ tsp
Partridges, oven-ready and with the giblets		

234

reserved	4	4
Water	900ml/1½ pints	3¾ cups
Whole cloves	4	4
Fresh root ginger, peeled and finely chopped	2½cm/1in piece	1in piece
Garlic cloves, chopped	4	4
Onion, halved	1	1
Butter	50g/2oz	4 Tbs
Medium onions, finely chopped	2	2
Ground coriander	2 tsp	2 tsp
Cayenne pepper	1 tsp	1 tsp
Single (light) cream	300ml/10floz	1¼ cups
Ground almonds	125g/4oz	⅔ cup
Cardamom seeds, crushed	1 tsp	1 tsp
Saffron threads, soaked in 2 Tbs boiling water	¼ tsp	¼ tsp

Mix the lemon juice with 1 teaspoon of salt, then rub the mixture all over the partridges. Set aside while you make the stock.

Bring the giblets, water, cloves, ginger, garlic and halved onion to the boil in a saucepan. Reduce the heat to low, cover the pan and simmer for 1½ hours. Remove from the heat and strain into a bowl. Rinse and dry the pan. Return the stock to the pan and bring to the boil again. Boil until it reduces to about 300ml/10floz (1¼ cups).

Melt the butter in a flameproof casserole. Add the chopped onions and fry until they are golden brown. Stir in the coriander and cayenne and cook for 3 minutes, stirring constantly. Add the partridges and fry until they are deeply and evenly browned.

Pour over the reserved stock and season with the remaining salt. Bring to the boil, reduce the heat to low and cover the pan. Simmer for 20 minutes. Uncover, increase the heat to moderately low and simmer for a further 25 minutes, or until the partridges are cooked through and tender and the liquid has evaporated.

Preheat the oven to cool 150°C (Gas Mark 2, 300°F).

Combine the cream, almonds, cardamom and the saffron mixture. Pour the mixture over the partridges and stir to mix. Bring to the boil, cover the casserole and put into the oven. Cook for 20 minutes, then serve at once.

4 Servings

DUCK CURRY

This basic curry combines the rich taste of duck with a vinegar-based masala and coconut milk— and the result is absolutely superb!

	Metric/U.K.	U.S.
Ghee or clarified butter	75g/3oz	6 Tbs
Duck, cut into serving pieces	1x3kg/6lb	1x6lb
Mustard seeds	1 tsp	1 tsp
Medium onions, finely chopped	3	3
Garlic cloves, finely chopped	2	2
Fresh root ginger, peeled and finely chopped	4cm/1½in piece	1½in piece
Green chilli, finely chopped	1	1
Ground cumin	1 tsp	1 tsp
Hot chilli powder	1 tsp	1 tsp
Ground coriander	1 Tbs	1 Tbs
Garam masala	1 Tbs	1 Tbs
Turmeric	1 tsp	1 tsp
Salt	½ tsp	½ tsp
Vinegar	3 Tbs	3 Tbs
Coconut milk	350ml/12floz	1½ cups

Melt the ghee or clarified butter in a large saucepan. Add the duck pieces and fry until they are evenly browned. Transfer them to a plate.

Add the mustard seeds to the pan, cover and fry them until they begin to pop. Add the onions and fry until they are golden brown. Add the garlic, ginger and chilli and fry for 3 minutes, stirring frequently.

Put the cumin, chilli powder, coriander, garam masala, turmeric and salt into a bowl and stir in the vinegar to make a smooth paste. Add the paste to the saucepan and fry for 8 minutes, stirring constantly. Return the duck pieces to the pan and baste well with the paste. Fry for 3 minutes. Pour over the coconut milk and stir well to mix. Reduce the heat to low, cover the pan and simmer for 1 hour, or until the duck pieces are cooked through and tender, and the gravy is thick.

Transfer the mixture to a warmed serving dish and serve at once.

4 Servings

Fish and Seafood

Two fabulous deep-fried dishes: above Talawa Gosht, deep-fried lean lamb cubes and potatoes (recipe page 216); below Tali Machee, deep-fried spiced sole fillets.

BANGRA MASALA
(Spiced Herrings)

This dish is from the west coast of India, where fish is abundant and plays an important part in the staple diet. Bangra is a fish found around the coasts; it looks and tastes somewhat like herrings, which is why we have suggested them as a substitute here.

	Metric/U.K.	U.S.
Herrings, cleaned and gutted	4	4
Salt	2½ tsp	2½ tsp
Juice of ½ lemon		
Flour	3 Tbs	3 Tbs
Turmeric	1 tsp	1 tsp
Vegetable oil	50ml/2floz	¼ cup
STUFFING Vegetable oil	3 Tbs	3 Tbs
Small onions, finely minced (ground)	2	2
Large garlic clove, crushed	1	1
Fresh root ginger, peeled and finely chopped	4cm/1½in piece	1½in piece
Turmeric	1 tsp	1 tsp
Ground coriander	1 tsp	1 tsp
Hot chilli powder	½ tsp	½ tsp
Garam masala	1 tsp	1 tsp
Tomato purée (paste)	75g/3oz	⅜ cup
Juice of ½ lemon		

Sprinkle the insides of the herrings with the salt and set aside.

To make the stuffing, heat the oil in a frying-pan. Add the onions and fry until they are golden brown. Add the garlic and ginger and fry for 2 minutes, stirring constantly. Stir in the turmeric, coriander, chilli powder and garam masala and fry for 8 minutes, stirring constantly. Add a spoonful or two of water if the mixture becomes too dry. Add the tomato purée (paste) and lemon juice and cook for 3 minutes. Divide the stuffing into four portions and stuff into the fish. Secure with a trussing needle and thread.

Make slits along the sides of the herrings and rub in a little lemon juice. Mix the flour, turmeric and a little salt on a plate and coat the fish in the mixture, shaking off any excess.

Heat the oil in a large frying-pan. Add the fish and fry for 10 to 15 minutes, or until they are crisp and the flesh flakes easily.

Transfer to a warmed serving dish and serve at once.

4 Servings

TALI MACHEE
(Deep-Fried Spiced Fish)

	Metric/U.K.	U.S.
Lemon sole fillets	8	8
Salt and pepper to taste		
Juice of 2 lemons		
Sufficient vegetable oil for deep-frying		
BATTER Chick-pea flour	75g/3oz	¾ cup
Rice flour	25g/1oz	¼ cup
Turmeric	1 tsp	1 tsp
Hot chilli powder	1 tsp	1 tsp
Cold water	125ml/4floz	½ cup

Cut each fillet in half, then rub all over with salt and pepper. Put the fish pieces in a large bowl and sprinkle over the lemon juice. Set aside to marinate for 1 hour.

Meanwhile, to make the batter, sift the flour, rice flour, turmeric and chilli powder into a bowl. Stir in the water until the mixture forms a smooth batter.

Remove the fish from the marinade and pat dry with kitchen towels. Dip each fish piece in the batter and set aside.

Fill a deep-frying pan one-third full with vegetable oil and heat until it reaches 180°C (350°F) on a deep-fat thermometer, or until a small cube of stale bread dropped into the oil turns golden in 55 seconds. Carefully lower the fish pieces into the oil, a few at a time, and fry for 5 minutes, or until they are crisp and golden brown. Remove from the oil and drain on kitchen towels.

Transfer to a warmed serving dish and serve at once.

4 Servings

TANDOORI MACHEE
(Marinated Spiced Fish)

The traditional items cooked in a tandoor, or clay oven, include breads and chicken; fish is a late addition and is usually only cooked in this manner in India around the west coast, where the fish and seafood are plentiful.

	Metric/U.K.	U.S.
Large red mullets, or any oily fish, cleaned and gutted	4	4
Juice of 2 lemons		
Butter, melted	75g/3oz	6 Tbs
Ground cumin	2 tsp	2 tsp
Lemon, thinly sliced	1	1
MARINADE Yogurt	50ml/2floz	$\frac{1}{4}$ cup
Garlic cloves, crushed	2	2
Fresh root ginger, peeled and finely chopped	4cm/1$\frac{1}{2}$in piece	1$\frac{1}{2}$in piece
Coriander seeds	1 Tbs	1 Tbs
Garam masala	1 tsp	1 tsp
Dried red chillis	2	2
Red food colouring	$\frac{1}{4}$ tsp	$\frac{1}{4}$ tsp

Make slits along both sides of the fish, about 2$\frac{1}{2}$cm/1in apart. Rub all over with the lemon juice and set aside for 10 minutes.

To make the marinade, put all the ingredients, except the food colouring, into a blender and purée until smooth. Stir in the food colouring. Put the fish into a large bowl and spoon over the marinade, turning the fish in it to coat thoroughly. Set aside to marinate at room temperature for 6 hours, basting occasionally.

Preheat the oven to fairly hot 190°C (Gas Mark 5, 375°F).

Remove the fish from the marinade and arrange them on individual skewers. Put into a rack in a deep roasting pan and put the pan into the oven. Roast the fish for 10 minutes. Combine the melted butter and ground cumin together, then brush over the fish. Return the

fish to the oven and roast for a further 5 to 8 minutes, or until the flesh flakes easily.

Remove from the oven and slide the fish on to a warmed serving dish. Garnish with the lemon slices and serve at once.

4 Servings

TAMATAR MACHEE
(Tomato Fish)

	Metric/U.K.	U.S.
Turmeric	2 tsp	2 tsp
Salt	1 tsp	1 tsp
Firm white fish fillets, skinned, boned and cubed	1kg/2lb	2lb
Vegetable oil	50ml/2floz	¼ cup
Medium onions, sliced	2	2
Hot chilli powder	1 tsp	1 tsp
Sugar	1 tsp	1 tsp
Garam masala	2 tsp	2 tsp
Ground coriander	1 Tbs	1 Tbs
Tomatoes, blanched, peeled, seeded and chopped	½kg/1lb	1lb
Sour cream	2 Tbs	2 Tbs
Lemon juice	1 Tbs	1 Tbs
Green chillis, slit in half lengthways and seeded	4	4

Mix 1½ teaspoons of turmeric and the salt on a plate. Rub the mixture over the fish cubes and set aside.

Heat the oil in a deep frying-pan. Add the fish cubes and fry until they are evenly browned. Transfer the cubes to a plate.

Jhinga Kari I, a delicious prawn (shrimp) curry from the west coast of India.

238

Add the onions to the pan and fry until they are golden brown. Stir in the chilli powder, sugar, garam masala, coriander and remaining turmeric. Cook for 2 minutes, stirring constantly. Stir in the tomatoes, sour cream, lemon juice and chillis and bring to the boil. Reduce the heat to low and simmer for 15 minutes.

Return the fish cubes to the pan and baste well to coat them with the sauce. Simmer for a further 10 minutes, or until the fish flakes easily.

Transfer the mixture to a warmed serving dish and serve at once.

6 Servings

WHITE FISH CURRY

	Metric/U.K.	U.S.
Vegetable oil	3 Tbs	3 Tbs
Medium onions, chopped	2	2
Garlic cloves, crushed	4	4
Fresh root ginger, peeled and finely chopped	2½cm/1in piece	1in piece
Green chillis, halved and seeded	6	6
Turmeric	1 tsp	1 tsp
Ground coriander	2 tsp	2 tsp
Black pepper	¼ tsp	¼ tsp
Thin coconut milk	300ml/10floz	1¼ cups
Cod steaks	1kg/2lb	2lb
Thick coconut milk	450ml/15floz	2 cups
Salt	1 tsp	1 tsp
Lemon juice	2 Tbs	2 Tbs
Sugar	1 tsp	1 tsp
Chopped coriander leaves	1 Tbs	1 Tbs

Heat the oil in a large saucepan. Add the onions and fry until they are golden brown. Add the garlic, ginger and chillis and fry for 3 minutes, stirring frequently. Add the turmeric, coriander and pepper and fry for 2 minutes. Pour over the thin coconut milk and stir to mix. Add the fish and bring to the boil. Cook for 5 minutes. Carefully stir in the thick coconut milk and salt and reduce the heat to low. Simmer for 20 minutes, or until the fish flakes easily. Remove from the heat and stir in the lemon juice and sugar.

Transfer the curry to a warmed serving dish. Sprinkle over the coriander leaves and serve at once.

6 Servings

JHINGA KARI I
(Prawn or Shrimp Curry)

This recipe is an adaptation of a recipe from the west coast of India, where large fresh prawns (shrimps) from the Indian Ocean are used. They are usually marinated in vinegar before being cooked; here we have suggested using cooked prawns or shrimps, more common in the West.

	Metric/U.K.	U.S.
Vegetable oil	50ml/2floz	4 Tbs
Fresh root ginger, peeled and finely chopped	4cm/1½in piece	1½in piece
Garlic cloves, crushed	3	3
Onions, finely chopped	3	3
Green chillis, finely chopped	3	3
Ground coriander	2 Tbs	2 Tbs
Turmeric	2 tsp	2 tsp
Wine vinegar	3 Tbs	3 Tbs
Salt	1 tsp	1 tsp
Large cooked prawns or shrimps, shelled	1kg/2lb	2lb
Hot coconut milk	450ml/15floz	2 cups

Heat the oil in a large saucepan. Add the ginger and garlic and fry for 1 minute, stirring constantly. Add the onions and fry until they are golden brown. Stir in the chillis and fry for 30 seconds. Stir in the coriander and turmeric, reduce the heat to moderately low and fry for a further 4 minutes, stirring constantly. Add the vinegar and salt and fry for 30 seconds.

Stir in the prawns or shrimps and fry for 2 to 3 minutes, stirring and tossing the prawns or shrimps until they are thoroughly coated. Pour in the milk, increase the heat to moderate and bring to the boil, stirring constantly. Reduce the heat to low, cover the pan and simmer the mixture for 5 minutes.

Transfer the curry to a warmed serving dish and serve at once.

6 Servings

Sondhia is a delicate dish of spiced large Dublin Bay prawns (large Gulf shrimps).

JHINGA KARI II
(Prawn or Shrimp and Vegetable Curry)

This colourful dish is both easy and quick to make —and is a meal in itself with plain boiled rice or lentils.

	Metric/U.K.	U.S.
Vegetable oil	3 Tbs	3 Tbs
Medium onions, chopped	2	2
Garlic cloves, crushed	2	2
Fresh root ginger, peeled and finely chopped	2½cm/1in piece	1in piece
Green chillis, seeded and finely chopped	2	2
Turmeric	1 tsp	1 tsp
Ground coriander	2 Tbs	2 Tbs
Paprika	2 tsp	2 tsp
Ground fennel	1 tsp	1 tsp
Aubergines (eggplants), cubed	2	2
Canned peeled tomatoes	425g/14oz	14oz
Salt	1 tsp	1 tsp
Creamed coconut	½cm/¼in slice	¼in slice
Juice of ½ lemon		
Water	300ml/10floz	1¼ cups
Prawns or shrimps, shelled	½kg/1lb	1lb
Green chillis, slit lengthways	2	2

Heat the oil in a large saucepan. Add the onions and fry until they are golden brown. Add the garlic, ginger and chopped chillis and fry for 3 minutes, stirring constantly. Stir in the turmeric, coriander, paprika and fennel and fry for 5 minutes, stirring frequently.

Add the aubergines (eggplants) and fry for 3 minutes, stirring frequently. Add the tomatoes and can juice, the salt, coconut, lemon juice and water, and bring to the boil, stirring constantly. Reduce the heat to low, cover the pan and simmer the curry for 30 minutes.

Stir in the prawns or shrimps and the two slit chillis. Re-cover and simmer for a further 15 minutes.

Transfer the curry to a warmed serving dish and serve at once.

4 Servings

SONDHIA
(Spiced Prawns or Shrimps)

Sondhia is a classic dish from the west coast of India.

	Metric/U.K.	U.S.
Uncooked Dublin Bay prawns (large Gulf shrimps)	1kg/2lb	2lb
Hot chilli powder	1 tsp	1 tsp
Ground cumin	1 tsp	1 tsp
Turmeric	2 tsp	2 tsp
Salt	1½ tsp	1½ tsp
Garlic cloves, crushed	3	3
Green chillis, finely chopped	3	3
Lemon juice	50ml/2floz	¼ cup
Water	300ml/10floz	1¼ cups
Vegetable oil	50ml/2floz	¼ cup
Finely chopped coriander leaves	2 Tbs	2 Tbs

Shell the prawns (shrimps) and reserve the shells. De-vein, then run the prawns (shrimps) under cold running water. Pat them dry with kitchen towels and transfer them to a large mixing bowl. Set aside.

Combine the chilli powder, cumin, turmeric, salt, garlic and chillis, then stir in just enough lemon juice to make a paste. Rub the paste into the prawns (shrimps) and set them aside for 1 hour.

Meanwhile, put the prawn (shrimp) shells and water into a saucepan and bring to the boil. Reduce the heat to low, cover the pan and simmer the shells for 20 minutes. Remove from the heat and strain the stock into a measuring cup. Discard the shells and reserve 250ml/8floz (1 cup) of strained stock.

Heat the oil in a large frying-pan. Add the prawns (shrimps), reduce the heat to low and simmer the prawns (shrimps), turning them occasionally, for 5 minutes, or until they turn pink. Stir in the reserved stock and bring to the boil. Reduce the heat to low and simmer for 20 minutes, stirring occasionally, or until the prawns (shrimps) are cooked through and tender. Stir in the remaining lemon juice and the coriander leaves.

Transfer the curry to a warmed serving dish and serve at once.

4-6 Servings

A colourful, satisfying mixture of vegetables, turmeric-flavoured rice and prawns (shrimps), that's Vegetable Pulao with Prawns or Shrimps.

JHINGA TIKKA
(Prawn or Shrimp Patties)

These little patties can either be served as part of an Indian meal, or as a snack or appetizer with drinks.

	Metric/U.K.	U.S.
Prawns or shrimps, shelled and chopped	275g/10oz	10oz
Medium onion, finely chopped	1	1
Fresh root ginger, peeled	1cm/½in	½in
and finely chopped	piece	piece
Green chilli, chopped	1	1
Finely chopped coriander leaves	1 Tbs	1 Tbs
Salt	¾ tsp	¾ tsp
Lemon juice	1 Tbs	1 Tbs
Fresh white breadcrumbs	2 Tbs	2 Tbs
Turmeric	¼ tsp	¼ tsp
Black pepper	¼ tsp	¼ tsp
Egg	1	1

	Metric/U.K.	U.S.
Dry breadcrumbs	75g/3oz	1 cup
Vegetable oil	50ml/2floz	¼ cup

Put the prawns or shrimps, onion, ginger, chilli, coriander leaves, salt, lemon juice, fresh breadcrumbs, turmeric, pepper and egg into a mixing bowl and knead until the ingredients are well mixed. Divide the mixture into eight portions, then shape into flat, round patties.

Dip the patties in the dry breadcrumbs, coating them thoroughly and shaking off any excess.

Heat the oil in a large frying-pan. Add the patties and fry for 5 to 7 minutes on each side, or until they are golden brown and cooked through.

Transfer the patties to a warmed serving dish and serve at once.

4-6 Servings

VEGETABLE PULAU WITH PRAWNS OR SHRIMPS

	Metric/U.K.	U.S.
Large uncooked prawns or shrimps, shelled and de-veined	½kg/1lb	1lb
Salt	1½ tsp	1½ tsp
Cayenne pepper	½ tsp	½ tsp
Juice of ½ lemon		
Butter	40g/1½oz	3 Tbs
Medium onions, sliced	2	2
Garlic cloves, sliced	2	2
Cumin seeds	1 tsp	1 tsp
Turmeric	1 tsp	1 tsp
French beans, trimmed and sliced	125g/4oz	⅔ cup
Carrots, sliced	3	3
Small courgettes (zucchini), sliced	2	2
Long-grain rice, soaked in cold water for 30 minutes and drained	350g/12oz	2 cups
SAUCE		
Vegetable oil	2 Tbs	2 Tbs
Medium onion, chopped	1	1
Garlic clove, crushed	1	1
Fresh root ginger, peeled and finely chopped	4cm/1½in piece	1½in piece
Green chillis, chopped	2	2
Turmeric	1 tsp	1 tsp
Ground coriander	1 Tbs	1 Tbs
Cayenne pepper	½ tsp	½ tsp
Paprika	2 tsp	2 tsp
Canned peeled tomatoes, rubbed through a strainer with the can juice	700g/1½lb	1½ lb
Sugar	1 tsp	1 tsp
Salt	1 tsp	1 tsp
Creamed coconut	4cm/1½in slice	1½in slice

Put the prawns or shrimps on a plate and rub them all over with ½ teaspoon of salt, the cayenne and lemon juice. Set aside for 30 minutes.

Meanwhile, make the sauce. Heat the oil in a saucepan. Add the onion, garlic, ginger and chillis and fry until the onion is golden brown. Stir in the turmeric, coriander, cayenne and paprika. Cook for 2 minutes and add the strained tomatoes, sugar and salt. Bring to the boil. Reduce the heat to low, cover the pan and simmer the sauce for 20 minutes. Stir in the creamed coconut until it has dissolved, then bring to the boil again. Cover the pan and simmer for a further 20 minutes.

Meanwhile, melt the butter in a large saucepan. Add the prawns or shrimps and fry, turning them frequently, for 5 minutes, or until they turn slightly pink. Transfer to a plate. Add the onions and garlic to the pan and fry until the onions are golden brown. Add the cumin seeds and turmeric and stir to mix. Add the beans, carrots and courgettes (zucchini). Reduce the heat to low, cover the pan and simmer for 10 minutes, or until the vegetables are almost tender. Stir in the rice and remaining salt and fry for 2 minutes, stirring constantly. Return the prawns or shrimps to the pan and stir well. Pour over enough boiling water to cover the prawns or shrimps by about 1cm/½in. Bring to the boil, reduce the heat to low and cover the pan. Simmer for 15 to 20 minutes, or until the rice is tender and the liquid has been absorbed.

Transfer the rice mixture to a warmed serving dish. Pour the sauce into a warmed bowl and serve, with the rice mixture.

6 Servings

Accompaniments

ADRAK CHATNI
(Ginger Chutney)

This recipe is quick and easy to make, especially if you have a blender. It does not, however, keep very well and should be eaten within two days of preparation. It goes particularly well with lamb dishes.

	Metric/U.K.	U.S.
Juice of 2 lemons		
Sugar	4 tsp	4 tsp
Fresh root ginger, peeled and finely chopped	125g/4oz	4oz
Sultanas or seedless raisins	75g/3oz	$\frac{1}{2}$ cup
Garlic clove	1	1
Salt	1$\frac{1}{2}$ tsp	1$\frac{1}{2}$ tsp

Put the juice of 1$\frac{1}{2}$ lemons, 2 teaspoons of the sugar and all the remaining ingredients into a blender and blend to a smooth purée. Taste and, if necessary, stir in the juice of the remaining $\frac{1}{2}$ lemon and the remaining sugar. Alternatively, chop all the ingredients finely and mix together.

Transfer the mixture to a small bowl and serve.

6 Servings

LIME PICKLE

	Metric/U.K.	U.S.
Whole limes	20	20
Green chillis	20	20
Coarse rock salt	6 Tbs	6 Tbs
Bay leaves, crumbled	4	4
Fresh root ginger, peeled and cut into thin matchstick shapes	175g/6oz	6oz
Lime juice	300ml/10floz	1$\frac{1}{4}$ cups

Wash the limes in cold water and dry on kitchen towels. Make four cuts through the limes to quarter them to within $\frac{1}{2}$cm/$\frac{1}{4}$in of the bottom. Remove the pips (stones).

Slit the chillis lengthways and scrape out the seeds, leaving the chillis whole with their stalks.

Arrange a layer of limes on the bottom of a large pickling jar. Sprinkle with salt and crumbled bay leaves. Add 2 or 3 chillis and about 2 tablespoons of the ginger. Repeat these layers until all the ingredients, except half the salt, are used up. Pour over the lime juice and give the jar a good shake to settle the contents.

Cover the mouth of the jar with a clean cloth and tie in place with string. Put the jar in a sunny place for at least 6 days, adding half a tablespoon of the remaining salt each day. Shake the jar at least twice a day. Each night, put the jar in a dry place in the kitchen. Be sure to turn the jar each day so that all sides are exposed to the sun's rays.

After six days, keep the pickle on a shelf for 10 days. Cover with a lid and shake the jar every day. The pickle will be ready to eat after 10 days.

About 1$\frac{1}{2}$kg/3 pounds

TAMATAR CHATNI
(Tomato Chutney)

	Metric/U.K.	U.S.
Tomatoes, blanched, peeled and chopped	1kg/2lb	2lb
White wine vinegar	450ml/15floz	2 cups
Onions, finely chopped	2	2
Salt	1 Tbs	1 Tbs
Soft brown sugar	350g/12oz	2 cups
Fresh root ginger, peeled and finely chopped	5cm/2in piece	2in piece
Garlic cloves, finely chopped	4	4
Dried red chillis, finely chopped (or use 2 tsp hot chilli powder)	4	4
Whole cloves	12	12

A selection of the many spices used in Indian pickles and chutneys. It includes coconut, cumin seeds, coriander leaves, chillis, cloves, root ginger and garlic. The yellow powder to the left of the picture is turmeric.

244

	Metric/U.K.	U.S.
Cinnamon bark	2 pieces	2 pieces
Cardamom seeds, crushed	½ tsp	½ tsp
Vegetable oil	50ml/2floz	¼ cup
Mustard seeds	1 Tbs	1 Tbs

No really good Indian meal is quite complete without the accompaniments, especially chutney. The particular chutney pictured here is Date and Banana.

Combine all the ingredients together, except the oil and mustard seeds, in a saucepan. Bring to the boil, reduce the heat to moderately low and simmer for 5 hours, stirring occasionally, or until the mixture is thick.

Meanwhile, heat the oil in a small frying-pan. Add the mustard seeds and cover. Fry until they begin to pop, then tip the seeds and oil into the saucepan. Cook for a further 15 minutes.

Remove from the heat and spoon the chutney into clean, dry jam or preserving jars. Serve when cool, or store, covered with vinegar-resistant paper, in a cool place or in the refrigerator.

About 400ml/14floz (1¾ cups)

CUCUMBER CHUTNEY

	Metric/U.K.	U.S.
Small cucumber, peeled, finely chopped and dégorged	1	1
Large onion, finely chopped	1	1
Garlic clove, crushed	1	1
Salt and pepper to taste		
Wine vinegar	4 Tbs	4 Tbs

Combine all the ingredients together and beat well to blend.

Transfer the mixture to a small bowl and use as required.

6-8 Servings

DATE AND BANANA CHUTNEY

	Metric/U.K.	U.S.
Bananas, peeled and sliced	6	6
Medium onions, chopped	4	4
Dates, stoned (pitted) and chopped	225g/8oz	1⅓ cups
Vinegar	300ml/10floz	1¼ cups
Ground coriander	½ tsp	½ tsp
Turmeric	¼ tsp	¼ tsp
Ground cumin	¼ tsp	¼ tsp
Ground ginger	¼ tsp	¼ tsp
Crystallized (candied) ginger, chopped	125g/4oz	4oz

	Metric/U.K.	U.S.
Salt	½ tsp	½ tsp
Black treacle or molasses	250ml/8floz	1 cup

Put the bananas, onions, dates and vinegar into a saucepan and cook for 15 minutes, stirring occasionally, or until the onions are cooked. Remove from the heat and mash to a pulp. Alternatively, put the mixture into a blender and blend to a purée.

Stir in the coriander, turmeric, cumin, ground ginger, crystallized (candied) ginger, salt and treacle or molasses and return the mixture to moderate heat. Cook for 15 to 20 minutes, stirring occasionally with a wooden spoon, or until the mixture is a rich brown colour.

Remove from the heat and spoon the chutney into clean, warmed jam or preserving jars. Cover with vinegar-resistant paper, cover, label and store in a cool, dry place until you wish to use.

About 1½kg/3 pounds

MANGO CHUTNEY

The cooking time for this chutney varies considerably depending on the quality of fruit used, and the yield given is therefore only approximate for the same reason. This chutney improves with keeping and should be stored for three or four weeks before using.

	Metric/U.K.	U.S.
Green mangoes, peeled, halved and stoned (pitted)	1½kg/3lb	3lb
Salt	6 Tbs	6 Tbs
Water	1¾l/3 pints	4 pints
Sugar	½kg/1lb	2 cups
Vinegar	600ml/1 pint	2½ cups
Fresh root ginger, peeled and finely chopped	75g/3oz	3oz
Garlic cloves, finely chopped	10	10
Hot chilli powder	2 tsp	2 tsp
Cinnamon stick	1x10cm/4in	1x4in
Raisins	125g/4oz	⅔ cup
Stoned (pitted) dates, chopped	125g/4oz	⅔ cup

Cut the mangoes into cubes. Dissolve the salt in the water in a large bowl. Stir in the mango cubes, cover and set aside at room temperature for 24 hours. Drain the cubes in a colander and set aside.

Dissolve the sugar in the vinegar over low heat, stirring frequently. When it has dissolved, bring the mixture to the boil. Add the mango cubes, ginger, garlic, chilli powder, cinnamon, raisins and dates and bring back to the boil, stirring occasionally. Reduce the heat to moderately low and simmer the chutney for 1½ to 2 hours, or until it is thick.

Remove from the heat. Remove the cinnamon stick. Spoon the chutney into clean, warmed jam or preserving jars. Cover with vinegar-resistant paper, cover, label and store in a cool, dry place until you wish to use.

About 2kg/4 pounds

TAMARIND SAUCE

This sweet-sour sauce from southern India is often served with Pakoras (page 198). If raw sugar is unobtainable, use soft brown sugar or molasses or dark treacle instead.

	Metric/U.K.	U.S.
Tamarind	225g/8oz	1 cup
Boiling water	900ml/1½ pints	3¾ cups
Salt	1 tsp	1 tsp
Fresh root ginger, peeled and finely chopped	2½cm/1in piece	1in piece
Raw sugar	2 Tbs	2 Tbs
Hot chilli powder	1 tsp	1 tsp

Put the tamarind into a bowl and pour over the boiling water. Set aside until the mixture is cool. Pour the mixture through a fine strainer into a saucepan, using the back of a wooden spoon to push through as much of the softened tamarind pulp as possible. Discard the contents of the strainer. Stir the salt, ginger, sugar and chilli powder into the pan and simmer gently for 20 minutes, stirring occasionally.

Remove from the heat and spoon into a warmed sauceboat. Set aside to cool slightly before serving.

About 425ml/14floz (1¾ cups)

RAITA I
(Yogurt Salad)

	Metric/U.K.	U.S.
Yogurt	600ml/1 pint	2½ cups
Cucumber, washed, sliced and dégorged	½	½
Spring onions, (scallions), finely chopped	4	4
Salt and pepper to taste		
Green chilli, finely chopped	1	1
Paprika	¼ tsp	¼ tsp

Put the yogurt into a mixing bowl and beat

until it is smooth. Stir in the cucumber, spring onions (scallions), and seasoning to taste. Pour the mixture into a serving bowl.

Cover the bowl and chill in the refrigerator for 1 hour, or until thoroughly chilled. Remove from the refrigerator and discard the covering. Sprinkle over the chilli and paprika and serve.

4-6 Servings

RAITA II
(Yogurt Salad)

If fresh mangoes are unavailable, this raita tastes just as good with canned ones. Or substitute guavas if you prefer.

	Metric/U.K.	U.S.
Yogurt	600ml/1 pint	2½ cups
Ripe fresh mangoes, peeled, stoned and diced	2	2
Salt	½ tsp	½ tsp
Ghee or clarified butter	1 Tbs	1 Tbs
Mustard seeds	1 tsp	1 tsp
Green chilli, finely chopped	1	1
Finely chopped coriander leaves	2 tsp	2 tsp

Put the yogurt into a mixing bowl and beat until it is smooth. Stir in the mangoes and salt. Set aside.

Melt the ghee or clarified butter in a small frying-pan. Add the mustard seeds and cover. Fry until they begin to pop. Add the chilli and fry for 20 seconds, stirring constantly. Remove from the heat and stir the mustard and chilli mixture into the yogurt. Stir well to mix. Pour the mixture into a serving bowl.

Cover the bowl and chill in the refrigerator for 1 hour, or until thoroughly chilled. Remove from the refrigerator and discard the covering. Sprinkle over the coriander leaves and serve at once.

4-6 Servings

SAMBAL I

This sambal is usually served with fish or vegetable curries.

	Metric/U.K.	U.S.
Peeled cooked shrimps, chopped	175g/6oz	6oz
Hard-boiled eggs, sliced	2	2
Medium onion, finely chopped	1	1
Green chilli, finely chopped	1	1
Fresh root ginger, peeled	2½cm/1in	1in

Indian 'salads' are usually yogurt based and provide a cool, refreshing complement to the hotter, spicier dishes. Two particularly delightful raitas are pictured here: on the left Raita I, with yogurt, cucumber and spring onions (scallions) and Raita II, yogurt, mangoes and mustard seeds.

249

	Metric/U.K.	U.S.
and finely chopped	piece	piece
Hot chilli powder	$\frac{1}{4}$ tsp	$\frac{1}{4}$ tsp
Thick coconut milk	2 Tbs	2 Tbs
Cumin seeds, coarsely crushed	$\frac{1}{4}$ tsp	$\frac{1}{4}$ tsp

Combine all the ingredients, except the cumin seeds, in a shallow serving dish and mix well. Sprinkle the crushed cumin seeds over the top.

Cover the bowl and chill in the refrigerator until you are ready to serve.

3-4 Servings

SAMBAL II

	Metric/U.K.	U.S.
Medium tomatoes, blanched, peeled and chopped	2	2
Medium onion, finely chopped	1	1
Green chilli, finely chopped	1	1
Lime or lemon juice	2 Tbs	2 Tbs
Salt and pepper to taste		
Grated fresh coconut or desiccated (shredded) coconut	2 Tbs	2 Tbs

Combine the tomatoes, onion and chilli in a small bowl. Pour over the lime or lemon juice and season to taste. Spoon into a shallow serving dish and scatter over the coconut.

Cover the bowl and chill in the refrigerator until you are ready to serve.

3-4 Servings

Sambals also make popular accompaniments to various Indian dishes—on the left, a pungent mixture of shrimps, hard-boiled eggs and onion, and on the right a mixture of tomatoes, onion and grated or desiccated (shredded) coconut.

Breads

PURIS
(Deep-fried Bread)

	Metric/U.K.	U.S.
Wholewheat (wholemeal) flour	225g/8oz	2 cups
Salt	½ tsp	½ tsp
Ghee or clarified butter	1 Tbs	1 Tbs
Warm water	50ml/2floz	¼ cup
Sufficient vegetable oil for deep-frying		

Combine the flour and salt in a bowl. Add the ghee or clarified butter and, using your fingertips, rub into the flour until it is absorbed. Add the water and, using your hands, knead the mixture until it forms a stiff dough, adding more water if necessary.

Turn the dough out on to a lightly floured board and knead it for 10 minutes, or until it is smooth and elastic.

Shape into a ball, return to the bowl, cover and set aside at room temperature for 30 minutes.

Turn out on to the floured board and pinch off small pieces of the dough. Roll them into balls, then flatten and roll out into rounds about 10cm/4in in diameter.

Fill a deep-frying pan one-third full with oil and heat until it reaches 180°C (350°F) on a deep-fat thermometer, or until a small piece of stale bread dropped into the oil turns golden in 55 seconds.

Carefully lower the rounds, one or two at a time, into the oil and, using a fish slice or spatula, press down. Fry for 1 minute, turn over and press down again. Fry for 30 seconds or until the puri is puffed up and golden brown.

Remove from the pan and drain on kitchen towels. Serve hot or warm.

About 12 Puris

One of the more exotic Indian breads, deep-fried Puris, made from wholewheat (wholemeal) flour.

PARATHA
(Fried Wholewheat Bread)

Paratha is a layered fried bread, formed by brushing the dough with ghee or clarified butter and folding and rolling it a number of times. The dough may be prepared in advance and kept for several hours in the refrigerator, covered with a damp cloth. They can also be cooked, then re-heated either in the frying-pan or in a hot oven before serving.

	Metric/U.K.	U.S.
Wholewheat (wholemeal) flour	225g/8oz	2 cups
Salt	1 tsp	1 tsp
Ghee or clarified butter	125g/4oz	8 Tbs
Water	50-125ml/ 2-4floz	¼-½ cup

Combine the flour and salt in a bowl. Add 2 tablespoons of the ghee or clarified butter and, using your fingertips, rub the butter into the flour until it is absorbed. Pour in 50ml/2floz (¼ cup) of the water and, using your hands, knead the mixture until it forms a soft dough. If it is too dry, add the remaining water, a little at a time, until the dough is soft and comes away from the sides of the bowl.

Turn out on to a lightly floured board and knead for 10 minutes, or until it is smooth and elastic. Pat into a ball and return to the bowl. Cover and set aside at room temperature for 1 hour.

Turn the dough out on to the floured board and divide into four portions. Shape each portion into a ball and roll out into a thin round shape. Brush each round with a little of the remaining ghee or clarified butter. Fold the rounds in half, then in quarters. Roll out into rounds again, brush with a little more of the ghee or butter, fold and repeat the process again until all but 2 tablespoons of the ghee or clarified butter has been used up.

Now roll out each dough piece into a round about 18cm/7in in diameter.

Using a little of the remaining ghee or clarified butter, lightly grease a heavy frying-pan and heat it over moderate heat. Add a paratha and cook it, moving it with your fingertips occasionally, for 3 to 4 minutes, or until the underside is lightly browned. Brush the top of the paratha with a little of the remaining clarified butter, turn over and continue cooking for a further 2 to 3 minutes or until it

is browned all over.

Remove from the pan and keep hot while you cook the remaining parathas in the same way.

Serve hot.

4 Parathas

CHAPPATIS
(Unleavened Bread)

Chappatis is probably the most popular of all the Indian breads and, although you can obtain them ready-made from Indian provision stores or even the larger supermarkets, it is very easy to make your own—and much more satisfying, of course! Serve them instead of rice for a lighter meal, or with a selection of dishes.

	Metric/U.K.	U.S.
Wholewheat (wholemeal) flour	225g/8oz	2 cups
Salt	½ tsp	½ tsp
Butter or vegetable fat	50g/2oz	4 Tbs
Water	150ml/5floz	⅝ cup
Ghee or clarified butter, melted	1 Tbs	1 Tbs

Pour the flour and salt into a bowl. Add the butter or fat and rub into the flour with your fingertips. Make a well in the centre and pour in 75ml/3floz (⅜ cup) of the water. Mix with your fingers and add the rest of the water gradually. Form the dough into a ball and turn out on to a lightly floured board. Knead the dough for 10 minutes, or until it becomes smooth and elastic. Put the dough into a bowl, cover and set aside at room temperature for 30 minutes.

Turn out on to a floured board and divide the dough into eight portions. Roll out each piece into a thin, round shape, about the size of a small plate.

Meanwhile, heat a heavy frying-pan over moderate heat. Put one portion of dough in the pan and, when small blisters appear on the surface, press the chappati to flatten it. Turn over and cook until it is a pale golden colour.

Remove the chappati from the pan and brush with a little ghee or clarified butter. Put on a plate and cover with a second plate to keep hot until all the chappatis are cooked. Serve warm.

8 Chappatis

Sweetmeats

GULAB JAMUN
(Deep-fried Dough Balls)

Desserts in the western sense are unknown in India but there is a natural sweet tooth—as can be seen from the selection of sweetmeats which follows. Sweetmeats are traditionally served after the main meal in India.

	Metric/U.K.	U.S.
Powdered milk	125g/4oz	½ cup
Flour	2 Tbs	2 Tbs
Baking powder	1 tsp	1 tsp
Ghee or clarified butter, melted	1 Tbs	1 Tbs
Water	50ml/2floz	¼ cup
Sufficient vegetable oil for deep-frying		
SYRUP Sugar	225g/8oz	1 cup
Boiling water	125ml/4floz	½ cup

First make the syrup. Dissolve the sugar in the water over moderate heat, stirring constantly. Simmer for 10 minutes, stirring frequently with a wooden spoon, or until the mixture has thickened slightly.

Meanwhile, combine all the dry ingredients together, and, using your fingertips, beat in the ghee or clarified butter. Add the water and knead until the mixture forms a slightly soft dough. Set aside at room temperature for 30 minutes. Using your hands, shape the mixture into small balls.

Fill a deep-frying pan one-third full with oil and heat until it reaches 180°C (350°F) on a deep-fat thermometer, or until a small cube of stale bread dropped into the oil turns golden in 55 seconds. Carefully lower the balls into the .oil, a few at a time, and fry for 3 to 4 minutes, or until they are golden brown and crisp, and rise to the surface. As they brown, transfer the balls to the syrup mixture. When all the balls are cooked, remove the syrup from the heat and set aside to cool.

Chill in the refrigerator for at least 30 minutes before serving.

4-6 Servings

HALVA
(Semolina Dessert)

	Metric/U.K.	U.S.
Sugar	400g/14oz	1¾ cups
Cardamom seeds	4	4
Cinnamon sticks	3x10cm/4in	3x4in
Butter	225g/8oz	16 Tbs
Semolina	225g/8oz	2 cups
Sultanas or seedless raisins	125g/4oz	⅔ cup
Blanched almonds, slivered	125g/4oz	1 cup

Dissolve the sugar in 900ml/1½ pints (3¾ cups) of boiling water and add the cardamom and cinnamon. Cook for 10 minutes, or until the mixture becomes syrupy.

Melt the butter in a second saucepan and stir in the semolina. Simmer for 20 minutes, stirring frequently. Add the sultanas or seedless raisins, almonds and the sugar syrup and bring to the boil. Boil for 5 minutes, stirring constantly. Discard the cardamom and cinnamon.

Pour the mixture into a shallow dish and set aside to cool.

Serve cold.

4-6 Servings

KULFI
(Ice-Cream)

	Metric/U.K.	U.S.
Mango juice	450ml/15floz	2 cups
Double (heavy) cream	150ml/5floz	⅝ cup
Sugar	2 Tbs	2 Tbs

Combine all the ingredients and spoon the mixture into six small moulds. Tightly cover with foil and put into the freezing compartment of the refrigerator. Shake the moulds three times during the first hour of freezing.

When the mixture is firm and set, remove from the refrigerator and dip the bottoms quickly in boiling water. Invert on to serving plates, giving the moulds a sharp shake. Serve at once.

6 Servings

A selection of popular Indian sweetmeats—top left Halva, a semolina fudge like dessert ; centre Gulab Jamun, small deep-fried dough balls in syrup ; and bottom left Kulfi, mango juice ice-cream.

Glossary

Asafoetida: Dried gum resin used as a spice in Indian cooking. Obtainable from Indian provision stores. No substitute, but it may be omitted from any recipe if it is unobtainable.

Chick-Pea Flour: Used extensively for batters in Indian cooking. Sold as *gram* or *besan* flour from Indian provision stores. Or you can grind chick-peas, then sift, until they are sufficiently refined.

Chilli: Small hot red or green pepper, often used in Indian cooking. Obtainable from Indian or Mexican provision stores. To reduce the fieriness of any dish, either reduce the number of chillis used, or seed them before adding them to the dish (the seeds are the hottest part). If fresh or dried chillis are not available, hot chilli powder may be substituted: allow about $\frac{1}{2}$ teaspoon per 1 chilli. When preparing chillis for cooking, always wear rubber gloves for protection and chop, seed etc well away from your eyes.

Coconut Milk: The milk of the coconut. If unobtainable, an acceptable substitute can be made by dissolving creamed coconut in boiling water. Use about 5cm/2in slice for every 450ml/15floz (2 cups) of water and stir until it dissolves. For thick coconut milk, add a little extra creamed coconut, for thin milk, a little less.

Coriander Leaves: Used as a condiment in Indian cooking. A member of the parsley family, and chopped parsley makes an acceptable substitute, especially if it is to be sprinkled over food after it has been cooked. Fresh coriander leaves can be obtained from Indian, Greek or Mexican food stores.

Curry Powder: Virtually unknown in India, but can be used as a short-cut to cooking Indian dishes. Available, in various strengths, from delicatessens or supermarkets. What is sold as curry powder is usually a combination of coriander, cumin, turmeric and hot chilli powder, perhaps with ground ginger and other spices as well.

Dhal: The word used to describe legumes or pulses. Lentils, which are a type of dhal, come in many varieties in India and form an important part of the diet, especially in the South. Substitute with any type of lentil obtainable in the West if you cannot find the Indian types mentioned.

Garam Masala: A type of 'dry' masala or mixture of ground spices. Sold commercially in Indian provision stores and larger supermarkets. To make your own, experiment with combinations of black pepper, cumin, cinnamon, cardamom, cloves, nutmeg and coriander.

Ghee: A type of clarified butter very popular in Indian cooking. Available in cans from Indian provision stores. To make at home, put about 450g/1lb (2 cups) of butter into a heavy-based saucepan and melt very slowly over low heat, being careful not to let it brown. Heat to just below boiling point then simmer for 30 minutes, or until the moisture in the butter evaporates and the protein sinks to the bottom, leaving the pure clear fat on top. Remove the pan from the heat and carefully strain the clear fat through several thicknesses of cheesecloth into a jar. Cover tightly and store in a cool place. It will solidify as it cools.

Ginger root: Knobbly and light brown, root ginger is an almost indispensable ingredient in Indian cooking. It can be readily obtained from Indian provision stores, or oriental delicatessens (it is widely used in Chinese cooking, too). To store fresh ginger, wrap it tightly, unpeeled, in plastic film and store in the refrigerator for up to six weeks. If fresh ginger is unobtainable, ground ginger can be substituted, although the taste is not quite the same: use about $\frac{1}{2}$ teaspoonful to 4cm/1$\frac{1}{2}$in piece of root ginger.

Pannir: A white curd cheese used for cooking in India. It is made from milk, soured milk and lemon juice. *Feta*, a Greek cheese, is somewhat similar in texture and can be substituted, as can any type of goat's cheese.

Tamarind: The dried fruit of the tamarind tree, which is used in South Indian cooking. The pulp is soaked in hot water and the seeds and fibre extracted before being used.

Yogurt: natural (plain) yogurt is a very popular ingredient in many Indian dishes and although commercial yogurt can be used, it is quite easy to make your own. Pour 1$\frac{1}{4}$l/2 pints (5 cups) of milk into a saucepan and bring to the boil. Remove from the heat and cool to 43°C (110°F) on a sugar thermometer, or until you can immerse a finger in the liquid for 10 seconds without discomfort. Meanwhile, beat 2 tbs of yogurt or yogurt culture until it is smooth, then beat in 3 tbs of the warmed milk until blended, then cover, wrap in a towel and keep in a warm, draught-free place for 8 hours, or until thickened. Store in the refrigerator until ready to use.

Italy

Italy was described by a nineteenth century Mrs. Beeton as having no specially characteristic article of food. And so the uninformed have dismissed it ever since—and thus denied themselves some marvellous meals. It was not, in fact, until the recent upsurge in tourism permitted many people to visit Italy and by necessity to eat its food, that it became obvious that there was a bit more to Italian cooking than oily tomato sauces and endless varieties of pasta. When these first tourists came back, stomachs intact and palates fairly tingling with all the good things they had tasted, the word began to spread: Italian food was superb, varied—AND inexpensive.

It took a long time for the message to sink in, for the Italians were fine cooks long before they were Italians; the ancient Romans were rather famous for their feasts, and their greed was so legendary that they had the dubious distinction of inventing the vomitorium in order to indulge themselves fully. It may have said negative things about their character, but it was probably an excellent reference for their cooks!

The classical Romans are also credited with producing one of the very first cook books. It is attributed to the nobleman and gourmet, Apicius, and is positively crammed with good advice: how to turn red wine into white (according to Apicius you add egg whites and stir and stir and stir), how to make 'bad' honey 'good'. (Honey, in fact, was one of the most indispensable ingredients in those early kitchens for not only was it included in many of their sauces but it was also widely used as a preservative.)

Although Apicius' book was written in the first centuries AD, the version which survives was not published officially until the late fifteenth century—significantly, for the Renaissance saw not only a resurgence of interest in the arts and learning, but also in food and cooking. The great ruling families of the city states patronized not only the Leonardos and Michelangelos, but also countless anonymous chefs, who evolved a cuisine second to none in the world of their time. Even the French reluctantly concede that it was the Italian cooks attached to the

An Italian farm familty eats a quick picnic lunch during harvesting.

court of Catherine de Medici (who married the French King Henry II), who laid the foundations of modern French *haute cuisine*.

There are, of course, strong regional influences, and since Italy did not become one nation until the nineteenth century, each has developed individually for a lot longer than they have evolved together. In the South, in Sicily, conquered in turn by the Greeks, Carthaginians, Arabs and Normans and ruled over by Hapsburgs, Bourbons and even Bonapartes, the influence of the invaders can still be seen: there is a dish called cuscusu which is recognizably a version of the North African couscous.

The Sicilians are generally given credit for inventing pasta, with which Italian cuisine is almost synonymous, but the art of drying it and preserving it was originally Neapolitan and, not surprisingly, so are many of the most famous of the pasta sauces. Pizza, which now threatens to rival even pasta in popularity outside Italy, started life as a sort of modest,

primitive bread snack with a topping, and although versions of it are found from Sicily in the south to Genoa in the north, its home remains Naples.

Rome is the heart and soul of Italy and its cooking is renowned throughout the world. Its specialities are legion, from abbacchio (baby lamb—they are supposed to be not more than a month old when killed) to young tender artichokes called carciofi, fresh in spring, cooked in oil and not to be missed. The ancient tradition is continued with some of the wines, one of which, Falerno, can be traced back to classical times. Another, Est! Est!! Est!!!, which originated in Montefiascone near Rome, is reputed to have been popularized in the Middle Ages by a Bishop of Augsburg. Frascati, an excellent white wine, is grown in the area around the city, and is one of the carafe wines of Rome.

Tuscany to the north of Rome is where the Renaissance blazed in all its glory, and it is now the home of Italian cattle farming. Its

cooking therefore veers to the excellent but simple—bistecca alla fiorentina, a succulent grilled (broiled) steak exemplifies the style and also the substance of Tuscan cooking. Tuscany is also the home of Italy's best known wine, Chianti and, although it can vary wildly in quality, the Chianti Classico (distinguished by its hallmark, the black cockerel) which is produced within a legally defined area between the cities of Florence and Siena, is excellent in quality.

Emilia-Romagna is also rich in history and the city of Bologna has the reputation of having the finest restaurants in the whole country, with the possible exception of Rome. Bologna is the home of the mortadella sausage, one of the delicatessen splendours of the country, and also of a rather piquant red wine called Lambrusco which is unique in that it is supposed to be served slightly chilled. And very good it is too, when complementing the rich food of the city. Nearby Parma has its ham and cheese (served grated on practically everything!) and the tradition again is one of excellence.

In the north-west the tradition changes again: in Piedmont, proximity to France and Switzerland has meant that these two countries have influenced both the cultural and eating habits of the people. There is a local version of fondue, called fonduta, and the truffle reigns supreme, for the truffle of Piedmont is both cheaper than its Périgord cousin and less of an acquired taste. The wines cultivated around the great lakes region are particularly good and they travel well so that they can be appreciated outside their native habitat—Barbera, Barolo and the Italian answer to Champagne, Asti Spumante.

Lombardy is the rice bowl of Italy and here risottos are more popular than pasta and soups are nearly as popular as risottos (zuppa pavese is said to have been created for the French King Francis I in a peasant's hut near Milan). Saffron is one of the characteristics of local cooking ('gilding' food was considered to be health-giving in the Middle Ages and saffron was as near as the poor could get to gold) and butter is said to have been invented here and its edible potential first appreciated (the ancient Romans, apparently, used to smear it over their bodies as a sort of war paint).

Venice and Genoa owed a good deal of their early wealth and pre-eminence to their geographical position—as sea ports they were among the first to sample the produce and particularly the spices of the orient. The Venetians are especially proud of their contribution to Italian cuisine in general and to table manners in particular (they are reputed to have introduced the fork as an eating implement) and it was their eager cooks who first converted shiploads of maize from the newly discovered Americas into polenta, now a staple of the Venetian diet. In Genoa a stuffed pasta, called ravioli, was invented and, as was usually the case, other areas rapidly recognized a good idea when they saw it, adopted, adapted, called it by another name and claimed it for their own (and so the noodle is variously referred to in different parts of Italy as tagliatelle, fettuccine, tagliolini or trenette).

All in all, there's more than several things for everyone in Italian cooking—the variety is endless, the tastes delightful and, with an increasing number of delicatessens and supermarkets selling what were once esoteric Italian products, it is becoming easier—and more economical—to recreate the Italian taste in your own kitchen.

Soups and Antipasta

Two more delicious soups —Zuppa di Cozze (Mussel Soup) and Zuppa di Fagioli Fiorentina (Bean and Macaroni Soup).

Minestrone—the most famous of Italian soups. It is a filling mixture of beans, vegetables, macaroni and herbs and, served with crusty bread, is a meal in itself.

MINESTRONE (Vegetable and Pasta Soup)

	Metric/U.K.	U.S.
Water	900ml/ 1½ pints	3¾ cups
Dried kidney beans	125g/4oz	⅔ cup
Dried chick-peas	50g/2oz	⅓ cup
Salt pork, cubed	175g/6oz	6oz
Olive oil	50ml/2floz	4 Tbs
Medium onions, chopped	2	2
Garlic clove, crushed	1	1
Medium potatoes, diced	2	2
Carrots, sliced	4	4
Celery stalks, sliced	4	4
Small cabbage, finely shredded	½	½
Medium tomatoes, blanched, peeled, seeded and chopped	6	6
Chicken stock	2½l/4 pints	10 cups
Bouquet garni	1	1
Salt and pepper to taste		
Fresh peas, weighed after shelling	225g/8oz	1⅓ cups
Macaroni	125g/4oz	4oz
Parmesan cheese, grated	50g/2oz	½ cup

Bring the water to the boil over high heat. Add the beans and chick-peas and boil for 2 minutes. Remove from the heat and set aside to soak for 1½ hours.

Return the pan to high heat and bring to the boil again. Reduce the heat to low and simmer the beans for 1½ hours, or until they are almost tender. Drain the beans and peas in a colander and set aside.

Fry the salt pork cubes in a saucepan until they resemble small croûtons and have rendered most of their fat. Transfer the salt pork to a plate. Add the oil to the saucepan and stir in the onions and garlic. Fry until the onions are soft. Stir in the potatoes, carrots and celery and fry for 5 minutes, then add the cabbage and tomatoes. Cook for a further 5 minutes.

Pour over the stock, then add the bouquet garni, reserved beans and chick-peas, salt pork and salt and pepper. Bring to the boil, reduce the heat to low and simmer the soup for 35 minutes. Uncover and remove and discard the bouquet garni. Add the fresh peas and macaroni and cook for a further 10 to 15 minutes, or until the macaroni is 'al dente', or just tender.

Pour the soup into serving bowls and sprinkle over the grated Parmesan before serving.

8 Servings

ZUPPA DI COZZE (Mussel Soup)

	Metric/U.K.	U.S.
Olive oil	2 Tbs	2 Tbs
Medium onion, grated	1	1
Celery stalk, chopped	1	1
Garlic cloves, crushed	2	2
Salt and pepper to taste		
Dried basil	1 tsp	1 tsp
Dried oregano	½ tsp	½ tsp
Tomatoes, blanched, peeled, seeded and chopped	700g/1½lb	1½lb
Dry white wine	175ml/6floz	¾ cup
Water	300ml/10floz	1¼ cups
Mussels, scrubbed	2l/2½ pints	3 pints
Parsley, chopped	2 Tbs	2 Tbs

Heat the oil in a large saucepan. Add the onion, celery and garlic and fry until the vegetables are soft. Stir in the seasoning and herbs and cook for a further 1 minute. Stir in the tomatoes and cook for 5 minutes.

Pour over the wine and water and bring to the boil. Reduce the heat to low and simmer the mixture for 10 minutes, or until the tomatoes become pulpy. Add the mussels and cook over moderate heat, shaking the pan occasionally, for about 10 minutes, or until the shells open. (Discard any shells that do not open.) Transfer the mussels from the pan and remove and discard the top shell. Transfer the mussels to a large, warmed tureen and keep hot.

Strain the soup into a bowl, pressing on the vegetables with the back of a wooden spoon to extract all the juice. Return the strained soup to the pan and bring to the boil. Cook for 2 minutes, then pour over the mussels. Sprinkle over the parsley and serve at once.

4 Servings

ZUPPA DI FAGIOLI FIORENTINA (Bean and Macaroni Soup)

	Metric/U.K.	U.S.
Dried white haricot (dried white) beans, soaked overnight in cold water and drained	275g/10oz	1⅔ cups
Large macaroni, broken into 10cm/4in pieces	125g/4oz	4oz
Bacon, chopped into 2½cm/1in pieces	450g/1lb	1lb
Large onion, grated	1	1
Large garlic clove, crushed	1	1
Medium tomatoes, quartered	4	4
Vegetable stock	1¾l/3 pints	7½ cups
Bouquet garni	1	1
Salt and pepper to taste		
Button mushrooms, finely chopped	50g/2oz	½ cup
Finely chopped parsley	2 Tbs	2 Tbs

Put all the ingredients, except the parsley, into a large saucepan and bring to the boil, stirring frequently. Reduce the heat to low and simmer for 1½ to 2 hours, or until the beans are cooked through. Taste the soup and adjust the seasoning if necessary.

Transfer to a warmed tureen, sprinkle over the parsley and serve at once.

6 Servings

ZUPPA DI FONTINA (Bread and Cheese Soup)

	Metric/U.K.	U.S.
Butter	75g/3oz	6 Tbs
French or Italian bread	12 slices	12 slices
Fontina cheese	12 slices	12 slices
Boiling beef stock	1¾l/3 pints	7½ cups

Melt the butter in a heavy-bottomed saucepan. Add the bread slices and fry for 3 to 4 minutes on each side, or until they are golden brown and crusty. Remove the slices from the pan and drain on kitchen towels.

Preheat the oven to moderate 180°C (Gas Mark 4, 350°F).

Arrange the bread slices in an ovenproof tureen or individual bowls and arrange a slice of cheese over each one. Pour over the stock and put the tureen or bowls into the oven. Cook for 10 minutes, or until the cheese has melted.

Remove from the oven and serve at once.

4 Servings

INSALATA DI POMODORI E SALAME (Tomato and Salami Salad)

This is one of the simplest and one of the most typical of Italian antipasta dishes. Serve with lots of crusty bread to mop up the sauce, and some mellow Chianti Classico wine.

	Metric/U.K.	U.S.
Tomatoes, thinly sliced	½kg/1lb	1lb
Salami, thinly sliced	175g/6oz	6oz
Black olives, chopped	6	6
Olive oil	6 Tbs	6 Tbs
White wine vinegar	3 Tbs	3 Tbs
Lemon juice	1 tsp	1 tsp
Large garlic clove, crushed	1	1
Salt and pepper to taste		
Chopped fresh basil	1 Tbs	1 Tbs

Arrange the tomato and salami slices in a serving dish. Separate the rows with the chopped olives.

Combine all the remaining ingredients, except the basil, in a screw-top jar and shake well to blend. Pour the dressing over the tomato mixture.

Chill in the refrigerator for 15 minutes. Sprinkle over the chopped basil before serving.

6 Servings

together and stir the mixture into the vegetables. Reduce the heat to low and simmer the mixture, covered, for 15 minutes. Stir in all the remaining ingredients, then return the aubergine (eggplant) dice to the pan and stir to blend thoroughly. Simmer the mixture for 20 minutes.

Transfer the caponata to a serving bowl. Chill in the refrigerator for 2 hours before serving.

4-6 Servings

FAGIOLI AL TONNO (Beans with Tuna Fish)

Beans are something of a local speciality in Tuscany and they are cooked and served in many different and very appetizing ways. This sturdy dish is now popular all over Italy—and beyond as well. Although it is served in Italy as an antipasta, with crusty bread and a mixed salad, it also makes an excellent light summer luncheon dish.

	Metric/U.K.	U.S.
Canned white haricot (white) beans, drained	450g/1lb	1lb
Medium onion, finely chopped	1	1
White wine vinegar	½ Tbs	½ Tbs
Olive oil	2 Tbs	2 Tbs
Lemon juice	1 tsp	1 tsp
Garlic clove, crushed	1	1
Salt and pepper to taste		
Chopped fresh basil	2 Tbs	2 Tbs
Canned tuna fish, drained and coarsely flaked	200g/7oz	7oz
Black olives, stoned (pitted)	6	6

Put the beans and onion into a medium serving dish. Put the vinegar, oil, lemon juice, garlic, seasoning and basil into a screw-top jar and shake vigorously to blend. Pour the dressing over the beans and onions and toss gently to blend.

Arrange the tuna fish and olives on top and serve at once.

4 Servings

Fagioli al Tonno is an unusual mixture of beans and tuna fish with a tart dressing. It is usually served as an antipasta.

CAPONATA (Augergines [Eggplants] in Sweet and Sour Sauce)

This superbly aromatic dish comes from Sicily and is usually served as an hors d'oeuvre, although it can be served as an accompaniment to cold meats as well. If possible, use a good-quality vinegar, otherwise the blend of flavours will not be so delicate.

	Metric/U.K.	U.S.
Olive oil	125ml/4floz	½ cup
Small aubergines (eggplants), chopped and dégorged	4	4
Celery stalks, finely chopped	4	4
Large onions, finely chopped	4	4
Tomato purée (paste)	125g/4oz	½ cup
Water	50ml/2floz	¼ cup
Capers	1 Tbs	1 Tbs
Green olives, chopped	50g/2oz	½ cup
Red wine vinegar	75ml/3floz	⅜ cup
Sugar	1 Tbs	1 Tbs

Heat three-quarters of the oil in a large frying-pan. Add the aubergine (eggplant) dice and fry for 8 to 10 minutes, stirring occasionally, or until they are soft and brown. Remove the dice from the pan and transfer them to drain on kitchen towels.

Add the remaining oil to the pan. Stir in the celery and onions and fry until they are soft. Blend the tomato purée (paste) and water

Pasta, Pizze and Risottos

CANNELLONI CON RICOTTA
(Pasta Stuffed with Ricotta and Ham)

	Metric/U.K.	U.S.
Cannelloni tubes	350g/12oz	12oz
Parmesan cheese, grated	50g/2oz	½ cup
SAUCE		
Olive oil	2 Tbs	2 Tbs
Large onion, finely chopped	1	1
Garlic cloves, crushed	2	2
Canned peeled tomatoes	700g/1½lb	1½lb
Tomato purée (paste)	1 Tbs	1 Tbs
Dried basil	1½ tsp	1½ tsp
Salt and pepper to taste		
FILLING		
Ricotta cheese	225g/8oz	8oz
Thick cooked ham, diced	2 slices	2 slices
Egg	1	1
Salt and pepper to taste		

First make the sauce. Heat the oil in a saucepan. Add the onion and garlic and fry until the onion is soft. Stir in the tomatoes and can juice, tomato purée (paste), basil and salt and pepper, and bring to the boil. Reduce the heat to low and simmer the sauce for 30 minutes, or until it is smooth and thick.

Meanwhile, cook the cannelloni tubes in boiling, salted water for 10 to 12 minutes, or until 'al dente', or just tender. Using a slotted spoon, transfer the tubes to a large plate.

Mix all the filling ingredients together until they are thoroughly blended. Using a small teaspoon, carefully stuff the filling into the tubes until they are well filled. Arrange the tubes in a well-greased shallow ovenproof casserole.

Preheat the oven to moderate 180°C (Gas

Cannelloni con Ricotta is one of those superb pasta dishes that is technically served before the main meat dish but, in fact, can make a filling main meal in itself. The filling is rich and the sauce light, and the overall result is very appetizing indeed.

Mark 4, 350°F).

Pour the tomato sauce over the tubes and sprinkle over the grated Parmesan. Put the casserole into the oven and bake for 30 minutes, or until the top is browned and bubbling.

Serve at once.

4 Servings

FETTUCCINE ALLA BOLOGNESE (Noodles with Bolognese Sauce)

Bologna is one of the gastronomic centres of Italy, and ragu bolognese is probably one of its most notable contributions to Italian cuisine. The fettuccine which traditionally is served with it, is supposed to have been created in honour of the marriage of Lucretia Borgia to the Duke of Farrara.

	Metric/U.K.	U.S.
Fettuccine	½kg/1lb	1lb
Butter	25g/1oz	2 Tbs
Parmesan cheese, grated	50g/2oz	½ cup
RAGU BOLOGNESE		
Butter	25g/1oz	2 Tbs
Olive oil	1 Tbs	1 Tbs
Lean ham, finely chopped	125g/4oz	4oz
Medium onion, finely chopped	1	1
Carrot, finely chopped	1	1
Celery stalk, finely chopped	1	1
Minced (ground) beef	225g/8oz	8oz
Chicken livers, cleaned and chopped	125g/4oz	4oz
Canned peeled tomatoes, drained	425g/14oz	14oz
Tomato purée (paste)	3 Tbs	3 Tbs
Dry white wine	150ml/5floz	⅝ cup
Chicken stock	300ml/10floz	1¼ cups
Dried basil	1 tsp	1 tsp
Bay leaf	1	1
Salt and pepper to taste		

First make the ragu. Melt the butter with the oil in a saucepan. Add the ham and vegetables and fry, stirring and turning occasionally, until the vegetables are brown. Stir in the minced (ground) beef and fry until it loses its pinkness. Add all the remaining ingredients and bring to the boil, stirring occasionally. Reduce the heat to low, cover the pan and simmer the ragu for 1 hour, or until it is very thick and smooth. Remove the bay leaf. (For an extra smooth finish, the sauce may be puréed in a blender.)

Meanwhile, cook the fettuccine in boiling, salted water for 5 to 7 minutes, or until 'al dente', or just tender. Drain the fettuccine in a colander, then transfer to a warmed, deep serving bowl. Add the butter and, using two large spoons, toss gently until the butter melts.

Pour over the ragu and serve at once, with the grated cheese.

4-6 Servings

FETTUCCINE CON PROSCIUTTO (Noodles with Ham)

	Metric/U.K.	U.S.
Fettuccine	½kg/1lb	1lb
Butter	50g/2oz	4 Tbs
SAUCE		
Prosciutto, cut into thin strips	125g/4oz	4oz
Lean cooked ham, cut into strips	50g/2oz	2oz
Garlic sausage, cut into thin strips	175g/6oz	6oz
Large tomatoes, blanched, peeled, seeded and chopped	3	3
Dried basil	1 tsp	1 tsp
Salt and pepper to taste		

Cook the fettuccine in boiling, salted water for 5 to 7 minutes, or until 'al dente', or just tender.

Mix together the prosciutto, ham, garlic sausage, tomatoes, basil and seasoning.

Drain the fettuccine in a colander, then transfer to a warmed, deep serving bowl. Add the butter and, using two large spoons, toss gently until the butter melts.

Stir in the ham mixture until the pasta is thoroughly coated and served at once.

4-6 Servings

The variations on pasta are endless, and each one seems more exciting than the last. Noodles, particularly, come in many shapes and forms and can be made very simply into almost 'instant' meals—as here with Fettuccine con Prosciutto.

LASAGNE (Pasta Sheets with Beef and Cheese Filling)

	Metric/U.K.	U.S.
Olive oil	50ml/2floz	¼ cup
Lasagne	½kg/1lb	1lb
Mozzarella cheese, sliced	½kg/1lb	1lb
Ricotta cheese	½kg/1lb	1lb
Parmesan cheese, grated	125g/4oz	1 cup
SAUCE		
Olive oil	50ml/2floz	¼ cup
Large onions, chopped	2	2
Garlic cloves, crushed	2	2
Minced (ground) beef	1kg/2lb	2lb
Canned tomato sauce	425g/14oz	14oz
Canned peeled tomatoes	700g/1½lb	1½lb
Tomato purée (paste)	75g/3oz	3oz
Salt and pepper to taste		
Sugar	2 tsp	2 tsp
Dried basil	1 tsp	1 tsp
Bay leaves	2	2
Mushrooms, sliced	225g/8oz	2 cups

First prepare the sauce. Heat the oil in a large saucepan. Add the onions and garlic and fry until the onions are soft. Stir in the beef and cook until it loses its pinkness. Stir in all the remaining sauce ingredients, except the mushrooms, and bring to the boil. Reduce the heat to low and simmer the sauce for 2 hours, stirring occasionally. Stir in the mushrooms and simmer for a further 30 minutes. Remove and discard the bay leaves.

Meanwhile, half-fill a large saucepan and pour in half the oil. Bring to the boil over high heat. Add half the lasagne, sheet by sheet, and cook for 12 to 15 minutes, or until 'al dente', or just tender. Remove the sheets from the pan with tongs, being careful not to tear them. Add the remaining oil to the pan and cook the remaining lasagne in the same way.

Preheat the oven to moderate 180°C (Gas Mark 4, 350°F).

Put a layer of pasta over the bottom of a large, deep ovenproof casserole. Cover with a layer of meat sauce, then with alternating layers of Mozzarella, ricotta and Parmesan cheese. Continue making layers in this way until all the ingredients have been used up, ending with a layer of pasta sprinkled liberally with Parmesan.

Put the casserole into the oven and bake for 45 minutes. Serve at once.

6-8 Servings

SPAGHETTI ALLA CARBONARA (Spaghetti with Bacon and Egg Sauce)

This is one of the most popular—and most delicious—of all pasta dishes. Although the eggs are added to the pasta mixture raw, the heat will 'cook' them slightly.

	Metric/U.K.	U.S.
Spaghetti	½kg/1lb	1lb
Butter	40g/1½oz	3 Tbs
Lean bacon, chopped	125g/4oz	4oz
Double (heavy) cream	3 Tbs	3 Tbs
Eggs	3	3
Parmesan cheese, grated	125g/4oz	1 cup
Salt and pepper to taste		

Cook the spaghetti in boiling, salted water for 10 to 12 minutes, or until 'al dente', or just tender.

Meanwhile, melt one-third of the butter in a frying-pan. Add the bacon and fry until it is crisp. Remove from the heat and stir in the cream. Set aside.

Beat the eggs and half of the grated cheese together until they are well blended. Stir in salt and pepper to taste.

Drain the spaghetti in a colander then transfer to a warmed, deep serving bowl. Add the remaining butter and, using two large spoons, toss gently until the butter melts. Stir in the bacon mixture and toss gently until the spaghetti is well coated. Finally, pour over the egg mixture and toss gently until the spaghetti is well coated.

Serve at once, with the remaining grated cheese.

4-6 Servings

SPAGHETTI COL PESTO (Spaghetti with Basil and Pine Nut Sauce)

This is the great dish of the city of Genoa, which claims to grow better sweet basil than any other city in Italy! The pasta traditionally used in Genoa are trenette or egg noodles, but spaghetti has been substituted here because trenette are difficult to obtain outside Italy. Fresh basil MUST be used if the full flavour of this dish is to be preserved, but walnuts may be substituted for the pine nuts if you prefer.

	Metric/U.K.	U.S.
Spaghetti or other pasta	½kg/1lb	1lb
Butter	25g/1oz	2 Tbs
PESTO SAUCE		
Garlic cloves, crushed	2	2
Finely chopped fresh basil	50g/2oz	1 cup
Finely chopped pine nuts	3 Tbs	3 Tbs
Salt	½ tsp	½ tsp
Pepper to taste		
Olive oil	250ml/8floz	1 cup
Parmesan cheese, grated	50g/2oz	½ cup

Cook the spaghetti in boiling, salted water for 10 to 12 minutes, or until 'al dente', or just tender.

Meanwhile, crush the garlic, basil, pine nuts and salt and pepper together in a mortar until the mixture forms a smooth paste. Gradually pound in the oil, then the cheese, until the sauce is thick and smooth.

Drain the spaghetti in a colander then transfer to a warmed, deep serving bowl. Add the butter and, using two large spoons, toss gently until the butter melts. Pour the sauce over the pasta and, using the spoons, toss the ingredients gently until the pasta is thoroughly coated.

Serve at once.

4-6 Servings

Spaghetti alla Carbonara is an unlikely combination of pasta, bacon, eggs, cream and grated Parmesan cheese and it is one of the glories of the cuisine. Serve with some red wine, salad and crusty bread for a superb—and inexpensive—meal or serve, as the Italians do, as a prelude to a light meat dish, such as Scaloppine al Limone (page 288).

BASIC PIZZA DOUGH

Pizza originated in Naples but has now spread, not only to the other regions of Italy, but all over the world—there's scarcely a city of any size, anywhere, that doesn't boast a pizzeria, or other pizza eating place.

Pizza originated in Naples but its popularity is now world-wide. Pizza Margherita is a rather patriotic variation on the theme since it incorporates the colours on the Italian flag (tomatoes representing red, Mozzarella cheese representing white and chopped fresh basil for the green).

	Metric/U.K.	U.S.
Fresh yeast	15g/½oz	1 Tbs
Sugar	¼ tsp	¼ tsp
Lukewarm water	125ml/4floz plus 3 tsp	½ cup plus 3 tsp
Flour	225g/8oz	2 cups
Salt	1 tsp	1 tsp

Crumble the yeast into a small bowl and mash in the sugar. Add the 3 teaspoons of water and cream the mixture together. Set aside in a warm, draught-free place for 15 to 20 minutes, or until the mixture is puffed up and frothy.

Sift the flour and salt into a large, warmed bowl. Make a well in the centre and pour in the yeast mixture and remaining lukewarm water. Using a spatula or wooden spoon, gradually draw the flour into the liquid. Continue mixing until the flour is incorporated and the dough comes away from the sides of the bowl.

Turn out on to a lightly floured board and knead for 10 minutes. The dough should be elastic and smooth. Rinse and dry the bowl and return the dough to it. Cover with a damp cloth and set the bowl in a warm, draught-free place. Leave for 45 minutes to 1 hour, or until the dough has risen and almost doubled in bulk.

Turn the risen dough on to the floured surface and knead it for a further 3 minutes.

The dough is now ready for use.

225g/8oz dough (enough for 2 medium pizze)

PIZZA MARGHERITA (Pizza with Tomatoes and Cheese)

This delicious dish was created to honour Queen Margherita, Queen of Italy and is a patriotic combination of the colours on the Italian flag (red = tomatoes, white = Mozzarella and green = basil). Dried basil may be used if fresh is unavailable.

	Metric/U.K.	U.S.
Basic pizza dough	225g/8oz	8oz
FILLING		
Tomatoes, thinly sliced	6	6
Mozzarella cheese, sliced	175g/6oz	6oz
Chopped fresh basil	2 Tbs	2 Tbs
Salt and pepper to taste		
Olive oil	2 tsp	2 tsp

Preheat the oven to very hot 230°C (Gas Mark 8, 450°F).

Cut the pizza dough in half and roll out each piece into a circle about ½cm/¼in thick. Arrange the circles, well spaced apart, on a well greased baking sheet. Arrange the tomato slices in decorative lines over each circle, and separate them with overlapping Mozzarella slices. Sprinkle the basil generously over the top and season to taste. Dribble over the olive oil.

Put the baking sheet into the oven and bake for 15 to 20 minutes, or until the dough is cooked through and the cheese has melted.

Serve at once.

2-4 Servings

PIZZA NAPOLETANA (Pizza with Tomatoes, Cheese and Anchovies)

This is the classic Neapolitan version of pizza.

	Metric/U.K.	U.S.
Basic pizza dough	225g/8oz	8oz
FILLING		
Tomato purée (paste)	3 Tbs	3 Tbs
Medium tomatoes, blanched, peeled, seeded and chopped	4	4
Mozzarella cheese, sliced	225g/8oz	8oz
Anchovy fillets, halved	8	8
Pepper to taste		
Dried oregano	1 tsp	1 tsp
Olive oil	2 tsp	2 tsp

Preheat the oven to very hot 230°C (Gas Mark 8, 450°F).

Cut the pizza dough in half and roll out each piece into a circle about ½cm/¼in thick. Arrange the circles, well spaced apart, on a well greased baking sheet. Spoon half the tomato purée (paste) on to each circle and spread it out. Decorate each circle with half the tomatoes, cheese and anchovy fillets and sprinkle over pepper to taste and half the oregano. Dribble over the olive oil.

Put the baking sheet into the oven and bake for 15 to 20 minutes, or until the dough is cooked through and the cheese has melted.

Serve at once.

2-4 Servings

Pizza Napoletana, with its delicious topping of tomatoes, cheese and anchovies, is one of the basic, traditional pizze of Naples.

Pizza Quattrostagione has
a more complicated
topping—it is divided into
quarters and each one is
garnished with distinctive
mixtures.

PIZZA QUATTROSTAGIONE
(Four Seasons Pizza)

*This pizza is more elaborate than most and isn't
really economical unless you are making it for at
least 6 people.*

	Metric/U.K.	U.S.
Basic pizza dough	450g/1lb	1lb
BASE TOPPING		
Cheddar cheese, grated	225g/8oz	2 cups
Parmesan cheese, grated	50g/2oz	½ cup
TOMATO TOPPING		
Tomatoes, blanched, peeled, seeded and chopped	½kg/1lb	1lb
Dried basil	½ tsp	½ tsp
Anchovy fillets, cut into strips	6	6
Black olives, halved and stoned (pitted)	24	24
ARTICHOKE TOPPING		
Prosciutto, halved	6 slices	6 slices
Canned artichoke hearts, drained and sliced	175g/6oz	6oz
SHRIMP TOPPING		
Mozzarella cheese, sliced	175g/6oz	6oz
Shrimps, shelled	175g/6oz	6oz
Canned asparagus tips, drained and chopped	175g/6oz	6oz
Salt and pepper to taste		
MUSHROOM AND PEPPERONI TOPPING		
Mushrooms, sliced and sautéed for 3 minutes in 25g/1oz (2 Tbs) butter	125g/4oz	1 cup
Pepperoni sausage, cut into 1cm/½in lengths	175g/6oz	6oz
Olive oil	1½ Tbs	1½ Tbs

Preheat the oven to very hot 230°C (Gas
Mark 8, 450°F).

Divide the pizza dough into seven pieces and
set one piece aside. Roll out the remaining
pieces into a circle about ½cm/¼in thick.
Arrange the circles, well spaced apart, on well
greased baking sheets. Top each circle with
equal amounts of grated Cheddar and
Parmesan cheese.

Roll out the remaining piece of dough to a
rectangle and divide into long strips, about
½cm/¼in wide by about 20cm/8in long. Use
these strips to divide the pizze into quarters.

On one quarter of each pizza, place the
tomato topping, sprinkling the tomatoes with
basil, then scattering anchovies and olives on
top. On the second quarter, arrange the
prosciutto and artichoke slices and on the third
the Mozzarella slices, in overlapping layers.
Cover the cheese slices with shrimps and
asparagus, and salt and pepper to taste.
Arrange the mushrooms and pepperoni pieces
on the fourth quarter. Dribble over the oil.

Put the baking sheets into the oven and bake
for 15 to 20 minutes, or until the dough is
cooked through and the cheese has melted.

Serve at once.

6 Servings

PIZZA PEPPERONI (Pizza with Sausage)

*If you cannot obtain pepperoni sausage, chorizo,
garlic or any type of hot Italian sausage will be
just as good.*

	Metric/U.K.	U.S.
Basic pizza dough	225g/8oz	8oz
Olive oil	2 tsp	2 tsp
FILLING		
Olive oil	2 Tbs	2 Tbs
Small onion, sliced	1	1
Garlic clove, crushed	1	1
Canned peeled tomatoes	425g/14oz	14oz
Salt and pepper to taste		
Tomato purée (paste)	2 Tbs	2 Tbs
Dried oregano	1 tsp	1 tsp
Bay leaf	1	1
Mozzarella cheese, sliced	175g/6oz	6oz
Pepperoni sausage, thinly sliced	1	1

First make the filling. Heat 2 tablespoons of the
oil in a saucepan. Add the onion and garlic and
fry until the onion is soft. Stir in the tomatoes
and can juice, salt and pepper, tomato purée
(paste), half the oregano and the bay leaf, and
bring to the boil. Reduce the heat to low and
simmer for 30 minutes, or until the sauce is
thick. Remove the bay leaf.

Rice is one of the staples of Italian cooking and in fact in parts of northern Italy it is more popular than pasta. To make a truly authentic risotto, Italian rice such as Avorio or Crystalo should be used, and the resulting dish will be creamier than long-grain rice and slightly nutty to taste. The two dishes pictured on the right are Risi e Bisi, a popular Venetian risotto and Risotto alla Bolognese, a combination of rice, ham and Bolognese sauce.

Preheat the oven to very hot 230°C (Gas Mark 8, 450°F).

Cut the pizza dough in half and roll out each piece into a circle about ½cm/¼in thick. Arrange the circles, well spaced apart, on a well greased baking sheet. Spoon the sauce over the dough and arrange the cheese slices on top. Sprinkle over the remaining oregano and arrange the pepperoni slices over the top. Dribble over the remaining olive oil.

Put the baking sheet into the oven and bake for 15 to 20 minutes, or until the dough is cooked through and the cheese has melted.

Serve at once.

2-4 Servings

GNOCCHI DI POLENTA (Corn Meal Dumplings with Mushroom and Ham Sauce)

Polenta is one of the staple foods of northern Italy, particularly the regions of Lombardy and Veneto. It is used in a variety of ways, including gnocchi as here.

	Metric/U.K.	U.S.
Milk	900ml/ 1½ pints	3¾ cups
Corn meal	175g/6oz	1 cup
Egg	1	1
Parmesan cheese, grated	125g/4oz	1 cup
SAUCE		
Butter	25g/1oz	2 Tbs
Small onion, chopped	1	1
Cooked ham, finely chopped	50g/2oz	½ cup
Button mushrooms, sliced	125g/4oz	1 cup
Canned peeled tomatoes	425g/14oz	14oz
Red wine	125ml/4floz	½ cup
Salt and pepper to taste		
Dried rosemary	1 tsp	1 tsp

Bring the milk to the boil, then sprinkle over the corn meal. Cook for 30 minutes, stirring constantly, or until the meal is thick. (If the meal thickens before 30 minutes, continue to cook for that time, stirring constantly to prevent it from sticking to the pan.) Stir in the egg and grated cheese.

Rinse a baking sheet with water, then turn out the mixture on to the sheet and smooth out the top (the mixture should be about 1cm/½in thick). Chill in the refrigerator for 30 minutes.

Meanwhile, to make the sauce, melt half the butter in a saucepan. Add the onion and ham and cook until the onion is soft. Add the mushrooms and cook for 3 minutes. Stir in the remaining ingredients and bring to the boil. Reduce the heat to low, cover the pan and simmer for 20 minutes.

Preheat the oven to hot 220°C (Gas Mark 6, 425°F).

Remove the mixture from the refrigerator. Cut the mixture into squares or rounds and arrange them in a well greased ovenproof dish. Cut the remaining butter into small pieces and scatter over the top. Put the dish into the oven and bake for 10 to 15 minutes, or until the top is golden brown. Serve at once.

4 Servings

RISI E BISI (Rice with Peas)

Italian rice tastes different from any other type of rice—and it's cooked differently too. Don't be alarmed if, at the end of cooking time, the rice is still quite 'creamy'—it's supposed to be like that. This particular dish is one of the classic dishes of Veneto, the region around Venice.

	Metric/U.K.	U.S.
Olive oil	1 Tbs	1 Tbs
Lean bacon, chopped	175g/6oz	6oz
Butter	50g/2oz	4 Tbs
Onion, thinly sliced	1	1
Fresh peas, weighed after shelling	½kg/1lb	1lb
Italian rice	½kg/1lb	2⅔ cups
Dry white wine	75ml/3floz	⅜ cup
Boiling chicken stock	1¼l/2 pints	5 cups
Salt and pepper to taste		
Parmesan cheese, grated	125g/4oz	1 cup

Heat the oil in a large saucepan. Add the bacon and fry until it is crisp. Transfer the bacon to kitchen towels to drain.

Add 25g/1oz (2 tablespoons) of butter to the pan and melt it over moderate heat. Add the onion and fry until it is soft. Add the peas and rice to the pan, reduce the heat to low and

274

simmer, stirring frequently, for 5 minutes. Pour over the wine and approximately one-third of the stock. Regulate the heat so that the rice is bubbling all the time. Stir the rice occasionally with a fork. When the rice swells and the liquid is absorbed, add another one-third of the stock. Continue cooking the rice in this way until it is tender and moist but still firm.

Stir in the bacon, the remaining butter, salt and pepper and grated cheese and mix well to blend. Simmer for 1 minute, stirring frequently.

Serve at once.

4-6 Servings

RISOTTO ALLA BOLOGNESE
(Braised Rice with Ham and Bolognese Sauce)

	Metric/U.K.	U.S.
Butter	125g/4oz	8 Tbs
Medium onion, thinly sliced	1	1
Parma ham, chopped	125g/4oz	4oz
Italian rice	½kg/1lb	2⅔ cups
Dry white wine	75ml/3floz	⅜ cup
Boiling beef stock	1¼l/2 pints	5 cups
Parmesan cheese, grated	25g/1oz	¼ cup
BOLOGNESE SAUCE		
Butter	25g/1oz	2 Tbs
Lean cooked ham, chopped	50g/2oz	2oz
Small onion, chopped	1	1
Carrot, chopped	½	½
Celery stalk, chopped	1	1
Lean minced (ground) beef	125g/4oz	4oz
Chicken livers, chopped	50g/2oz	2oz
Canned peeled tomatoes, drained	225g/8oz	8oz
Tomato purée (paste)	2 Tbs	2 Tbs
Dry white wine	75ml/3floz	⅜ cup
Chicken stock	175ml/6floz	¾ cup
Dried basil	½ tsp	½ tsp
Salt and pepper to taste		

First make the sauce. Melt the butter in a large saucepan. Add the ham, onion, carrot and

celery and fry until they are soft. Stir in the beef and cook until it loses its pinkness. Add all the remaining sauce ingredients and stir well to blend. Reduce the heat to low, cover and simmer the mixture for 1 hour.

Meanwhile, make the rice. Melt 75g/3oz (6 tablespoons) of butter in a large saucepan. Add the onion and fry until it is soft. Add the ham and rice, reduce the heat to low and cook, stirring frequently, for 5 minutes. Pour over the wine and approximately one-third of the boiling stock. Regulate the heat so that the rice is bubbling all the time. Stir the rice occasionally with a fork. When the rice swells and the liquid is absorbed, add another one-third of the stock. Continue cooking the rice in this way until it is tender and moist but still firm.

Stir in the remaining butter, the bolognese sauce and grated cheese and mix well to blend. Simmer for 1 minute, stirring frequently.

Serve at once.

4-6 Servings

RISOTTO ALLA MILANESE
(Braised Saffron Rice)

As the name suggests, this dish is a speciality of the city of Milan, in northern Italy; it is the classic accompaniment to Osso Buco.

	Metric/U.K.	U.S.
Butter	50g/2oz	4 Tbs
Chopped beef marrow	2 Tbs	2 Tbs
Onion, thinly sliced	1	1
Italian rice	½kg/1lb	2⅔ cups
Dry white wine	75ml/3floz	⅜ cup
Boiling beef stock	1¼l/2 pints	5 cups
Crushed saffron threads, soaked in 1 Tbs hot water	½ tsp	½ tsp
Parmesan cheese, grated	50g/2oz	½ cup

Melt 40g/1½oz (3 tablespoons) of butter in a large saucepan. Add the marrow and onion and fry until the onion is soft. Add the rice to the pan, reduce the heat to low, and cook, stirring frequently, for 5 minutes. Pour over the wine and approximately one-third of the stock. Regulate the heat so that the liquid is bubbling all the time. Stir the rice occasionally with a fork. When the rice swells and the liquid is absorbed, add another one-third of the stock.

Continue cooking the rice in this way until it is tender and moist but still firm.

Stir in the saffron mixture, the remaining butter and the grated cheese. Simmer for 1 minute, stirring frequently.

Serve at once.

4-6 Servings

GAMBERI CON RISO (Rice with Shrimps)

	Metric/U.K.	U.S.
Butter	50g/2oz	4 Tbs
Olive oil	2 Tbs	2 Tbs
Large onion, finely chopped	1	1
Garlic clove, crushed	1	1
Medium red pepper, pith and seeds removed and chopped	1	1
Button mushrooms, chopped	125g/4oz	1 cup
Dried basil	1 tsp	1 tsp
Salt and black pepper to taste		
Italian rice	350g/12oz	2 cups
Frozen shrimps, shelled	350g/12oz	12oz
Boiling fish stock or water	900ml/ 1½ pints	3¾ cups
Parmesan cheese, grated	50g/2oz	½ cup

Melt half the butter with the oil in a frying-pan. Add the onion, garlic and pepper and fry until they are soft. Stir in the mushrooms, basil, salt and pepper and cook for 5 minutes. Add the rice, reduce the heat to low and cook, stirring frequently, for 5 minutes. Stir in the shrimps and cook for 1 minute. Add approximately one-third of the stock. Regulate the heat so that the rice is bubbling all the time. Stir the rice occasionally with a fork. When the rice swells and the liquid is absorbed, add another one-third of the stock. Continue cooking the rice in this way until it is tender and moist but still firm.

Stir in the remaining butter and the cheese and mix well to blend. Simmer for 1 minute, stirring frequently.

Serve at once.

3-4 Servings

Fish and Seafood

Trote sulla Brace is a very simple dish of grilled (broiled) trout. Serve with stuffed tomatoes and rice for a delicious meal.

TROTE SULLA BRACE
(Grilled [Broiled] Trout)

	Metric/U.K.	U.S.
Medium trout, cleaned and with the eyes removed	4	4
Salt and pepper to taste		
Garlic cloves, halved	2	2
Rosemary sprays	4	4
Olive oil	3 Tbs	3 Tbs
Lemon, cut into 8 wedges	1	1

Preheat the grill (broiler) to moderate.

Place the fish on a flat surface and rub them all over with salt and pepper. Put half a garlic clove and a rosemary spray in the cavity of each fish. Make three shallow cuts on each side and arrange the trout in the lined grill (broiler) pan.

Lightly coat the fish with the oil, then grill (broil) the fish for 5 minutes. Remove the pan from the heat and turn the fish over. Brush with the remaining oil and grill (broil) for a further 5 to 6 minutes, or until the flesh flakes easily.

Transfer to a warmed serving dish and remove the garlic and rosemary. Garnish with lemon wedges and serve at once.

4 Servings

SOLGLIOLE ALLA VENEZIANA (Sole Marinated in Wine and Vinegar)

Venice is known as the Queen of the Sea and her diet reflects this—fish is if not the most important single ingredient in Venetian cooking, then one of the most important. This is a typical dish of the region. For economy's sake, any firm-fleshed white fish fillets, such as plaice (flounder) or whiting could be substituted for the sole.

	Metric/U.K.	U.S.
Sole fillets, skinned	8	8
Flour	50g/2oz	½ cup
Olive oil	75ml/3floz	⅜ cup
Salt	2 tsp	2 tsp
Large onion, sliced into rings	1	1
White wine vinegar	175ml/6floz	¾ cup
Dry white wine	175ml/6floz	¾ cup
Garlic cloves, crushed	2	2
Fresh marjoram	1 Tbs	1 Tbs
Fresh chopped rosemary	½ Tbs	½ Tbs
Pine nuts (optional)	3 Tbs	3 Tbs

Coat the fish fillets in the flour, shaking off any excess.

Heat the oil in a large frying-pan. Add the fillets and fry for 3 minutes on each side, or until the flesh flakes easily. Transfer to kitchen towels to drain and sprinkle over the salt. Add the onion rings to the pan and fry gently until they are soft. Transfer them to kitchen towels to drain.

Pour the vinegar and wine into a saucepan and bring to the boil. Reduce the heat to low and simmer.

Transfer the fish to a shallow, earthenware dish and scatter over the onion rings. Stir the remaining ingredients into the wine and vinegar mixture, then pour over the fillets. Set aside to cool to room temperature, then chill in the refrigerator for 4 hours, basting occasionally. Serve cold.

4-6 Servings

CACCIUCCO
(Seafood Stew)

Considered to be one of the glories of Tuscan cooking, this spicy fish stew is the speciality of the port of Livorno, or Leghorn, near Florence. To be really authentic—and sensible!—serve it in soup bowls; although it is technically a 'stew' it resembles the great, thick fish soups, such as Bouillabaisse, of the Mediterranean.

	Metric/U.K.	U.S.
Olive oil	125ml/4floz	½ cup
Garlic cloves, chopped	2	2
Red chilli, chopped and seeds removed	1	1
Shelled shrimps	225g/8oz	8oz
Squid, skinned, cleaned and chopped	225g/8oz	8oz
Dry white wine	125ml/4floz	½ cup
Tomato purée (paste)	3 Tbs	3 Tbs
Water	450ml/15floz	2 cups
Salt	½ tsp	½ tsp
Cod fillet, cut into pieces	225g/8oz	8oz
Haddock, cut into pieces	225g/8oz	8oz
Italian or French bread, toasted	4 slices	4 slices
Garlic clove, halved	1	1
Chopped pimiento	2 Tbs	2 Tbs

Heat the oil in a large saucepan or flameproof casserole. Add the chopped garlic and chilli and fry until the garlic is lightly browned. Stir in the shrimps and squid, reduce the heat to low and cover. Simmer for 30 minutes, stirring occasionally.

Pour in the wine and simmer, uncovered, for a further 15 minutes. Stir in the tomato purée (paste), water and salt, and bring to the boil. Stir in the cod and haddock pieces, cover, reduce the heat to low again and simmer for 15 minutes, or until the fish flakes easily.

Meanwhile, rub the toasted bread slices with

Cacciucco is a seafood stew from Livorno, a port in Tuscany near Florence. It is a mixture of shrimps, squid and firm-fleshed white fish, all cooked in a wine and garlic sauce.

The Italians are particularly fond of deep-frying mixtures of food and have several dishes where different meats and vegetables are cooked together. This is one of the classics, Fritto Misto di Mare, where a mixture of fish and shellfish are deep-fried in batter.

the garlic halves, then arrange a slice on the bottom of four individual bowls. Pour over the hot stew, sprinkle with the pimiento and serve at once.

4 Servings

IMPANATA DI PESCE SPADA
(Swordfish with Piquant Tomato Sauce)

Swordfish fishing is one of the major industries of Sicily, and the fish is cooked in a variety of interesting ways—in stews, casseroles, or cut into steaks and grilled (broiled). Since it can be somewhat difficult to obtain outside the Mediterranean, fresh tuna steaks or even cod may be substituted, although the tastes will be quite different.

	Metric/U.K.	U.S.
Dry white breadcrumbs	75g/3oz	1 cup
Dried oregano	1 tsp	1 tsp
Salt and pepper to taste		
Eggs, lightly beaten	2	2
Swordfish steaks	4	4
Butter	50g/2oz	4 Tbs
SAUCE		
Olive oil	50ml/2floz	¼ cup
Medium onions, sliced	2	2
Garlic cloves, crushed	2	2
Canned peeled tomatoes	425g/14oz	14oz
Capers	1 Tbs	1 Tbs
Cayenne pepper	¼ tsp	¼ tsp
Salt and pepper to taste		
Black olives, chopped	40g/1½oz	⅓ cup

First make the sauce. Heat the oil in a saucepan. Add the onions and garlic and fry until the onions are soft. Stir in all the remaining ingredients, except the black olives, and bring to the boil. Reduce the heat to low and simmer the sauce for 15 minutes.

Meanwhile, combine the breadcrumbs, oregano, salt and pepper together in a bowl. Put the eggs in a second shallow bowl. Dip the swordfish steaks first in the eggs, then in the breadcrumbs, shaking off any excess.

Melt the butter in a large frying-pan. Add the steaks to the pan and fry them, turning occasionally, for 6 to 8 minutes, or until they are lightly and evenly browned.

Transfer the steaks to the tomato sauce and carefully stir in the olives. Simmer for a further 15 minutes, basting the steaks occasionally, or until the flesh flakes easily.

Transfer the mixture to a warmed serving dish and serve at once.

4 Servings

FRITTO MISTO DI MARE
(Deep-fried Fish and Shellfish)

This is one of the great classics of Italian cooking, and can be found in restaurants and trattoria all around the coast. The fish used below are merely suggestions and are among those most widely used in Italy, but of course this is one of those dishes where you can add and subtract according to availability, season—and purse!

	Metric/U.K.	U.S.
Sufficient oil for deep-frying		
Plaice (flounder) fillets, skinned and cut into strips	2	2
Whiting fillets, skinned and cut into strips	2	2
Small scallops	4	4
Large frozen prawns or shrimps, thawed and shelled but with the tails left on	225g/8oz	8oz
Parsley sprigs	8	8
Lemon, quartered	1	1
BATTER		
Flour	125g/4oz	1 cup
Salt	¼ tsp	¼ tsp
Egg yolk	1	1
Vegetable oil	1 Tbs	1 Tbs
Milk	250ml/8floz	1 cup
Egg whites	2	2

To prepare the batter, sift the flour and salt into a bowl. Make a well in the centre and put in the egg yolk and oil. Mix the egg yolk and oil together, gradually incorporating the flour, then add the milk, a little at a time. Cover the bowl and set it aside in a cool place for 30 minutes.

Beat the egg whites until they form stiff

peaks. Quickly fold the egg whites into the batter.

Fill a large deep-frying pan about one-third full with oil and heat until it reaches 190°C (375°F) on a deep-fat thermometer, or until a small cube of stale bread dropped into the oil turns light brown in 40 seconds.

Using tongs, dip the fish pieces first into the batter, then into the oil. Fry them for 3 to 4 minutes or until they are crisp and golden brown. As each piece is cooked, remove from the pan and drain on kitchen towels. Transfer to a warmed serving dish and keep hot while you fry the remaining fish.

Garnish with parsley sprigs and lemon quarters and serve at once, piping hot.

4-6 Servings

ANGUILLA ALLA FIORENTINA (Eels with Breadcrumbs)

Eels are a great favourite in all of the countries of the Mediterranean, although this simple recipe is Italian in origin. Serve with fresh vegetables and salad, and a lightly chilled white wine, such as Toscano Bianco.

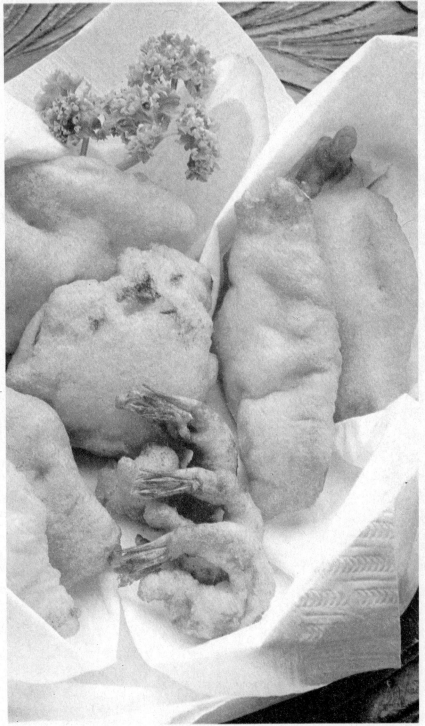

	Metric/U.K.	U.S.
Flour	75g/3oz	$\frac{3}{4}$ cup
Salt and pepper to taste		
Cayenne pepper	$\frac{1}{4}$ tsp	$\frac{1}{4}$ tsp
Paprika	$\frac{1}{2}$ tsp	$\frac{1}{2}$ tsp
Milk	2 Tbs	2 Tbs
Egg yolk	1	1
Dry white breadcrumbs	225g/8oz	$2\frac{2}{3}$ cups
Eels, skinned, washed, and cut into $7\frac{1}{2}$cm/3in pieces	1kg/2lb	2lb
Butter	75g/3oz	6 Tbs
Chopped parsley	2 Tbs	2 Tbs
Lemons, quartered	2	2

Combine the flour and seasonings in a large, shallow plate. Beat the milk and egg yolk together in a saucer and, on a third, large plate, spread out the breadcrumbs.

Roll the eel pieces, first in the flour, then in the milk mixture and, finally, in the bread-crumbs, shaking off any excess.

Melt two-thirds of the butter in a large, heavy frying-pan. Add the eel pieces and fry for 10 minutes on each side, or until they are cooked through and the outside is crisp and golden brown. Transfer them to a warmed serving dish.

Add the parsley and remaining butter to the pan. Reduce the heat to low and simmer, stirring constantly, until the butter has melted. Pour over the eels and garnish with the lemon quarters before serving.

4 Servings

281

CALAMARI RIPIENI
(Stuffed Squid)

This strongly flavoured dish can be served either as a filling first course, or as a light main dish, with salad.

Squid is a favourite fish in all the Mediterranean countries and it frequently forms part of Italian seafood dishes. In Calamari Ripieni, squid are stuffed with a spicy mixture of breadcrumbs, grated cheese and garlic.

	Metric/U.K.	U.S.
Medium squid, cleaned and skinned with the tender parts of the tentacles reserved	6	6
Fresh breadcrumbs	3 Tbs	3 Tbs
Finely chopped parsley	2 Tbs	2 Tbs
Grated Parmesan cheese	6 Tbs	6 Tbs
Garlic cloves, crushed	2	2
Egg, lightly beaten	1	1
Olive oil	50ml/2floz	¼ cup
Cayenne pepper	⅛ tsp	⅛ tsp
Salt and pepper to taste		
Garlic cloves, whole	4	4
Canned peeled tomatoes	425g/14oz	14oz
Dried rosemary	½ tsp	½ tsp
Dry white wine	50ml/2floz	¼ cup

Chop the tentacles finely and put them in a bowl. Add the breadcrumbs, parsley, cheese, 1 crushed garlic clove, the egg, 1 tablespoon of oil, the cayenne and salt and pepper, and mix well. Spoon the mixture into the squid, then with a thick needle and thread, sew up the openings.

Heat the remaining oil in a large, deep frying-pan. Add the whole garlic and fry for 5 minutes. Remove and discard the garlic. Add the squid to the pan and brown on all sides. Stir in the tomatoes and can juice, remaining crushed garlic, and the remaining ingredients. Reduce the heat to low, cover and simmer gently for 25 minutes.

Transfer the squid to a warmed serving dish and remove the thread. Slice and arrange the slices on a warmed serving dish. Pour over the sauce and serve.

3-4 Servings

Meat and Poultry

STUFATINO ALLA ROMANA
(Roman Beef Stew)

This traditional Roman dish is easy to cook—and quite delicious. Cardoons, a favourite vegetable in the area around Rome, are often added.

	Metric/U.K.	U.S.
Top rump (bottom round) of beef, cut into cubes	1kg/2lb	2lb
Seasoned flour (flour with salt and pepper to taste)	50g/2oz	½ cup
Olive oil	1 Tbs	1 Tbs
Streaky (fatty) bacon, chopped	175g/6oz	6oz
Medium onion, thinly sliced into rings	1	1
Garlic cloves, crushed	2	2
Celery stalks, thinly sliced	2	2
Fresh marjoram	1 Tbs	1 Tbs
Red wine	250ml/8floz	1 cup
Beef stock	125ml/4floz	½ cup
Tomato purée (paste)	2 Tbs	2 Tbs

Coat the cubes in the seasoned flour, shaking off any excess.

Heat the oil in a large flameproof casserole. Add the bacon pieces and fry until they are crisp and have rendered all of their fat. Transfer them to kitchen towels to drain.

Add the onion, garlic and celery to the casserole and fry until the onion is soft. Add the beef cubes and fry until they are evenly browned. Stir in the marjoram and reserved bacon, and pour over the wine and stock. Bring to the boil, reduce the heat to low and simmer the stew, uncovered, for 30 minutes, or until the liquid has reduced by about half. Stir in the tomato purée (paste) and continue to simmer for a further 30 minutes, moistening the meat with a little more stock if it becomes too dry. (It should be very tender and the sauce very thick and dark by the time the stufatino is cooked.) Serve at once.

4-6 Servings

The Italians are famous for their stews called stufatos or stufatinos, and this Roman version using beef is particularly rich and delicious. Serve with potatoes and courgettes (zucchini) for a delightful meal.

BISTECCA ALLA FIORENTINA
(Grilled [Broiled] Steak)

Tuscany is the cattle raising part of Italy and it is there that the tenderest beef—and the largest steaks!—are found. Bistecca is, quite simply, the glory of Florentine cuisine. Traditionally the steaks are cooked over a charcoal grill (broiler) but if you do not have one, the grill (broiler) of a household stove is fine.

	Metric/U.K.	U.S.
T-bone steaks, cut about 2½cm/1in thick	4	4
Butter	25g/1oz	2 Tbs
Salt and pepper to taste		
Olive oil	4 Tbs	4 Tbs

Preheat the grill (broiler) to its highest setting.

Arrange the steaks on a lined grill (broiler) pan. Cut the butter into small pieces and scatter half over the steaks. Cook for 3 minutes, then turn over and scatter over the remaining butter. Cook for a further 3 minutes.

Reduce the heat to moderate and cook for a further 3 minutes on each side. This will produce rare steaks; double the cooking time for well-done. About 1 minute before the end of cooking time, rub salt and pepper over the steaks and brush them with the olive oil.

When the steaks are cooked to your liking, transfer them to individual serving plates and serve at once.

4 Servings

ABBACCHIO BRODETTATO
(Lamb with Egg Sauce)

Abbacchio is the Roman word for sucking lamb, which is considered to be one of the great delicacies of the area. Kid is sometimes substituted in this dish.

	Metric/U.K.	U.S.
Butter	25g/1oz	2 Tbs
Vegetable oil	2 Tbs	2 Tbs
Lean lamb (leg if possible), cut into cubes	1kg/2lb	2lb
Small onion, finely chopped	1	1
Garlic cloves, crushed	2	2
Chopped fresh sage	2 tsp	2 tsp
Salt and pepper to taste		
Dry white wine	175ml/6floz	¾ cup
Chicken stock	125ml/4floz	½ cup
Lemons	2	2
Egg yolks	2	2
Parsley sprigs (to garnish)		

Melt the butter with the oil in a flameproof casserole or saucepan. Add the lamb and fry until it is evenly browned. Transfer to a plate.

Add the onion and garlic to the casserole and fry until the onion is soft. Stir in the sage, seasoning, wine and stock, and bring to the boil. Return the meat to the casserole, reduce the heat to low and cover. Simmer the mixture, stirring occasionally, for 1½ hours, or until the meat is cooked through and tender.

Meanwhile, grate the rind of one of the lemons and set aside. Beat the egg yolks and juice from both lemons together until they are mixed. Stir in the rind and seasoning to taste.

Stir about 3 tablespoons of cooking liquid from the casserole into the egg yolk mixture and mix well. Whisk the mixture gently into the simmering casserole and cook gently for 1 minute, or until the sauce has thickened slightly but not curdled.

Serve at once, garnished with parsley.

4-6 Servings

COSTOLETTA DI MAIALE ALLA PIZZAIOLA
(Pork Chops in Pizzaiola Sauce)

Pizzaiola is one of the most popular sauces in Italian cuisine and, in spite of the name, is used not only as a pizza topping but as a sauce for fish, meat (particularly pork as here) and even with noodles.

	Metric/U.K.	U.S.
Pork loin chops, about 2½cm/1in thick	6	6
Salt and pepper to taste		
Vegetable oil	50ml/2floz	¼ cup
Garlic cloves, crushed	2	2
Dried basil	1 tsp	1 tsp
Dried thyme	1 tsp	1 tsp

Costolette di Maiale de Pizzaiola is a superb dish of pork chops covered with classic pizzaiola sauce, a mixture of peppers, mushrooms and tomatoes.

	Metric/U.K.	U.S.
Bay leaf	1	1
Red wine	75ml/3floz	⅜ cup
Canned peeled tomatoes, drained and chopped	450g/1lb	1lb
Tomato purée (paste)	3 Tbs	3 Tbs
Butter	40g/1½oz	3 Tbs
Medium green peppers, pith and seeds removed and chopped	3	3
Medium onion, sliced	1	1
Button mushrooms, quartered if large	225g/8oz	2 cups
Cornflour (cornstarch), blended with 1 Tbs water	1½ Tbs	1½ Tbs
Chopped parsley	1 Tbs	1 Tbs

Rub the chops with salt and pepper.

Heat the oil in a large frying-pan. Add the chops to the pan, a few at a time, and fry until they are evenly browned. Transfer them to a plate.

Pour off all but a thin film of oil from the pan. Add the garlic and herbs, and stir to mix. Pour over the wine and bring to the boil. Stir in the tomatoes and tomato purée (paste). Return the chops to the pan and baste thoroughly with the sauce. Reduce the heat to low, cover the pan and simmer for 40 minutes, basting occasionally.

About 10 minutes before the chops are cooked through, prepare the vegetables. Melt the butter in a frying-pan. Add the peppers and onion and fry until they are soft. Stir in the mushrooms and cook for a further 3 minutes.

Transfer the vegetables to the frying-pan containing the meat. Simmer, uncovered, for 15 minutes, or until the chops are cooked through and tender. Transfer the chops to a warmed serving dish. Stir the cornflour (cornstarch) mixture into the sauce and cook, stirring constantly, for 2 minutes, or until it has thickened. Remove the bay leaf.

Pour the sauce over the chops, sprinkle over the parsley.

Serve at once.

6 Servings

COSTOLETTE DE MAIALE ALLA MILANESE (Breaded Pork Cutlets)

	Metric/U.K.	U.S.
Pork cutlets, trimmed of excess fat	4	4
Lemon juice	3 Tbs	3 Tbs
Seasoned flour (flour with salt and pepper taste)	40g/1½oz	⅓ cup
Eggs, lightly beaten	2	2
Fine dry breadcrumbs	50g/2oz	⅔ cup
Parmesan cheese, very finely grated	25g/1oz	¼ cup
Butter	50g/2oz	4 Tbs
Lemon, quartered	1	1

Put the cutlets on a shallow dish and sprinkle over the lemon juice. Set aside for 10 minutes. Pat dry with kitchen towels. Dip the cutlets, one by one, in the seasoned flour, shaking off any excess.

Put the eggs in a shallow dish. Combine the breadcrumbs and grated cheese in a second dish. Dip the cutlets, first in the eggs then in the breadcrumb mixture to coat them thoroughly. Chill in the refrigerator for 15 minutes.

Melt the butter in a large frying-pan. Add the cutlets and fry for 6 to 12 minutes on each side (depending on the thickness of the cutlets), or until they are cooked through and tender.

Transfer the cutlets to a warmed serving dish and garnish with the lemon quarters before serving.

4 Servings

SCALOPPINE ALLA MARSALA (Veal escalopes with Marsala)

Marsala is a slightly sweet, fortified wine which is produced on the island of Sicily and much used in the Italian kitchen.

Serve with fresh vegetables and salad, and a lightly chilled white wine, such as Toscano Bianco.

	Metric/U.K.	U.S.
Veal escalopes, pounded thin	4	4
Lemon juice	3 Tbs	3 Tbs
Salt and pepper to taste		
Flour	25g/1oz	¼ cup

Saltimbocca, a melt-in-the-mouth mixture of tender veal escalope, proscuitto and fresh sage, is a speciality of the city of Rome.

Butter	50g/2oz	4 Tbs
Marsala	125ml/4floz	½ cup
Beurre manié (two parts flour and one part butter blended)	1 Tbs	1 Tbs

Sprinkle the escalopes with two-thirds of the lemon juice and set aside for 30 minutes, basting occasionally. Dry on kitchen towels and rub them with salt and pepper. Dip them into the flour, shaking off any excess.

Melt the butter in a large frying-pan. Add the escalopes to the pan and fry them for 3 to 4 minutes on each side, or until they are lightly and evenly browned. Pour over the remaining lemon juice and Marsala and cook for a further 2 minutes, stirring occasionally. Stir in the beurre manié, a little at a time, until the sauce thickens.

Transfer the escalopes and sauce to a warmed serving dish.

Serve at once.

4 Servings

SALTIMBOCCA
(Veal Escalopes with Prosciutto and Sage)

In Italian, saltimbocca means literally 'jump in the mouth' which is what this classic Roman dish does, it's so good!

	Metric/U.K.	U.S.
Veal escalopes, pounded thin	4	4
Lemon juice	2 Tbs	2 Tbs
Salt and pepper to taste		
Chopped fresh sage	2 tsp	2 tsp
Prosciutto	4 slices	4 slices
Butter	50g/2oz	4 Tbs
Dry white wine	50ml/2floz	¼ cup

Sprinkle the escalopes with lemon juice and set aside for 30 minutes, basting occasionally. Dry the escalopes on kitchen towels and rub them with salt and pepper and half the sage.

Put one slice of ham over each escalope and

trim to fit. Secure them together with wooden cocktail sticks.

Melt the butter in a large frying-pan. Add the remaining sage and fry, stirring constantly, for 1 minute. Add the escalopes to the pan and fry them for 3 to 4 minutes on each side, or until they are lightly and evenly browned. Pour over the wine and cook for a further 2 minutes.

Transfer the escalopes and pan juices to a warmed serving dish and remove the cocktail sticks. Serve at once.

4 Servings

SCALOPPINE AL LIMONE
(Veal Escalopes with Lemon Sauce)

	Metric/U.K.	U.S.
Veal escalopes, pounded thin	4	4
Lemon juice	4 Tbs	4 Tbs
Salt and pepper to taste		
Butter	50g/2oz	4 Tbs
Dry white wine or chicken stock	175ml/6floz	¾ cup
Beurre manié (one part butter and two parts flour blended)	1 Tbs	1 Tbs
Large lemon, thinly sliced	1	1
Chopped parsley	1 tsp	1 tsp

Sprinkle the escalopes with 2 tablespoons of the lemon juice and set aside for 30 minutes, basting occasionally. Dry on kitchen towels and rub them with salt and pepper.

Melt the butter in a large frying-pan. Add the escalopes to the pan and fry them for 3 to 4 minutes on each side, or until they are lightly and evenly browned. Transfer them to a plate and keep hot while you make the sauce.

Pour the remaining lemon juice and wine or stock into the pan and bring to the boil, stirring constantly. Boil for 5 minutes or until the liquid has reduced slightly. Reduce the heat to moderate and return the escalopes to the pan. Cook for 1 minute. Stir in the beurre manié, a little at a time, until the sauce thickens.

Transfer to a serving dish, garnish with lemon and parsley and serve at once.

4 Servings

INVOLTINI ALLA MARITO
(Veal Escalopes Stuffed with Cheese and Herbs)

	Metric/U.K.	U.S.
Grated Parmesan cheese	4 Tbs	4 Tbs
Chopped fresh sage	1 tsp	1 tsp
Dried oregano	½ tsp	½ tsp
Salt and pepper to taste		
Veal escalopes, pounded thin	4	4
Flour	4 Tbs	4 Tbs
Butter	50g/2oz	4 Tbs
Garlic cloves, crushed	2	2
Marsala	50ml/2floz	¼ cup
Red wine	150ml/5floz	⅝ cup

Combine the grated cheese, sage, oregano and salt and pepper to taste in a small bowl. Lay out the escalopes on a flat surface and spread a little cheese mixture over each escalope. Roll up Swiss (jelly) roll style and secure with wooden cocktail sticks.

Coat the rolls in the flour, shaking off any excess.

Melt the butter in a large frying-pan. Add the garlic and fry for 1 minute, stirring constantly. Add the veal rolls and fry until they are golden brown all over. Transfer to a plate and keep hot.

Pour the Marsala and wine into the pan and bring to the boil, stirring constantly. Return the rolls to the pan. Reduce the heat to low, cover the pan and simmer for 20 minutes.

Using a slotted spoon, transfer the rolls to a warmed serving dish. Strain the pan juices over the rolls and serve at once.

4 Servings

NOCE DE VITELLO FARCITO
(Veal Stuffed with Meat)

	Metric/U.K.	U.S.
Large veal escalopes	1kg/2lb	2lb
Lemon juice	1 Tbs	1 Tbs
Olive oil	125ml/4floz	½ cup
STUFFING Chicken meat, cut into strips	225g/8oz	8oz

Vitello Tonnato is a classic dish of cold roast veal served with a sauce of tuna fish and mayonnaise.

	Metric/U.K.	U.S.
Calf's liver, cut into strips	50g/2oz	2oz
Cooked ham, cut into strips	75g/3oz	3oz
Medium cooking apple, peeled, cored and grated	1	1
Marsala	125ml/4floz	½ cup
Egg yolks	2	2
Salt and pepper to taste		
French beans, trimmed, blanched and drained	125g/4oz	⅔ cup

First make the stuffing. Combine the meats and apple together. Pour over the Marsala and set aside to soak for 15 minutes.

Drain the meats and apple and return them to the bowl. Add the egg yolks and seasoning, and beat well.

Preheat the oven to moderate 180°C (Gas Mark 4, 350°F).

Lay the escalopes out on a board, over-lapping the edges slightly to make a 30cm/12in square. Using a meat mallet or your clenched fist, beat the edges together to form a slight seal. Sprinkle with salt and pepper and lemon juice.

Arrange one-third of the stuffing in the middle of the meat. Cover with half the French beans and cover these with another one-third of the stuffing. Repeat the layers to use up the remaining ingredients. Fold the top and bottom sides of the escalope square over the stuffing so that they just meet. Turn in the sides to make a neat parcel. Tie the meat with string in four or five places along its length and twice around its width.

Put the meat in a roasting pan. Pour over the oil and place the pan in the oven. Roast the meat for 1 hour, or until a skewer inserted into the centre passes easily through the stuffing.

Remove from the oven, remove the meat from the pan and transfer to a warmed serving platter. Remove and discard the string and serve at once.

6-8 Servings

VITELLO ALLA PIEMONTESE
(Veal with Truffles)

	Metric/U.K.	U.S.
Veal escalope	1x700g/1½lb	1x1½lb
Veal escalope	1x½kg/1lb	1x1lb
Prosciutto, thinly sliced	125g/4oz	4oz
Pork fat, cut into thin strips	50g/2oz	2oz
Carrots, cut lengthways into thin strips	3	3
Salt and pepper to taste		
Liver sausage	175g/6oz	6oz
Truffle, finely chopped	1	1
Small green pepper, pith and seeds removed and cut into thin strips	½	½
Butter	50g/2oz	4 Tbs
Shallots, chopped	6	6
Marsala	175ml/6floz	¾ cup
Veal or beef stock	175ml/6floz	¾ cup
Beurre manié (one part butter and two parts flour blended).	1 Tbs	1 Tbs

Slice both the escalope pieces through the centre crosswise to within 1cm/½in of the end of the meat. Pull apart and lay flat on a working surface. Cover the meat with a layer of grease-proof or waxed paper and pound for 2 to 3 minutes or until the meat is slightly thinner. Remove the paper and trim the edges to neaten them. On the larger piece place the prosciutto, pork fat and carrots, and season with salt and pepper. Lay the smaller piece on top, then spread over the liver sausage. Arrange the truffle and pepper lengthways down the centre and roll up Swiss (jelly) roll style, tying firmly with string at about 2½cm/1in intervals.

Preheat the oven to moderate 180°C (Gas Mark 4, 350°F).

Melt the butter in a large flameproof casserole. Add the shallots and fry until they are soft. Add the meat and fry until it is evenly browned. Pour over the Marsala and stock and bring to the boil. Cover and transfer the casserole to the oven. Cook for 1 to 1¼ hours, or until the veal is cooked through and tender. Remove from the oven and transfer the meat to a warmed serving dish. Untruss and keep hot while you finish the sauce.

Bring the cooking liquid to the boil, then boil briskly for 5 minutes, or until it has reduced slightly. Reduce the heat to low and stir in the beurre manié, a little at a time, until the sauce thickens and becomes smooth.

Pour into a warmed sauceboat and serve at once, with the meat.

6 Servings

VITELLO TONNATO
(Cold Veal with Tuna Fish Sauce)

	Metric/U.K.	U.S.
Boned leg or loin of veal	1x1½kg/3lb	1x3lb
Anchovy fillets, halved	3	3
Garlic cloves, halved	3	3
Canned tuna fish, oil reserved	200g/7oz	7oz
Medium onion, sliced	1	1
Carrots, sliced	2	2
Veal or chicken stock	300ml/10floz	1¼ cups
Dry white wine	175ml/6floz	¾ cup
White wine vinegar	3 Tbs	3 Tbs
Bay leaves	2	2
Dried basil	1 tsp	1 tsp
Chopped parsley	1 Tbs	1 Tbs
Salt and pepper to taste		
SAUCE Mayonnaise	125ml/4floz	½ cup
Hard-boiled egg yolks, strained	2	2
Double (heavy) cream, stiffly beaten	3 Tbs	3 Tbs
GARNISH Capers	2 tsp	2 tsp
Green or black olives, halved and stoned (pitted)	6	6

Preheat the oven to moderate 180°C (Gas Mark 4, 350°F).

Put the veal on a working surface and make six incisions in the meat. Insert half an anchovy fillet and half a garlic clove in each incision. Transfer the veal to a large flame-proof casserole and add the tuna fish with its oil, the vegetables, stock, wine, vinegar, herbs and seasoning. Mix well and bring to the boil. Cover and transfer the casserole to the oven. Cook for 1½ to 1¾ hours, or until the veal is cooked through and tender. Remove from the oven and set aside to cool in the casserole.

Remove the veal from the casserole and put it on a carving board. Carve into thin slices, then arrange the slices, slightly overlapping, on a large serving dish. Set aside.

Strain the casserole liquids into a bowl, rubbing the fish, vegetables and flavourings through with the back of a wooden spoon. Pour off all but 250ml/8floz (1 cup) of the

liquid, then beat in the mayonnaise, strained egg yolks and cream until the sauce is smooth. Taste and add more seasoning if necessary.

Pour the sauce over the veal slices to cover them and carefully cover the dish with foil or greaseproof or waxed paper. Chill in the refrigerator for 8 hours, or overnight.

Remove from the refrigerator and remove the covering. Garnish with the capers and olives and serve at once.

6-8 Servings

OSSOBUCO
(Stewed Veal Knuckle or Shank)

Ossobuco is one of the great dishes of Milan, although it is now found throughout Italy. The gremolada, a spicy mixture of lemon rind, garlic and parsley, is a specifically Milanaise addition to the dish. When you put the veal pieces into the casserole, try to arrange them in one layer if possible, so that they will retain the marrow in the centre. It is traditionally served with Risotto alla Milanese.

	Metric/U.K.	U.S.
Veal knuckle or shank, sawn into 7½cm/3in pieces	1kg/2lb	2lb
Seasoned flour (flour with salt and pepper to taste)	75g/3oz	¾ cup
Butter	125g/4oz	8 Tbs
Large onion, thinly sliced	1	1
Canned peeled tomatoes	425g/14oz	14oz
Tomato purée (paste)	4 Tbs	4 Tbs
Dry white wine	175ml/6floz	¾ cup
Salt and pepper to taste		
Sugar	1 tsp	1 tsp
GREMOLADA		
Finely grated lemon rind	1 Tbs	1 Tbs
Garlic cloves, crushed	2	2
Finely chopped parsley	1½ Tbs	1½ Tbs

Dip the veal pieces in the seasoned flour, shaking off any excess.

Melt the butter in a very large, shallow flameproof casserole. Add the veal pieces and fry until they are lightly and evenly browned. Transfer them to a plate.

Add the onion to the casserole and fry until it is soft. Stir in the tomatoes and can juice and the tomato purée (paste), and cook for a further 3 minutes. Pour over the wine, salt, pepper and sugar and bring to the boil.

Return the veal pieces to the casserole and stir well. Reduce the heat to low, cover the casserole and simmer the veal for 2 to 2½ hours, or until the meat is almost falling off the bone.

Meanwhile, to make the gremolada, combine all the ingredients. Stir the gremolada into the veal mixture and cook for a further 1 minute.

Serve at once, straight from the casserole.

6 Servings

FRITTO MISTO
(Deep-fried Meat and Vegetables)

Fritto Misto is the Italian for 'mixed fry' and that is exactly what this dish is—the Italians are very fond of this method of cooking. Almost any type of meat and/or vegetables may be used, but the ingredients used below are typically Italian.

	Metric/U.K.	U.S.
Calf's sweetbreads, soaked in cold water for 1 hour and drained	2	2
Lemon juice	1 Tbs	1 Tbs
Salt	1 tsp	1 tsp
Aubergine (eggplant), peeled, sliced and dégorged	1	1
Courgettes (zucchini), sliced and dégorged	½kg/1lb	1lb
Sufficient vegetable oil for deep-frying		
Chicken breasts, boned and cut into strips	4	4
Medium mushrooms	8	8
Lemons, quartered	2	2
BATTER		
Flour	125g/4oz	1 cup
Salt	¼ tsp	¼ tsp
Eggs, lightly beaten	2	2
Vegetable oil	1 Tbs	1 Tbs
Milk	250ml/8floz	1 cup

To prepare the batter, sift the flour and salt into a bowl. Make a well in the centre and put in the

Ossobuco is a rich stew of veal knuckle or shanks and white wine. It originated in Milan although it is now popular throughout the country. Traditionally it is served with Risotto alla Milanese (page 276).

293

eggs and oil. Mix the eggs and oil together, gradually incorporating the flour, then add the milk, a little at a time. Cover and keep in a cool place for 30 minutes.

Put the sweetbreads in a saucepan and pour over enough water to cover. Add the lemon juice and salt. Bring to the boil, reduce the heat to moderate and cook for 15 minutes. Remove from the heat and drain the sweetbreads in a colander. Rinse well under cold running water. Carefully remove and discard the outer membrane, then cut out the tubes and any gristle. Cut the sweetbreads into 2½cm/1in cubes.

Dry the aubergine (eggplant), courgettes (zucchini) and sweetbreads with kitchen towels.

Preheat the oven to very cool 140°C (Gas Mark 1, 275°F). Line a large baking dish with kitchen towels.

Fill a large deep-frying pan one-third full with oil and heat until it reaches 190°C (375°F) on a deep-fat thermometer, or until a small cube of stale bread dropped into the oil turns golden in 40 seconds.

Using tongs, dip the chicken strips first into the batter, then carefully lower into the oil. Fry for 5 minutes. Transfer the pieces to the baking dish and keep hot in the oven.

Dip the aubergine (eggplant), courgettes (zucchini), mushrooms and sweetbread pieces into the batter and then into the oil. Fry for 2 to 3 minutes each and keep hot while you finish frying.

Transfer the fritto misto to a warmed serving dish and garnish with the lemon quarters.

Serve at once.

8 Servings

FEGATO ALLA VENEZIANA
(Calf's Liver with Onions)

This is one of the classic dishes of the Veneto, although it is now found all over Italy. The calf's liver should be cut very thinly if possible. If you can't obtain calf's liver (or can't afford it—it tends to be a luxury item in most budgets these days) lamb's liver, again very thinly sliced and cut into strips, may be substituted.

	Metric/U.K.	U.S.
Butter	25g/1oz	2 Tbs
Olive oil	2 Tbs	2 Tbs
Large onions, thinly sliced into rings	3	3
Calf's liver, thinly sliced then cut into strips	700g/1½lb	1½lb
Salt and pepper to taste		
Chopped parsley	1 Tbs	1 Tbs

Melt the butter with the oil in a large, deep frying-pan. Add the onions, reduce the heat to low and simmer, stirring occasionally, for 15 to 20 minutes, or until they are very soft.

Meanwhile, rub the liver strips with salt and pepper. Add the strips to the pan, raise the heat to moderate and fry them for 4 to 6 minutes, turning them occasionally or until they are just cooked through and tender.

When all the liver has been cooked, transfer the liver and onions to a warmed serving dish and sprinkle over the parsley.

Serve at once.

6 Servings

FEGATO DI VITELLO AL POMODORO
(Calf's Liver with Tomatoes, Mushrooms and Onions)

	Metric/U.K.	U.S.
Calf's liver, thinly sliced	700g/1½lb	1½lb
Lemon juice	3 Tbs	3 Tbs
Butter	75g/3oz	6 Tbs
Medium onions, sliced	2	2
Garlic cloves, crushed	2	2
Canned peeled tomatoes	425g/14oz	14oz
Large button mushrooms, sliced	4	4
Dried sage	1 tsp	1 tsp
Dried basil	1 tsp	1 tsp
Seasoned flour (flour with salt and pepper to taste)	25g/1oz	¼ cup

Sprinkle the liver slices with lemon juice and set them aside for 30 minutes, basting occasionally.

Melt about one-third of the butter in a saucepan. Add the onions and garlic and fry until the onions are soft. Stir in the remaining ingredients, except the seasoned flour, and bring to the boil. Reduce the heat to low, cover the saucepan and simmer the sauce for 30 minutes.

Meanwhile, dry the liver slices on kitchen towels, then dip them into the seasoned flour, shaking off any excess.

Melt the remaining butter in a large frying-pan. Add the liver slices, a few at a time, and fry them gently for 2 to 3 minutes on each side, or until they are just cooked through and tender.

When all the liver has been cooked, transfer to a warmed serving dish. Pour over the sauce and serve at once.

6 Servings

CODA DI BUE CON SEDANO
(Braised Oxtail with Celery)

This dish is particularly good if you make it the day before you plan to eat it, chill overnight in the refrigerator, then heat through.

	Metric/U.K.	U.S.
Oxtails, cut into 7½cm/3in pieces	2	2
Seasoned flour (flour with salt and pepper to taste)	50g/2oz	½ cup
Olive oil	5 Tbs	5 Tbs
Large onion, chopped	1	1

Fegato di Vitello al Pomodoro is calf's liver with tomato sauce. Serve with mashed potatoes and salad—and some good robust red wine.

295

Garlic cloves, crushed	2	2
Red wine	175ml/6floz	¾ cup
Beef stock	250ml/8floz	1 cup
Canned tomatoes, drained and chopped	425g/14oz	14oz
Tomato purée (paste)	2 Tbs	2 Tbs
Bouquets garnis	2	2
Celery, chopped	1 bunch	1 bunch
Boiling water	450ml/15floz	2 cups
Cornflour (cornstarch), blended with 1 Tbs water	2 tsp	2 tsp

Preheat the oven to warm 170°C (Gas Mark 3, 325°F). Coat the oxtail pieces in the seasoned flour, shaking off any excess.

Heat half the oil in a large frying-pan. Add the oxtail pieces and fry until they are evenly browned. Transfer the pieces to a large flameproof casserole. Wipe the pan clean and pour in the rest of the oil. Add the onion and garlic and fry until the onion is soft. Pour over the wine and bring to the boil, stirring constantly. Boil until the liquid has reduced by about half. Pour the stock into the pan and cook for 2 minutes. Pour the mixture over the oxtail.

Stir the tomatoes, tomato purée (paste) and bouquets garnis into the casserole and bring to the boil. Cover and transfer to the oven. Braise for 3½ hours.

Just before the end of the cooking period, blanch the celery pieces in boiling water for 5 minutes. Drain and stir into the casserole. Re-cover and braise for a further 30 minutes.

Remove from the oven and skim the scum from the surface. Set over moderate heat and stir in the cornflour (cornstarch) mixture. Bring to the boil and cook, stirring constantly, for 2 minutes, or until the liquid thickens and is smooth.

6 Servings

SALSICCE CON FAGIOLI
(Sausages with Beans)

This unassuming dish is particularly good when made with a mixture of Italian hot and sweet sausages if these are available. If they are not, use ordinary beef sausages and a little garlic sausage, chopped.

Salsicce con Fagioli is a filling casserole based on a mixture of Italian sausages and beans. It is marvellously easy to prepare and inexpensive, too.

	Metric/U.K.	U.S.
Dried white haricot (dried white) beans, soaked overnight and drained	450g/1lb	2⅔ cups
Water	1¼l/2 pints	5 cups
Olive oil	2 Tbs	2 Tbs
Italian or other sausages	700g/1½lb	1½lb
Medium onions, chopped	2	2
Garlic cloves, crushed	2	2
Medium green peppers, pith and seeds removed and chopped	2	2
Canned peeled tomatoes	425g/14oz	14oz
Water	250ml/8floz	1 cup
Dried sage	1 tsp	1 tsp
Tomato purée (paste)	1 Tbs	1 Tbs
Sugar	2 tsp	2 tsp
Salt and pepper to taste		

Put the beans and water into a saucepan and bring to the boil. Reduce the heat to low and simmer the beans for 45 minutes, or until they are just tender. Drain and set aside.

Heat the oil in a flameproof casserole. Add the sausages and fry until they are lightly and evenly browned and have rendered some of their fat. Transfer to a plate and keep hot.

Pour off all but about 2 tablespoons of oil from the casserole. Add the onions, garlic and peppers and fry until they are soft. Stir in the tomatoes and can juice and water, and bring to the boil. Reduce the heat to low and cook for a further 3 minutes. Stir in all the remaining ingredients and add the beans and sausages. Reduce the heat to low and cover the pan. Simmer for 1 hour, stirring occasionally, or until the sausages are cooked through and the mixture is fairly dry.

Either serve at once or allow to cool completely and chill overnight in the refrigerator.

6-8 Servings

POLLO PARMIGIANA
(Chicken with Grated Cheese)

	Metric/U.K.	U.S.
Chicken, cut into serving pieces	1x2kg/4lb	1x4lb
Salt and pepper to taste		
Olive oil	125ml/4floz	½ cup
Mushrooms, sliced	125g/4oz	1 cup
Medium green pepper, pith and seeds removed and thinly sliced	1	1
Medium onions, sliced	3	3
Garlic, crushed	2	2
Dried oregano	1 tsp	1 tsp
Canned peeled tomatoes, chopped	425g/14oz	14oz
Dry white wine or sherry	4 Tbs	4 Tbs
Parmesan cheese, grated	75g/3oz	¾ cup

Preheat the oven to moderate 180°C (Gas Mark 4, 350°F). Rub the chicken pieces with salt and pepper and set aside.

Heat the olive oil in a large flameproof casserole. Add the chicken pieces and fry until they are evenly browned. Add the mushrooms, pepper, onions, garlic, oregano, tomatoes and can juice and wine or sherry, and bring to the boil, stirring occasionally. Cover the casserole and transfer it to the oven. Bake for 1½ to 1¾ hours, or until the chicken is cooked through and tender.

Sprinkle one-third of the grated cheese over the top of the mixture and serve at once, with the remaining grated cheese.

4-6 Servings

BOLLITO MISTO (Boiled Chicken, Beef and Sausage)

The stock from this dish is often served as a separate soup course.

	Metric/U.K.	U.S.
Veal knuckle	1	1
Salt	1 tsp	1 tsp
Chicken	1x2kg/4lb	1x4lb
Topside (top round) of beef	1x700g/1½lb	1x1½lb
Black peppercorns	6	6
Bay leaves	2	2
Dried basil	1½ tsp	1½ tsp
Dried thyme	½ tsp	½ tsp

Leeks, coarsely chopped	2	2
Celery stalks, chopped	2	2
Carrots, sliced	½kg/1lb	1lb
Small white onions, peeled and left whole	12	12
Medium white cabbage, quartered	1	1
Potatoes, sliced	1kg/2lb	2lb
Italian boiling sausage	1	1

Put the veal knuckle into a very large, heavy saucepan and half-fill the pan with water. Add the salt and bring to the boil, skimming any scum from the surface. Boil the knuckle for 45 minutes. Add the chicken, beef, peppercorns and herbs, and bring to the boil again. Reduce the heat to low, cover the pan and simmer for 1½ hours.

Add the vegetables and boiling sausage and top up the water if necessary so that it almost covers them. Bring to the boil again. Reduce the heat to low and simmer for a further 1 hour, or until the meat and vegetables are cooked through and tender. Remove and discard the veal knuckle and bay leaves. Remove the meat, chicken and sausage to a chopping board. Carve the meat into slices, the chicken into serving pieces and the sausage into bite-sized portions. Arrange them on a heated platter and surround them with the vegetables. Moisten the meat and vegetables with about 5 tablespoons of the stock and serve at once.

8-10 Servings

POLLO ALLA CACCIATORA
(Chicken with Wine, Tomatoes and Mushrooms)

	Metric/U.K.	U.S.
Butter	15g/½oz	1 Tbs
Olive oil	2 Tbs	2 Tbs
Garlic cloves, crushed	2	2
Spring onions (scallions), finely chopped	2	2
Mushrooms, sliced	175g/6oz	1½ cups
Chicken, cut into serving pieces	1x2kg/4lb	1x4lb
Salt and pepper to taste		
Dry white wine	175ml/6floz	¾ cup
Chicken stock	50ml/2floz	¼ cup

Medium tomatoes, blanched, peeled, seeded and chopped	6	6
Large bay leaf	1	1
Beurre manié (one part butter and two parts flour blended)	2 tsp	2 tsp
Chopped parsley	1 Tbs	1 Tbs

Melt the butter with the oil in a flameproof casserole. Add the garlic and spring onions (scallions) and fry until they are soft. Add the mushrooms and fry for a further 3 minutes. Transfer the vegetables to a plate.

Add the chicken pieces to the casserole and fry until they are evenly browned. Stir in the seasoning, wine, stock, tomatoes, bay leaf and vegetable mixture, and bring to the boil. Reduce the heat to low, cover and simmer the mixture for 40 to 50 minutes, or until the chicken pieces are cooked through and tender. Remove from the heat and transfer the chicken pieces to a warmed serving dish. Keep hot.

Return the casserole to moderate heat and boil the sauce until it has reduced slightly. Stir in the beurre manié, a little at a time, and cook for a further 2 to 3 minutes, or until the sauce is smooth and fairly thick. Remove from the heat and discard the bay leaf.

Pour the sauce over the chicken, sprinkle over the parsley and serve at once.

4-6 Servings

POLLA ALLA BOLOGNESE
(Chicken Breasts with Ham and Cheese)

	Metric/U.K.	U.S.
Chicken breasts, skinned and boned	4	4
Seasoned flour (flour with salt and pepper to taste)	25g/1oz	4 Tbs
Butter	50g/2oz	4 Tbs
Smoked ham, thinly sliced and cut a little smaller than the chicken	8 slices	8 slices
Parmesan cheese, grated	50g/2oz	½ cup

Cut each chicken breast in half, crosswise. Place each piece between greaseproof or waxed paper and pound with a mallet to flatten.

Two superb examples of the Italian way with chicken—Pollo alla Bolognese (chicken breasts with ham and cheese) and Pollo alla Cacciatora (chicken stewed in wine, tomatoes and mushrooms).

Remove from the paper and coat with the seasoned flour, shaking off any excess.

Melt half the butter in a large frying-pan. Add the chicken pieces and fry for 10 to 15 minutes, or until they are lightly and evenly browned and cooked through.

Meanwhile, melt the remaining butter in a small saucepan. Remove from the heat.

Place a slice of ham on each chicken piece and sprinkle over about one-quarter of the grated cheese. Pour over the melted butter. Return the frying-pan to moderate heat, cover and cook the mixture for 3 to 4 minutes or until the cheese has melted.

Using a slotted spoon, transfer the chicken mixture to a warmed serving dish and serve at once, with the remaining cheese.

4 Servings

POLLO ALLA DIAVOLA
(Grilled [Broiled] Chicken with Herbs)

	Metric/U.K.	U.S.
Chickens, cut in half lengthways	2x1kg/2lb	2x2lb
Large garlic clove, halved	1	1
Salt and pepper to taste		
Butter	125g/4oz	8 Tbs
Olive oil	2 Tbs	2 Tbs
Lemon juice	1 Tbs	1 Tbs
Chopped parsley	1 Tbs	1 Tbs
Dried basil	1½ tsp	1½ tsp

Preheat the grill (broiler) to moderate.

Rub the chicken halves all over with the garlic clove halves, then with salt and pepper. Discard the garlic.

Melt the butter with the oil in a small saucepan. Remove from the heat and stir in the lemon juice, parsley and basil. Brush the chicken all over with the butter and herb mixture, then place the halves, skin side down, on the lined grill (broiler) rack.

Put under the grill (broiler) and grill (broil) for 7 to 10 minutes on each side, basting frequently with the butter mixture. After 15 minutes, test the chicken for doneness by inserting a skewer into one of the thighs; if the juices run clear the birds are cooked.

Remove the chicken halves to a warmed serving dish and spoon over any remaining

butter and herb mixture. Serve at once.

4 Servings

CONIGLIO AL VINO BIANCO
(Rabbit in White Wine)

	Metric/U.K.	U.S.
Water	1¾l/3 pints	7½ cups
Malt vinegar	1 Tbs	1 Tbs
Rabbit, cleaned and cut into serving pieces	1x2kg/4lb	1x4lb
Butter	50g/2oz	4 Tbs
Onions, sliced	2	2
Garlic cloves, crushed	2	2
Carrots, chopped	2	2
Celery stalks, chopped	3	3
Dry white wine	350ml/12floz	1½ cups
Dried rosemary	½ tsp	½ tsp
Dried oregano	½ tsp	½ tsp
Salt and pepper to taste		
Beurre manié (one part butter and two parts flour blended)	1 Tbs	1 Tbs

Pour the water and vinegar into a large bowl. Add the rabbit pieces and baste well. Marinate at room temperature for 8 hours, or overnight. Remove the rabbit from the bowl and discard the marinade. Pat dry with kitchen towels.

Preheat the oven to moderate 180°C (Gas Mark 4, 350°F).

Melt the butter in a flameproof casserole. Add the rabbit pieces and fry until they are evenly browned. Transfer them to a plate. Add the onions and garlic to the casserole and fry until they are soft. Add the carrots and celery and fry for 5 minutes. Pour over the wine, herbs and seasoning. Bring to the boil.

Return the rabbit pieces to the casserole and baste well. Cover and transfer the casserole to the oven. Cook for 1 to 1¼ hours, or until the rabbit is cooked through and tender.

Remove from the oven and transfer the rabbit pieces to a warmed serving dish. Keep hot while you finish the sauce. Put the casserole over high heat and bring the juices to the boil. Reduce the heat to low and add the beurre manié, a little at a time, stirring constantly until the sauce thickens. Serve at once.

6 Servings

Vegetables and Salads

ZUCCHINI RIPIENI
(Stuffed Courgettes)

	Metric/U.K.	U.S.
Dried mushrooms	15g/½oz	¼ cup
Medium courgettes (zucchini), trimmed	12	12
Fresh white breadcrumbs, soaked in 4 Tbs milk	50g/2oz	1 cup
Eggs, lightly beaten	2	2
Salt and pepper to taste		
Dried oregano	1 tsp	1 tsp
Parmesan cheese, grated	175g/6oz	1½ cups
Prosciutto, chopped	50g/2oz	2oz
Olive oil	50ml/2floz	¼ cup

Put the mushrooms in a bowl, pour over enough water to cover and soak for 30 minutes. Drain, chop and reserve.

Bring a large saucepan of salted water to the boil. Add the courgettes (zucchini) and boil for 7 to 8 minutes, or until they are just tender. Drain in a colander. Slice the vegetables in half lengthways and scoop out the flesh, taking care not to break the skins. Set aside.

Squeeze any excess moisture out of the breadcrumbs and place them in a bowl. Add the reserved courgette (zucchini) flesh, the eggs, salt, pepper, oregano, half the cheese, the prosciutto and reserved mushrooms. Mix all the ingredients together.

Preheat the oven to fairly hot 200°C (Gas Mark 6, 400°F). Lightly grease a shallow ovenproof casserole with a little of the oil. Arrange the courgette halves in the dish.

Spoon a little stuffing into each courgette (zucchini) half and sprinkle over the remaining cheese. Sprinkle over the remaining oil.

Put the casserole into the oven and bake for 20 minutes, or until the cheese has melted and the courgettes (zucchini) are golden on top. Serve at once.

6-12 Servings

Zucchini Ripieni is a dish of courgettes stuffed with breadcrumbs, ham and mushrooms, then covered with cheese. Serve with salad and crusty bread as a light snack lunch, or as a superb vegetable accompaniment to steak or chops.

FAGIOLI AL FORNO
(Tuscan Baked Beans)

Dried white haricot (dried white) beans are immensely popular in northern Italy, particularly in Tuscany, where they form part of many of the classic dishes of the area.

	Metric/U.K.	U.S.
Dried white haricot (dried white) beans, soaked overnight and drained	½kg/1lb	2⅔ cups
Garlic cloves, crushed	3	3
Chopped fresh basil	3 Tbs	3 Tbs
Salt and pepper to taste		
Ground cinnamon	½ tsp	½ tsp
Streaky (fatty) bacon, coarsely chopped	8 slices	8 slices

Preheat the oven to very cool 140°C (Gas Mark 1, 275°F).

Place the beans, garlic, basil, seasoning, cinnamon and bacon in a large ovenproof casserole. Stir and add just enough water to cover the mixture. Cover and put the casserole into the oven. Bake for 3 to 3½ hours, or until the beans are very tender but still firm.

Remove from the oven, strain off any excess liquid and serve at once.

6 Servings

CAVOLO IN AGRODOLCE
(Sweet and Sour Cabbage)

The Italians are very fond of the 'sweet and sour' taste in food, especially game and vegetables—rabbit and hare for instance and courgettes (zucchini) are also cooked in this way.

	Metric/U.K.	U.S.
Vegetable oil	50ml/2floz	¼ cup
Medium onion, chopped	1	1
Small green cabbage, finely shredded	1	1
Tomatoes, blanched, peeled, seeded and chopped	4	4
White wine vinegar	2 Tbs	2 Tbs
Salt and pepper to taste		
Sugar	1 Tbs	1 Tbs

Heat the oil in a deep frying-pan. Add the onion and fry until it is soft. Stir in the cabbage, a handful at a time, and, as it goes down, add the next. Then stir in the tomatoes, vinegar, salt and pepper. Reduce the heat to low and simmer for 15 to 20 minutes, or until the cabbage is cooked.

Stir in the sugar and cook for 1 minute longer. Transfer to a warmed serving dish and serve at once.

4 Servings

CROCCHETTINE DI PATATE
(Potato Croquettes with Cheese and Ham)

	Metric/U.K.	U.S.
Potatoes	1kg/2lb	2lb
Butter, softened	25g/1oz	2 Tbs
Eggs, lightly beaten	4	4
Parmesan cheese, grated	75g/3oz	¾ cup
Cooked ham, finely diced	50g/2oz	2oz
Salt and pepper to taste		
Grated nutmeg	½ tsp	½ tsp
Fine dry breadcrumbs	75g/3oz	1 cup
Sufficient vegetable oil for deep-frying		

Boil the potatoes in salted water for 15 to 20 minutes, or until they are tender. Drain and mash them. Transfer to a large bowl. Beat in the butter, half the beaten egg mixture, the grated cheese, ham, seasoning and nutmeg until the mixture is well blended.

Using your hands, form the mixture into sausage shapes about 5cm/2in long. Arrange on a baking sheet and chill in the refrigerator for 15 minutes.

Put the remaining beaten egg in one shallow dish and the breadcrumbs in another. Remove the croquettes from the refrigerator and dip them, one by one, first in the eggs then in the breadcrumbs, shaking off any excess.

Fill a large deep-frying pan one-third full with oil and heat until it reaches 190°C (375°F) on a deep-fat thermometer, or until a small cube of stale bread dropped into the oil turns golden in 40 seconds.

Carefully lower the croquettes into the oil, a few at a time, and fry for 3 to 4 minutes, or until they are golden brown. As they are cooked, transfer to kitchen towels to drain and keep hot while you cook the remaining croquettes in the same way.

Serving piping hot.

4-6 Servings

MELANZANE ALLA PARMIGIANA
(Aubergine [Eggplant] Parmesan)

This delicious and filling dish is almost more popular in the United States than in its native land. In Italy, Parma ham is sometimes substituted for the Mozzarella used in this recipe, and a meat sauce (similar to ragù Bolognese) can also be substituted for tomato sauce if you wish the dish to be more substantial.

	Metric/U.K.	U.S.
Olive oil	about 175ml/ 6floz	about ¾ cup
Aubergines (eggplants), sliced and dégorged	4	4
Mozzarella cheese, sliced	175g/6oz	6oz
Parmesan cheese, grated	75g/3oz	¾ cup
SAUCE		
Olive oil	3 Tbs	3 Tbs
Medium onions, chopped	2	2
Garlic cloves, crushed	2	2
Tomatoes, blanched, peeled and chopped	½kg/1lb	1lb
Tomato purée (paste)	4 Tbs	4 Tbs
Dried basil	2 tsp	2 tsp
Salt and pepper to taste		

To make the sauce, heat the oil in a saucepan. Add the onions and garlic and fry until the onions are soft. Stir in the tomatoes, tomato purée (paste) and the remaining ingredients, and bring to the boil. Reduce the heat to low, cover the pan and simmer the sauce for 30 minutes, or until it is thick and rich. Remove from the heat.

Meanwhile, heat about 50ml/2floz (4 tablespoons) of olive oil in a large frying-pan. Add a few of the aubergine (eggplant) slices and fry until they are golden brown on both sides. Transfer them to a plate. Cook the remaining slices in the same way, adding more oil as necessary.

Preheat the oven to moderate 180°C (Gas

Mark 4, 350°F).

Arrange about one-third of the aubergine (eggplant) slices on the bottom of an ovenproof casserole. Cover with half the Mozzarella slices and a third of the sauce. Top with a generous sprinkling of grated cheese. Continue making layers in this way until all the ingredients are used up, finishing with a layer of aubergine (eggplant) slices covered with sauce and grated cheese.

Put the dish into the oven and bake for 45 minutes.

Serve at once.

4-6 Servings

PEPERONATA
(Red Pepper and Tomato Stew)

This dish is one of the classics of Italian cuisine and can be served as an accompaniment to lamb, veal or chicken.

	Metric/U.K.	U.S.
Butter	25g/1oz	2 Tbs
Olive oil	2 Tbs	2 Tbs
Large onion, thinly sliced	1	1
Garlic clove, crushed	1	1
Red peppers, pith and seeds removed and cut into strips	½kg/1lb	1lb
Tomatoes, blanched, peeled and chopped	½kg/1lb	1lb
Salt and pepper to taste		
Bay leaf	1	1

Peperonata is a classic stew of red peppers and tomatoes. Serve with veal escalopes, or sliced liver.

Melt the butter with the oil in a large saucepan. Add the onion and garlic and fry until the onion is soft. Stir in the red peppers, reduce the heat to low and cover. Simmer for 15 minutes. Stir in the tomatoes, seasoning and bay leaf, and simmer, uncovered, for a further 20 minutes. If there is too much liquid in the pan, increase the heat to moderately high and cook for 5 minutes, or until the mixture is thick and some liquid has evaporated.

Remove from the heat and discard the bay leaf. Serve at once, if you are serving the peperonata hot. (This dish is equally good served cold.)

4-6 Servings

Peppers are very popular in Italy and are incorporated into many meat dishes, as well as being served by themselves as a vegetable. In this Peperoni Ripieni, they are stuffed with a tomato, tuna, anchovy and olive mixture, and could be served as a light snack meal as well as a filling vegetable accompaniment.

PEPERONI RIPIENI
(Peppers Stuffed with Tomatoes, Tuna, Anchovies and Olives)

This dish can be served as a first course, as an accompaniment to steak dishes, or even (if you serve two per person) as a light lunch.

	Metric/U.K.	U.S.
Large green peppers	4	4
Olive oil	4 Tbs	4 Tbs
Medium onion, thinly sliced	1	1
Garlic cloves, crushed	2	2
Canned peeled tomatoes	700g/1½lb	1½lb
Tomato purée (paste)	2 Tbs	2 Tbs
Dried basil	½ tsp	½ tsp
Dried oregano	½ tsp	½ tsp
Salt and pepper to taste		
Chopped parsley	1 Tbs	1 Tbs
Canned tuna, drained and flaked	350g/12oz	12oz
Anchovy fillets, chopped	4	4
Black olives, chopped	6	6
Capers	2 tsp	2 tsp
Parmesan cheese, grated	25g/1oz	¼ cup

Slice off about 2½cm/1in from the wider end of each pepper. Carefully remove and discard the pith and seeds. Set aside. Remove and discard the stems from the sliced tops and chop the flesh into small dice. Set aside.

Heat half the oil in a large frying-pan. Add the onion, garlic and pepper dice and fry until the onion is soft. Stir in the tomatoes and can juice, tomato purée (paste), herbs, salt and pepper. Cover and cook, stirring occasionally, for 25 minutes, or until the mixture has thickened. Stir in the remaining ingredients, except the cheese, and cook the mixture for 5 minutes.

Preheat the oven to warm 170°C (Gas Mark 3, 325°F).

Remove from the heat and spoon the sauce into the peppers, filling them to within about 1cm/½in of the top.

Brush a baking pan with about 1 tablespoon of the remaining oil. Arrange the peppers in the pan and put the pan into the oven. Bake for 45 minutes, basting occasionally with the remaining oil. After 45 minutes, sprinkle the tops of the peppers with the grated cheese and bake for a further 15 minutes, or until the cheese is brown and bubbly. Remove from the oven and serve at once.

4 Servings

PISELLI AL PROSCIUTTO
(Peas with Prosciutto)

This dish is Roman in origin although it is found throughout Italy now. Use fresh petits pois if at all possible; frozen if necessary. It can be served as a vegetable accompaniment or as an hors d'oeuvre, with lots of crusty bread.

	Metric/U.K.	U.S.
Butter	50g/2oz	4 Tbs
Small onion, finely chopped	1	1
Fresh peas, weighed after shelling	½kg/1lb	1lb
Salt and pepper to taste		
Chicken stock	50ml/2floz	¼ cup
Prosciutto, cut into strips	175g/6oz	6oz

Melt the butter in a saucepan. Add the onion and fry until it is soft. Stir in the peas, seasoning and stock, and bring to the boil. Reduce the heat to low and simmer the peas for 8 to 10 minutes, or until they are just tender. Add the prosciutto strips and simmer the mixture for a further 3 minutes, stirring from time to time.

Transfer the contents of the pan to a warmed serving dish.

Serve at once.

4 Servings

ZUCCA ALLA PARMIGIANA
(Pumpkin, Parma-Style)

Pumpkin is a popular vegetable all over Italy and this is a particularly delicious way of cooking it. It is fairly rich, so serve with a light main dish, such as veal escalope or grilled (broiled) lamb and lots of mixed salad.

	Metric/U.K.	U.S.
Eggs, lightly beaten	2	2
Dry breadcrumbs	50g/2oz	⅔ cup
Pumpkin flesh, sliced	1kg/2lb	2lb
Butter	50g/2oz	4 Tbs
Parmesan cheese, finely grated	25g/1oz	¼ cup
SAUCE		
Olive oil	2 Tbs	2 Tbs
Onion, finely chopped	1	1
Garlic clove, crushed	1	1
Canned peeled tomatoes	425g/14oz	14oz
Tomato purée (paste)	2 Tbs	2 Tbs
Chopped fresh basil	1 Tbs	1 Tbs
Chopped parsley	1 Tbs	1 Tbs
Sugar	1 tsp	1 tsp
Salt and pepper to taste		

To make the sauce, heat the oil in a saucepan. Add the onion and garlic and fry until the onion is soft. Stir in the tomatoes and can juice, tomato purée (paste), herbs, sugar and seasoning, and bring to the boil. Reduce the heat to low and simmer the sauce for 15 minutes. Remove the pan from the heat and keep hot.

Preheat the oven to moderate 180°C (Gas Mark 4, 350°F).

Put the eggs in one dish and the breadcrumbs in another. Dip the pumpkin slices first in the eggs then in the breadcrumbs, shaking off any excess.

Melt the butter in a large frying-pan. Add the pumpkin slices, a few at a time, and fry until they are evenly browned. Transfer the slices to a well-greased ovenproof baking dish. Pour over the sauce and sprinkle over the cheese. Put the dish into the oven and bake for 30 minutes, or until the cheese is golden brown and bubbling.

Remove the dish from the oven and serve at once.

6 Servings

INSALATA DI FUNGHI
(Mushroom Salad)

	Metric/U.K.	U.S.
Olive oil	3 Tbs	3 Tbs
Lemon juice	1 Tbs	1 Tbs
Salt and pepper to taste		
Button mushrooms, thinly sliced	225g/8oz	2 cups
Cooked peas	50g/2oz	⅓ cup
Lettuce, shredded	1	1

Combine the oil, lemon juice, salt and pepper in a screw-top jar and shake to blend thoroughly.

Arrange the mushrooms and peas in a bowl and pour over the dressing. Toss thoroughly and chill in the refrigerator for at least 30 minutes.

Line a serving dish with the lettuce. Pile the mushroom mixture into the centre and serve at once.

4 Servings

FUNGHI MARINATE
(Marinated Mushrooms)

	Metric/U.K.	U.S.
Small button mushrooms, stalks removed	½kg/1lb	1lb
MARINADE Salt	1 tsp	1 tsp
Black peppercorns, coarsely crushed	½ tsp	½ tsp
Dried dill	1 tsp	1 tsp
Tarragon vinegar	4 Tbs	4 Tbs
Lemon juice	1 Tbs	1 Tbs
Olive oil	50ml/2floz	¼ cup

Combine all the marinade ingredients in a shallow bowl. Stir in the mushrooms and baste them with the liquid. Cover the dish and set aside in a cool place to marinate for 2 hours, basting frequently.

Drain off and discard the marinade and pile the mushrooms on a serving dish. Serve at once.

6 Servings

INSALATA D'ARANCIA
(Orange Salad)

	Metric/U.K.	U.S.
Lettuce, shredded	1 crisp	1 crisp
Oranges, peeled, pith removed and separated into segments	2	2
Large tomato, thinly sliced	1	1
Lemon juice	1 Tbs	1 Tbs
Vegetable oil	1 Tbs	1 Tbs
Chopped chives	1 tsp	1 tsp
Salt and pepper to taste		

Arrange the lettuce on a serving plate.

Put the orange segments and tomato slices in a bowl. Combine all the remaining ingredients in a screw-top jar and shake well to blend. Pour over the fruit and toss well to blend.

Arrange the fruit and dressing mixture over the lettuce and chill in the refrigerator for 15 minutes before serving.

4 Servings

INSALATA DI FINOCCHIO
(Fennel Salad)

	Metric/U.K.	U.S.
Fennel, trimmed	1 head	1 head
Chicory (French or Belgian endive), outer leaves removed	1 head	1 head
Tomatoes, thinly sliced	4	4
Olive oil	4 Tbs	4 Tbs
White wine vinegar	2 Tbs	2 Tbs
Garlic clove, crushed	1	1
Salt and pepper to taste		

Thinly slice the fennel and chicory (endive) and arrange them in a serving dish. Add the tomatoes.

Combine all the remaining ingredients in a screw-top jar and shake well to blend. Pour the dressing over the fennel mixture and toss gently to blend. Chill in the refrigerator for 30 minutes before serving.

4-6 Servings

Salads can either be accompaniments to the main dish or antipasta in Italy and these two delightful dishes are no exception : Insalata di Funghi, a refreshing mushroom and pea salad at the top, and Insalata d'Arancia, an orange and tomato salad at the bottom.

Desserts and Cakes

CILIEGE AL MARSALA
(Cherries in Marsala)

	Metric/U.K.	U.S.
Canned stoned (pitted) Morello cherries, drained	1kg/2lb	2lb
Marsala	150ml/5floz	$\frac{5}{8}$ cup
Grated nutmeg	$\frac{1}{2}$ tsp	$\frac{1}{2}$ tsp
Sugar	1 Tbs	1 Tbs
Double (heavy) cream, stiffly beaten	150ml/5floz	$\frac{5}{8}$ cup

Put the cherries, Marsala, nutmeg and sugar into a saucepan and bring to the boil, stirring until the sugar has dissolved. Reduce the heat to low and simmer gently for 10 minutes. Remove from the heat and transfer the cherries to a serving dish.

Return the pan to the heat and boil the liquid briskly for 3 to 4 minutes, or until it is thick and syrupy. Pour the syrup over the cherries.

Chill the dish in the refrigerator for at least 1 hour. Top the cherries with the cream before serving.

4 Servings

RICOTTA AL CAFFE
(Ricotta Cheese with Coffee)

Ricotta cheese is a very popular cooking ingredient all over Italy, and it is used equally in both savoury dishes, such as Lasagne (page 268) and sweet dishes such as the recipe below. If you cannot obtain ricotta, cottage cheese may be substituted.

	Metric/U.K.	U.S.
Ricotta cheese	350g/12oz	12oz
Castor (superfine) sugar	175g/6oz	$\frac{3}{4}$ cup
Freshly percolated strong black coffee	50ml/2floz	$\frac{1}{4}$ cup
Dark rum	50ml/2floz	$\frac{1}{4}$ cup
Walnuts, halved	2	2

Rub the cheese through a strainer, using the back of a wooden spoon. Beat the sugar, coffee and rum into the cheese and continue beating until the mixture is smooth and thick. Set aside at room temperature for 1 hour.

Spoon the mixture into individual serving glasses and chill in the refrigerator for 1 hour. Decorate each glass with half a walnut before serving.

4 Servings

GELATA DI PISTACCHIO
(Pistachio Ice-cream)

You will need either an ice-cream maker with paddles or a churn for this recipe. Serve with crisp wafers or, to be really authentic, little amoretti biscuits (cookies).

	Metric/U.K.	U.S.
Single (light) cream	250ml/8floz	1 cup
Pistachio nuts, shelled, chopped and blanched	125g/4oz	1 cup
Double (heavy) cream	250ml/8floz	1 cup
Almond essence (extract)	$\frac{1}{2}$ tsp	$\frac{1}{2}$ tsp
Egg yolks	3	3
Sugar	50g/2oz	$\frac{1}{4}$ cup
Water	75ml/3floz	$\frac{3}{8}$ cup
Egg whites, stiffly beaten	3	3

Put the single (light) cream and nuts in a blender and blend until the nuts are puréed. Spoon the mixture into a small saucepan and stir in the double (heavy) cream. Place over low heat and simmer gently until the mixture is hot. Remove from the heat, cover and set aside to cool.

Pour the mixture into a medium-sized bowl, beat in the almond essence (extract) and set aside.

Beat the egg yolks until they are well blended.

Dissolve the sugar in the water over low heat, stirring constantly. Increase the heat to moderate and boil the syrup until the temperature reaches 140°C (220°F) on a sugar thermometer or until a little of the syrup spooned out of the pan and cooled will form a short thread when drawn out between your index finger and thumb. Remove from the heat and let the syrup stand for 1 minute.

Pour the syrup over the egg yolks in a steady stream, whisking constantly. Continue whisking until the mixture is thick and fluffy. Mix in the cooled cream mixture, then fold in the beaten egg whites.

Pour the mixture into an ice-cream container equipped with paddles or into a hand-propelled ice-cream churn, and freeze according to manufacturers' instructions.

Store in the frozen food storage compartment of the refrigerator and serve as required.

4 Servings

BODINO DI RICOTTA
(Cheese and Almond Pudding)

	Metric/U.K.	U.S.
Butter	1 tsp	1 tsp
Fine dry breadcrumbs	1 Tbs	1 Tbs
Sultanas or seedless raisins	1 Tbs	1 Tbs
Chopped mixed candied peel	2 Tbs	2 Tbs
Rum	50ml/2floz	$\frac{1}{4}$ cup
Ricotta cheese	$\frac{1}{2}$kg/1lb	1lb
Eggs	4	4
Ground almonds	75g/3oz	$\frac{1}{2}$ cup
Slivered almonds	50g/2oz	$\frac{1}{3}$ cup
Ground cinnamon	$\frac{1}{2}$ tsp	$\frac{1}{2}$ tsp
Grated lemon rind	1 Tbs	1 Tbs
Sugar	50g/2oz	$\frac{1}{4}$ cup

Preheat the oven to moderate 180°C (Gas Mark 4, 350°F). Lightly grease a large baking dish with the butter, then sprinkle over the breadcrumbs.

Put the sultanas or raisins and candied peel in a small bowl. Cover with rum and set aside to soak for 10 minutes.

Using the back of a wooden spoon, rub the ricotta through a strainer into a large bowl. Beat in the eggs, then gradually add the sultana or raisin mixture and all of the remaining ingredients.

Turn the mixture into a baking dish and put the dish into the oven. Bake for 45 minutes to 1 hour, or until the top is light brown. Remove from the oven and set aside to cool. When the mixture is cold, transfer it to the refrigerator and chill for at least 1 hour.

To serve, run a knife around the edge of the dish and quickly invert the mixture on to a serving dish.

4-6 Servings

Simplicity itself, yet a deliciously satisfying dessert, is Ciliege al Marsala, cherries in Marsala.

ZABAGLIONE
(Egg Yolk and Wine Dessert)

This has rightly been called the queen of Italian desserts, and there's scarcely a self-respecting Italian housewife or restaurant chef who doesn't have at least one version of it at her fingertips. It is traditionally served warm, but if you prefer, it can be chilled in the refrigerator.

	Metric/U.K.	U.S.
Egg yolks	4	4
Castor (superfine) sugar	4 Tbs	4 Tbs
Marsala	4 Tbs	4 Tbs
Grated lemon rind	2 tsp	2 tsp

Beat the egg yolks and sugar together in a heatproof bowl until they thicken and become pale yellow. Place the bowl over a saucepan one-third full of boiling water and put the pan over moderate heat. Add the Marsala and lemon rind and continue beating until the mixture rises slightly and stiffens. Remove from the heat.

Spoon into individual serving glasses and serve at once.

4 Servings

ZUPPA INGLESE
(English Trifle)

Despite the name, this recipe is NOT a soup but a rather fanciful Italian idea of what constitutes a traditional English trifle!

	Metric/U.K.	U.S.
Sponge cakes, sliced in half crosswise	2x18cm/7in	2x7in
Marsala	250ml/8floz	1 cup
Zabaglione (make double the quantity given in the recipe above)		
Double (heavy) cream, stiffly beaten	475ml/16floz	2 cups
Maraschino cherries	16	16

Place one-half of the sponge, cut side up, on a serving plate. Sprinkle over about a quarter of the Marsala, then spread over one-third of the zabaglione. Continue making layers in this way until all the ingredients are used up, ending with a layer of sponge.

Spread the cream over the top and sides of the trifle. Arrange the cherries decoratively over the surface and chill in the refrigerator for 1 hour.

Remove the plate from the refrigerator and serve at once.

6 Servings

ZUPPA A DUE COLORI
(Two-Coloured Sponge Pudding)

This stunning dessert looks fabulous—and complicated—when it is assembled but in actual fact it is quite easy to make. It is very rich to eat, so serve after a fairly light main dish such as veal or chicken.

	Metric/U.K.	U.S.
Chocolate sponge cake, thinly sliced	2x20cm/8in	2x8in
Chocolate-flavoured liqueur	125ml/4floz	½ cup
Sponge cake, thinly sliced	1x18cm/7in	1x7in
Rum	125ml/4floz	½ cup
Thick custard	350ml/12floz	1½ cups
Double (heavy) cream, stiffly beaten	300ml/10floz	1¼ cups
Dark cooking (semi-sweet) chocolate, grated	50g/2oz	2 squares
Flaked hazelnuts, toasted	125g/4oz	1 cup
CHOCOLATE CREAM		
Dark cooking (semi-sweet) chocolate, broken into pieces	½kg/1lb	16 squares
Butter	25g/1oz	2 Tbs
Rum	50ml/2floz	¼ cup
Eggs, lightly beaten	5	5

First make the cream. Put the chocolate, butter and rum into a heatproof bowl placed over a pan of simmering water. Set the pan over low heat and cook, stirring constantly, until the chocolate and butter have melted. Beat in the eggs, one at a time and, beating constantly, cook the cream for 12 to 15 minutes, or until it

begins to thicken. Remove the pan from the heat and the bowl from the pan. Set the cream aside.

Place half the chocolate sponge slices in a layer on the bottom of a deep, glass serving bowl. Pour over one-half of the chocolate-flavoured liqueur. Using a flat-bladed knife, spread half the chocolate cream over the sponge. Place half the plain sponge slices over the cream and sprinkle with half the rum.

Spoon all of the custard over and continue making layers in this way, ending with the plain sponge.

Put the pudding in the refrigerator to chill for 1 hour. Remove from the refrigerator. Spoon over the cream, sprinkle with the grated chocolate and hazelnuts.

Serve at once.

8 Servings

Zabaglione is one of the glories of Italian cuisine and has carried the reputation of its excellence throughout the world. It is very easy to make, too, being a simple mixture of egg yolks, sugar, Marsala and grated lemon rind.

313

ZUCCOTTO
(Pumpkin-Shaped Cream and Sponge Dessert)

This rich dessert makes a superb ending to a dinner party, and can be made ahead of time, if you prefer.

	Metric/U.K.	U.S.
Double (heavy) cream, stiffly beaten	600ml/1 pint	2½ cups
Icing (confectioners') Sugar	25g/1oz plus 2 Tbs	¼ cup plus 2 Tbs
Hazelnuts, toasted	50g/2oz	½ cup
Fresh cherries, halved and stoned (pitted)	225g/8oz	2 cups
Dark dessert (semi-sweet) chocolate, chopped or grated	124g/4oz	4 squares
Brandy	50ml/2floz	¼ cup
Orange-flavoured liqueur	50ml/2floz	¼ cup
Chocolate sponge cakes, halved horizontally	2x20cm/ 8in	2x8in
Cocoa powder	2 Tbs	2 Tbs

Combine the cream and 25g/1oz (¼ cup) of icing (confectioners') sugar in a bowl. Fold in the hazelnuts, cherries and chocolate and chill the mixture in the refrigerator.

Mix together the brandy and orange-flavoured liqueur.

Line a 1¼l/2 pint (1½ quart) pudding basin with three-quarters of the sponge, cutting it into pieces so that it fits the shape of the basin. Sprinkle the brandy mixture over the sponge lining. Spoon the cream mixture into the sponge cake, then use the remaining sponge to cover the top. Chill the mixture in the refrigerator for 2 hours.

Remove from the refrigerator and run a knife around the edge of the pudding to loosen it. Invert a serving plate over the basin and, holding the two together, reverse them. The zuccotto should slide out easily.

Sprinkle half of the remaining icing (confectioners') sugar over one-quarter of the pudding and half the cocoa powder over a second quarter, then repeat these over the other half of the pudding so that the zuccotto has four alternating segments of colour.

Serve at once.

8-10 Servings

CASSATA ALLA SICILIANA
(Sponge Cake with Chocolate Icing)

	Metric/U.K.	U.S.
Fresh Madeira (pound) cake, about 23cm/9in long by 7½cm/3in wide	1	1
Ricotta cheese	½kg/1lb	1lb
Double (heavy) cream	2 Tbs	2 Tbs
Sugar	50g/2oz	¼ cup
Orange-flavoured liqueur	2 Tbs	2 Tbs
Chopped mixed candied fruit	2 Tbs	2 Tbs
Chopped pistachio nuts	1 Tbs	1 Tbs
Dark cooking (semi-sweet) chocolate, grated	50g/2oz	2 squares
ICING		
Dark cooking (semi-sweet) chocolate, cut into small pieces	350g/12oz	12 squares
Black coffee	175ml/6floz	¾ cup
Unsalted butter, cut into small pieces and chilled	225g/8oz	16 Tbs

Cut the cake, lengthways, into 1cm/½in slices.

Using the back of a wooden spoon, rub the ricotta through a strainer into a bowl, then beat until it is smooth. Beat in the cream, sugar and liqueur. Fold in the candied fruit, pistachios and grated chocolate.

Put the bottom cake slice on a flat serving plate and spread it evenly with a fairly thick layer of the ricotta mixture. Cover with another slice of cake on top and spread with the ricotta mixture. Continue making layers in this way until all the ingredients are used up, ending with a slice of cake on top. Gently press the 'loaf' together. Wrap the cake in foil and chill in the refrigerator for 3 hours, or until the filling is set and firm.

Melt the chocolate with the coffee in a small saucepan over low heat, stirring constantly. Remove from the heat and beat in the butter, a piece at a time. Continue beating until the mixture is smooth. Transfer the icing to a bowl and allow to cool until it reaches a thick, spreading consistency.

Reserve a little icing for decoration, then cover the top and sides of the cake with the remainder, swirling it on with a flat-bladed knife. Fill a piping bag with the reserved icing

Zuccotto, a classic pumpkin-shaped cream, cherry and chocolate sponge dessert.

Cassata alla Siciliana is a rich cake dessert which makes a spectacular end to any meal.

and pipe it decoratively over the top and sides.

Cover the cake loosely with foil and chill in the refrigerator for 12 hours before serving.

8-10 Servings

CROSTATA DI RICOTTA
(Cheese Cake)

	Metric/U.K.	U.S.
PASTRY		
Butter, cut into small pieces	175g/6oz	12 Tbs
Flour	225g/8oz	2 cups
Salt	¼ tsp	¼ tsp
Egg yolks, lightly beaten	4	4
Sugar	2 Tbs	2 Tbs
Marsala	5 Tbs	5 Tbs
Grated lemon rind	1½ tsp	1½ tsp
FILLING		
Ricotta cheese	1¼kg/2½lb	2½lb
Sugar	125g/4oz	½ cup
Flour	2 Tbs	2 Tbs
Vanilla essence (extract)	½ tsp	½ tsp
Grated rind of 1 orange		
Grated rind and juice of 2 lemons		
Raisins	3 Tbs	3 Tbs
Finely chopped candied peel	2 Tbs	2 Tbs
Slivered almonds	2 Tbs	2 Tbs
Egg white, lightly beaten	1	1

Lightly grease a 23cm/9in springform pan with a little butter. Set aside.

To make the pastry, sift the flour and salt into a large bowl. Make a well in the centre and drop in the remaining butter, the egg yolks, sugar, Marsala and lemon rind. Using your fingertips, lightly combine all the ingredients, then knead the dough until it is smooth and can be formed into a ball. Do not overhandle. Cover the dough and chill in the refrigerator for about 1 hour, or until it is fairly firm.

Break off about a quarter of the dough. Dust it with flour, cover and return to the refrigerator. Reshape the rest of the dough into a ball, then flatten into a circle. Roll out to a circle about 5cm/2in wider than the pan. Using the rolling pin, gently ease the dough into the pan to form a case, trimming off any excess.

Preheat the oven to moderate 180°C (Gas Mark 4, 350°F).

To make the filling, beat all the ingredients together, except the almonds and egg white, until they are well blended. Spoon into the dough case and sprinkle over the almonds.

Remove the reserved dough from the refrigerator and roll out to a rectangle at least 25cm/10in long. Cut the dough into long strips, then arrange the strips across the filling to make a lattice pattern. Brush with the egg white.

Put the pie into the oven and bake for 1 hour, or until the crust is golden and the filling is firm to touch. Remove from the oven and transfer to a wire rack. Remove the pie from the pan and leave to cool. Serve cold, in wedges.

6-8 Servings

CENCI
(Deep-Fried Pastry Fritters)

These delightful fritters look like lovers' knots and are served as a snack, or as an accompaniment to ice-creams and fruit salads.

	Metric/U.K.	U.S.
Flour	275g/10oz	2½ cups
Icing (confectioners') sugar	1½ Tbs	1½ Tbs
Salt	½ tsp	½ tsp
Eggs	2	2
Egg yolks	2	2
Rum or red wine	2 Tbs	2 Tbs
Sufficient vegetable oil for deep-frying		

Sift 225g/8oz (2 cups) of the flour with a third of the sugar and the salt into a bowl. Make a well in the centre and pour in the eggs, egg yolks and rum or wine. Using a wooden spoon, gradually draw the flour into the liquids, stirring gently until the mixture is blended to a smooth dough. Shape into a ball.

Spread about half the remaining flour over a working surface and knead the dough in the flour for about 10 minutes, or until it is shiny. Wrap in greaseproof or waxed paper and chill in the refrigerator for 1 hour.

Sprinkle the remaining flour over the surface. Cut the dough into quarters and roll out each piece until it is paper thin. Divide the

Crostata di Ricotta, one of the original cheesecakes and still one of the best. This version has a superb pastry, flavoured with Marsala, and a filling of ricotta cheese, grated orange and lemon rind and raisins. The end result is dripping with calories but unbelievably good!

dough into strips 1cm/½in wide by 12½cm/5in long, shaping the lengths into loose knots. Set aside.

Fill a large deep-frying pan one-third full with oil and heat until it reaches 180°C (350°F) on a deep-fat thermometer, or until a small piece of stale bread dropped into the oil turns golden in 50 seconds.

Drop the knots into the oil, a few at a time, and deep-fry until they are light brown and puffed up. Transfer them to kitchen towels to drain and keep hot while you fry the remaining dough knots.

Arrange the knots on a serving dish, sprinkle over the remaining sugar and serve warm.

4 Dozen

Pandolce is a sweet bread, one of the specialities of the port of Genoa in northern Italy. Serve it warm with butter, or on its own for a tasty snack.

PANDOLCE
(Genoese Sweet Bread)

This delicious sweet bread, flavoured with pine and pistachio nuts and fennel, is the speciality of Genoa, in northern Italy. Serve on its own or with lots of butter.

	Metric/U.K.	U.S.
Fresh yeast	25g/1oz	1oz
Sugar	175g/6oz	¾ cup
Lukewarm milk	425ml/14floz	1¾ cups
Flour	900g/2lb	8 cups
Salt	1 tsp	1 tsp
Orange-flower water	3 Tbs	3 Tbs
Butter, melted	75g/3oz	6 Tbs
Pine nuts	50g/2oz	⅓ cup
Pistachio nuts	50g/2oz	½ cup
Raisins, soaked in 3 Tbs Marsala for 30 minutes and drained	175g/6oz	1 cup
Fennel seeds, crushed	2 tsp	2 tsp
Aniseed, crushed	½ tsp	½ tsp
Candied lemon peel,		

chopped	50g/2oz	⅓ cup
Candied citron, chopped 50g/2oz		⅓ cup
Grated rind of 1 orange		

Crumble the yeast into a bowl and mash in ½ teaspoon of sugar with a fork. Add 4 tablespoons of the milk and cream the mixture together. Set the bowl aside in a warm, draught-free place for 15 to 20 minutes or until the yeast mixture is puffed up and frothy.

Sift the flour, salt and remaining sugar into a warmed mixing bowl. Make a well in the centre and pour in the yeast mixture, the remaining milk and the orange-flower water. Add the melted butter and, using your fingers or a spatula, gradually draw the flour mixture into the liquid. Continue mixing and beating briskly until all the flour is incorporated and the dough comes away from the sides of the bowl.

Turn the dough out on to a floured board or marble slab and knead it for 10 minutes, reflouring the surface if it becomes sticky. The dough should be elastic and smooth. Rinse, dry and lightly grease the bowl. Shape the dough into a ball and return it to the bowl. Cover with a damp cloth and set aside in a warm, draught-free place for 1 to 1½ hours, or until the dough has risen and almost doubled in bulk.

Turn the risen dough on to a floured surface. Using your fingers, push out the dough until it forms a square about 1cm/½in thick. Sprinkle over the nuts, raisins, fennel seeds, aniseed, peel, citron and orange rind. Roll up the dough Swiss (jelly) roll style. Push into a square again and, using the heel of your hand, flatten it out to about 2½cm/1in thick. Roll up Swiss (jelly) roll style again.

Shape the dough into a round and arrange on a well-greased baking sheet. Return the dough to the warm, draught-free place for 1 to 1¼ hours or until it has almost doubled in bulk.

Preheat the oven to fairly hot 190°C (Gas Mark 5, 375°F).

Make three cuts in the top of the dough to make a triangular shape. Put the baking sheet into the centre of the oven and bake the bread for 20 minutes. Reduce the oven temperature to warm 170°C (Gas Mark 3, 325°F) and continue to bake the bread for a further 1 hour.

Remove the sheet from the oven. Tip the bread off the baking sheet and rap the underside with your knuckles. If it sounds hollow, like a drum, it is cooked. If it does not sound hollow, return the bread, upside-down, to the oven and bake for a further 10 minutes.

Cool completely on a wire rack before serving.

One 1¼kg/2½lb Loaf

PANETTONE
(Breakfast Bread)

This bread is a speciality of the city of Siena, in Tuscany. Serve on its own or with lots of butter.

	Metric/U.K.	U.S.
Butter, softened	75g/3oz	6 Tbs
Fresh yeast	15g/½oz	½oz
Sugar	75g/3oz	⅜ cup
Lukewarm water	50ml/2floz	¼ cup
Flour	450g/1lb	4 cups
Salt	1½ tsp	1½ tsp
Lukewarm milk	175ml/6floz	¾ cup
Eggs, lightly beaten	3	3
Candied citron, chopped	75g/3oz	½ cup
Sultanas or seedless raisins	75g/3oz	½ cup
Raisins	3 Tbs	3 Tbs
Grated lemon rind	2 tsp	2 tsp
Butter, melted	25g/1oz	2 Tbs

Using 1 tablespoon of the softened butter, grease a 1kg/2lb coffee tin or a tall cylindrical mould about 15cm/6in in diameter and about 18cm/7in high. Line with greaseproof or waxed paper greased with another 1 tablespoon of softened butter. Allow the excess paper to come up over the rim of the tin. Set the tin aside.

Crumble the yeast into a small bowl and mash in ½ teaspoon of sugar. Add the water and cream the water and yeast together. Set aside in a warm, draught-free place for 15 to 20 minutes, or until the mixture is puffed up and frothy.

Sift the flour, the remaining sugar and the salt into a large bowl. Make a well in the centre and pour in the yeast mixture and the milk. Using a spatula, gradually draw the flour into the liquids until all the flour is incorporated and the dough comes away from the sides of the bowl. Turn the dough out on to a lightly floured surface and knead for 10 minutes. The dough should be elastic and smooth.

Rinse, dry and lightly grease the mixing bowl. Shape the dough into a ball and return it to the bowl. Cover with a damp cloth and set in a warm, draught-free place for 2 hours, or until the dough has risen and almost doubled in bulk. Beat in the remaining softened butter, the eggs, citron, sultanas or seedless raisins, raisins and lemon rind until they are well blended. Re-cover the bowl and return to the warm place for a further 1 hour, or until the dough has risen slightly.

Put the dough into the prepared tin or mould. Brush the top with a little melted butter. Set aside in the warm, draught-free place for 30 minutes, or until the dough has risen slightly.

Preheat the oven to fairly hot 200°C (Gas Mark 6, 400°F). Brush the dough with a little more of the melted butter. Put the tin or mould into the oven and bake for 30 minutes. Reduce the oven temperature to moderate 180°C (Gas Mark 4, 350°F) and bake the bread for a further 30 minutes, brushing once more during the cooking time with the remaining melted butter.

Zeppole are mouth-watering doughnuts from Naples. Serve as a snack with milk or freshly percolated coffee.

Remove the bread from the oven and allow to cool in the tin for 20 minutes. Remove from the tin and transfer to a wire rack to cool, upright, until it is completely cold.

10-12 Servings

ZEPPOLE (Neapolitan Doughnuts)

These delightful little doughnuts are a speciality of the city of Naples, and are much easier to cook than most doughnuts

	Metric/U.K.	U.S.
Water	725ml/ 1¼ pints	3 cups
Salt	½ tsp	½ tsp
Sugar	50g/2oz	¼ cup
Brandy	2 Tbs	2 Tbs
Flour	350g/12oz	3 cups
Sufficient vegetable oil for deep-frying		
Icing (confectioners') sugar	50g/2oz	½ cup
Ground cinnamon	2 tsp	2 tsp

Pour the water, salt, sugar and brandy into a large saucepan. Set the pan over moderate heat and bring the mixture to the boil. Using a wooden spoon, stir in the flour until the mixture comes away from the sides of the pan. Remove from the heat and beat vigorously until the dough becomes light and elastic.

Turn out the dough on to a lightly floured surface and shape into a ball. Beat with a pestle or rolling pin for 10 minutes, reshaping it into a ball whenever it becomes flat. Divide the dough into 16 pieces and roll each one into a sausage shape about 25cm/10in long. Shape the pieces into rings and press the ends together to seal. Prick each ring with a form.

Fill a large saucepan one-third full with oil and heat until it reaches 190°C (375°F) on a deep-fat thermometer, or until a small cube of stale bread dropped into the oil turns golden in 40 seconds. Carefully lower the dough rings into the oil, a few at a time, and fry for about 5 minutes or until they are golden brown. Remove from the oil and drain on kitchen towels.

Sift the icing (confectioners') sugar and cinnamon together in a small bowl. Sprinkle over the zeppole.

16 doughnuts

Spain and Mexico

Spain and Mexico are literally oceans apart. But the Spanish conquest of Mexico over 300 years ago has assured some similarities—the language and religion are the same, and they share an enthusiasm for bull-fighting, guitars and long, lazy siestas. And *machismo*, it is worth noting, is also a Spanish word, applicable equally to the old country and the new. There is also a common interest in food: before the conquest, the Mexicans boiled everything, existing on a diet which consisted mainly of corn, potatoes, tomatoes and chocolate, all liberally laced with highly potent chillis; now they fry most things and live on a diet of corn, potatoes, tomatoes and chocolate, all liberally laced with highly potent chillis. Spain did, however, contribute lard to make the frying easier.

Spanish cuisine is sadly under-rated. Those who dismiss it as 'greasy, oily muck' are probably those who have suffered from package holiday hotel food, a situation almost guaranteed to produce gastronomical disasters in most countries. The true cuisine owes much to Spain's geographical position as co-inhabitor of the land mass in south-western Europe known as the Iberian Peninsula. Bordered as it is on three sides by the ocean, fish forms an important part of the diet, and the cuisine in general is plain and uncluttered, relying on good-quality fresh products for its excellence. Olive oil is used almost exclusively as a cooking agent—rather understandably since Spain is the largest producer of that commodity in the world.

The foundations of modern Spanish cuisine were laid down by the Romans, who conquered Spain and brought with them olive trees and garlic. Of the later conquerors, the most important were the Moors, a mixtures of tribes from northern Africa, who dominated southern Spain for over seven hundred years and who left behind them not only cities of unsurpassed beauty but a national taste for saffron, citrus fruit and nuts, especially pine nuts.

For most of its history, Spain has been a conglomeration of rival kingdoms, roughly corresponding to the present-day regions,

321

The general store plus client of a small, rural town in Mexico. It will often be the only shop for miles around and stock everything from safety pins to broom sticks.

so that cultural and gastronomic development have taken place separately rather than together. As a result, there is no acknowledged 'national' cuisine, although the better-known dishes from one region have, of course, travelled to and been incorporated into the eating habits of many others.

The northeastern borders with France house two of the most important of these regional cuisines, the Basque and the Catalan. In both areas live people who have their own language, customs and habits which seem unrelated to those of the rest of Spain, and in both there is a distinct cultivation of this 'separate' identity. The coastline of the Basque provinces yields an abundance of fish and it is therefore in the cooking of this food that the reputation of the excellence of Basque cooking is based. But cooking in general is an occupation which is treated with great seriousness (and because of this has traditionally been dominated by men in Basque society); all of the leading cities of the province boast all-male gastronomic societies, where the traditions of excellence are fiercely upheld—as is the unisexual nature of the institutions. In Catalonia, the tradition is also strong and the cuisine is somewhat similar to that of France, with an emphasis on sauces and herbs.

To the south of Catalonia and the Basque provinces are Castile and Aragon, famous in history as the dual kingdom ruled over by Ferdinand and Isabella. In Castile, there is the Rioja, the main wine-producing area of Spain, and certainly the best. The full-bodied red wines of the region, particularly, age beautifully, travel well and are among the relatively few Spanish wines not dismissed by the experts as *vin très ordinaire*. In Castile too, there is the region called La Mancha, the setting of Cervantes' novel *Don Quixote*. In the novel, mention is made of a medieval stew/soup called Olla Podrida (page 348), which survives today although it is now sometimes known as Cocido Madrileño. Aragon is the home of another of those famous Spanish stew/soups—this one called Fabada (page 347).

Galicia and Asturias are the other northern provinces, over on the western side just above Portugal. Galicia is bordered on two sides by the ocean and because of this, fish features prominently in the cuisine. The food tends to the hearty and uncomplicated and there are many robust and filling soups. Galicia is also the home of the Spanish Empanada (page 352)—not to be confused

with the smaller, spicier Mexican version—which is a filling double-crust pie filled with practically anything that takes your fancy.

Andalusia in the south is the tourist 'dream' of Spain, all dusty, forgotten Moorish castles, melancholy guitar music and the lost, haunted sound and rhythm of the flamenco. It was here that the Moorish influence was strongest, and can still be seen. It lingers in the construction of some of the older cities, and in the cultivation of oranges, a fruit introduced by the Moors and which is now one of the main crops of the region. Andalusia is also the home of the Paella, although that dish is probably the nearest the Spaniards have to a national dish and versions of it are found in many other provinces, and of sherry, a fortified wine which owes its name to foreign inability to pronounce the name of the city from which it comes, Jerez.

Although its origins are as ancient as those of Spain, Mexico is part of the New World. It occupies a prominent position on the Central American Peninsula, north of Guatemala and Honduras, south of the

southwestern states of the United States. It is a country created by a series of highly advanced Indian civilizations, which until the early sixteenth century had never seen a white man.

In 1519 all that was changed when Hernando Cortès, a native of Extremadura in western Spain, marched into Tenochtitlan (modern-day Mexico City), then the largest city in the world and the capital of the Aztec empire. The Aztec leader, called Montezuma, in his innocence thought of the Spaniards as special pale gods. The Spaniards in their wisdom thought Mexico an uncivilized land inhabited by primitive pagans and ripe only for plunder. But while their main concern was for gold and other precious metals, some of that plunder did take rather an unusual form: chocolate, tomatoes, corn and capsicums were all native to Mexico and all were unknown in Europe until taken back by the *conquistadors*.

The basis of Mexican cuisine, both before and after the Spanish conquest, was corn, a plant sacred to the Aztecs and possibly to the Mayas before them. It was used in many ways but most importantly to make the flat unleavened bread called tortilla, which is still widely used in Mexico today both as a bread and as the basis for many savoury snack dishes. Originally cooked on a sort of flat griddle called a *comal*, now—the price of progress—it is more usually manufactured on special tortilla-making machines. No part of the ear of corn was wasted; even the outer husks were used (and still are) in making *tamales*, little parcels of corn dough stuffed with mixtures such as Picadillo (page 337) or Frijoles Refritos (page 371) and then tucked into the husks. In earliest times, the husks were usually cooked over an open fire; nowadays they are more likely to be thrust into a colander and steamed in a pan of boiling water.

Chillis were used by all of the Indian civilizations of Central and South America but nowhere did they become as popular as in Mexico. Over thirty varieties are used there, ranging from mild to pretty lethal. Some are merely local varieties, unobtainable outside their narrow region, others are available and used widely throughout the world. Most Mexican food is very hot, so the recipes in this book, while every endeavour has been made to assure their authenticity, have been scaled down in 'heat' slightly as an act of kindness to protect the non-Mexican palate!

Mexican food, like Spanish, does vary quite widely from region to region, although there are some standard dishes that are found throughout the country. Where the regional differences occur, they are often due to geographical conditions: in Yucatan, for instance, much of the province is bound by the sea and fish therefore figures largely in the local diet. In the states which border on the United States, with access to the cattle country there and with a similar geography, meat, particularly beef, is favoured and many of the dishes owe much to Texas and the outdoor way of life. In Jalisco province, the plant called *aguey* is grown which, when refined and fermented, becomes the great white spirit of Mexico, *tequila*. Although it has the reputation of having a powerful 'kick' to it, commercial varieties are in fact usually no stronger than whisky.

Both cuisines offer enormous range and variety of eating pleasure and both particularly suit the modern way of life in that complicated dishes requiring much preparation and careful cooking are on the whole avoided.

Soups and Dips

SOPA DE ALBONDIGAS
(Meatball Soup)

This spicy Mexican soup is traditionally served with hot tortillas. A clear consommé base may be substituted for the tomato one used here and ½ teaspoon of hot chilli powder may be substituted for the chilli pepper.

	Metric/U.K.	U.S.
Butter	25g/1oz	2 Tbs
Onion, chopped	1	1
Small dried hot red chillis, crumbled	2	2
Dried oregano	½ tsp	½ tsp
Tomatoes, blanched, peeled and puréed	1kg/2lb	2lb
Water	1¼l/2pints	5 cups
Salt	1½ tsp	1½ tsp
MEATBALLS		
Minced (ground) beef	350g/12oz	12oz
Cooked rice	4 Tbs	4 Tbs
Small onion, grated	1	1
Small egg	1	1
Ground cumin	¼ tsp	¼ tsp
Finely chopped coriander leaves	1 tsp	1 tsp
Salt and pepper to taste		

Melt the butter in a large saucepan. Add the onion and fry until it is soft. Stir in the chillis and oregano and cook for 30 seconds. Stir in the tomatoes and water and add the salt. Bring to the boil and cook, uncovered, for 1 hour, or until the liquid has reduced by about half.

Meanwhile, combine all the meatball ingredients in a large bowl. Using your hands, roll the mixture into small, walnut-sized balls. Add the balls to the soup. Reduce the heat to low, cover and simmer the soup for 40 minutes, or until the meatballs are cooked through.

Transfer the mixture to a warmed tureen and serve at once.

6 Servings

CALDO DE CONGRIO
(Conger Eel Soup)

Spain has an abundance of seafood and many interesting dishes with a fish base. This particular soup is rich and filling and almost makes a meal in itself. Any firm, white-fleshed fish may be substituted for the eel, although the latter is the traditional main ingredient.

	Metric/U.K.	U.S.
Olive oil	1½ Tbs	1½ Tbs
Medium onions, sliced	3	3
Garlic clove, crushed	1	1
Tomatoes, blanched, peeled, seeded and chopped	700g/1½lb	1½lb
Tomato purée (paste)	1 Tbs	1Tbs
Dried oregano	½ tsp	½ tsp
Bay leaf	1	1
Salt and pepper to taste		
Potatoes, cut into 1cm/½ in wide strips	½kg/1lb	1lb
Fish stock	900ml/1½ pints	3¾ cups
Conger eel, cleaned and cut into 5cm/2in steaks	1 × 3kg/6lb	1 × 6lb
Ground coriander	1 tsp	1 tsp
Finely chopped parsley	2 Tbs	2 Tbs

Heat the oil in a large saucepan. Add the onions and garlic and fry until they are soft. Add the tomatoes, tomato purée (paste), oregano, bay leaf and seasoning and cook for 5 minutes, stirring constantly. Add the potatoes and fish stock and bring to the boil. Reduce the heat to low, cover and simmer the soup for 20 minutes.

Stir in the eel steaks and coriander. Recover and simmer for a further 12 minutes, or until the eel flesh flakes easily, and the potatoes are cooked and tender. Remove and discard the bay leaf.

Transfer the soup to a warmed tureen, sprinkle over the parsley and serve at once.

8 Servings

ESCUDELLA A LA CATALANA
(Catalan Sausage and Vegetable Soup)

This sturdy soup is from Catalonia and can be served as a meal in itself, with lots of crusty bread.

	Metric/U.K.	U.S.
Beef stock	1¾l/3 pints	7½ cups
Large potatoes, diced	2	2
Carrots, diced	3	3
Turnip, diced	1	1
Onion, chopped	1	1
Garlic cloves, crushed	2	2
Celery stalks, chopped	2	2
Salt and pepper to taste		
Bay leaf	1	1
Long-grain rice, soaked in cold water for 30 minutes and drained	2 Tbs	2 Tbs
Ground saffron	¼ tsp	¼ tsp
Chorizo sausage, thinly sliced	175g/6oz	6oz

Pour the stock into a large saucepan and bring to the boil. Add the vegetables, seasoning and bay leaf and bring to the boil again. Reduce the heat to low, cover the pan and simmer for 30 minutes.

Add the rice, saffron and sausage and simmer for a further 15 to 20 minutes, or until the rice is cooked. Remove from the heat and remove and discard the bay leaf.

Transfer to a warmed tureen and serve at once.

6 Servings

Spain is noted for her filling, delicious soups and Escudella a la Catalana, a mixture of vegetables and sausage, is one of the best.

CALDO HABA
(Broad [Fava or Lima] Bean Soup)

This hearty, filling soup contains the popular Spanish ingredients of broad (fava or lima) beans, Serrano ham and chorizo sausage. If you cannot obtain Serrano, any other type of ham may be substituted.

	Metric/U.K.	U.S.
Water	2½l/4 pints	5 pints
Broad beans (fava or lima beans), soaked in cold water overnight and drained	225g/8oz	1⅓ cups
Serrano ham	225g/8oz	8oz
Medium onion, chopped	1	1
Salt and pepper to taste		
Chorizo sausage	175g/6oz	6oz
Small turnip, chopped	1	1
Potatoes, chopped	2	2

Pour the water into a large saucepan and add the beans. Bring to the boil and boil for 2 minutes, skimming any scum from the surface of the soup. Cover the pan, remove from the heat and set aside for 1½ hours.

Return the pan to the heat and add the ham, onion and seasoning. Bring to the boil, skimming off any scum which rises to the surface. Reduce the heat to low, half-cover the pan and simmer for 1½ hours.

Prick the chorizo in one or two places with a fork and add to the soup with the remaining ingredients. Simmer for a further 30 minutes or until the potatoes are cooked and tender.

Using a slotted spoon, transfer the ham and chorizo to a chopping board and, when they are cool enough to handle, cut them into bite-sized pieces. Return them to the soup and simmer gently until they are heated through.

Transfer to a warmed tureen and serve at once.

6 Servings

CALDO TLALPENO
(Chicken and Bean Soup)

This Mexican soup contains an unusual mixture of ingredients, including avocado and cheese.

Any firm white cheese will do, such as Cheddar or California jack. Serve with hot tortillas for an authentic touch.

	Metric/U.K.	U.S.
Boiling chicken	1 × 2½kg/5lb	1 × 5lb
Medium onion, quartered	1	1
Carrot, sliced	1	1
Salt	2 tsp	2 tsp
Peppercorns	4	4
Bouquet garni	1	1
Water	3l/5 pints	6 pints

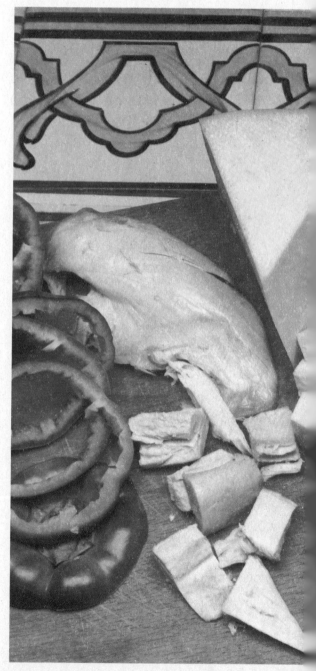

Green peppers, pith and seeds removed and sliced	2	2
Large onion, thinly sliced into rings	1	1
Canned chick-peas, drained	425g/14oz	14oz
Black pepper	$\frac{1}{4}$ tsp	$\frac{1}{4}$ tsp
Firm white cheese, cubed	225g/8oz	8oz
Avocado, peeled, stoned, sliced and sprinkled with lemon juice	1	1

Put the chicken into a large saucepan and add the quartered onion, carrot, 1 teaspoon of salt, the peppercorns and bouquet garni. Pour over the water, adding more if necessary to cover the chicken completely. Bring to the boil, then reduce the heat to moderately low and simmer the chicken for 2 hours, or until it is cooked through and tender. Remove the chicken from the pan and transfer to a chopping board. Cover with foil to keep hot.

Increase the heat to moderately high and bring the pan liquid to the boil. Boil for 15 minutes, or until it has reduced slightly. Strain, discarding the contents of the strainer. Rinse out the saucepan and return the strained liquid to it. Return to the boil, skimming off

Caldo Tlalpeno is a traditional Mexican soup whose basic ingredients are chicken, beans and avocado.

One of the most famous of Spanish classics, Gazpacho — a delicious soup served cold with a variety of garnishes.

any scum which rises to the surface. Add the sliced peppers and onion rings, reduce the heat to moderately low and simmer for 10 minutes. Stir in the chick-peas and simmer for a further 5 minutes.

Meanwhile, cut the chicken into serving pieces and return to the saucepan. Add the remaining salt and the pepper and simmer for a further 5 minutes, or until the chicken pieces are heated through. Stir in the cheese cubes.

As soon as the cheese melts, transfer the soup to a warmed tureen and add the avocado slices. Serve at once.

6–8 Servings

SOPA DE AJO CON HUEVOS
(Garlic Soup with Eggs)

This is a Spanish classic, found throughout the

country and with almost as many versions as there are regions. At its simplest, it is bread and garlic fried in oil with water added. This version adds tomatoes and beaten eggs, and is one of the most popular variations on the theme.

	Metric/U.K.	U.S.
Olive oil	50ml/2floz	¼ cup
Garlic cloves, chopped	4	4
French or Italian bread, crusts removed and cubed or chopped	4 slices	4 slices
Paprika	1 tsp	1 tsp
Salt and pepper to taste		
Water	1¼l/2 pints	5 cups
Tomatoes, blanched, peeled and chopped	3	3
Eggs, lightly beaten	2	2

Heat the oil in a large saucepan. Add the

garlic and fry for 2 minutes, stirring constantly. Add the bread pieces and fry until they are lightly and evenly browned. Stir in the paprika and seasoning, then pour over the water and tomatoes. Bring to the boil, reduce the heat to low and cover the pan. Simmer for 15 to 20 minutes, or until the bread is very soft, and beginning to break up.

Carefully pour in the beaten eggs, in a steady stream, and simmer gently for about 1 minute, taking care not to let the soup come to the boil or the eggs will curdle. Serve at once.

4–6 Servings

SOPA AL CUARTO DE HORA
(Quarter-of-an-Hour Soup)

This quaintly named Spanish soup is a filling mixture of seafood, ham and vegetables. It is so named because the main stage of cooking takes quarter of an hour.

	Metric/U.K.	U.S.
Water	900ml/1½ pints	3¾ cups
Small clams, scrubbed	6	6
Olive oil	2 Tbs	2 Tbs
Medium onion, chopped	1	1
Garlic clove, crushed	1	1
Tomatoes, blanched, peeled and chopped	2	2
Long-grain rice, soaked in cold water for 30 minutes and drained	25g/1oz	⅙ cup
Lemon juice	1 Tbs	1 Tbs
Shelled shrimps	225g/8oz	8oz
Serrano or other ham, chopped	50g/2oz	2oz
Hard-boiled egg, finely chopped	1	1

Pour the water into a large saucepan and bring to the boil. Add the clams, cover and cook for 6 to 8 minutes, or until the shells open (discard any clams that do not open). Using a slotted spoon, transfer the clams to a serving plate and keep hot. Either remove one or both shells, according to taste. Reserve the clam cooking liquid.

Heat the oil in a small saucepan. Add the onion and garlic and fry until they are soft. Stir in the tomatoes and fry gently until the mixture is thick and pulpy. Remove from the heat.

Strain the clam liquid into a fresh saucepan, and bring to the boil. Stir in the tomato mixture, rice and lemon juice, and bring to the boil again. Reduce the heat to low and simmer the soup for 15 minutes.

Stir in the remaining ingredients, including the reserved clams, and simmer for a further 2 to 3 minutes, or until the shrimps and clams are heated through.

Transfer the soup to a warmed tureen and serve at once.

6 Servings

GAZPACHO ✓
(Chilled Tomato Soup)

There are many versions of what is perhaps one of the two or three Spanish 'classic' dishes. This is a simple, basic version. It is traditionally served with a variety of accompaniments, such as croûtons, chopped olives, cucumbers, hard-boiled eggs and onions. Each diner sprinkles a little of the accompaniments over his Gazpacho before eating.

	Metric/U.K.	U.S.
Brown bread, cut into cubes	3 slices	3 slices
Canned tomato juice	300ml/10floz	1¼ cups
Garlic cloves, crushed	2	2
Cucumber, peeled and finely chopped	½	½
Green pepper, pith and seeds removed and chopped	1	1
Red pepper, pith and seeds removed and chopped	1	1
Large onion, chopped	1	1
Tomatoes, blanched, peeled and chopped	700g/1½lb	1½lb
Olive oil	75ml/3floz	⅜ cup
Red wine vinegar	2 Tbs	2 Tbs
Salt and pepper to taste		
Dried marjoram	¼ tsp	¼ tsp
Dried basil	¼ tsp	¼ tsp

	Metric/U.K.	U.S.
Ice cubes (optional)	4	4

Put the bread cubes in a bowl and pour over the tomato juice. Leave to soak for 5 minutes, then squeeze to extract the excess juice. Transfer to a large bowl and reserve the juice.

Add the garlic, cucumber, peppers, onion and tomatoes to the soaked bread and stir to mix. Put the mixture into a blender and blend to a smooth paste, or push through a food mill until the mixture is smooth. Stir in the reserved tomato juice.

Add all the remaining ingredients, except the ice cubes, to the mixture and stir well. The soup should be the consistency of single (light) cream so add more tomato juice if necessary.

Transfer the soup to a deep serving bowl and chill in the refrigerator for 1 hour. Just before serving, stir well and float in the ice cubes, if you are using them.

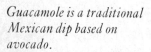

Guacamole is a traditional Mexican dip based on avocado.

4–6 Servings

GUACAMOLE
(Avocado Dip)

This is one of the most popular of Mexican dishes and is almost as well-known outside the country as inside. It is much easier and quicker to make if you have a blender, but the traditional method of putting it together is given below. Serve with a variety of raw vegetables.

	Metric/U.K.	U.S.
Medium ripe avocados	3	3
Lemon juice	1 Tbs	1 Tbs
Olive oil	2 tsp	2 tsp
Salt and pepper to taste		
Ground coriander	$\frac{1}{2}$ tsp	$\frac{1}{2}$ tsp
Hard-boiled egg, chopped	1	1
Small green pepper, pith and seeds removed and chopped	$\frac{1}{2}$	$\frac{1}{2}$

Small dried hot red chillis, crumbled	1½	1½
Spring onions (scallions), chopped	2	2
Tomato, blanched, peeled, seeded and chopped	1	1

Halve the avocados and remove the stones. Peel and transfer the flesh to a large bowl. Mash with a fork until it is smooth, then gradually beat in the lemon juice, olive oil, seasoning and coriander. Beat in all the remaining ingredients. Chill in the refrigerator for 1 hour.

Transfer the mixture to a serving bowl and serve at once if possible.

4–6 Servings

SALSA DE CHILE ROJO
(Red Chilli Sauce)

There are several distinctive types of chilli used in Mexican cooking, ranging from mild to fiery hot. The types most usually used in this classic sauce are ancho, *a mild but pungent chilli or* péquin *a small, much hotter variety. Péquin or other small dried red chilli has been suggested for the recipe given below, but if you prefer to substitute* ancho *chillis, double the quantity and soak them in boiling water for 30 minutes before draining and using. This sauce is used in many ways—as an accompaniment to tortillas, tacos, or enchiladas, or either served with meat and poultry or cooked with them.*

	Metric/U.K.	U.S.
Small dried red *péquin* or other similar chillis, crumbled	5	5
Boiling water	3 Tbs	3 Tbs
Canned peeled tomatoes, chopped and drained but with the juice reserved	425g/14oz	14oz
Vegetable oil	50ml/2floz	¼ cup
Onion, chopped	1	1
Garlic cloves, crushed	2	2
Tomato purée (paste)	2 Tbs	2 Tbs
Ground cumin	1 tsp	1 tsp
Wine vinegar	1½ Tbs	1½ Tbs

Sugar	½ tsp	½ tsp

Put the chillis, water and chopped tomatoes into a blender and blend to a smooth purée. Pour into a jug and set aside.

Heat the oil in a saucepan. Add the onion and garlic and fry until they are soft. Stir in the tomato mixture, the reserved tomato can juice and the remaining ingredients, and bring to the boil. Reduce the heat to low, cover and simmer the sauce for 10 minutes.

The sauce is now ready to be added to other ingredients, or to be served.

About 600ml/1 pint (2½ cups)

SALSA DE TOMATILLO VERDE
(Green Tomato Sauce)

This unusual sauce is a popular accompaniment to tortilla dishes in Mexico, particularly tacos and enchiladas, but it could also be used as an accompaniment to roast or grilled (broiled) meat, particularly lamb. Canned green tomatoes are available from Mexican provision stores.

	Metric/U.K.	U.S.
Vegetable oil	2 Tbs	2 Tbs
Large onion, chopped	1	1
Canned Mexican green tomatoes	450g/1lb	1lb
Canned green chillis, drained and chopped	2	2
Finely chopped coriander leaves	1 Tbs	1 Tbs
Chicken stock	250ml/8floz	1 cup

Heat the oil in a small frying-pan. Add the onion and fry until it is soft. Remove from the heat.

Put the onion, tomatoes and can juice, chillis and coriander leaves into a blender and blend to a smooth purée. Pour into a saucepan and set over low heat. Gradually add the chicken stock, stirring constantly. Cook until the sauce comes to the boil. Reduce the heat to low and simmer the sauce for 5 minutes.

The sauce is now ready to be added to other ingredients, or to be served.

About 725ml/25floz (3 cups)

Tortillas

TORTILLAS
(Flat Corn Bread)

Tortillas were popular in Mexico long before the Spaniards arrived, and they have remained one of the staple foods ever since. They are traditionally made on a clay griddle called a comal, although below a frying-pan is recommended for obvious reasons. The masa harina suggested below is the type of corn meal flour usually used for making tortillas and can be obtained from Mexican and some Spanish provision stores.

	Metric/U.K.	U.S.
Masa harina (corn-meal flour)	225g/8oz	2 cups
Lukewarm water	300ml/10floz	1¼ cups

Put the masa harina into a bowl and gradually beat in the water until the mixture is well blended. Using your hands, knead the dough until it is smooth and elastic. Divide the dough into 12 equal pieces.

Put each piece between two large pieces of greaseproof or waxed paper and lay on a flat surface. Using a rolling pin, carefully roll out the dough until it is about ⅛cm/1/16in thick and about 15cm/6in in diameter. Trim the dough into shape if necessary. As each piece is rolled out put to one side, still between the paper.

To cook the tortillas, heat an ungreased heavy-based frying-pan over moderate heat. Peel off the greaseproof or waxed paper from one side of one tortilla and put it, paper side up, into the pan. Cook for about 1½ minutes or until it becomes lightly speckled. Peel off the remaining paper, turn over the tortilla and cook on the second side for 1½ minutes, or until the underside is lightly browned. Wrap in a hot towel or foil and keep hot while you cook the remaining tortillas in the same way. Serve hot. (The tortillas may be cooked ahead of time, especially if they are to be served with fillings such as tacos or enchiladas; in this case, when you wish to reheat the tortillas just follow the instructions in the respective recipes.)

12 Tortillas

HUEVOS RANCHEROS
(Ranch-Style Eggs)

This classic Mexican dish is often served with Frijoles Refritos (page 371) for a filling meal.

	Metric/U.K.	U.S.
Vegetable oil	1 Tbs	1 Tbs
Tortillas	6	6
Salsa de Chile Rojo (red chilli sauce) (page 11)	450ml/15floz	2 cups
Fried eggs, kept hot	6	6
Avocado, peeled, stoned and thinly sliced	1	1

Brush a large frying-pan with some of the oil and heat over moderate heat. Holding a tortilla between your finger and thumb, dip it into the chilli sauce, shaking off any excess. Carefully arrange the tortilla in the hot frying-pan and fry for 1 to 2 minutes on each side or until it is golden brown. Using a spatula or tongs, transfer the tortilla to a large serving platter or individual serving plate and keep hot while you cook the remaining tortillas in the same way.

Pour a little of the remaining sauce over the tortillas and top each one with a fried egg. Garnish with the avocado slices. Pour the remaining sauce into a warmed sauceboat and serve at once, with the tortillas and eggs.

6 Servings

TACOS WITH CHILLI SAUCE AND MEAT FILLING

Tacos are just shaped, filled tortillas and although the most popular type is the U or half-moon shaped taco, you can, if you prefer, roll or fold the tortillas around the filling. Garnishes are also traditional and many can be used in addition to those suggested below—sliced avocado or grated cheese, for instance. Although we have suggested frying tortillas into taco shapes below, you can buy prepared tacos which have already been fried and shaped.

	Metric/U.K.	U.S.
Sufficient oil for shallow-frying		
Tortillas	12	12

SAUCE FILLING		
Vegetable oil	50ml/2floz	$\frac{1}{4}$ cup
Small onion, chopped	1	1
Minced (ground) beef	$\frac{1}{2}$kg/1lb	1lb
Salsa de Chile Rojo (red chilli sauce) (page 331)	450ml/15floz	2 cups
GARNISHES		
Tomatoes, finely chopped	4	4
Cucumber, diced	$\frac{1}{4}$	$\frac{1}{4}$
Crisp lettuce, shredded	$\frac{1}{2}$	$\frac{1}{2}$

First make the sauce filling. Heat the oil in a large saucepan. Add the onion and fry until it is soft. Stir in the meat and fry until it loses its pinkness. Add the sauce and bring to the boil. Reduce the heat to low and simmer for about 40 minutes.

Meanwhile, pour enough oil into a shallow frying-pan to make a 1$\frac{1}{2}$cm/$\frac{3}{4}$in layer. When it is hot, carefully arrange one tortilla in the oil and, using tongs, fold over one side, keeping a generous space between the upper and lower sides for the filling. Cook the tortilla in this way, turning it occasionally, until it is crisp throughout. Remove from the oil and keep hot while you make the other tacos in the same way.

To serve the tacos, fill each shell about two-thirds full with the filling and top with the garnishes. Serve at once.

4 Servings

ENCHILADAS
(Stuffed Tortillas with Tomato Sauce)

This is one of the most popular tortilla-based dishes both inside and outside Mexico. Although we have given the classic method of cooking the dish, that is dipping the tortillas in sauce then frying prior to stuffing, this can be rather a messy process and, if you prefer, it would not radically alter the texture of the dish to fry first and dip in sauce later.

	Metric/U.K.	U.S.
Vegetable oil	1 Tbs	1 Tbs
Tortillas	18	18
Salsa de Chile Rojo (red chilli sauce)		

(page 331)	450ml/15oz	2 cups
Grated Parmesan cheese	3 Tbs	3 Tbs
FILLING		
Butter	25g/1oz	2 Tbs
Onion, finely chopped	1	1
Minced (ground) beef	225g/8oz	8oz
Cheddar or jack cheese, grated	50g/2oz	$\frac{1}{2}$ cup
Salt and pepper to taste		
Small dried hot red chilli, crumbled	1	1

First prepare the filling. Melt the butter in a frying-pan. Add the onion and fry until it is soft. Stir in the meat and fry until it loses its pinkness. Remove the pan from the heat and transfer the mixture to a bowl. Stir in the remaining filling ingredients until they are thoroughly blended. Set aside.

Preheat the oven to moderate 180°C (Gas Mark 4, 350°F).

Brush a large frying-pan with some of the oil and heat over moderate heat. Holding a tortilla between your finger and thumb, dip it into the chilli sauce, shaking off any excess. Carefully arrange the tortilla in the hot frying-pan and fry for 30 seconds on each side. Using a spatula or tongs, transfer the cooked tortilla to a large plate. Spoon about a table-spoon of filling into the centre, and roll up Swiss (jelly) roll style. Arrange the roll in a large, greased baking dish. Keep hot while you cook and stuff the remaining tortillas in the same way.

When all the tortillas have been stuffed, pour the remaining sauce over them and sprinkle over the grated Parmesan. Put the dish into the oven and bake for 15 to 20 minutes, or until the sauce has browned and is bubbling. Remove from the oven and serve at once.

6 Servings

ENCHILADAS VERDES
(Stuffed Tortillas with Green Tomato Sauce)

The previous recipe is the 'basic' Enchilada recipe, but there are many, many variations on the theme and, in fact, the tortillas may be stuffed with almost anything you fancy— Frijoles Refritos (page 371) and grated or cream cheese, to name only two. This particular recipe

uses cooked chicken in a green tomato sauce, a very popular combination in Mexico.

	Metric/U.K.	U.S.
Vegetable oil	3 Tbs	3 Tbs
Onion, chopped	1	1
Chicken breasts, skinned and boned	3	3
Salsa de Tomatillo Verde (green tomato sauce) (page 331)	725ml/25floz	3 cups
Small dried hot red chillis, crumbled	3	3
Tortillas	12	12
Grated Parmesan cheese	3 Tbs	3 Tbs
Grated Cheddar or jack cheese	3 Tbs	3 Tbs

Heat 2 tablespoons of the oil in a large frying-pan. Add the onion and fry until it is soft. Add the chicken breasts and fry until they are evenly browned. Pour over the sauce, crumble in the chillis and bring to the boil. Reduce the heat to low and simmer for 30 minutes, or until the chicken is cooked through and tender. Remove from the heat and, using a slotted spoon, transfer the chicken to a chopping board. Chop very finely or cut into shreds and set aside.

Preheat the oven to moderate 180°C (Gas Mark 4, 350°F).

Brush a large frying-pan with some of the remaining oil and heat over moderate heat. Holding a tortilla between your finger and thumb, dip it into the green tomato sauce, shaking off any excess. Carefully arrange the tortilla in the hot frying-pan and fry for 30 seconds on each side. Using a spatula or tongs, transfer the cooked tortilla to a large plate. Spoon about 1 tablespoon of shredded chicken into the centre and sprinkle over a little Parmesan cheese. Fold into a neat parcel and arrange the parcel, seam side down, in a large, greased baking dish. Keep hot while you cook and stuff the remaining tortillas in the same way.

When all the tortillas have been stuffed, pour the remaining sauce over them and sprinkle over the grated Cheddar or jack cheese. Put the dish into the oven and bake for 15 to 20 minutes, or until the sauce has browned and is bubbling.

Remove the dish from the oven and serve at once.

4 Servings

Another, more formal variation on tortillas, Enchilladas: tortillas stuffed with a beef mixture then baked in a tomato and cheese sauce.

Meat and Poultry

EMPANADAS
(Meat-Filled Pasties)

These tasty pasties are popular all over Latin America although they originated in Mexico. Picadillo (page 337) can also be used as a filling if you would like a change. Although they are baked in this version, they are also often deep-fried.

Empanadas are small meat-filled pasties popular all over Latin America.

	Metric/U.K.	U.S.
Frozen puff pastry, thawed	425g/14oz	14oz
FILLING		
Butter	25g/1oz	2 Tbs
Medium onion, finely chopped	1	1
Tomatoes, blanched, peeled, seeded and chopped	2	2
Small green pepper, pith and seeds removed and chopped	½	½
Minced (ground) beef	225g/8oz	8oz
Sultanas or seedless raisins	50g/2oz	⅓ cup
Salt and pepper to taste		
Small dried hot red chilli, crumbled	1	1
Ground cumin	½ tsp	½ tsp

To make the filling, melt the butter in a frying-pan. Add the onion, tomatoes and pepper and fry until they are soft. Stir in the meat and fry until it loses its pinkness. Stir in the remaining ingredients and bring to the boil. Reduce the heat to low and cook the mixture for 10 minutes, stirring occasionally. Remove from the heat and set aside.

Preheat the oven to fairly hot 190°C (Gas Mark 5, 375°F).

Roll out the dough on a lightly floured surface into a large square. Using a 13cm/5in pastry cutter, cut the dough into eight circles.

Put about 1 tablespoon of the beef mixture on one side of each circle and fold over the dough to enclose it. Dampen the edges with water and crimp to seal.

Transfer the pasties to a well-greased baking sheet and put the sheet into the oven. Bake for 35 minutes, or until the pastry is cooked and golden brown.

Remove from the oven and serve at once.

4 Servings

PICADILLO
(Minced [Ground] Beef with Apples, Raisins and Olives)

This traditional Mexican dish can be served in any of several ways—by itself with rice for an informal meal or as a filling for tortillas or empanadas (see previous page).

	Metric/U.K.	U.S.
Vegetable oil	3 Tbs	3 Tbs
Large onion, chopped	1	1
Garlic clove, crushed	1	1
Minced (ground) beef	1kg/2lb	2lb
Canned peeled tomatoes	425g/14oz	14oz
Tomato purée (paste)	2 Tbs	2 Tbs
Large cooking apple, peeled, cored and chopped	1	1
Canned Jalapeño chillis, drained and chopped	2	2
Sultanas or seedless raisins	50g/2oz	⅓ cup
Stuffed olives, sliced	10	10
Ground cinnamon	½ tsp	½ tsp
Ground cloves	¼ tsp	¼ tsp
Salt and pepper to taste		
Slivered almonds, toasted	3 Tbs	3 Tbs

Heat the oil in a large saucepan. Add the onion and garlic and fry until they are soft. Stir in the meat and fry until it loses its pinkness. Stir in all the remaining ingredients, except the almonds, and bring to the boil. Reduce the heat to low and simmer for 40 minutes.

Transfer the mixture to a warmed serving dish and scatter over the toasted almonds. Serve at once.

6 Servings

CHILLI CON CARNE I
(Minced [Ground] Beef with Chillis)

This hot, spicy dish could claim dual nationality since tradition has it that it was 'invented' in what are now the border states of the United States and Mexico. Whatever its origins, it remains a popular dish in both the United States and Mexico.

	Metric/U.K.	U.S.
Olive oil	2 Tbs	2 Tbs
Medium onions, finely chopped	2	2
Garlic cloves, crushed	2	2
Minced (ground) beef	700g/1½lb	1½lb
Canned peeled tomatoes	225g/8oz	8oz
Tomato purée (paste)	4 Tbs	4 Tbs
Bay leaf	1	1
Ground cumin	1 tsp	1 tsp
Dried oregano	1 tsp	1 tsp

Chilli con Carne — one of the great classics of Mexican cooking and now enjoyed all over the world.

Calderete al Jerez is a Spanish lamb stew cooked with sherry.

	Metric/U.K.	U.S.
Cayenne pepper	¼ tsp	¼ tsp
Mild chilli powder	1 Tbs	1 Tbs
Salt and pepper to taste		
Beef stock	250ml/8floz	1 cup
Canned red kidney beans, drained	425g/14oz	14oz

Heat the oil in a large saucepan. Add the onions and garlic and fry until they are soft. Stir in the meat and fry until it loses its pinkness. Stir in the tomatoes and can juice, tomato purée (paste), seasonings and stock, and bring to the boil. Reduce the heat to low and cover the pan. Simmer for 1 hour, stirring occasionally.

Stir in the kidney beans, re-cover the pan and simmer for a further 30 minutes. Remove and discard the bay leaf and serve at once.

6 Servings

CHILLI CON CARNE II
(Braising Steak with Chillis)

This fiery variation of Chilli con Carne is the one most popular in Mexico itself. If you prefer a milder taste, seed the chillis before using them, or use mild chilli powder (about 1 to 1½ table-spoons) instead. If you prefer to use milder ancho chillis, use three or four instead of the number indicated below.

	Metric/U.K.	U.S.
Vegetable oil	2 Tbs	2 Tbs
Onion, thinly sliced	1	1
Garlic clove, crushed	1	1
Red pepper, pith and seeds removed and cut into rings	1	1
Small dried hot red chilli, crumbled or canned Jalapeño chilli, drained and chopped	1	1
Braising (chuck) steak, cubed	1kg/2lb	2lb
Salsa de Chile Rojo (red chilli sauce) (page 331)	450ml/15floz	2 cups
Canned red kidney beans, drained	425g/14oz	14oz
Dark brown sugar	25g/1oz	2 Tbs
Salt and pepper to taste		
Finely chopped coriander leaves or parsley	1 Tbs	1 Tbs

Heat the oil in a large saucepan. Add the onion, garlic and pepper and fry until they are soft. Stir in the crumbled or chopped chilli. Add the beef cubes to the pan and fry until they are evenly browned. Stir in all the remaining ingredients, except the coriander or parsley, and bring to the boil. Reduce the heat to low, cover the pan and simmer the stew for 2 hours, or until the meat is cooked through and tender. Uncover for the last 15 minutes of cooking time if you wish to thicken the sauce.

Transfer the mixture to a warmed serving dish and sprinkle over the coriander or parsley. Serve at once.

4-6 Servings

CALDERETA AL JEREZ
(Lamb Stew with Sherry)

	Metric/U.K.	U.S.
Dry sherry	300ml/10floz	1¼ cups
Garlic cloves, crushed	2	2
Boned lamb, cut into cubes	1½kg/3lb	3lb

Salt and pepper to taste		
Ground cumin	1 tsp	1 tsp
Vegetable oil	50ml/2floz	¼ cup
Medium onions, sliced	2	2
Flour	2 Tbs	2 Tbs

Combine the sherry and garlic in a mixing bowl. Add the lamb cubes and baste well. Cover and set aside to marinàte at room temperature for 3 hours, basting occasionally. Remove the cubes from the marinade and pat dry with kitchen towels. Reserve the marinade.

Rub the cubes with salt and pepper to taste, then the cumin.

Heat the oil in a large saucepan. Add the lamb and fry until it is evenly browned. Add the onions and fry until they are soft. Stir in the flour until it is well blended, then pour over the reserved marinade, stirring constantly. Bring to the boil. (If the sauce is too thick, add a little water.) Reduce the heat to low, cover the pan and simmer the stew for 1 to 1¼ hours, or until the lamb is cooked through and tender. Remove from the heat and serve at once.

6–8 Servings

CHULETAS DE CORDERO A LA NAVARRA
(Lamb Chops with Ham and Chorizo in Tomato Sauce)

This dish is a speciality of the region of Navarre in the Pyrenees near the French border. Although the ham is traditional to the recipe, it can be omitted if you prefer.

	Metric/U.K.	U.S.
Lamb cutlets	8	8
Salt and pepper to taste		
Olive oil	50ml/2floz	¼ cup
Large onion, chopped	1	1
Garlic cloves, crushed	2	2
Cooked ham, finely chopped	125g/4oz	4oz
Canned peeled tomatoes, chopped	425g/14oz	14oz
Chorizo sausage, thinly sliced	175g/6oz	6oz

Rub the cutlets all over with salt and pepper to taste.

Heat the oil in a large frying-pan. Add the cutlets, a few at a time, and fry until they are evenly browned. Using a slotted spoon or tongs, transfer the cutlets to a baking dish large enough to take them in one layer.

Preheat the oven to moderate 180°C (Gas Mark 4, 350°F).

Add the onion, garlic and ham to the oil remaining in the frying-pan and fry until the onions are soft. Pour over the tomatoes and can juice and bring to the boil, stirring occasionally. Stir in seasoning to taste. Pour the mixture over the lamb cutlets and put the baking dish into the oven. Bake for 20 minutes.

Remove from the oven and arrange the sausage slices over the mixture. Return the dish to the oven for a further 15 minutes, or until the cutlets are cooked through and tender.

Remove from the oven and serve at once.

4 Servings

Tinga de Cerdo y Ternera is a Mexican speciality of pork and veal cubes cooked in a sauce of green tomatoes.

TINGA DE CERDO Y TERNERA
(Pork and Veal Stew with Green Tomatoes)

This Mexican stew incorporates one of the specialities of the country, green tomatoes.

	Metric/U.K.	U.S.
Butter	50g/2oz	4 Tbs
Vegetable oil	2 Tbs	2 Tbs
Pork, cubed	1kg/2lb	2lb
Lean veal, cubed	1kg/2lb	2lb
Onions, finely chopped	2	2
Garlic cloves, crushed	3	3
Green tomatoes, blanched, peeled and chopped	1kg/2lb	2lb
Green peppers, pith and seeds removed and chopped	3	3
California green chillis, chopped	4	4
Tomato purée (paste)	2 Tbs	2 Tbs
Chopped fresh marjoram	1 Tbs	1 Tbs
Chopped chives	1 Tbs	1 Tbs
Chopped fresh basil	1 Tbs	1 Tbs
Grated nutmeg	2 tsp	2 tsp
Salt and pepper to taste		
Sugar	1 tsp	1 tsp
Chicken stock	250ml/8floz	1 cup
Dry sherry	250ml/8floz	1 cup
Double (heavy) cream	75ml/3floz	⅜ cup

Melt the butter with the oil in a large flameproof casserole. Add the meat and fry until it is evenly browned. Transfer to a plate. Add the onions and garlic to the casserole and fry until they are soft. Stir in the tomatoes, peppers, chillis, tomato purée (paste), herbs, seasoning and sugar and cook for 5 minutes, stirring constantly.

Return the meat to the casserole and pour over the stock and sherry. Bring to the boil. Reduce the heat to low, cover the casserole and simmer the stew for 1½ hours, or until the meat is cooked through and tender.

Remove from the heat and stir in the cream. Serve at once, straight from the casserole.

8–10 Servings

ARROZ CON CERDO
(Mexican Rice and Pork)

	Metric/U.K.	U.S.
Vegetable oil	2 Tbs	2 Tbs
Medium onion, chopped	1	1
Minced (ground) pork	½kg/1lb	1lb
Sausagemeat	225g/8oz	8oz
Celery stalks, cut into 2½cm/1in pieces	2	2
Small green pepper, pith and seeds removed and cut into rings	1	1
Sultanas or seedless raisins	75g/3oz	½ cup
Garlic clove, crushed	1	1
Ground cumin	½ tsp	½ tsp
Small dried hot red chilli, crumbled	1	1
Salt and pepper to taste		
Long-grain rice, soaked in cold water for 30 minutes and drained	175g/6oz	1 cup
Canned peeled tomatoes	425g/14oz	14oz
Water	125ml/4floz	½ cup
Tomato purée (paste)	2 Tbs	2 Tbs
Juice of ½ lemon		
Pine nuts	3 Tbs	3 Tbs

Preheat the oven to moderate 180°C (Gas Mark 4, 350°F).

Heat the oil in a flameproof casserole. Add the onion and fry until it is soft. Stir in the pork and sausagemeat and fry until they lose their pinkness. Stir in the vegetables, sultanas or raisins, garlic, cumin, chilli, seasoning and rice and fry for 5 minutes, stirring constantly. Stir in the tomatoes and can juice, water and tomato purée (paste) and bring to the boil. Reduce the heat to low, cover the casserole and simmer for 10 minutes. Transfer the casserole to the oven and bake for 25 minutes.

Remove the casserole from the oven and sprinkle the lemon juice and pine nuts over the top. Return to the oven and bake, uncovered, for a further 10 minutes.

Remove from the oven and serve at once, straight from the casserole.

4–6 Servings

Arroz con Cerdo is a Mexican dish of pork and rice.

341

LOMO DE CERDO CON VINO BLANCO
(Loin of Pork with White Wine Sauce)

	Metric/U.K.	U.S.
Boned loin of pork, rolled	1 × 1kg/2lb	1 × 2lb
Garlic cloves, crushed	3	3
Salt and pepper to taste		
Olive oil	3 Tbs	3 Tbs
Onions, sliced	2	2
Dry white wine	300ml/10floz	1¼ cups
Bouquets garnis	2	2
Cornflour (cornstarch), blended with 3 Tbs water	1 Tbs	1 Tbs

Rub the pork all over with the garlic and salt and pepper to taste, and set aside for 30 minutes.

Heat the oil in a flameproof casserole or large saucepan. Add the pork and fry until it is evenly browned. Add the onions and fry until they are soft. Pour over the wine and add the bouquets garnis. Bring to the boil, reduce the heat to low and cover the casserole. Simmer for 2¼ hours, or until the pork is cooked through and tender.

Transfer the pork to a warmed serving dish and keep hot. Bring the pan liquid to the boil, stirring constantly. Add the cornflour (cornstarch) mixture and cook, stirring constantly, for 2 minutes, or until the sauce thickens and is smooth.

Pour a little of the sauce over the pork and transfer the rest to a warmed sauceboat. Serve at once, with the meat.

4–6 Servings

COCHINILLO ASADO
(Roast Suckling Pig)

This is one of the great specialities of Castile, and of Segovia in particular. Stuffings vary from cook to cook, but almost any fairly light one would be suitable instead of the ingredients suggested below. The pig should be roasted for about 20 minutes per half kilo (pound).

Suckling pig is one of the great festive dishes of Spain, and particularly of the province of Castile. In Cochinillo Asado the pig has been stuffed with garlic, onions and herbs, but if you prefer, any stuffing of your choice may be used.

	Metric/U.K.	U.S.
Garlic cloves, crushed	3	3

Onions, chopped	2	2
Bouquets garnis	2	2
Chopped parsley	1 bunch	1 bunch
Suckling pig, prepared	1 × 7¼kg/16lb	1 × 16lb
Salt and pepper to taste		
Olive oil	50ml/2floz	¼ cup
Lemon juice	125ml/4floz	½ cup
GARNISH		
Small red apple	1	1
Fresh herbs to taste		
Large oranges, sliced	4	4
Black grapes, seeded and halved	125g/4oz	1 cup

Put the garlic, onions, bouquets garnis and parsley into the pig and close the cavity with skewers or a trussing needle and thread. Rub the pig all over with salt and pepper. Then rub over half the olive oil and lemon juice. Set aside for 1 hour, then rub the remaining oil and juice into the skin of the pig, using your fingertips.

Preheat the oven to hot 220°C (Gas Mark 7, 425°F).

Place a small piece of wood or a ball of aluminium foil in the mouth of the pig to wedge it open, and place balls of foil in the eye sockets. Cover the ears with foil and curl the tail and secure it with a wooden cocktail stick. Pull the front legs forwards and the back legs forwards and tie them with string.

Transfer the pig, on its stomach, to a deep roasting pan and place the pan in the oven. Roast for 30 minutes. Reduce the oven temperature to warm 170°C (Gas Mark 3, 325°F) and roast the pig for a further 5½ to 6 hours, basting frequently with the pan juices. Drain off the cooking juices occasionally, leaving about a 1cm/½in depth.

Increase the oven temperature to hot 220°C (Gas Mark 7, 425°F) and roast the pig for a final 20 minutes, or until the skin is crisp. Remove from the oven.

To serve the pig, untie the legs and remove the wood or foil from the mouth, eye socket and ears. Untie the tail. Transfer the pig to a large serving platter and surround with the garnishes. Insert the apple into the pig's mouth if you wish, or you can cut it into slices and arrange with the orange.

Serve at once.

14–16 Servings

TERNERA AL JEREZ
(Veal Escalopes with Olives and Sherry)

This festive dish features two of Spain's most popular products—olive oil and sherry, together with one of her favourite meats, veal.

	Metric/U.K.	U.S.
Olive oil	75ml/3floz	⅜ cup
Shallots, chopped	3	3
Garlic cloves, crushed	3	3
Small green pepper, pith and seeds removed and chopped	1	1
Button mushrooms, sliced	125g/4oz	1 cup
Tomatoes, blanched, peeled and chopped	3	3
Lean smoked ham, chopped	50g/2oz	2oz
Green olives, stoned (pitted) and blanched	8	8
Veal escalopes, pounded until thin	4	4
Seasoned flour (flour with salt and pepper to taste)	50g/2oz	½ cup
Dry sherry	50ml/2floz	¼ cup
Water	50ml/2floz	¼ cup

Heat half the oil in a frying-pan. Add the shallots, garlic and green pepper and fry until they are soft. Add the mushrooms, tomatoes, ham and olives and cook for 20 minutes, stirring occasionally, until the mixture has thickened.

Coat the escalopes in the seasoned flour, shaking off any excess.

Heat the remaining oil in a large, deep casserole. Add the escalopes and cook for 3 to 4 minutes on each side, or until they are cooked through and tender. Using tongs, transfer the veal to a plate.

Pour the sherry and water into the casserole and bring to the boil. Stir in the tomato mixture and return the escalopes to the casserole, basting them with the mixture. Reduce the heat to low, cover the casserole and simmer for 5 minutes.

Transfer the mixture to a warmed serving dish and serve at once.

4 Servings

TERNERA A LA VALENCIANA

(Spanish Veal Escalopes with Orange and Sherry Sauce)

	Metric/U.K.	U.S.
Veal escalopes, pounded thin	4	4
Salt and pepper to taste		
Lean smoked ham	4 slices	4 slices
Olive oil	50ml/2floz	¼ cup
Onion, sliced	1	1
Grated orange rind	1 tsp	1 tsp
Orange juice	175ml/6floz	¾ cup
Dry sherry	125ml/4floz	½ cup
Cornflour (cornstarch), blended with 2 Tbs water	2 tsp	2 tsp

Rub the escalopes with salt and pepper. Lay the ham slices over the escalopes, trimming to fit if necessary. Roll up Swiss (jelly) roll style, securing with wooden cocktail sticks or thread.

Heat the oil in a large frying-pan. Add the rolls and fry until they are evenly browned. Using a slotted spoon, transfer the rolls to a plate.

Add the onion to the pan and fry until it is soft. Stir in the orange rind, juice and sherry and bring to the boil. Reduce the heat to low and return the rolls to the pan. Simmer for 15 to 20 minutes, turning the rolls in the sauce occasionally, or until the meat is cooked through and tender.

Transfer the rolls to a warmed serving dish and keep hot while you finish the sauce.

Stir the cornflour (cornstarch) mixture into the pan liquid and cook, stirring constantly, until it thickens and is smooth. Pour over the rolls and serve at once.

4 Servings

RINONES AL JEREZ

(Kidneys in Sherry Sauce)

	Metric/U.K.	U.S.
Olive oil	50ml/2floz	¼ cup
Lambs' kidneys, cleaned, prepared and chopped into small pieces	16	16
Salt and pepper to taste		
Small onion, finely chopped	1	1
Garlic cloves, crushed	2	2
Flour	1 Tbs	1 Tbs
Chicken stock	125ml/4floz	½ cup
Dry sherry	125ml/4floz	½ cup

Heat half the oil in a frying-pan. Add the kidneys and seasoning and fry until they are cooked through and tender. Using a slotted spoon, transfer the pieces to a plate. Keep warm.

Add the onion and garlic to the pan and fry until they are soft. Remove from the heat and keep hot.

Sherry not unnaturally is used extensively in Spanish cooking and nowhere more successfully than in this dish of lambs' kidneys, Rinones al Jerez. Served, as in the picture, on a bed of saffron rice it makes a delightful and colourful main dish.

Heat the remaining oil in a small saucepan. Remove the pan from the heat and stir in the flour to form a smooth paste. Gradually add the stock, stirring constantly. Return the pan to the heat and bring to the boil, stirring constantly. Cook for 2 minutes, stirring constantly, or until the sauce is smooth and thick. Stir in the reserved onion and garlic, reduce the heat to low and simmer for 3 minutes. Remove the pan from the heat.

Return the frying-pan to the heat, add the sherry and bring to the boil. Add the kidneys and onion sauce and bring to the boil, stirring constantly. Reduce the heat to low and simmer for a further 5 minutes.

Transfer the mixture to a warmed serving dish and serve at once.

4 Servings

JAMON CON NABOS
(Spanish Ham and Turnip Stew)

Serrano ham is the traditional ingredient for this warming Spanish stew, but if it is not available any other smoked ham or, in fact, any cooked ham, may be substituted.

	Metric/U.K.	U.S.
Vegetable oil	50ml/2floz	¼ cup
Onion, chopped	1	1
Garlic clove, chopped	1	1
Serrano ham, coarsely chopped	½kg/1lb	1lb
Flour	1 Tbs	1 Tbs
Water	600ml/1 pint	2½ cups
Salt and pepper to taste		
Bay leaf	1	1
Chopped parsley	1 Tbs	1 Tbs
Turnips, diced	½kg/1lb	1lb

Heat the oil in a large saucepan. Add the onion and garlic and fry until they are soft. Add the ham and fry for a further 5 minutes, stirring frequently. Stir in the flour until it forms a smooth paste. Fry for 2 minutes, stirring constantly.

Add all of the remaining ingredients and bring to the boil. Reduce the heat to low, cover the pan and simmer for 1½ hours, or until the turnips are cooked and tender.

Transfer the mixture to a warmed serving dish. Remove and discard the bay leaf and serve at once.

4-6 Servings

FABADA ASTURIANA
(Bean and Sausage Stew)

This classic dish is one of the national dishes of the province of Asturias in northwestern Spain and is a cross between a soup and a stew. The traditional alubia beans are sometimes difficult to obtain outside Spain and haricot (dried white) beans may be substituted.

	Metric/U.K.	U.S.
Water	1¾l/3 pints	7½ cups
Dried white alubia beans, soaked overnight in cold water and drained	225g/8oz	1⅓ cups
Dried broad (fava or lima) beans, soaked overnight in cold water and drained	225g/8oz	1⅓ cups
Large onion, chopped	1	1
Garlic cloves, crushed	2	2
Morcilla or blood sausage, sliced	125g/4oz	4oz
Dried oregano	1 tsp	1 tsp
Small chorizo sausages, sliced	2	2
Bacon, chopped	2 slices	2 slices
Serrano ham, chopped	50g/2oz	2oz
Ground saffron	½ tsp	½ tsp
Salt and pepper to taste		

Pour the water into a large saucepan and bring to the boil. Add the alubia and broad (fava or lima) beans, onion and garlic and bring back to the boil. Reduce the heat to low, cover the pan and simmer for 45 minutes to 1 hour, or until the beans are cooked and tender.

Add the morcilla or blood sausage, oregano, chorizo sausages, bacon, ham, saffron and seasoning and stir to mix. Simmer for a further 30 minutes.

Transfer the mixture to a warmed serving bowl and serve at once.

6-8 Servings

Fadaba Asturiana comes from northwestern Spain and is one of several Spanish classics that could correctly be described as a cross between a soup and a stew — in either case it is fabulous to eat and practically a meal in itself.

CALLOS VIZCAINOS
(Tripe in Wine Sauce)

	Metric/U.K.	U.S.
Chicken stock	300ml/10floz	1¼ cups
Dry white wine	300ml/10floz	1¼ cups
Dried thyme	½ tsp	½ tsp
Bay leaf	1	1
Medium onions, 1 left whole and 2 finely chopped	3	3
Tripe, blanched, and cut into strips about 5cm/2 in long	1kg/2lb	2lb
Tomatoes, blanched, peeled, seeded and chopped	4	4
Tomato purée (paste)	2 Tbs	2 Tbs
Celery stalk, chopped	1	1
Salt and pepper to taste		

Put the stock, wine, herbs, whole onion and tripe into a large saucepan and bring to the boil. Reduce the heat to low and simmer slowly for about 1 hour, or until the tripe is cooked through and tender. Using a slotted spoon, transfer the tripe to a plate and keep hot.

Add the tomatoes, tomato purée (paste), celery and chopped onions to the liquid and simmer for a further 30 minutes. Remove from the heat and strain the mixture into a bowl. Remove and discard the bay leaf. Mash the vegetables with the back of a wooden spoon to extract all the juices.

Return the tripe and strained sauce to the pan and season to taste. Simmer gently for 20 minutes. Remove from the heat, transfer to a warmed serving dish.

Serve at once.

4 Servings

OLLA PODRIDA
(Meat and Vegetable Stew)

This filling Spanish dish predates the Inquisition and was, in fact, originally Jewish. It was altered during the Inquisition by the Jewish community to include pork to convince the skeptical (and particularly their Inquisitors!) of their commitment to Christianity.

	Metric/U.K.	U.S.
Dried chick-peas, soaked in cold water overnight and drained	½kg/1lb	2⅔ cups
Large onions, sliced	2	2
Garlic cloves, crushed	2	2
Bouquet garni	1	1
Boned shoulder butt or leg of pork, cubed	½kg/1lb	1lb
Bacon, cubed	½kg/1lb	1lb
Stewing (chuck) beef, cubed	225g/8oz	8oz
Small boiling chicken, cut into serving pieces	1 × 2kg/4lb	1 × 4lb
Salt and pepper to taste		
Leeks, white part only, thinly sliced	2	2
Large carrots, thinly sliced	2	2
Cabbage, shredded	1	1
Large potatoes, cubed	2	2
Tomatoes, blanched, peeled and chopped	4	4
Chorizo sausage, sliced	1	1
Chopped parsley	2 Tbs	2 Tbs

Put the chick-peas in a large saucepan and pour over just enough cold water to cover. Set the pan over moderate heat and bring to the boil. Reduce the heat to low and simmer for 2 to 2½ hours or until the chick-peas are very tender, skimming off any scum that rises to the surface with a slotted spoon.

Add the onions, garlic, bouquet garni, meat, chicken pieces and seasoning. Add more cold water so that the meats are almost covered. Bring back to the boil, skimming off any scum that rises to the surface. Reduce the heat to low and simmer for 2 hours, or until all the meats are cooked through and tender. Remove from the heat and transfer to a large bowl. Set aside in a cool place until a layer of fat forms on top. Skim off and discard the fat.

Return the mixture to the saucepan and stir in the vegetables and sausage. Return to moderate heat and cook for 30 minutes, or until the vegetables are cooked and tender.

Transfer the stew to a large serving bowl. Sprinkle over the parsley and serve at once.

8–10 Servings

POLLO A LA ESPANOLA
(Spanish Chicken)

	Metric/U.K.	U.S.
Olive oil	50ml/2floz	¼ cup
Chicken, cut into 8 serving pieces	1 × 2kg/4lb	1 × 4lb
Medium onions, thinly sliced	2	2
Garlic cloves, crushed	1	1
Large red pepper, pith and seeds removed and chopped	1	1
Canned artichoke hearts, drained	425g/14oz	14oz
Chicken stock	450ml/15floz	2 cups
Salt and pepper to taste		
Cayenne pepper	¼ tsp	¼ tsp
Saffron threads, soaked in 1 Tbs water	½ tsp	½ tsp
Stuffed olives, halved	16	16
Beurre manié (one part butter and two parts flour blended)	25g/1oz	2 Tbs

Pollo a la Espanola is a simple chicken stew enlivened with stuffed olives and saffron.

Preheat the oven to moderate 180°C (Gas Mark 4, 350°F).

Heat the oil in a large, deep frying-pan. Add the chicken pieces and fry until they are evenly browned. Using tongs, transfer the pieces, as they brown, to a large flameproof casserole.

Add the onions, garlic and pepper to the pan and fry until they are soft. Add the artichoke hearts and fry for a further 2 minutes. Pour over the stock and stir in the seasoning, cayenne and saffron mixture. Bring to the boil, stirring occasionally. Pour the mixture over the chicken pieces.

Put the casserole into the oven and cook for 1 hour, or until the chicken pieces are cooked through and tender. Remove from the oven and transfer the chicken pieces to a

warmed serving dish. Keep hot while you finish the sauce.

Add the olives to the casserole and place over moderate heat. Bring to the boil, stirring occasionally. Stir in the beurre manié, a little at a time, until the sauce has thickened and is smooth.

Pour the sauce over the chicken pieces and serve at once.

4 Servings

ARROZ CON POLLO
(Chicken with Saffron Rice)

	Metric/U.K.	U.S.
Vegetable oil	3 Tbs	3 Tbs
Streaky (fatty) bacon, chopped	6 slices	6 slices
Chicken, cut into serving pieces	1 × 2½kg/5lb	1 × 5lb
Seasoned flour (flour with salt and pepper to taste)	40g/1½oz	⅓ cup
Onions, chopped	2	2
Garlic clove, crushed	1	1
Canned peeled tomatoes	425g/14oz	14oz
Canned pimientos, drained	75g/3oz	3oz
Paprika	2 tsp	2 tsp
Ground saffron	¼ tsp	¼ tsp
Salt	1 tsp	1 tsp
Water	600ml/1 pint	2½ cups
Long-grain rice, soaked in cold water for 30 minutes and drained	225g/8oz	1⅓ cups
Frozen peas, thawed	175g/6oz	1 cup

Heat the oil in a flameproof casserole. Add the bacon and fry until it is crisp and has rendered its fat. Transfer the bacon to kitchen towels to drain.

Coat the chicken pieces in the seasoned flour, shaking off any excess. Add the pieces to the casserole and fry until they are evenly browned. Using tongs, transfer the pieces to a plate.

Preheat the oven to moderate 180°C (Gas Mark 4, 350°F).

Drain off most of the oil from the casserole and add the onions and garlic. Fry until they

are soft. Arrange the chicken pieces over the onions and add the tomatoes and can juice, the pimientos, paprika, saffron, salt and water. Bring to the boil, then stir in the rice. Cover the casserole and put into the oven. Cook for 35 minutes. Stir in the peas and bacon and cook for a further 15 to 20 minutes, or until the chicken pieces are cooked through and tender.

Remove the casserole from the oven and serve at once.

4–6 Servings

POLLO AL CHILINDRON
(Chicken with Peppers and Tomatoes)

This is a popular dish from Aragon in Spain. Lamb and pork are also often cooked in this way.

	Metric/U.K.	U.S.
Chicken, cut into serving pieces	1 × 2kg/4lb	1 × 4lb
Seasoned flour (flour with salt and pepper to taste)	40g/1½oz	⅓ cup
Olive oil	50ml/2floz	¼ cup
Large onion, chopped	1	1
Garlic cloves, crushed	2	2
Large red peppers, pith and seeds removed and chopped (or 425g/14oz canned pimientos, drained and chopped)	2	2
Serrano ham, chopped	50g/2oz	2oz
Canned peeled tomatoes	425g/14oz	14oz
Saffron threads, soaked in 2 Tbs water	½ tsp	½ tsp
Cayenne pepper	¼ tsp	¼ tsp
Salt and pepper to taste		

Coat the chicken pieces in the seasoned flour, shaking off any excess.

Heat the oil in a large, heavy-based saucepan. Add the chicken pieces and fry until they are evenly browned. Using tongs, transfer to a plate.

Add the onion, garlic and red peppers and fry until they are soft. Stir in the ham, tomatoes and can juice, saffron mixture, cayenne and seasoning and bring to the boil. Return the chicken pieces to the pan and

Arroz con Pollo was originally Spanish but is now just as popular in Mexico — one of the kinder legacies of the conquest. It is a mixture of chicken pieces, saffron rice, bacon and peas.

351

reduce the heat to low. Cover and simmer for 1 hour, or until the chicken pieces are cooked through and tender.

4–6 Servings

POLLO RELLENO
(Stuffed Chicken, Andalusian-Style)

	Metric/U.K.	U.S.
Chicken	1 × 2kg/4lb	1 × 4lb
Butter	50g/2oz	4 Tbs
Olive oil	1 Tbs	1 Tbs
Large onion	1	1
Bouquet garni	1	1
Flour	1 Tbs	1 Tbs
Tomato purée (paste)	2 Tbs	2 Tbs
Salt and pepper to taste		
Dry white wine	125ml/4floz	½ cup
STUFFING		
Cooked rice	125g/4oz	2 cups
Cooked ham, diced	125g/4oz	4oz
Paprika	2 tsp	2 tsp
Salt	1 tsp	1 tsp
GARNISH		
Vegetable oil	2 Tbs	2 Tbs
Large onion, thinly sliced into rings	1	1
Green peppers, pith and seeds removed and sliced into rings	2	2
Tomatoes, blanched, peeled and chopped	½kg/1lb	1lb
Salt and pepper to taste		

Rub the chicken inside and out with kitchen towels. Mix all of the stuffing ingredients together and spoon into the cavity. Close the cavity with a skewer or a trussing needle and thread.

Melt the butter with the oil in a large, heavy-based saucepan. Add the chicken and fry until it is evenly browned. Add the onion and bouquet garni and reduce the heat to low. Cover and simmer the chicken for about 1 to 1¼ hours, or until it is cooked through and tender.

Meanwhile, to make the garnish, heat the oil in a large frying-pan. Add the onion and

fry until it is soft. Add all of the remaining ingredients and cook gently until they are soft. Remove from the heat and keep hot.

Remove the chicken from the pan and arrange it on a large, warmed serving dish. Discard the onion and bouquet garni. Bring the pan juices to the boil, then sprinkle over the flour, stirring constantly. Stir in the tomato purée (paste), seasoning and wine and bring to the boil. Cook, stirring constantly, for 2 to 3 minutes, or until the sauce thickens and is smooth.

Arrange the garnish around the chicken, then pour over the sauce. Serve at once.

4 Servings

EMPANADA GALLEGA
(Chicken and Ham Pie)

Empanadas in Mexico are small turnover-like pasties, but in Spain they are usually more substantial, large pies that can constitute a main dish. Galicia is particularly famous for its empanadas and small empanadas called empanadillas, and they can have a variety of fillings—pork is very popular as are fresh sardines. The filling below is another popular one, of chicken and ham.

	Metric/U.K.	U.S.
PASTRY		
Flour	450g/1lb	4 cups
Salt	1 tsp	1 tsp
Ground cloves	¼ tsp	¼ tsp
Olive oil	75ml/3floz	⅜ cup
Cold water	175ml/6floz	¾ cup
Egg white, beaten with 2 Tbs milk	1	1
FILLING		
Chicken, cut into serving pieces	1 × 1½kg/3lb	1 × 3lb
Onion, quartered	1	1
Bouquet garni	1	1
Peppercorns	1 tsp	1 tsp
Olive oil	50ml/2floz	¼ cup
Leek, white part only, chopped	1	1
Garlic cloves, crushed	2	2
Green pepper, pith and seeds removed and		

finely chopped	1	1
Serrano ham, chopped	125g/4oz	4oz
Tomatoes, blanched, peeled, seeded and chopped	4	4

First make the filling. Put the chicken into a large saucepan and just cover with water or stock. Add the onion, bouquet garni and peppercorns and bring to the boil, skimming off any scum which rises to the surface. Reduce the heat to low, cover the pan and simmer the chicken for 1 hour, or until it is cooked through and tender. Remove the chicken from the pan and set aside until it is cool enough to handle. Discard the cooking liquid and flavourings.

Meanwhile, to make the pastry, sift the flour, salt and cloves into a large bowl. Make a well in the centre and pour over the oil and water. Gradually incorporate the flour into the liquid, beating until it comes away from the sides of the bowl. Turn the dough out on to a lightly floured surface and knead lightly until it is smooth and elastic. Cover with a damp cloth and set aside in the refrigerator for 30 minutes.

Cut the chicken into bite-sized pieces and discard any bones or skin.

Heat the oil in a large, deep frying-pan. Add the leek, garlic and pepper and fry until

A classic stuffed chicken dish from Andalusia in southern Spain, Pollo Relleno.

A Spanish dish of partridges cooked in white wine with vegetables, Perdices Estofadas.

they are soft. Stir in the ham, tomatoes and chicken and cook for 5 minutes, stirring constantly. Remove the pan from the heat.

Preheat the oven to moderately hot 190°C (Gas Mark 5, 375°F).

Divide the dough in half. On the lightly floured surface, roll out each half to a 23cm/9in circle. Carefully transfer one half to a well-greased baking sheet. Arrange the filling in the centre of the circle, leaving at least a a 2½cm/1in edge all the way round. Using a rolling pin, carefully arrange the second dough circle over the filling. Roll up the edges and crimp them to seal. Cut a deep slit in the centre of the top dough circle. Brush the top and sides of the dough with the egg white mixture and put the baking sheet into the oven. Bake for 30 to 40 minutes, or until the pie is golden brown.

Remove from the oven and transfer the pie to a warmed serving dish. Serve at once.

6 Servings

MOLE POBLANO
(Turkey with Chocolate Sauce)

This could almost be described as the Mexican

national dish and legend has it that it was invented by the nuns of a convent in honour of a visiting bishop—from scraps they had in a rather bare kitchen plus a turkey in the yard. The sauce traditionally is supposed to have thirty ingredients in it, although it is now usually simplified to more manageable proportions, as here.

	Metric/U.K.	U.S.
Turkey, cut into serving pieces	1 × 4½kg/10lb	1 × 10lb
Seasoned flour (flour with salt and pepper to taste)	125g/4oz	1 cup
Lard or butter	75g/3oz	6 Tbs
Salt	1 tsp	1 tsp
Bouquets garnis	2	2
SAUCE		
Large onion, finely chopped	1	1
Garlic clove, crushed	1	1
Sultanas or seedless raisins	75g/3oz	½ cup
Ground almonds	125g/4oz	1 cup
Tomatoes, blanched,		

peeled, seeded and chopped	3	3
Sesame seeds, toasted	4 Tbs	4 Tbs
Tortillas, crumbled	2	2
Aniseed	½ tsp	½ tsp
Ground cinnamon	½ tsp	½ tsp
Ground cloves	½ tsp	½ tsp
Ground coriander	½ tsp	½ tsp
Salt and pepper to taste		
Small dried hot red chillis, crumbled	3	3
Jalapeño chilli, chopped	1	1
Turkey stock (made from the giblets, etc)	600ml/1 pint	2½ cups
Dark cooking (semi-sweet) chocolate, crumbled	50g/2oz	2 squares

Coat the turkey pieces in the seasoned flour, shaking off any excess.

Melt half the lard or butter in a large, heavy-based saucepan. Add the turkey pieces and fry until they are deeply and evenly browned. Add enough water just to cover the pieces, then add the salt and bouquets garnis. Bring to the boil. Reduce the heat to low, cover the pan and simmer the turkey for 1½ hours, or until the pieces are cooked through and tender. Remove from the heat, drain the turkey pieces and set them aside.

Meanwhile, to make the sauce, melt the remaining fat in a large saucepan. Add the onion and garlic and fry until they are soft. Stir in the sultanas or raisins, almonds, tomatoes, half the sesame seeds, the tortillas, spices, seasoning and chillis and cook for 8 minutes, stirring occasionally. Add half the stock and bring to the boil. Remove from the heat.

Add the remaining stock and blend the mixture, a little at a time, in a blender until it forms a smooth purée. Return the purée to the saucepan. Add the chocolate and simmer gently, stirring constantly, until it melts and the sauce has thickened and is smooth.

Arrange the turkey pieces in a large serving dish and pour over a little of the sauce. Garnish with the remaining sesame seeds. Pour the remaining sauce into a warmed sauceboat and serve at once, with the turkey pieces.

8–10 Servings

PERDICES ESTOFADAS
(Partridges with White Wine and Vegetables)

	Metric/U.K.	U.S.
Partridges, trussed and larded	4	4
Salt and pepper to taste		
Butter	50g/2oz	4 Tbs
Lean bacon, chopped	4 slices	4 slices
Dry white wine	125ml/4floz	½ cup
Water	250ml/8floz	1 cup
Garlic cloves, crushed	3	3
Bouquet garni	1	1
Grated nutmeg	¼ tsp	¼ tsp
Grated lemon rind	2 tsp	2 tsp
Small onions, blanched	12	12
Small new potatoes, scraped	12	12
Small carrots, cut into quarters, lengthways	6	6
Green peas, weighed after shelling	50g/2oz	⅓ cup
Small courgettes (zucchini), sliced	4	4

Sprinkle the partridges with salt and pepper to taste.

Melt the butter in a flameproof casserole or large, heavy-based saucepan. Add the partridges and fry until they are evenly browned. Using tongs, transfer them to a plate and keep hot.

Add the bacon to the casserole and fry until it is crisp and has rendered its fat. Transfer the bacon to kitchen towels to drain. Pour off most of the cooking fat from the casserole.

Pour the wine and water into the casserole, then add the garlic, bouquet garni, nutmeg and lemon rind. Return the partridges to the casserole and bring the liquid to the boil. Stir in the onions, potatoes and carrots and reduce the heat to low. Simmer the mixture for 15 minutes. Add the remaining ingredients and reserved bacon and cook for a further 15 minutes, or until the partridges are cooked through and tender.

Remove from the heat and remove and discard the bouquet garni. Remove the trussing thread and lard.

Serve at once.

4 Servings

Fish and Seafood

MERO A LA NARANJA
(Fish with Orange Sauce)

The mero is a Mediterranean fish and is very popular in Spain. Halibut or grouper may be substituted if it is unavailable.

Mero is a Mediterranean fish and not always available outside that part of the world, but this delightful fish with orange sauce can be made with halibut or even cod or whiting if mero is not available.

	Metric/U.K.	U.S.
Mero steaks	6	6
Butter	50g/2oz	4 Tbs
Flour	2 Tbs	2 Tbs
Chicken stock	250ml/8floz	1 cup
Orange juice	150ml/5floz	⅝ cup
Salt and pepper to taste		
Orange, thinly sliced	1	1

Preheat the grill (broiler) to high.

Arrange the fish steaks in the lined grill (broiler) pan. Cut half the butter into small pieces and dot over and around the fish. Place the pan under the grill (broiler) and grill (broil) for 3 to 5 minutes on each side. Using tongs, transfer the fish steaks to a large, warmed serving dish. Keep hot while you prepare the sauce.

Melt the remaining butter in a small saucepan. Remove from the heat and stir in the flour to form a smooth paste. Gradually stir in the stock, orange juice and seasoning and return the pan to low heat. Bring to the boil, stirring constantly. Cook for 2 to 3 minutes, stirring constantly, or until the sauce is thick and smooth.

Pour the sauce over the fish and garnish with the orange slices.

Serve at once.

6 Servings

MERLUZA A LA MARINERA
(Hake Fillets in Tomato and Almond Sauce)

If hake is unavailable, cod fillets may be substituted in this Spanish dish.

	Metric/U.K.	U.S.
Olive oil	3 Tbs	3 Tbs
Small onion, chopped	I	I
Garlic cloves, crushed	2	2
Ground almonds	50g/2oz	½ cup
Fresh breadcrumbs	15g/½oz	¼ cup
Chopped parsley	4 Tbs	4 Tbs
Tomatoes, blanched, peeled, seeded and chopped	½kg/1lb	1lb
Hake fillets	1kg/2lb	2lb
Hot water	1¼l/2 pints	5 cups
Juice of ½ lemon		
Salt	½ tsp	½ tsp
Bouquet garni	I	I
Flaked almonds	2 Tbs	2 Tbs

Heat the oil in a large frying-pan. Add the onion and garlic and fry until they are soft. Remove the pan from the heat and stir in the ground almonds, breadcrumbs, 3 tablespoons of parsley and the tomatoes. Return to the heat and cook for 5 minutes, or until the liquid has evaporated and the mixture is thick. Remove from the heat and set aside.

Preheat the oven to moderate 180°C (Gas Mark 4, 350°F).

Arrange the fish fillets, in one layer, in a large baking pan. Pour over the hot water and lemon juice and add the salt and bouquet garni. Cover with foil and place the tin in the oven. Poach for 8 to 12 minutes, or until the flesh flakes easily. Remove from the oven and transfer the fillets to a warmed serving dish. Keep hot while you prepare the sauce.

Strain and reserve 75ml/3floz (⅜ cup) of the cooking liquid. Add it to the tomato and almond mixture in the frying-pan and stir well to blend. Set the pan over moderate heat and cook until the mixture is smooth, stirring constantly.

Pour the sauce over the fish and sprinkle over the flaked almonds and remaining parsley. Serve at once.

6 Servings

MERLUZA A LA GALLEGA
(Hake with Potatoes)

This classic dish is from Galicia, a province of Spain noted for the excellence of its fish. If hake is unobtainable, cod may be substituted.

	Metric/U.K.	U.S.
Potatoes	6	6
Olive oil	75ml/3floz	⅜ cup
Onion, chopped	I	I
Garlic cloves, crushed	2	2
Fish stock	1¼l/2 pints	5 cups
Hake fillets, skinned and halved	700g/1½lb	1½lb
Wine vinegar	1 Tbs	1 Tbs
Cayenne pepper	1 tsp	1 tsp

Parboil the potatoes in salted water for 5 minutes. Drain and set aside until they are cool enough to handle. Cut them into thick rounds.

Heat the oil in a large, deep frying-pan. Add the onion and garlic and fry until they are soft. Add the potato rounds and fry gently until they are evenly browned. Pour over 300ml/10floz (1¼ cups) of the fish stock and bring to the boil. Reduce the heat to low and simmer the mixture for 20 minutes.

Meanwhile, arrange the fish fillets in a shallow saucepan and pour over the remaining stock. Poach the fish over gentle heat for about 15 minutes, or until the flesh flakes easily. Drain and discard the stock.

Mix the vinegar and cayenne together and carefully stir into the potato mixture. Simmer for 1 minute. Remove from the heat and transfer the potato mixture to a shallow, warmed serving dish. Arrange the fish fillets on top and serve at once.

6 Servings

MERLUZA KOSKERA
(Hake with Clams and Asparagus)

	Metric/U.K.	U.S.
Clams, scrubbed	16	16
Hake or cod steaks	4	4
Seasoned flour (flour with salt and pepper to taste)	50g/2oz	½ cup
Olive oil	50ml/2floz	¼ cup
Garlic cloves, crushed	3	3
Chopped parsley	2 Tbs	2 Tbs

	Metric/U.K.	U.S.
Dry white wine	150ml/5floz	⅝ cup
Frozen peas, thawed	125g/4oz	⅔ cup
Frozen asparagus tips, thawed and trimmed to uniform length	8	8
Hard-boiled eggs, halved lengthways	2	2

Half-fill a large saucepan with water and bring to the boil. Add the clams, cover and cook for 6 to 8 minutes, or until the shells open (discard any clams that do not open). Drain and reserve about 125ml/4floz (½ cup) of the liquid. Set the clams aside, discard the shells and keep hot.

Coat the fish steaks in the seasoned flour, shaking off any excess. Heat the oil in a large, deep frying-pan. Add the garlic and fry for 1 minute, stirring constantly. Add the fish steaks and fry until they are evenly browned. Add the parsley, wine and reserved clam liquid and bring to the boil. Reduce the heat to low and cover the pan. Simmer for 10 minutes, or until the flesh flakes easily.

Stir in the peas, asparagus tips and reserved clams. Simmer for a further 3 minutes, or until they are heated through.

Transfer the mixture to a warmed serving dish, arranging the vegetables, clams and sauce decoratively over and around the fish. Garnish each fish steak with a hard-boiled egg half and serve at once.

4 Servings

BESUGO AL HORNO
(Baked Bream with Potatoes)

	Metric/U.K.	U.S.
Bream, each cleaned but with the head and tails left on	2 × 1kg/2lb	2 × 2lb
Salt	1½ tsp	1½ tsp
Lemon, cut into 6 sections	1	1
Small black olives	2	2
Fresh breadcrumbs	25g/1oz	½ cup
Garlic cloves, crushed	2	2
Paprika	1 Tbs	1 Tbs
Chopped parsley	1 Tbs	1 Tbs
Medium potatoes, cut into ½cm/¼in rounds	3	3
Black pepper	½ tsp	½ tsp
Water	250ml/8floz	1 cup
Olive oil	75ml/3floz	⅜ cup

Preheat the oven to moderate 180°C (Gas Mark 4, 350°F).

Wash and dry the fish on kitchen towels. Sprinkle over 1 teaspoon of salt and make three parallel, crosswise, cuts across each fish—they should be about 1cm/½in deep, about 7½cm/3in long and about 4cm/1½in apart. Insert a section of lemon, skin side up, into each cut and insert an olive in the eye socket of each fish.

Mix together the breadcrumbs, garlic, paprika and parsley. Spread the potato rounds evenly on the bottom of a large, shallow baking pan and sprinkle over the remaining salt and the pepper. Pour the water over the potatoes. Place the fish on top of the potatoes, then brush them all over with the oil. Sprinkle over the breadcrumb mixture.

Put the pan into the oven and bake for 30 minutes, or until the fish flesh flakes easily. Remove from the oven and serve at once.

4 Servings

CEVICHE
(Mackerel Fillets Marinated in Lemon Juice)

This traditional Mexican dish is now popular all over Central and South America, with slight variations from country to country. Originally limes were used, but since they can be difficult to obtain, fresh lemon juice is suggested instead. If you prefer to use limes, however, use 250ml/8floz (1 cup) of lime juice and 250ml/8floz (1 cup) of lemon juice, instead of the amount suggested below.

	Metric/U.K.	U.S.
Fresh lemon juice	450ml/15floz	2 cups
Dried small hot red chilli, crumbled	1	1
Large onions, thinly sliced into rings	2	2
Garlic clove, chopped	½	½
Salt and pepper to taste		

Escabeche is a Mediterranean dish of pickled cooked fish.

Large mackerels, filleted and cut into 2½cm/1in pieces	3	3
Large sweet potatoes, unpeeled	3	3
Crisp lettuces, separated into leaves and chilled	2	2
Fresh sweetcorn, outer husks and thread removed and cut crosswise into 5cm/2in rounds	4	4
Fresh red chilli, split, seeded and cut into thin pieces	1	1

Combine the lemon juice, dried chilli, onion rings, garlic and seasoning in a large pitcher.

Arrange the fish pieces in a shallow porcelain dish and pour the lemon juice over them. (Add more lemon juice if the mixture does not completely cover the fish pieces.) Cover the dish and transfer it to the refrigerator. Leave for at least 3 hours, or until it is opaque and white.

About 30 minutes before serving time, bring 1¾l/3 pints (7½ cups) of water to the boil in a large saucepan. Put the sweet potatoes into the pan and cover. Reduce the heat to moderate and cook for 30 to 35 minutes, or until they are cooked through and tender.

While the potatoes are cooking, arrange a bed of lettuce leaves on individual serving plates.

Remove the pan from the heat and drain the potatoes. Peel and cut each one into three slices. Keep hot while you cook the sweetcorn.

Pour 1¼l/2 pints (5 cups) of water into a saucepan and bring to the boil. Drop the corn rounds into the pan and boil for 4 to 5 minutes or until they turn bright yellow. Remove from the heat and drain the corn.

Remove the marinated fish from the refrigerator and divide it equally between the plates. Garnish with the onion rings and strips of fresh chilli pepper. Arrange the sweet potato slices and corn rounds around the fish and serve at once.

4 Servings

ESCABECHE
(Pickled Fish)

This Spanish (and Provençal) dish is probably the ancestor of the Mexican Ceviche and is used extensively throughout the Mediterranean countries to preserve fish when it is plentiful and cheap. Any type of fish fillet may be used, such as mackerel, cod, halibut or haddock, or even whole small fish such as red mullet.

	Metric/U.K.	U.S.
Flour	3 Tbs	3 Tbs
Salt	1½ tsp	1½ tsp
White fish fillets	700g-1kg/ 1½lb-2lb	1½-2lb
Olive oil	150ml/5floz	⅝ cup
Large onions, sliced	2	2
Red pepper, pith and seeds removed and cut into strips	1	1
Garlic cloves, chopped	2	2
Fresh red chilli, chopped	1	1
Bay leaves	3	3
Black peppercorns	¼ tsp	¼ tsp
Red wine vinegar	300ml/10floz	1¼ cups

Combine the flour and 1 teaspoon of salt on a plate. Coat the fish pieces in the flour, shaking off any excess.

Heat 75ml/3floz (⅜ cup) of oil in a large frying-pan. Add the fish and fry for 4 to 5 minutes on each side, or until they are golden brown and flake easily. Transfer the fish to kitchen towels to drain.

Pour off the oil and rinse out the pan. Pour the remaining oil into the pan and heat. Add the onions and fry until they are soft. Stir in the pepper, garlic, chilli, bay leaves, remaining salt, the peppercorns and vinegar and bring to the boil. Cook for 2 minutes.

Arrange the fish in an earthenware or heat-proof glass dish. Pour the mixture over the fish and cover the dish with a lid or foil. Allow to cool to room temperature, then transfer the dish to the refrigerator. Leave to marinate for 2 to 3 days. Serve straight from the dish.

4 Servings

HUACHINANGO VERACRUZANO
(Red Snapper, VeraCruz Style)

If red snapper is not available, gurnet or sea bream may be substituted.

	Metric/U.K.	U.S.
Vegetable oil	50ml/2floz	¼ cup
Large onion, chopped	1	1
Garlic clove, crushed	1	1
Canned peeled tomatoes	700g/1½lb	1½lb
Small dried hot red chillis, crumbled, or Jalapeño chillis, drained and chopped	2	2
Stuffed green olives, chopped	6	6
Black olives, stoned (pitted), and chopped	4	4
Red snapper fillets	700g/1½lb	1½lb
Seasoned flour (flour with salt and pepper to taste)	40g/1½oz	⅓ cup
Butter	50g/2oz	4 Tbs

Heat the oil in a large saucepan. Add the onion and garlic and fry until they are soft. Purée the tomatoes and can juice in a blender until they are soft (or push them through a food mill) and stir them into the onion mixture with the chillis and olives. Bring to the boil, reduce the heat to low and simmer the sauce for 20 minutes.

Meanwhile, coat the fillets in the seasoned flour, shaking off any excess.

Melt the butter in a large frying-pan. Add the fillets and fry for 4 to 6 minutes on each side or until they are evenly browned and the flesh flakes easily.

Another Latin American favourite which originated in Mexico, Ceviche is fillets of mackerel marinated in lemon or lime juice.

Transfer the fish to a warmed serving dish. Pour over the sauce and serve at once.

4 Servings

to time with the sauce mixture.

Remove from the heat and garnish with the avocado slices. Serve at once.

6 Servings

HUACHINANGO YUCATECO
(Red Snapper, Yucatan Style)

If red snapper is not available, gurnet or sea bream may be substituted.

	Metric/U.K.	U.S.
Butter	50g/2oz	4 Tbs
Medium onion, chopped	1	1
Garlic clove, crushed	1	1
Small red pepper, pith and seeds removed and chopped	1	1
Small green pepper, pith and seeds removed and chopped	1	1
Chopped coriander leaves	1 Tbs	1 Tbs
Ground cumin	1 tsp	1 tsp
Orange juice	125ml/4floz	½ cup
Grated orange rind	½ tsp	½ tsp
Salt and pepper to taste		
Red snapper, cleaned but with the head and tail left on	1 × 2½kg/5lb	1 × 5lb
Black or green olives, stoned (pitted) and chopped	6	6
Avocado, stoned (pitted) and thinly sliced	1	1

Melt half the butter in a frying-pan. Add the onion, garlic and peppers and fry until they are soft. Stir in the coriander, cumin, orange juice, orange rind and seasoning and bring to the boil. Simmer for 2 minutes, then remove the pan from the heat. Set aside.

Preheat the oven to moderate 180°C (Gas Mark 4, 350°F).

Cut the remaining butter into small dice and scatter it over the bottom of a large, shallow casserole dish. Arrange the fish on top and pour over the orange juice mixture. Scatter over the olives. Put the dish into the oven and bake for 25 to 30 minutes, or until the fish flesh flakes easily, basting the fish from time

SALMONETES ANDALUZA
(Red Mullet, Andalusian Style)

	Metric/U.K.	U.S.
Red mullets, cleaned and with the eyes removed	6	6
Juice of 1 lemon		
Ground pine nuts	75g/3oz	¾ cup
Garlic cloves, crushed	2	2
Small onion, finely chopped	1	1
Chopped parsley	4 Tbs	4 Tbs
Salt and pepper to taste		
Olive oil	3 Tbs	3 Tbs
Green pepper, pith and seeds removed and cut into ½cm/¼in strips	1	1
Medium tomatoes, blanched, peeled, seeded and sliced	6	6
Butter, cut into small pieces	25g/1oz	2 Tbs
Black olives	6	6

Put the mullets in a large shallow bowl and pour over the lemon juice. Set aside at room temperature for 15 minutes.

Preheat the oven to moderate 180°C (Gas Mark 4, 350°F).

Combine the pine nuts, garlic, onion, parsley and seasoning and gradually beat in the oil until the mixture is smooth and blended. Set aside.

Remove the fish from the marinade, discarding the marinating liquid and pat dry with kitchen towels. Arrange the fish, in one layer, in a large baking dish. Spread over the pine nut mixture making sure that each fish is evenly covered. Arrange the pepper strips over the fish and cover with the tomatoes. Dot over the butter and place the dish in the oven. Bake for 25 minutes, or until the fish flesh flakes easily.

Remove the dish from the oven and transfer the fish to a warmed serving dish. Place the

olives in the uppermost eye socket of each fish and serve at once.

6 Servings

MARMITAKO
(Tuna Steaks with Potatoes)

This delicious dish is a classic from the Basque country, bordering on France. If tuna steaks are not available, substitute halibut or cod instead.

	Metric/U.K.	U.S.
Olive oil	125ml/4floz	½ cup
Onions, chopped	2	2
Garlic clove, crushed	1	1
Medium potatoes, sliced into 1cm/½in thick rounds	3	3
Small red peppers, pith and seeds removed and cut into strips	2	2
Salt and pepper to taste		
Paprika	1½ tsp	1½ tsp
Tuna fish steaks, about 2½ cm/1in thick	4	4
Water	175ml/6floz	¾ cup

Heat the oil in a large, deep frying-pan. Add the onions and garlic and fry until they are soft. Add the potatoes and peppers and fry for 5 minutes, turning occasionally. Stir in the seasoning and paprika. Add the tuna steaks and fry until they are lightly browned on both sides. Pour over the water and bring to the boil.

Salmonetes Andaluzá — red mullets marinated in an oil and pine nut mixture then baked with pepper and tomatoes.

Reduce the heat to low, cover the pan and simmer for 15 minutes, or until the fish flesh flakes easily.

Remove the pan from the heat and transfer the mixture to a warmed serving dish. Serve at once.

4 Servings

BACALAO A LA VISCAINA
(Salt Cod, Biscay Style)

Estofado de Anguila — Spanish Eel Stew.

Salt cod is immensely popular all over Spain and it is cooked in a variety of delicious ways. This particular dish is a classic from the Basque country.

	Metric/U.K.	U.S.
Salt cod, soaked in cold water for 24 hours	1kg/2lb	2lb
Seasoned flour (flour with salt and pepper to taste)	40g/1½oz	⅓ cup
Olive oil	50ml/2floz	¼ cup
Large onions, chopped	2	2
Garlic cloves, crushed	2	2
Canned peeled tomatoes	700g/1½lb	1½lb
White bread, crusts removed	2 slices	2 slices
Fresh red or green chillis, seeded and chopped	2	2

	Metric/U.K.	U.S.
Canned pimientos, drained and cut into strips	425g/14oz	14oz
Fine dry breadcrumbs	3 Tbs	3 Tbs
Finely chopped parsley	1 Tbs	1 Tbs

Drain the salt cod and transfer to a large saucepan. Just cover with cold water. Set the pan over low heat and bring to the boil. Remove the pan from the heat and drain the salt cod. When it is cool enough to handle, remove the skin and bones and cut into 5cm/2in pieces. Coat the fish pieces in the seasoned flour, shaking off any excess and set aside.

Heat half the oil in a large, deep frying-pan. Add the onions and garlic and fry until they are soft. Add the tomatoes and can juice and reduce the heat to low. Simmer for 5 minutes.

Meanwhile, heat 1 tablespoon of the remaining oil in a small saucepan. Add the bread slices and fry until they are evenly browned. Remove from the heat and cut the bread into small pieces. Stir the bread pieces and chillis into the tomato mixture and simmer for a further 10 minutes.

Preheat the oven to moderate 180°C (Gas Mark 4, 350°F).

Spread half the tomato mixture over the bottom of a medium baking dish. Cover with the salt cod pieces, then top with the remaining tomato mixture. Arrange the pimiento strips over the top.

Mix the breadcrumbs and parsley together and sprinkle over the mixture, then pour over the remaining oil. Put the dish into the oven and cook for 15 to 20 minutes, or until the topping is browned.

Remove from the heat and serve at once.

6 Servings

ESTOFADO DE ANGUILA
(Eel Stew)

	Metric/U.K.	U.S.
Olive oil	3 Tbs	3 Tbs
Chopped blanched almonds	50g/2oz	½ cup
Large red pepper, pith and seeds removed and chopped	1	1
Large onion, sliced	1	1
Garlic cloves, crushed	3	3
Black pepper	¼ tsp	¼ tsp
Dried thyme	¼ tsp	¼ tsp
Paprika	1 tsp	1 tsp
Cayenne pepper	½ tsp	½ tsp
Eels, skinned and cut into serving pieces	1kg/2lb	2lb
Fish stock	900ml/1½ pints	3¾ cups
Cornflour (cornstarch), blended with 1 Tbs water	1 tsp	1 tsp

Heat the oil in a large, heavy-based saucepan. Add the almonds, pepper, onion and garlic and fry until the almonds are golden brown and the onion is soft. Add the pepper, thyme, paprika and cayenne and cook for 2 minutes, stirring constantly. Add the eel pieces and cook, turning them frequently, for 5 minutes. Pour over the fish stock and bring to the boil. Reduce the heat to low, cover the pan and simmer the mixture for 30 minutes.

Stir in the cornflour (cornstarch) mixture and simmer for 2 to 3 minutes, stirring constantly, until the sauce thickens and is smooth.

Remove the pan from the heat and serve at once.

6 Servings

CALAMARES EN SU TINTA
(Squid in its own Ink)

	Metric/U.K.	U.S.
Olive oil	75ml/3floz	⅜ cup
Squid, cleaned thoroughly and cut into 1cm/½in pieces (ink sacs reserved)	1½kg/3lb	3lb
Medium onion, finely chopped	1	1
Garlic cloves, crushed	2	2
Chopped parsley	1 Tbs	1 Tbs
Ground mace	⅛ tsp	⅛ tsp
Salt and pepper to taste		
Cold water	250ml/8floz	1 cup
Flour	2 Tbs	2 Tbs

The glory of Spain — a real, authentic and mouth-watering Paella (I).

Heat the oil in a large saucepan. Add the squid, onion, garlic and parsley and fry until they are lightly browned. Add the mace and seasoning and reduce the heat to low. Cover and simmer for 20 minutes.

Meanwhile, mash the ink sacs through a strainer set over a bowl to extract the ink. Pour over the water and mash again. Using a whisk, beat in the flour until the ink and water mixture is smooth.

Pour the sauce over the squid mixture and bring to the boil, stirring constantly. Reduce the heat to very low, cover and simmer for 5 minutes, stirring occasionally. Remove the pan from the heat and set aside, covered, for 5 minutes.

Transfer the mixture to a large, warmed serving dish.

Serve at once.

4–6 Servings

ALMEJAS A LA MARINERA
(Clams in Tomato and Garlic Sauce)

	Metric/U.K.	U.S.
Olive oil	3 Tbs	3 Tbs
Large onion, chopped	1	1
Garlic cloves, crushed	2	2
Fresh white breadcrumbs	40g/1½oz	¾ cup
Tomatoes, blanched, peeled, seeded and chopped	700g/1½lb	1½lb
Hard-boiled egg yolks, strained	2	2
Salt and pepper to taste		
Small clams, scrubbed	48	48
Dry white wine	450ml/15floz	2 cups
Chopped parsley	2 Tbs	2 Tbs
Hard-boiled egg whites, finely chopped	2	2
Lemons, cut into wedges	2	2

Heat the oil in a frying-pan. Add the onion and garlic and fry until they are soft. Add the breadcrumbs, tomatoes, egg yolks and seasoning and cook, stirring constantly, until the mixture forms a thick purée. Remove from the heat and set aside.

Put the clams into a large, heavy-based saucepan and pour over the wine. Bring to the boil, then reduce the heat to low. Cover the pan and steam the clams for 6 to 8 minutes, or until the shells open (discard any clams that do not open).

Transfer the clams to a large, warmed serving bowl. Strain the liquid from the pan and add to the tomato purée. Pour the sauce over the clams. Garnish with the parsley and egg whites and serve at once, accompanied by the lemon wedges.

4 Servings

PAELLA I
(Chicken and Seafood with Rice)

Paella is probably the single most famous dish from Spain and it is one of those dishes whose origins were modest and simple but which is now both rich and ornate to make. Almost any ingredient can be added or subtracted but saffron-flavoured rice is traditional as are the chicken and shrimps.

	Metric/U.K.	U.S.
Cooked lobster, shell split, claws cracked and grey sac removed	1 × 700g/1½lb	1 × 1½lb
Olive oil	2 Tbs	2 Tbs
Chicken, cut into serving pieces	1 × 1kg/2lb	1 × 2lb
Chorizo sausage, sliced	1	1
Medium onion, sliced	1	1
Garlic clove, crushed	1	1
Tomatoes, blanched, peeled, seeded and chopped	3	3
Large red pepper, pith and seeds removed and chopped	1	1
Salt and pepper to taste		
Paprika	1 tsp	1 tsp
Long-grain rice, soaked in cold water for 30 minutes and drained	350g/12oz	2 cups
Water	600ml/1 pint	2½ cups
Juice of 1 lemon		
Saffron threads, soaked in 125ml/4floz water	¼ tsp	¼ tsp

	Metric/U.K.	U.S.
Green peas, weighed after shelling	225g/8oz	1⅓ cups
Large prawns or shrimps, shelled	175g/6oz	6oz
Mussels, scrubbed, steamed for 6 to 8 minutes	20	20
Chopped parsley	1 Tbs	1 Tbs

Remove the lobster meat from the shell and claws and cut it into 2½cm/1in pieces. Set aside.

Heat the oil in a large, deep frying-pan. Add the chicken and chorizo and fry until the chicken is deeply and evenly browned. Using tongs, remove the chicken pieces and chorizo from the pan. Set aside and keep hot.

Add the onion and garlic to the pan and fry until they are soft. Add the tomatoes, pepper, seasoning and paprika and cook for 10 to 12 minutes, stirring occasionally, or until the mixture is thick.

Add the rice to the pan and, shaking the pan frequently, fry it for 3 minutes, or until it is transparent. Add the water, lemon juice and saffron mixture and bring to the boil. Reduce the heat to low and stir in the peas. Return the chicken and sausage to the pan and cook for 15 minutes, stirring occasionally. Add the lobster meat, prawns or shrimps and mussels and cook for a further 5 minutes, or until the chicken is cooked through and tender, and the cooking liquid has been absorbed.

Remove the pan from the heat. Sprinkle over the parsley and serve at once.

6 Servings

PAELLA II
(Chicken and Seafood with Rice)

This is a slightly more modest version of this Spanish favourite.

	Metric/U.K.	U.S.
Cooked lobster, shell split, claws cracked and grey sac removed	1 × 700g/1½lb	1 × 1½lb
Olive oil	75ml/3floz	⅜ cup
Chicken, cut into serving pieces	1 × 1½kg/3lb	1 × 3lb

Lean bacon, chopped	6 slices	6 slices
Large tomatoes, blanched, peeled, seeded and chopped	2	2
Garlic cloves, crushed	2	2
Mange-tout or green beans, cut into lengths	225g/8oz	2 cups
Long-grain rice, soaked in cold water for 30 minutes and drained	450g/1lb	2⅔ cups
Paprika	2 tsp	2 tsp
Water	1¼l/2 pints	5 cups
Salt	2 tsp	2 tsp
Ground saffron	¼ tsp	¼ tsp
Small clams, scrubbed and steamed for 6 to 8 minutes, and with one shell removed	12	12
Snails	6	6
Baby squid, cleaned thoroughly and chopped	225g/8oz	8oz
Lemon wedges	6	6

Remove the lobster meat from the shell and claws and cut it into 2½cm/1in pieces. Set aside.

Heat the oil in a large, deep frying-pan. Add the chicken pieces and bacon and fry until the chicken is deeply and evenly browned. Add the tomatoes, garlic and mange-tout or beans and fry for a further 5 minutes, stirring occasionally. Using a slotted spoon, transfer the mixture to a bowl. Set aside and keep hot.

Add the rice and paprika to the pan and cook for 3 minutes, stirring frequently, or until the rice is translucent. Add the water, salt and saffron and bring to the boil, stirring constantly. Reduce the heat to low and return the chicken and vegetable mixture to the pan. Cook for 10 minutes, stirring occasionally. Add the clams, snails, squid and lobster and cook for a further 5 to 10 minutes, or until the chicken is cooked through and tender and the cooking liquid has been absorbed.

Garnish with lemon wedges and serve.

6 Servings

ZARZUELA
(Fish Stew)

A frothy Catalan sea-food stew.

	Metric/U.K.	U.S.
Olive oil	150ml/5floz	⅝ cup
Large onion, sliced	1	1
Squid, cleaned thoroughly and cut into rings (sac removed)	225g/8oz	8oz
Tomatoes, blanched, peeled and chopped	6	6
Chopped fresh basil	2 tsp	2 tsp
Dry white wine	125ml/4floz	½ cup
Eel, cut into 2½cm/1in pieces	350g/12oz	12oz
Clams, scrubbed and steamed for 6 to 8 minutes	24	24
Salt and pepper to taste		
Fish stock	300ml/10floz	1¼ cups
Canned tuna fish, drained and flaked	200g/7oz	7oz
Sole fillets, skinned and cut into 2½cm/1in pieces	255g/8oz	8oz
Ground almonds	50g/2oz	½ cup
Chopped parsley	2 Tbs	2 Tbs
Ground saffron	½ tsp	½ tsp
Garlic cloves, crushed	2	2
White bread, fried in olive oil and quartered	2 slices	2 slices
Cooked prawns or shrimps, unpeeled	225g/8oz	8oz

Heat all but 1 tablespoon of the oil in a large saucepan. Add the onion and fry until it is golden brown. Add the squid, tomatoes, basil and wine and cook for 3 minutes, stirring occasionally. Add the eel, clams, salt, pepper and stock, reduce the heat to low and simmer for 10 minutes. Add the tuna fish and sole and simmer for a further 10 minutes.

Meanwhile, put the almonds, parsley, saffron, garlic, the remaining oil and one piece of bread into a mortar. Add 1 tablespoon of liquid from the fish mixture and pound the mixture with a pestle until it forms a paste.

Spread the paste on the bottom of a warmed serving dish. Remove the pan from the heat and pour the fish mixture into the serving dish. Garnish with the remaining fried bread and the prawns or shrimps.

Serve at once.

6 Servings

Zarzuela means operetta in Spanish, and the name of this frothy concoction of mixed seafood becomes all the more appropriate when you taste it.

Vegetables and Eggs

JUDIAS VERDES CON SALSA DE TOMATE
(Green Beans in Tomato Sauce)

Torrijas de Maiz Tierno — deep-fried sweetcorn fritters.

	Metric/U.K.	U.S.
Butter	25g/1oz	2 Tbs
Garlic cloves, crushed	2	2
Green or French beans, cut into 2½cm/1in lengths	1kg/2lb	5⅓ cups
Canned peeled tomatoes, chopped	700g/1½lb	1½lb
Finely chopped chives	1 Tbs	1 Tbs
Salt and pepper to taste		
Bay leaf	1	1
Chopped pine nuts	1 Tbs	1 Tbs
Lemon juice	1 Tbs	1 Tbs

Melt the butter in a large saucepan. Add the garlic and fry for 2 minutes, stirring constantly. Add the beans and cook for 4 minutes, stirring occasionally. Stir in the tomatoes and can juice, and all the remaining ingredients and bring to the boil, stirring constantly. Reduce the heat to low and simmer for 25 to 30 minutes or until the beans are very tender and the liquid has reduced a little.

Remove and discard the bay leaf. Transfer the mixture to a warmed serving dish and serve at once.

6 Servings

TORRIJAS DE MAIZ TIERNO
(Corn Fritters)

	Metric/U.K.	U.S.
Sweetcorn kernels	225g/8oz	1⅓ cups
Flour	50g/2oz	½ cup
Sugar	2 Tbs	2 Tbs
Salt and pepper to taste		
Eggs, lightly beaten	2	2
Grated Parmesan cheese	2 Tbs	2 Tbs
Sufficient vegetable oil for deep-frying		

Combine the sweetcorn, flour, sugar, seasoning, eggs and cheese until they are thoroughly blended. Set aside.

Fill a large deep-frying pan one-third full with oil and heat until it reaches 185°C (360°F) on a deep-fat thermometer, or until a small cube of stale bread dropped into the oil turns golden brown in 50 seconds. Carefully lower a few tablespoons of the sweetcorn mixture into the oil and fry for 3 to 4 minutes, or until the fritters are golden brown. Using a slotted spoon, transfer the fritters to kitchen towels to drain. Keep hot while you cook the remaining mixture in the same way.

Transfer the fritters to a warmed serving dish and serve at once.

4 Servings

GARBANZOS A LA MEXICANA
(Spicy Chick-Peas)

	Metric/U.K.	U.S.
Dried chick-peas, soaked overnight in cold water and drained	275g/10oz	1⅔ cups
Salt	1½ tsp	1½ tsp
Streaky (fatty) bacon, diced	6 slices	6 slices
Large onion, roughly chopped	1	1
Garlic clove, crushed	1	1
Small red pepper, pith and seeds removed and chopped	1	1
Black pepper	¼ tsp	¼ tsp
Small dried hot red chilli, crumbled	1	1
Dried oregano	½ tsp	½ tsp
Canned tomato sauce (not ketchup)	150g/5oz	5oz

Put the chick-peas and 1 teaspoon of salt into a saucepan and pour over enough water just to cover. Set over moderately high heat and bring to the boil. Reduce the heat to low and simmer for 1 hour, or until the chick-peas are cooked and tender. Drain the chick-peas and set aside.

Fry the bacon in a medium, heavy-based saucepan until it is crisp and has rendered all of its fat. Add the onion, garlic and pepper and fry until they are soft. Stir in the remaining salt, the pepper, chilli, oregano, tomato sauce and chick-peas. Bring to the boil and reduce the heat to low. Simmer for 10 minutes, stirring occasionally.

Transfer the mixture to a warmed serving dish and serve at once.

4 Servings

FRIJOLES REFRITOS
(Refried Beans)

This is one of the staple foods of Mexico and can be used in a variety of ways—as an accompaniment to meat, as a filling for tortillas or, as here, with the addition of sausage and cheese, as a filling meal on its own.

Frijoles Refritos (refried beans) is one of the staples of Mexico and is used as a snack, with the addition of sausages and cheese as a meal in itself, or as a filling for tortillas or empanadas.

	Metric/U.K.	U.S.
Dried kidney or pinto beans, soaked in cold water overnight and drained	225g/8oz	1⅓ cups
Salt	1 tsp	1 tsp
Small chorizo sausage, skinned and diced	1	1
Lard or vegetable fat	3 Tbs	3 Tbs
Onion, chopped	1	1
Medium tomatoes, blanched, peeled, seeded and chopped	3	3

Zapellitos Rellenos are courgettes (zucchini) stuffed with a mixture of cheese, breadcrumbs, garlic and basil.

Small dried hot red chillis, crumbled	2	2
Cheddar or jack cheese, grated	50g/2oz	½ cup

Put the beans and ½ teaspoon of salt into a saucepan and pour over enough water just to cover. Set over moderately high heat and bring to the boil. Reduce the heat to low, cover the pan and simmer for 1½ hours, or until the beans are cooked and tender. Drain the beans and purée them in a blender. Set aside.

Meanwhile, fry the chorizo in a small frying-pan for 5 minutes, stirring occasionally. Do not add any fat as the sausage will let out a good deal of its own. Using a slotted spoon, transfer the chorizo pieces to kitchen towels to drain. Set aside.

Melt the lard or fat in a large frying-pan. Add the onion and fry until it is soft. Stir in the tomatoes, remaining salt and chilli and cook, stirring frequently, for 5 minutes, or until the mixture becomes pulpy. Stir in the sausage, the puréed beans and the cheese and cook, stirring and turning frequently, for 10 minutes or until the cheese has melted.

Transfer the mixture to a warmed serving dish and serve at once.

4 Servings

ZAPELLITOS RELLENOS
(Stuffed Courgettes [Zucchini] Mexican Style)

	Metric/U.K.	U.S.
Courgettes (zucchini)	6	6
Garlic clove, crushed	1	1
Dry breadcrumbs	125g/4oz	1⅓ cups
Chopped fresh basil	1 Tbs	1 Tbs
Fontina, Cheddar or jack cheese, grated	175g/6oz	1½ cups
Salt and pepper to taste		
Eggs, lightly beaten	2	2
Butter, melted	50g/2oz	4 Tbs

Cut the courgettes (zucchini) in half lengthways and carefully hollow out the flesh to within ½cm/¼in of the skin. Set the shells aside.

Chop the flesh, then press with the back of a wooden spoon to extract as much juice as possible and drain it away. Set the flesh aside.

Preheat the oven to fairly hot 200°C (Gas Mark 6, 400°F).

Combine the courgette (zucchini) flesh, garlic, breadcrumbs, basil, cheese, seasoning, eggs and half the melted butter until they are thoroughly blended.

Arrange the courgette (zucchini) shells, skin side down, in a well-greased shallow baking dish. Stuff with the breadcrumb mixture and pour over the remaining melted butter. Put the dish into the oven and bake for 20 to 30 minutes, or until the top is brown and bubbling.

Remove the dish from the oven and serve at once.

6 Servings

COLACHE
(Courgettes [Zucchini], Sweetcorn and Tomatoes)

	Metric/U.K.	U.S.
Butter or lard	40g/1½oz	3 Tbs
Courgettes (zucchini), sliced crosswise	4	4
Onion, chopped	1	1
Garlic, crushed	1	1
Green pepper, pith and seeds removed and chopped	1	1
Medium tomatoes, blanched, peeled and chopped	2	2
Small dried hot red chilli, chopped	1	1
Water	125ml/4floz	½ cup
Sweetcorn kernels	175g/6oz	1 cup
Salt and pepper to taste		

Melt the butter or lard in a saucepan. Add the courgette (zucchini) slices and fry until they are evenly browned. Add the onion, garlic and pepper and fry until they are soft. Stir in the tomatoes, chilli and water and bring to the boil, stirring occasionally. Reduce the heat to low and simmer for 10 minutes.

Stir in the sweetcorn and seasoning and simmer for a further 5 to 10 minutes, or until the courgettes (zucchini) are cooked and tender.

Transfer the mixture to a warmed serving dish and serve at once.

4-6 Servings

PISTO MANCHEGO
(Mixed Vegetable Stew)

This dish is a variation on the Basque pipérade filling and variations of it are cooked all over northern Spain. Ham is sometimes added to the vegetables and with its addition, the dish becomes a light main dish rather than a filling accompaniment.

	Metric/U.K.	U.S.
Olive oil	50ml/2floz	¼ cup
Onions, chopped	2	2
Courgettes (zucchini), sliced crosswise	4	4
Large green pepper, pith and seeds removed and chopped	1	1
Large red pepper, pith and seeds removed and chopped	1	1
Canned peeled tomatoes	425g/14oz	14oz
Paprika	1½ tsp	1½ tsp
Salt and pepper to taste		
Eggs, lightly beaten	2	2

Heat the oil in a shallow saucepan. Add the onions, courgettes (zucchini) and peppers and fry until they are soft. Purée the tomatoes and can juice in a blender and stir into the vegetable mixture. Bring to the boil, reduce the heat to low and simmer the mixture, stirring occasionally, for 35 minutes, or until the vegetables are cooked and tender.

Combine the paprika, seasoning and eggs until they are thoroughly blended. Stir into the vegetable mixture and stir and beat until the eggs have scrambled.

Transfer the mixture to a warmed serving dish and serve at once.

4 Servings

CHILES RELLENOS I
(Stuffed Green Chillis)

Green, California-type chillis are often stuffed in Mexico, and with a variety of different materials. Picadillo (page 337) for instance, Frijoles Refritos (page 371), or, as here, simple sticks of cheese. The sauce is traditional to the dish but can be omitted if you prefer.

	Metric/U.K.	U.S.
Canned California green chillis	2 × 200g/7oz	2 × 7oz
Cheddar or jack cheese, cut into strips short enough to fit into the chillis	175g/6oz	6oz
Seasoned flour (flour with salt and pepper to taste)	50g/2oz	½ cup
Sufficient vegetable oil for deep-frying		
Salsa de Chile Rojo (red chilli sauce) (page 11)	300ml/10floz	1¼ cups
COATING		
Eggs, separated	3	3
Water	1 Tbs	1 Tbs
Cornflour (cornstarch)	3 Tbs	3 Tbs

Drain the chillis and gently cut a slit halfway down the side of each one. Remove any seeds and membrane and rinse under cold running water. Insert the cheese piece, then coat in the seasoned flour, shaking off any excess.

To make the coating, beat the yolks, water and cornflour (cornstarch) together until

they are well blended. Beat the egg whites until they form stiff peaks. Fold into the egg yolk mixture.

Fill a large saucepan one-third full with oil and heat until it reaches 185°C (360°F) on a deep-fat thermometer, or until a small cube of stale bread dropped into the oil turns golden in 50 seconds. Dip the chillis in the batter to coat them thoroughly and place them one by one in the hot oil (use a saucer to slide them in if necessary). Fry for 3 to 4 minutes, or until the coating is puffed up and lightly browned. Remove from the oil and drain on kitchen towels.

Transfer the cooked chillis to a warmed serving dish and pour over the sauce. Serve at once.

4 Servings

CHILES RELLENOS II
(Stuffed Peppers, Yucatan Style)

	Metric/U.K.	U.S.
Large green or red peppers	4	4
Olive oil	50ml/2floz	¼ cup
Medium onions, diced	2	2
Garlic cloves, crushed	2	2
Dried small hot red chillis, crumbled	2	2
Minced (ground) beef	½kg/1lb	1lb
Dried oregano	1 tsp	1 tsp
Salt	1 tsp	1 tsp
Bay leaves	2	2
Tabasco sauce	½ tsp	½ tsp
Flour	2 Tbs	2 Tbs
Beef stock	250ml/8floz	1 cup
Tomato purée (paste)	3 Tbs	3 Tbs
SAUCE		
Cream cheese	225g/8oz	1 cup
Single (light) cream	125ml/4floz	½ cup
Salt	1 tsp	1 tsp
Cayenne pepper	¼ tsp	¼ tsp
Seedless raisins	75g/3oz	½ cup

Cut the tops from the peppers and carefully scoop out the pith and seeds, leaving the peppers whole. Set aside. Remove and discard the stems from the tops and chop the flesh into small dice.

Heat the oil in a saucepan. Add the onions, garlic, chillis and diced pepper and fry until they are soft. Add the meat, oregano, salt, bay leaves and Tabasco and fry until the meat loses its pinkness. Stir in the flour, stock, tomato purée (paste) and bring to the boil. Reduce the heat to low, cover the pan and simmer for 30 minutes, stirring occasionally.

Preheat the oven to moderate 180°C (Gas Mark 4, 350°F).

Remove and discard the bay leaves from the beef mixture. Carefully spoon the mixture into the peppers and arrange the peppers in a shallow, well-greased baking dish. Put the dish into the oven and bake for 40 minutes.

Meanwhile, prepare the sauce. Put the cream cheese, cream, salt and cayenne into a small saucepan and simmer gently until the mixture is smooth, stirring constantly. Stir in the seedless raisins and simmer until the sauce is hot but not boiling. Remove from the heat. Pour the sauce over the peppers and cook for a further 15 minutes, or until the sauce is bubbling. Remove from the oven and serve at once.

4 Servings

CHILES EN NOGADA
(Stuffed Peppers with Walnut Cream Sauce)

This exotic dish is traditionally served in Mexico on Independence Day (September 15) because its main ingredients echo the colours of the Mexican flag. In Mexico, California green chillis are used (they can be obtained outside Mexico in cans if they are not available fresh), but green peppers can be substituted, as here, for a more substantial dish.

	Metric/U.K.	U.S.
Large firm green peppers	4	4
Vegetable oil	2 Tbs	2 Tbs
Onion, finely chopped	1	1
Garlic clove, crushed	1	1
Canned peeled tomatoes, drained and chopped	225g/8oz	8oz
Minced (ground) beef	½kg/1lb	1lb
Seedless raisins	3 Tbs	3 Tbs
Ground cinnamon	½ tsp	½ tsp
Ground cloves	½ tsp	½ tsp
Salt and pepper to taste		

Stuffed chillis or green peppers are found in many forms all over Mexico — this particular favourite is from Yucatan where the peppers are stuffed with a spicy minced (ground) beef mixture, then cooked with a sauce of cream cheese and cream.

SAUCE

	Metric/U.K.	U.S.
Single (light) cream	250ml/8floz	1 cup
Walnuts, shelled and ground	125g/4oz	1 cup
Ground almonds	1 Tbs	1 Tbs
Salt and pepper to taste		
Pomegranate seeds	50g/2oz	⅓ cup

Cut the tops from the peppers and carefully scoop out the pith and seeds, leaving the peppers whole. Cook them in boiling water for 5 minutes, drain and set aside.

Heat the oil in a saucepan. Add the onion and garlic and fry until they are soft. Add the tomatoes and bring to the boil. Stir in the meat until it loses its pinkness. Stir in the raisins, cinnamon, cloves and seasoning and bring to the boil. Reduce the heat to low and simmer the mixture for 10 minutes, or until it is thick and rich.

Preheat the oven to moderate 180°C (Gas Mark 4, 350°F).

Carefully spoon the meat mixture into the green peppers and arrange the peppers in a shallow, well-greased baking dish. Put the dish into the oven and cook for 30 minutes.

Meanwhile, to make the sauce, put the cream, walnuts, almonds and seasoning into a small saucepan. Simmer gently, stirring constantly, until it is hot but not boiling and has thickened.

Remove the dish from the oven and transfer the peppers to a warmed serving dish. Pour over the sauce and scatter over the pomegranate seeds. Serve at once.

4 Servings

HUEVOS A LA FLAMENCA
(Eggs Baked with Sausages, Onions and Pepper)

	Metric/U.K.	U.S.
Olive oil	50ml/2floz	¼ cup
Large onion, chopped	1	1
Garlic clove, crushed	1	1
Red pepper, pith and seeds removed and chopped	1	1
Potatoes, cooked and sliced	2	2
Canned peeled tomatoes	425g/14oz	14oz
Tomato purée (paste)	1 Tbs	1 Tbs
Green peas, weighed after shelling	125g/4oz	⅔ cup
Green beans, chopped	125g/4oz	⅔ cup
Eggs	8	8
Chorizo sausage, cut into 8 slices	125g/4oz	4oz
Serrano ham, cut into strips	125g/4oz	4oz
Canned asparagus tips, drained	225g/8oz	8oz

Heat 3 tablespoons of the oil in a large frying-pan. Add the onion, garlic and pepper and fry until they are soft. Add the potatoes and fry until they are lightly and evenly browned. Stir in the tomatoes and can juice, tomato purée (paste), peas and beans and bring to the boil. Simmer for 5 minutes.

Preheat the oven to moderate 180°C (Gas Mark 4, 350°F).

Spread the tomato mixture over the bottom of a large, shallow baking dish. Make eight hollows in the mixture and carefully break one egg into each one. Garnish around the eggs with the chorizo slices, ham strips and asparagus tips. Pour over the remaining oil. Put the dish into the oven and bake for 20 to 25 minutes, or until the eggs have set and are cooked.

4-8 Servings

Tortilla in Mexico might mean a type of bread made from corn meal but in Spain it describes a thick, flat omelet. This particular basic Tortilla has a filling of potatoes and onion but any vegetables or cooked meat can be used.

TORTILLA
(Basic Omelet)

Tortillas in Mexico are flat breads, usually made from corn meal, but in Spain the same word is used to denote an omelet, somewhat thicker and fuller than the traditional French type. This omelet below has a mixture of potatoes and onions as its filling, a mixture typical of Castile.

	Metric/U.K.	U.S.
Olive oil	2 tsp	2 tsp
Butter	15g/½oz	1 Tbs
Large onion, chopped	1	1
Medium potatoes, cooked and diced	4	4
Chopped parsley	1 Tbs	1 Tbs
Large eggs, lightly beaten	4	4
Salt and pepper to taste		

Heat the oil and butter in a medium omelet or frying-pan. Add the onion and fry until it is golden brown. Add the potatoes and cook for 2 minutes, stirring occasionally. Stir in the parsley. Combine the eggs and seasoning together. Increase the heat to high.

Pour the egg mixture into the pan, tilting it so that the bottom is evenly covered. Reduce the heat to moderate. Using a palette knife or spatula, lift the edges of the omelet and, at the same time, tilt the pan away from you so that the liquid egg escapes from the top and runs on to the pan. Put the pan down flat over the heat and leave until the omelet sets.

Slide the omelet carefully on to a plate, then return to the pan to cook the other side in the same way.

Serve cold.

2–3 Servings

TORTILLA ESPANOLA
(Spanish Omelet)

	Metric/U.K.	U.S.
Olive oil	2 Tbs	2 Tbs
Onion, finely chopped	1	1
Garlic cloves, crushed	3	3
Medium tomatoes, blanched, peeled, seeded and chopped	2	2
Canned pimientos, chopped	6 Tbs	6 Tbs
Eggs	6	6
Salt and pepper to taste		
Milk	1 Tbs	1 Tbs
Frozen green peas, thawed	50g/2oz	⅓ cup

Tortilla Espanola has a classic filling of onion, garlic, tomatoes, pimientos and peas.

Heat the oil in a medium omelet or frying-pan. Add the onion and garlic and fry until they are soft. Stir in the tomatoes and pimientos and fry for a further 3 minutes. Remove the pan from the heat and keep hot. Combine the eggs, seasoning and milk until they are well blended. Stir in the peas.

Preheat the grill (broiler) to high.

Return the pan to the heat and pour the egg mixture into the pan, tilting it so that the bottom is evenly covered. Reduce the heat to low. Using a palette knife or spatula, lift the edges of the omelet and, at the same time, tilt the pan away from you so that the liquid egg escapes from the top and runs on to the pan. Put the pan down flat over the heat until the omelet sets.

Remove the pan from the heat and place it under the grill (broiler). Grill (broil) for 2 minutes, or until the top of the omelet has set. Remove from the heat.

Carefully slide the omelet on to a serving dish and cut into wedges. Serve at once.

3 Servings

Desserts and Cookies

Naranjas al Kirsch is a Spanish dessert of fresh mixed fruit soaked in kirsch.

CALABAZA ENMIELADA
(Sweet Pumpkin)

This is one of the favourite desserts of Mexico. Marrow can be substituted for the pumpkin, if you prefer.

	Metric/U.K.	U.S.
Water	50ml/2floz	4 Tbs
Fresh pumpkin, peeled, and with fibre and seeds removed	1kg/2lb	2lb
Dark brown sugar	275g/10oz	1⅔ cups
Double (heavy) cream, stiffly beaten	250ml/8floz	1 cup

Pour the water into a shallow flameproof casserole, or deep frying-pan. Cut the pumpkin into eight equal pieces and arrange it, in one layer, in the casserole or pan. Sprinkle thickly with the sugar and set the casserole or pan over moderate heat. Bring to the boil. Reduce the heat to low and cover. Simmer for 45 to 50 minutes, basting occasionally or until the pumpkin is tender but still retains its shape.

Remove from the heat and set aside to cool completely. Using a slotted spoon, transfer the pumpkin pieces to a serving dish and spoon over the cooking liquid. Serve at once, garnished with cream.

4 Servings

NARANJAS AL KIRSCH
(Fruit Soaked in Kirsch)

	Metric/U.K.	U.S.
Medium oranges, peeled, pith removed and thinly sliced	6	6
Black cherries, stoned (pitted) and halved	125g/4oz	4oz
Raspberries	225g/8oz	8oz
Castor (superfine) sugar	2 Tbs	2 Tbs
Ground allspice	½ tsp	½ tsp
Flaked almonds	50g/2oz	½ cup
Kirsch	125ml/4floz	½ cup

Put the fruit, in alternating layers, in a medium shallow serving dish, sprinkling a little of the sugar, allspice and flaked almonds over each layer.

Pour over the kirsch. Cover the dish with aluminium foil and place it in the refrigerator. Marinate the fruit for 2 hours, basting occasionally with the kirsch.

Remove the dish from the refrigerator. Remove and discard the foil. Baste once with the kirsch and serve at once.

4 Servings

CAPIROTADA
(Mexican Bread Pudding)

	Metric/U.K.	U.S.
Water	250ml/8floz	1 cup
Dark brown sugar	225g/8oz	1⅓ cups
Ground cinnamon	1½ tsp	1½ tsp
Butter	50g/2oz	4 Tbs
Stale bread, crusts removed and cubed	10 slices	10 slices
Sultanas or seedless raisins	50g/2oz	⅓ cup
Walnuts, chopped	125g/4oz	1 cup
Cottage cheese	175g/6oz	¾ cup
Double (heavy) cream, stiffly beaten	250ml/8floz	1 cup

Put the water, sugar and half the cinnamon into a saucepan and cook over moderate heat, stirring constantly until the sugar has dissolved. Cook the mixture without stirring for 5 minutes.

Meanwhile, melt the butter in a large frying-pan. Add the bread cubes and fry gently until they are evenly browned. Remove from the heat and stir into the syrup mixture. Stir in the raisins, walnuts and cheese and simmer gently until the ingredients are thoroughly blended.

Preheat the oven to fairly hot 190°C (Gas Mark 5, 375°F).

Turn the mixture into a well-greased oven-proof baking dish and sprinkle over the remaining cinnamon. Put the dish into the oven and bake for 15 to 20 minutes, or until the pudding has set and is golden brown. Remove from the heat and serve warm, with the cream.

4 Servings

TORRIJAS
(Bread and Honey Dessert)

Torrijas is a must for everyone who enjoys heavy, rich puddings — bread and milk soaked with honey and sherry.

	Metric/U.K.	U.S.
White bread, crusts removed and cut into large strips	4 slices	4 slices
Milk	125ml/4floz	½ cup
Egg, lightly beaten	1	1
Butter	25g/1oz	2 Tbs
Clear honey	50ml/2floz	¼ cup
Dry sherry	50ml/2floz	¼ cup

Preheat the oven to warm 170°C (Gas Mark 3, 325°F).

Arrange the bread in a shallow dish and

Quesadillas can be a multitude of things in Mexican cooking — there is a dish of deep-fried stuffed tortillas which can be so called but it also refers to this delightful snack cake made from crisp pastry with a cheese and raisin filling.

pour over the milk. Set aside to soak for 4 minutes. Using a slotted spoon, transfer the bread to kitchen towels to drain. Dip the bread into the beaten egg, then set aside on a plate.

Melt the butter in a flameproof casserole. Add the bread and cook until it is lightly and evenly browned. Meanwhile, combine the honey and sherry. Pour into the casserole.

Put the casserole into the oven and bake for 20 to 25 minutes, or until the bread is golden brown. Remove from the oven and serve at once, or set aside to cool completely before serving.

2-3 Servings

QUESADILLAS
(Mexican Cheese Squares)

	Metric/U.K.	U.S.
PASTRY		
Flour	350g/12oz	3 cups
Salt	¼ tsp	¼ tsp
Butter, chilled	175g/6oz	12 Tbs
Small eggs, lightly beaten	2	2
Iced water	3-4 Tbs	3-4 Tbs
Milk	2 Tbs	2 Tbs
Sugar	2 Tbs	2 Tbs
FILLING		
Cottage cheese, strained	225g/8oz	1 cup
Egg, beaten with 2 egg yolks	1	1
Castor (superfine) sugar	125g/4oz	½ cup
Mixed spice or ground allspice	⅛ tsp	⅛ tsp
Currants	75g/3oz	½ cup
Lemon juice	1 tsp	1 tsp
Vanilla essence (extract)	¼ tsp	¼ tsp

Sift the flour and salt into a bowl. Add the butter and cut it into small pieces with a knife. With your fingertips, rub the butter into the flour until the mixture resembles fine breadcrumbs. Add the beaten eggs with 2 tablespoons of the iced water and mix into the flour mixture with the knife. Add more water if the dough is too dry. Knead the dough gently and form into a ball. Wrap in foil and chill in the refrigerator for 30 minutes.

Preheat the oven to fairly hot 200°C (Gas Mark 6, 400°F).

To make the filling, beat the ingredients together until they are well blended.

Remove the dough from the refrigerator and divide it in half. Roll out one-half of the dough on a lightly floured surface, to a rectangle large enough to line a 18cm/7in by 28cm/11in baking sheet. Lift the dough on a rolling pin and place over the sheet. Spoon over the filling, spreading it to within about ½cm/¼in of the edges. Using a pastry brush, moisten the edges of the dough with a little water.

Roll the remaining dough out to a rectangle large enough to cover the filling. Lift the dough on to the filling, pressing the edges together to seal. Cut a slit in the centre of the dough and trim the edges. Discard the trimmings. Using a pastry brush, brush the top of the dough with the milk and sprinkle over the sugar.

Put the baking sheet into the oven and bake the dough for 20 to 25 minutes, or until it is golden brown. Remove from the oven and set aside to cool completely. Using a sharp knife, cut the pastry into eight squares and serve.

8 Pastries

TORTAS DE ACEITE
(Sesame Seed and Aniseed Biscuits [Cookies])

	Metric/U.K.	U.S.
Vegetable oil	350ml/12floz	1½ cups
Thinly pared rind of ½ lemon		
Sesame seeds	1 Tbs	1 Tbs
Aniseed	1 Tbs	1 Tbs
Dry white wine	125ml/4floz	½ cup
Finely grated lemon rind	2 tsp	2 tsp
Finely grated orange rind	2 tsp	2 tsp
Sugar	125g/4oz	½ cup
Flour	575g/1¼lb	5 cups
Ground cinnamon	1 tsp	1 tsp
Ground cloves	1 tsp	1 tsp
Ground ginger	1 tsp	1 tsp
Flaked almonds	25g/1oz	¼ cup

Heat the oil in a saucepan. When it is hot, add the pared lemon rind, sesame seeds and aniseed and remove the pan from the heat. Set aside and leave to cool. Using a slotted spoon, remove the lemon rind. Pour the oil mixture into a large bowl and add the wine, lemon and orange rind and sugar, beating until all the ingredients are well blended.

Sift the flour and spices into a bowl. Gradually add the mixture to the oil mixture, beating with a wooden spoon until they form a stiff dough. Using your hands, lightly knead the dough until it is smooth. Form into a ball and wrap in greaseproof or waxed paper. Set aside at room temperature for 30 minutes.

Preheat the oven to fairly hot 200°C (Gas Mark 6, 400°F). Line two large baking sheets with non-stick silicone paper.

Remove the paper from the dough and divide the dough into 24 equal pieces. Roll the pieces into small balls and, using the palm of your hand, flatten them into flat round biscuits (cookies), about 1cm/½in thick. Arrange the biscuits (cookies) on the prepared sheets and press a few flaked almonds into the top of each one.

Put the sheets into the oven and bake for 15 to 20 minutes, or until the biscuits (cookies) are firm to the touch and golden brown around the edges. Remove the sheets from the oven

Spicy flavourful biscuits (cookies) filled with sesame seeds and aniseed — Tortas de Aceite.

and transfer the biscuits (cookies) to a wire rack to cool. Allow to cool completely before serving.

24 biscuits (cookies)

TURRON
(Almond Sweets [Candies])

	Metric/U.K.	U.S.
Blanched almonds, toasted	450g/1lb	4 cups
Sugar	225g/8oz	1 cup
Clear honey	125ml/4floz	½ cup
MARZIPAN		
Ground almonds	50g/2oz	½ cup
Icing (confectioners') sugar	40g/1½oz	⅓ cup
Sugar	15g/½oz	1½ Tbs
Egg yolk	½	½
Dash of almond essence (extract)		

To make the marzipan, sift the almonds, icing (confectioners') sugar and sugar into a bowl. Mix lightly together. Gradually beat in the egg yolk and almond essence (extract), using a knife or a spatula to stir them in. Lightly dust a working surface with icing (confectioners') sugar. Turn the marzipan mixture out on to the working surface and knead it, pressing down and away from you with the heel of your hand, for 5 minutes or until the mixture is very smooth. Set the marzipan aside.

Combine the almonds, sugar and honey in a large saucepan and set the pan over very low heat. Cook the mixture until the sugar has dissolved, stirring constantly. Increase the heat to moderate and bring to the boil. Cook for 3 minutes, stirring constantly. Remove the pan from the heat and stir in the marzipan. Beat the mixture until the ingredients are thoroughly combined.

Spoon the mixture into a well-greased 15cm/6in by 23cm/9in baking pan, and set aside to cool slightly. Mark the mixture into 4cm/1½in squares and leave aside to cool completely.

Remove the sweets (candies) from the pan and break them into squares. Either place the sweets (candies) on a serving plate, or wrap them in greaseproof or waxed paper and store until required.

About 24 sweets (candies)

CHURROS
(Fried Choux Pastries)

	Metric/U.K.	U.S.
Sufficient vegetable oil for deep-frying		
Icing (confectioners') sugar, sifted		
CHOUX PASTRY		
Water	150ml/5floz	⅝ cup
Butter, cut into small pieces	40g/1½oz	3 Tbs
Salt	½ tsp	½ tsp
Pinch of grated nutmeg		
Flour	150g/5oz	1¼ cups
Medium eggs	3	3

First make the pastry. Bring the water to the boil over moderate heat. Add the butter, salt and nutmeg. When the butter has melted,

remove the pan from the heat and beat in the flour. Continue beating until the mixture pulls away from the sides of the pan.

One by one, beat the eggs into the mixture, beating each one into the dough until it is well blended before adding the next. When the eggs have all been completely absorbed, the mixture should be thick and somewhat glossy. Set aside to cool. Spoon the dough into a piping bag with a 1cm/½in plain nozzle.

Fill a large saucepan one-third full with oil and heat until it reaches 180°C (350°F) on a deep-fat thermometer, or until a small cube of stale bread dropped into the oil turns golden in 55 seconds.

Holding the piping bag in your left hand, squeeze out 20cm/8in lengths of the dough into the hot oil, cutting the lengths with scissors. Do not cook more than two or three lengths at a time. Deep-fry the pastries for about 8 minutes, or until they are crisp and golden brown. Using a slotted spoon, carefully remove the churros from the oil and drain on kitchen towels.

Sprinkle with icing (confectioners') sugar and serve hot. Or set aside to cool, sprinkle with icing (confectioners') sugar and serve cold.

4 Servings

FIGOS RELLENOS
(Stuffed Figs)

These delicious little sweetmeats are eloquent testimony to the North African influence on Spanish cuisine. They are usually eaten after the meal, *perhaps with coffee or tea.*

	Metric/U.K.	U.S.
Dried figs, stalks removed	24	24
Ground almonds	125g/4oz	⅔ cup
Sultanas or seedless raisins	50g/2oz	⅓ cup
Dark cooking (semi-sweet) chocolate, grated	25g/1oz	1 square
Orange-flavoured liqueur	3 Tbs	3 Tbs
Whole blanched almonds, toasted	24	24

Preheat the oven to moderate 180°C (Gas Mark 4, 350°F).

Holding a fig in one hand, push your thumb into the hole at the top and rotate the fig so that the centre becomes hollowed out. Combine the ground almonds, sultanas or raisins, chocolate and liqueur.

Using one teaspoonful at a time, fill the hollowed figs with the almond mixture. When the figs are full, gently press the tops together with your fingertips.

Arrange the figs, open end up, in a 23cm/9in round baking pan or shallow casserole. Put the pan or casserole into the oven and bake for 10 minutes, or until the tops of the figs open a little. Remove the figs from the oven. Insert a whole almond halfway into the hole in each fig.

Set the stuffed figs aside to cool completely before serving.

24 Sweetmeats

Glossary

Chilli peppers: There are literally scores of different varieties of chilli pepper regularly used in Mexican cooking, from the reasonably mild to the suicidally hot. Many are interchangeable with one another, and in this book, the types recommended in specific recipes have been limited to those available outside Mexico. In general, when seeding or chopping chillis, care should be taken to wear gloves and to rinse the chillis in cold, running water—they can be very hot, and if the seeds particularly come into contact with skin, they can cause an unpleasant, burning sensation. The major types of chillis are:

Ancho, a mild, dark capsicum, usually obtained dried from Mexican food stores. They are much less hot than most of the others on the market and if they are to be substituted for any other type, the quantity should be doubled to obtain the equivalent hotness of taste.

California, usually sold in cans from Mexican or Spanish food stores. They are fairly mild, smooth skinned and green and are often sold merely as 'green chillis'. They are the peppers used traditionally in Chiles Relleños. They can be stored, in their can liquid, in a screw-top container in the refrigerator for up to one month.

Jalapeño, usually sold in cans from Mexican or Spanish food stores. They are smooth skinned, green and very hot indeed. Care should be taken when chopping or otherwise handling them. They can be stored, in their can liquid, in a screw-top container in the refrigerator for up to one month.

Small dried red, usually known in Mexico as the *hontaka* chilli. They are native to Japan but widely used in cooking all over Latin America. They are very hot. Usually bought in bags or small portions and can be stored dry indefinitely.

Péquin, as above, small dried red chillis somewhat similar in appearance to the *hontaka.* They are very hot indeed. Can sometimes be obtained from Mexican food stores but can be difficult to obtain outside Mexico. When unobtainable, substitute other small dried hot red chillis, such as *hontaka.*

Chorizo sausage: a coarse red sausage, obtainable from Spanish food stores or good quality delicatessens. There are several varieties, but usually one type can be substituted for another. If chorizo is unobtainable, Italian *pepperoni* sausage, which is somewhat similar in texture, can be substituted, or any type of garlic sausage.

Coriander leaves: used as a condiment in Mexican cooking. Available fresh from Mexican, Greek or Indian food stores, or parsley can be used as a substitute. Coriander leaves can also be grown from coriander seeds. Plant in pots, keep indoors in a warm place and water frequently until it flowers.

Morcilla sausage: a smoked blood sausage, very popular in Spain, especially as a soup ingredient. Obtainable from Spanish food stores. Any type of blood sausage can be substituted if morcilla is unobtainable.

Pine nuts: a popular ingredient in Spanish cooking, especially dishes with a Catalan origin. Available from health food stores or delicatessens. If unavailable, hazelnuts or even finely chopped walnuts or pecans may be substituted.

Pomegranate seeds: the bright red dried seeds of the pomegranate fruit, sometimes used as a garnish in Mexican cooking. Available from Mexican or Indian food stores.

Salt cod: a specially cured form of cod fillet vastly popular in Spain and all other parts of the Mediterranean. Usually obtainable from Spanish and some French food stores, or some speciality fish merchants. If unavailable, cod or any white fish fillets can be substituted—although in this case the initial soaking stage should be omitted.

Serrano ham: a specially smoked ham, eaten uncooked, popular all over Spain. Available from Spanish food stores, but difficult and expensive to obtain outside Spain. If unavailable, *prosciutto,* or any other type of smoked ham may be substituted.

Tomatillo verde: small green, rather piquant tomatoes, usually sold canned, and a very popular ingredient in Mexican cooking. There is really no substitute, but if unavailable the texture may be duplicated by using canned peeled Italian plum tomatoes. The taste, however, is not the same.

Index

Picture Credits

Dr. Hugh Baker 69;
Rex Bamber 28/9;
Black Star/John Launois 3;
Ole Brask 130;
Barry Bullough 269;
John Bulmer 258/9;
Camera Press 74; 270;
Patrick Cocklin 221;
Colorific/M. Desjardins 322/3;
Daily Telegraph Colour Library/Chris Bonnington 193;
Delu/Paf International 141; 148; 161; 165; 170; 171; 174; 178;
Douglas Dickens 66/7;
Alan Duns 6; 17; 26/7; 29; 35; 38/9; 47; 57; 59; 71; 112; 113; 121; 125; 136;
157; 173; 177; 182; 186; 188; 196; 213; 226; 228; 253; 254; 271; 273; 283;
285; 296; 330; 336; 337; 350; 377;
Melvin Grey 109;
Robert Harding Associates/Christina Gascoigne 194/5; John G. Ross 257;
Bryn Cambell/John Hillelson Agency 129;
Denis Hughes-Gilbey 50; 230;
Frank Keating 2L;
Paul Kemp 49; 85; 100/1; 143, 144; 199; 201; 241; 305; 306; 310; 320; 372;
376;
Don Last 53; 62; 160; 359;
John Lees 383;
Max Logan 164; 246; 316;
Magnum/Marc Ribaud 65; 68; /Eric Lessing 130/1; /Élliott Erwit 133;
David Meldrum 11; 121; 153; 184; 353;
Toby Molinaar 321;
Key Nilson 43;
Stanli Opperman 371;
Roger Phillips 4; 7; 8; 10; 12; 14; 20/1; 22; 24; 25; 31; 33; 36; 38; 40; 44; 46;
55; 63; 72; 77; 79; 80; 86; 91–99; 102; 104; 107; 110/1; 116/7; 120/1; 126;
134; 135; 146; 147; 150; 154; 156; 159; 162; 167; 181; 183; 191; 203; 204;
207; 210; 214; 217; 218; 222; 225; 234; 237; 238; 245; 248/9; 250; 251; 260;
261; 263; 264; 265; 266; 275; 277; 278; 281; 282; 288; 291; 292; 295; 298;
301; 311; 313; 317; 318; 326/7; 328; 333; 335; 338; 339; 340; 342/3; 345;
346; 354; 360; 361; 363; 364; 367; 368; 370; 379; 381; 382;
Picturepoint 2R; 132;
Rapho/George Hall 1;
M. M. Rathore 194;
Iain Reid 15; 18; 32; 114; 119; 127; 168; 174/5; 200; 208; 233; 242; 287; 303;
314; 325; 349; 356; 375; 378; 380;
David Smith 54; 60; 83; 211;
John Turner 139;
ZEFA 88;